HOW
THE
WORLD
RUNS

Copyright © 2023 by Generations

All rights reserved.
Printed in the United States of America
2nd Printing, 2023

ISBN: 978-1-954745-31-5

Unless otherwise noted, Scripture is taken from the New King James Version®.
Copyright © 1982 by Thomas Nelson. Used by permission.
All rights reserved.

Cover Design: Justin Turley
Interior Layout Design: Rei Suzuki Design, Ltd.
Published by:
Generations
19039 Plaza Drive Ste 210
Parker, Colorado 80134
www.generations.org

For more information on this and
other titles from Generations,
visit www.generations.org or call 888-389-9080.

HOW THE WORLD RUNS

BY KEVIN SWANSON

Chapter 5 authored by Rory Groves

CONTENTS

INTRODUCTION VII

1 HUMAN MOTIVATION—
WHAT MAKES THE WORLD RUN? 1

2 THE LAWS OF
SUPPLY AND DEMAND 15

3 WEALTH INEQUALITY—
WHY SOME NATIONS ARE RICH
AND OTHERS ARE POOR 35

4 THORNS AND THISTLES—
THE REALITY OF SIN,
THE EFFECTS OF SIN,
AND JUDGMENT 65

5 ECONOMIC THEORIES—
BIBLICAL ECONOMICS AND THE ECONOMIC SYSTEMS OF MEN 87

6 GETTING YOUR JOB—WORK IN THE ECONOMY 117

7 BANKING AND YOUR MONEY— HOW THE WORLD ROBS, CHEATS, AND
STEALS 155

8 INVESTMENTS—DON'T BURY YOUR TALENTS IN THE GROUND! 201

9 SEEKING GOOD GOVERNMENT
—HOW GOVERNMENTS RUIN ECONOMIES 249

10	HOW TO BE SUCCESSFUL IN BUSINESS	295
11	MAKING WISE PURCHASING CHOICES	345
12	HOW BUSINESSES RUN	385
13	YOUR CALLING IN LIFE	421
	ENDNOTES	455
	INDEX	464

INTRODUCTION

The Bible contains over two thousand verses that deal with the subject of money. About forty percent of Jesus' parables have something to do with economics. Plainly, God is interested in how we make use of our time and money.

The time is right for young people and Christian families to make this study a priority. When it comes to preparing a child for life, an economics course will be more important and useful than science and mathematics. Many of us will use science and mathematics now and then throughout our lives, but economics applies to real life every day. By what we find in the fourth commandment (Ex. 20:9-11), apparently God expects us to work six days a week, and all work ties into economics. Each day of our lives, we are either consuming or producing, or both.

Consider the following reasons why economics is an essential study for every young person growing up in Christian homes.

1. The Apostle Paul has rather grim words for a young man who does not make material provision for his own family or for his widowed mother or grandmother in their old age. Such a one has "denied the faith and is worse than an unbeliever" (1 Tim. 5:8). This is such a crucial issue that a failure to materially provide for one's family is a matter of church discipline. In 2 Thessalonians 3, Paul reiterates that the church should withdraw from the person who does not work. Then he says, "If anyone will not work, neither shall he eat" (2 Thess. 3:10).

2. Young women are called to be keepers of the home or managers of the home economy. The Greek word for "keeper of the home" is "oikos-despoteo" (1 Tim. 5:14, Tit. 2:5). A direct translation of this word is "one who directs the home's day-to-day activities." Here is a God-inspired, definitive description of a woman's role (for those women who do not dedicate themselves to singleness). She is the manager of the economic program in the home. Likewise, the Prov-

erbs 31 woman is described in similar language: "The heart of her husband safely trusts her; so he will have no lack of gain" (Prov. 31:11). Economics is for everybody—man and woman alike.

3. Jesus said, "You cannot serve God and money." Money or mammon takes the role of the ultimate "master" or "lord" in the world's mind. Thus, it is helpful to know how the world views money. Within the same economy of the world, Christians are to be found serving God rather than money. There is a marked worldview difference between how the world views money and how Christians view money, and our Christian young people need to understand the difference.

4. As modern nations abandon Christian values, the consequences will be very bad. Now more than ever, this generation is witnessing the destructive work of bad economic ideas. If there will be any recovery, it will only happen by those who return to biblical principles (especially in the area of economics). While it may seem impossible to change the whole nation on a macro scale, consider that our Christian families may be able to retain some sound practices in micro communities. Most surveys of economics address the national economy and government policies. As Christians, however, we cannot leave the study of economics in the hypothetical. We are called to be doers of the Word and not hearers only. Therefore, the student must never study macroeconomics as applied to government policy without applying that study to direct his/her own life according to the will of God. I sincerely hope these studies will produce a profound reformation of thought and life for the Christian family.

5. If education is of any use to prepare a person for life, then every young person would do well to know something about how the world works and that with which they will be engaged for ninety percent of their adult life. If a young woman has a "very good education" by the time she is twenty-six years old, she knows the derivative of a cosine. She knows how Freudian psychology differs from Skinner's. She knows who Rome fought in the Punic Wars.

She knows that Plato asserts ideal forms as an absolute and eternal reality of which the phenomena of the world are a transitory reflection. She knows how pinocytic vesicles function in an amoeba. She knows how to parse just about any Latin verb—on the assumption that she still remembers any of this after she has completed her "very good education." Unfortunately, all too often the young woman still wouldn't have a clue how to manage a staff of seven in a home or how to handle a budget of $100,000 a year without running the household into the ground. She hasn't learned how to cook a meal, how to hire a contractor, how to raise children, how to change diapers, how to calm a baby, how to nurture a two-year-old, how to exercise authority, how to create a budget, how to cut food costs by forty percent without increasing time for shopping, or how to train a five-year-old in social skills. She doesn't know the best way to maintain vehicles. She doesn't know how to assess value in products and services. She doesn't know how to decorate a house. She doesn't know how to engage in hospitality with skill, wisdom, and grace. She doesn't know how to do ninety percent of life. Her education hasn't taught her that. The same applies to most young men.

Life isn't about school. Life is about work, money, eating, buying stuff, rest, business, sales, government, church, and family. Because life isn't about school, school shouldn't be about school either. It should be about life. That in a nutshell is the purpose of this economics course. This is a course about life.

1

HUMAN MOTIVATION— WHAT MAKES THE WORLD RUN?

A feast is made for laughter,
And wine makes merry;
But money answers everything.
(Eccl. 10:19)

When it comes to the questions of life (whether philosophical or practical), the best place to begin is with the basics. What makes the world go 'round? Well, of course, everybody should know that God makes the earth go around by His creative power and providential guidance. For the purpose of this study, we aren't talking about the physical earth, though. We are talking about human beings and human action. Look at the world of people outside your door. What do you see? There they are, moving here and there—all appearing to be very busy. What makes this world of people move, produce, and develop as it does?

> For of Him and through Him and to Him are all things, to whom be glory forever. Amen. (Rom. 11:36)

Once again, the answer for the Christian is that God is the first cause or, as some thoughtful person put it, the Prime Mover. God is in control. Nothing happens outside of His oversight and purpose. While this is true, this little book will focus on human action. We will look at what humans purpose to do, what motivates them, and how they do it.

WHY DO PEOPLE GET OUT OF BED IN THE MORNING?

If men and women are going to move around and do things, they must be energized by some source within them. Of course, physical energy comes by eating food and your body processing the calories into muscle movement. But let's start with a simple question. Why do people get out of bed in the morning? Now there is a difference between the world and the Christian, and you need to keep this in mind.

The average man of the world gets out of bed on Monday morning and runs off to work for two reasons: He is motivated by money and pleasure. Most of the time, it takes money to take a

3 HOW THE WORLD RUNS

Money motivates

vacation and have a good time. So almost everybody is motivated by money. The most powerful motivators are power and the praise of others, but not everybody is equally motivated by these things.

Pain is another motivator. In some communist prison camps, people are forced to work each day. If they do not work, they are beaten. Some young men sign up for the armed forces. They aren't allowed to sleep in until 10:00 a.m. on Monday morning. If they try something like that, they would be punished. They fear negative repercussions, so they get out of bed and go to work.

But some people just won't get out of bed to go to work. How does this happen? When nations are on the rise, lots of people seek wealth. They want to buy bigger houses and nicer cars. They build their towers in the big cities. They empower stronger governments. They believe in man, and they want to seek more powerful kingdoms.

As with all the kingdoms of men, these towers eventually fall. At first, many men and women are excited and motivated to build bigger and better houses and kingdoms, but they will lose that motivation. Money is no longer a strong enough motivator for them. Building their own kingdoms and living for their own glory just doesn't motivate them as it did in the past. They discover that they can't find the ultimate good. They cannot overcome pain and death. They finally come to realize that they can't find the ultimate purpose for life. So they step over the line into despair. The only goal in life becomes escape or even suicide. First, people will turn to games, fantasy, and entertainment. They lose interest in making money, raising children, and building big homes. Now all they want to do is play games and watch movies. This is why they don't get out of bed to go to work. They get out of bed to play games, and that is how the kingdoms of men fall apart. This happened recently to nations like the United States and Canada.

HOPE

More basically, people get out of bed because they have hope. They hope that work will give them money and that money will get them what they want in life. They hope they will have a good time on the weekend. They hope the pleasures they buy will make them happy. A husband hopes his wife will be happy with the money he earns. He hopes that if she is happy, she will make him happy too. That's basically how the world works.

Thus, the prime motivator for most of the world is money. "Money answers everything." As we learn from Ecclesiastes 10, people do seek after wine and feasting to make them happy. But money pays for the wine and the feasting. Money makes things happen. Money helps us build houses, barns, companies, cars, boats, and roads. Money makes men more powerful. Money enables governments to pay for guns and battleships to defend their nation from enemies who attack them. If people believe this present world is all there is in life, then the thing that matters most to them is money.

Christ's parable contained in Luke 16 is very helpful to better understand how the world runs. It teaches us that:
1. God wants us to be faithful with money.

2. God wants us to be faithful with other people's money.
3. God wants us to produce an increase with the talents we are given.
4. God doesn't want us to serve money and materials as our god or an ultimate master.
5. God wants us to use whatever resources possible to bless others, especially with the good news of eternal life.

HOW DO YOU INCREASE RICHES?

[Jesus] also said to His disciples: "There was a certain rich man who had a steward, and an accusation was brought to him that this man was wasting his goods. So he called him and said to him, 'What is this I hear about you? Give an account of your stewardship, for you can no longer be steward.'

"Then the steward said within himself, 'What shall I do? For my master is taking the stewardship away from me. I cannot dig; I am ashamed to beg. I have resolved what to do, that when I am put out of the stewardship, they may receive me into their houses.'

"So he called every one of his master's debtors to him, and said to the first, 'How much do you owe my master?' And he said, 'A hundred measures of oil.' So he said to him, 'Take your bill, and sit down quickly and write fifty.' Then he said to another, 'And how much do you owe?' So he said, 'A hundred measures of wheat.' And he said to him, 'Take your bill, and write eighty.' So the master commended the unjust steward because he had dealt shrewdly. For the sons of this world are more shrewd in their generation than the sons of light.

"And I say to you, make friends for yourselves by unrighteous mammon, that when you fail, they may receive you into an everlasting home. He who is faithful in what is least is faithful also in much; and

> he who is unjust in what is least is unjust also in much. Therefore if you have not been faithful in the unrighteous mammon, who will commit to your trust the true riches? And if you have not been faithful in what is another man's, who will give you what is your own?
>
> "No servant can serve two masters; for either he will hate the one and love the other, or else he will be loyal to the one and despise the other. You cannot serve God and mammon." (Luke 16:1-13)

While teaching His disciples these lessons, Jesus also takes note of the worldly wisdom in the steward's actions. Why was the owner happy with the steward? Evidently, the rich man wanted access to some amount of his capital which had been tied up with the borrowers. None of the borrowers were paying him back with interest or principal. The money wasn't doing anything for the rich man, and in the end, he was happy with the steward for returning some of his capital to him.

The bottom line is this: people want to increase their wealth. They seek reproduction. They want to see their efforts in life produce something and then continue to reproduce year after year. They hope to see an increase of their riches. In this way, at least, people reflect the heart of God. This world's vegetation and other life forms are highly reproducible. It's commendable to use money as a tool to get more things done and bless more people. We get into trouble when we become so fixated on money that we believe the end goal to all of life is making more money.

The first principle of worldly economics is to use time and money to make more money and get more productive things done.

But how should we do this? Where do we invest our time and money? Where can we best provide for needs in the market?

SUPPLY THE DEMAND

The second principle in worldly economics is to find a demand and offer to supply that demand for a profit. In order to supply some product

or service for a demand or market need, one must:
1. Identify the demand.
2. Assemble the capital, the know-how, and the time and work to produce the product or service.
3. Bring the product or service to the market where the demand is to be found, and sell it for a profit.

There is one other factor to contend with, and that is competition. Usually, there are others in the same market that are providing the same product or service. That product or service may be of better or worse quality, it may be sold for a higher or lower price, but it is still a competitor.

Suppose you had an apple tree in your yard bearing 100 apples a day. And all 100 people living on your street learned that an apple a day keeps the doctor away. This creates a demand for apples, and you have a supply. If everybody on the street figured they could afford to pay $1.00 for an apple, then you could make $100 a day in your apple stand.

But if your neighbor had an apple tree bearing 100 apples a day, he could set up a stand across the street from you. He might drop the price to 50 cents per apple and sell 100 apples a day. Then you would have to drop

Trading apples for money

your price to 50 cents per apple, and both you and your neighbor would probably sell 50 apples a day. This would lower your income to $25 per day. What happened here? Well, the supply of apples doubled, but the demand remained the same. The market is happier because they are getting apples for a lower price, but the suppliers are making less money overall.

Now, you could improve the quality of your apples to increase your price and the quantity you would sell. Suppose your neighbor's apples were filled with worms and pecking holes caused by birds. But you were more careful to use the right chemicals and netting to keep worms and birds away from your tree. You might be able to increase the price for your apples because the demand for better looking apples was high and the supply was lower on your street. Now, this introduces a few options for you.

You could increase your price to $1.00 an apple while your neighbor still sells his crummy apples for 50 cents each. But the difference is pretty high, so you would only sell 60 apples a day at that price. And you would earn $60 every day instead of just $25 because you are selling a higher quality apple.

But if you only increase the price to 75 cents an apple, you discover that you would sell 90 apples a day. This means that you are making $67.50 a day. And that's how you maximize your market share.

Then some of the neighbors tell their friends about your apples. They say yours are the best apples they've ever seen. And so people from the surrounding neighborhood crowd in to buy your apples. So you plant a second apple tree. Before you know it, you are selling 200 apples a day at $1.00 per apple. That amounts to $200 per day in apple sales.

When you improved the quality of your apples, this increased the value of your apples, and at the same time it increased the demand for your apples.

> **Supply** is the amount of goods offered for sale at a certain price under certain quality conditions.
>
> **Demand** is the amount of goods bought at a certain price under certain quality conditions.

WHAT DOES THIS MEAN FOR CHRISTIANS?

While presenting the worldly way in economics, we also want to present the "Wordly" way. What does God's Word say about the Christian's participation in the economy? What biblical principles do we need to know? What is the Jesus way? It is important to understand how the world behaves and how the world thinks about life and money. But how should we think about it?

Here's the bottom line. The Christian's highest goal is not to get more money. While the whole world is motivated by money, we're not. Our highest purpose in life is to glorify God and to enjoy Him forever. And our highest motive is—you got it—loving God with all our heart, soul, mind, and strength. We aren't supposed to be loving money or ourselves with all our heart, soul, mind, and strength. Love for others and love for God is the strongest driving force in the world. Nothing will motivate you to get out of bed and get to work as love for God and love for your family.

Consider the work accomplished by Jesus Christ as a powerful example of this motive. When our Lord was faced with all the force of the devil's temptations, He didn't budge a bit. As He followed through on the will of the Father to die on the cross for our sins, He was empowered by love.

> "I will no longer talk much with you, for the ruler of this world is coming, and he has nothing in Me. But that the world may know that I love the Father, and as the Father gave Me commandment, so I do." (John 14:30-31)

Jesus said, "You cannot serve God and money." We are not servants of money, and we do not obey the call of this master for making money when we hear the call. First and foremost, we hear God's call. We listen to God's Word. We submit to God's law. And we serve God.

> Again, the devil took Him up on an exceedingly high mountain, and showed Him all the kingdoms of the world and their glory. And he said to Him, "All these things I will give You if You will fall down and worship me." Then Jesus said to him, "Away with you, Satan! For it is

> written, 'You shall worship the Lord your God, and Him only you shall serve.'" (Matt. 4:8-10)

This means that there will be money-making opportunities we will pass up. When an opportunity conflicts with God's revealed will for our lives and other priorities, we will refuse to take advantage of it.

The Christian's second motive that drives him is a sense of duty to God. He realizes his identity as the servant of Christ. After a hard day of serving Jesus, we still say, "We are unprofitable servants" (Luke 17:7-10). We are not our own. We are bought with a price, and we are Christ's slaves (1 Cor. 7:23-24).

One of the reasons we get out of bed in the morning to do the will of Christ is because we are not our own. We belong to Him. When a new army recruit decides to sleep in on a Saturday morning, his sergeant will rudely interrupt the young man's beauty sleep with a harsh word. The recruit might inform his commander that he chose to sleep in for the weekend because he needs the extra sleep. At this point, the sergeant would point out with a fair degree of ardor: "You don't get that choice! We own you. Young man, you may have forgotten this, but let me remind you: You are a soldier in the US army, and we own you." The realization of one's identity forms the basis for life's purpose and motive. The same principle applies to the Christian who serves the Lord.

> Let nothing be done through selfish ambition or conceit, but in lowliness of mind let each esteem others better than himself. Let each of you look out not only for his own interests, but also for the interests of others. (Phil. 2:3-4)

A SECONDARY MOTIVE FOR CHRISTIANS IS SERVICE TO OTHERS.

As Jesus came to relieve suffering, God calls us to relieve the suffering of others as well.

As it turns out, the major metric of success for Christians is not how much money we make in life. That is, in fact, a fairly unimportant measurement. We don't ignore money, but our greater interest is in blessing others, honoring our superiors, providing food and clothing for our loved ones, and helping the poor. These things render more satisfaction to our lives than making money. Our ultimate satisfaction is still found in our heart-filled service, our work done for the Lord Jesus.

> Bondservants, be obedient to those who are your masters according to the flesh, with fear and trembling, in sincerity of heart, as to Christ; not with eyeservice, as men-pleasers, but as bondservants of Christ, doing the will of God from the heart, with goodwill doing service, as to the Lord, and not to men. (Eph. 6:5-7)

What part then does money play in the Christian's economic mindset? The world sees money as an earned reward received for work accomplished, but the Christian thinks differently. For us, all material blessings are blessings or gifts from God. In the ultimate sense, Christians do not see their rewards coming from the markets or an employer. Rewards come from God. "Every good gift and every perfect gift is from above, and comes down from the Father of lights" (Jas. 1:17). Christians consider money to be a blessing from God, but it is also an added responsibility placed on us by God. Money is merely another resource on loan from God. Money is intended for investing, giving, or capitalizing to accomplish more of God's will in our work.

The Word of God also warns us about the desire to be rich. Seeking to be rich is a terrible trap. The goal of the Christian must never be to become rich. For men to desire wealth is sinful and lustful, and this desire will most certainly drown them "in destruction and perdition" (1 Tim. 6:9). Working hard and investing the talents God has given us may result in more responsibility, more wealth, and more capital to invest. But we should count all of this as a gift from God. Our goals therefore will focus in on being good stewards of God's gifts, ever being thankful for His good gifts, and blessing others with our time, resources and talents.

Seeking to be rich is a terrible trap.

> Command those who are rich in this present age not to be haughty, nor to trust in uncertain riches but in the living God, who gives us richly all things to enjoy. Let them do good, that they be rich in good works, ready to give, willing to share, storing up for themselves a good foundation for the time to come, that they may lay hold on eternal life. (1 Tim. 6:17–19)

Hope plays an important part for the motivation of Christians in their work, but their hope is in God. Nobody wants their work to be fruitless and meaningless. Without consideration of God, or failing to consider ourselves His servants would reduce all work to futility. This was Solomon's conclusion about his work in Ecclesiastes 2:

> Then I looked on all the works that my hands had done
> And on the labor in which I had toiled;
> And indeed all was vanity and grasping for the wind.
> There was no profit under the sun.
> Then I turned myself to consider wisdom and madness and folly;
> For what can the man do who succeeds the king?—
> Only what he has already done. . .
> Therefore I turned my heart and despaired of all the labor in which I had toiled under the sun. For there is a man whose labor is with wisdom, knowledge, and skill; yet he must leave his heritage to a man who has not labored for it. This also is vanity and a great evil. For what has man for all his labor, and for the striving of his heart with which he has toiled under the sun? For all his days are sorrowful, and his work burdensome; even in the night his heart takes no rest. This also is vanity. (Eccl. 2:11-12, 17-19

For Solomon, even his work was all in vain. This was the great conclusion for this wisest of all earthly men.

Yet, in the final analysis, only God can turn our work into something of eternal benefit. Only God brings forth the increase; and real and substantial increase can only be that which has an eternal benefit. Otherwise, our legacy is only that of the grass of the field - here today and gone tomorrow. We apply ourselves to our work each day, hoping that God will bless the work of our hands and the output of our lives. These are the final words of Moses, contained in Psalm 90:

> And let the beauty of the Lord our God be upon us,
> And establish the work of our hands for us;
> Yes, establish the work of our hands. (Ps. 90:17)

HUMAN MOTIVATION—WHAT MAKES THE WORLD RUN? 14

2

THE LAWS OF SUPPLY AND DEMAND

Not that I speak in regard to need, for I have learned in whatever state I am, to be content: I know how to be abased, and I know how to abound. Everywhere and in all things I have learned both to be full and to be hungry, both to abound and to suffer need. I can do all things through Christ who strengthens me. (Phil. 4:11-13)

Economies are actively moving wealth and value from one person to another, but that only happens when people realize their needs and desires.

If people are going to want to purchase goods or services, they need to desire those goods or services. But why do people want a particular product or service?

First of all, they need to see some value in it. There are three kinds of values: **real useful value, perceived useful value**, and **exchange value**.

Something that is **really useful** has a practical benefit to human life. Food and clothing are basic useful products.

Some things are needful for life, and other things are luxuries. Luxuries might increase the comfort level of a particular lifestyle. And what may be useful to one person may not be useful to another. People who buy goods on the basis of useful value will assess an item's value on the basis of its usefulness to their lives. They plan to consume the product or use it for their own benefit instead of selling it to somebody else. This is the basis of most retail sales.

A **perceived useful value** is something that is presented as having useful value, but once it is purchased the thing has very little, if any, useful value to the consumer. Its value quickly fades after the purchase. Advertising can often impress the customer with the idea that a product has higher useful value than it really does.

Exchange value is that value set on a product by the market. In this case, the purchaser is not thinking in terms of what he is willing to pay for the product for his own use. He is concerned with the market price—what the market is willing to pay for it. The exchange value varies month to month, week to week, and day to day depending on the overall supply and the overall demand in any given market.

But what really contributes to a market demand? What enters into people's hearts to make them want to buy things? Some of these impulses are sinful, and others are not, to include:

1. Advertising and fads created by famous athletes, pop stars, and movie stars will affect tastes and preferences among consumers. By the endorsement of the celebrities, the product is associated with a certain image. This especially applies to items like tennis shoes, hair care products, jeans, soft drinks, and diet products.
2. Idolatry in the hearts of men and women as well as addictions (to media, gambling, alcohol, food, etc.) will increase a market for certain products.
3. Covetousness—when men and women see the better conditions of others and desire this for themselves—will provide market demand.
4. Immediate bodily needs for food, clothing, and shelter, coupled with an increased population in a certain area, will increase demand.
5. Competing scientific studies and folk wisdom (especially relating to health) will sometimes produce an increased demand for certain kinds of food, medicines, and supplements. For example, by 2018, the organic food market in the United States increased to about six percent of the total food supply. Switzerland, Den-

Celebrity basketball star Michael Jordan was known for marketing tennis shoes in the 1990s.

Organic food was popular in grocery stores in the 2000s.

mark, Sweden, Germany, France, Canada, Norway, the United Kingdom, and China contributed large demand for organic foods.

6. Increases in take-home pay and family income (as God blesses a community economically) can result in increased demand for certain goods. This may also open a demand for higher quality goods. Whereas the community may have favored cheap soft-serve ice cream and popsicles, now they want high-end ice cream made from real cream.

7. Proven conveniences which make life more comfortable or more functional open a demand for new markets. For example, washing machines and clothes dryers are proven to be more efficient than washing clothes by hand. Once the word gets out about these helpful inventions, it's not long before everybody wants to purchase them.

8. Innovations and improvements of existing goods with added bells and whistles and helpful conveniences can also produce more demand. For example, the development of certain shampoos to eliminate dandruff would generate a demand from people with dandruff problems. Or new technical improvements to cars (like automated speed control, backup cameras, etc.) will create demand for the new car market.

Modern car interior

9. Things that go wrong in a society or smaller community can produce a change in demand. For example, an increase in certain diseases in a community will result in a demand for medical solutions. Increased crime rates encourage a demand for gun purchases.

Now, as Christians, we are careful to observe God's commandments when it comes to buying stuff or contributing to market demand. God forbids covetousness with the tenth commandment. This sin is to desire something that God has not given you nor given you the power to get. Covetousness is discontentment and ingratitude with God's recent provisions. To covet means to desire something that belongs to your neighbor or to set your heart on getting something you're not supposed to get or something you're not sure you should get. According to the instructions of 1 Timothy 6:6-8, you should be content with just your food and clothing. If you have a little extra money, there would be nothing wrong with enjoying other conveniences. But if not, you should be just as grateful with little or much.

> Now godliness with contentment is great gain. For we brought nothing into this world, and it is certain we can carry nothing out. And having food and clothing, with these we shall be content. (1 Tim. 6:6-8)

This is not the mindset of the world. Greed, lust, discontentment, and ingratitude are normal attitudes of the world. These attitudes are fueled by idolatry and a rebellion against God. The worship of materials, wine, food, and money permeates our world around us. These are unhealthy elements that drive market demands. Proverbs, the Wisdom of God, reminds us that the excessive use of luxuries, wine, and food is sin (drunkenness, gluttony, and laziness).

> Hear, my son, and be wise;
> And guide your heart in the way.
> Do not mix with winebibbers,
> Or with gluttonous eaters of meat;
> For the drunkard and the glutton will come to poverty,
> And drowsiness will clothe a man with rags. (Prov. 23:19-21)

The Scripture also warns us about the love of money which is the root of all kinds of evil (1 Tim. 6:10). We want to be careful not to spoil ourselves and our families with too many treats, luxuries, and unnecessary gifts. When we reach the point where we are less grateful to the Giver (God) and grabbing more after the gifts, we have given way to idolatry. When our focus is upon the gift more than the Giver, we have become too materialistic. We are serving mammon more than we serve God.

INCREASING DEMAND—HOW MUCH IS THIS THING WORTH?

What is the value of a product or service? What would you charge for the product if you were selling it? What price would you put on it? In the final analysis, you could only charge what somebody was willing to pay for it. If there was only one of this thing (like a rare piece of art), and nobody else could market the same art, you would still need somebody who wanted to buy it from you. If nobody wanted it, the price would be $0.00. If there were three buyers, then you could auction the product to the highest bidder. Auctions help to identify the person who wants something more than

Diamonds are both scarce and considered aesthetically pleasing.

everybody else. Only by competitive bidding could we understand the real demand for the product in the hearts of the buyers in the market.

Some people place value on products for aesthetic reasons. They think the art piece is beautiful, for example. They may place value on products for sentimental reasons, as in the case of antiques. But most people place value on products for their **utility** or **usefulness.** The value is determined by **utility** and **scarcity (availability).**

Suppose you were to make cooking pots out of cardboard. Nobody would want to buy this silly product because it would burn up the minute you turned on the stove burner. **Usefulness** is really the degree of satisfaction people get from owning a product or receiving a service.

Scarcity also drives the market. Wealthy people living in rich communities purchase large diamond rings not always because they find a lot of utility in them but more so because of the scarcity of large diamonds.

The price of a product is decided by the amount a person or business is willing to sell it for, and what somebody is willing to pay for it. We call it robbery when a mobster forces a merchant to sell a product for a certain price against his will or if the civil government sets the price of goods and services by force.

The price a customer is willing to pay is related to the amount of satisfaction he would get out of the product as well as the degree of the product's availability on the market. For example, a starving man on a desert

Market stall of fruits and vegetables

island might be willing to give $500 for a sandwich because of two reasons. First, he would get a lot of satisfaction out of it, and secondly, there aren't any other sandwiches on the island available for purchase.

A FREE MARKET EXCHANGE

> She considers a field and buys it;
> From her profits she plants a vineyard. (Prov. 31:16)

Buying and selling is really a form of trade. And, the most rudimentary form of trade is bartering in which one useful thing is traded for some different, useful thing. Most of the time, people don't exchange one thing for the very same thing. That is, I wouldn't trade a red ball for another red ball (that looks just like mine).

Trade is defined as a transaction where one party gives up something to get something else from another party.

A free market trade occurs when one party gives up something to a second party to get something else he wants more than the thing he is giving up. The same applies to the second party. Each party gives up something he considers less useful or important for something he considers more desirable. In the case of buying and selling, the buyer is willing to give his money for a product. The seller would rather have the money than the product he is selling. Often, the reason for this is that the seller has more of that product than he can use himself. The farmer who sells his apples at a stand on the side of the road could not possibly eat 1,000 apples. He would rather have money than apples because he could use the money to buy other things needful for himself and his family.

> "[The product] is good for nothing," cries the buyer;
> But when he has gone his way, then he boasts. (Prov. 20:14)

For most exchanges today, the prices are already fixed. There is no bargaining at the grocery store when you purchase fruit and vegetables. But in open markets, the prices are more negotiable. The buyer wants to know the lowest price for which the seller would part with his goods. The seller wants to know the highest price for which the buyer would purchase his goods. In the case of Proverbs 20:14, the buyer tries to conceal his valuation of the product. He wants the seller to think he would place a lower value on the product than he really does. He hopes the seller will give up some of his profit and lower the price for the exchange. Therefore the buyer doesn't want the seller to know how much he wants the product. Christians must not lie about their need or interest in a product. It would be better to know the market price of the product in your local area and to know something of the motivation of the seller. If the market has been slow on a given day, the seller will be more interested in lowering his price to get some profit for his labors.

But how do most sellers know how much to charge for something? That's simple in our society. We check out three sellers on the Internet.

If, for example, we want to sell a used car, we look at how much other sellers are trying to get for the same model-and-year car. There are several factors that affect the price of the car.

1. **Location.** A car sold in one part of the country for a certain price may be twenty percent more or less expensive in another part of the country. These differences are affected by average incomes and the preferences of the consumers.
2. **Reputation of the seller or dealer.** Some dealers may be able to get more for their products because they provide better service and they have made a good reputation for themselves. Some people will pay more for more dependable and higher quality service.
3. **Financing.** Some people will pay more for a product if the dealer or seller is willing to finance the sale. This means that the consumer is borrowing money to buy the product.
4. **Quality of the product.** The same car sold somewhere else might have higher quality parts, more bells and whistles, fancier hubcaps, a better maintenance record, a better paint job, less dings on the body, and lower mileage. Cars that have been in an accident are usually priced lower because damage to the body of the car could result in more problems later on.

As you can see, there are quite a few factors that go into the pricing of a used car or any other product. We as Christians are called to be plain and honest in the representation of whatever we are trying to sell.

UNDERCUTTING THE MARKET

Pre-owned cars

Now, suppose you wanted to undercut the market by lowering the price of a product or service. While other window washers were charging $5.00 per window, you decide you will do it for $1.00 per window. You hope this will increase your business such that you will put the other window washers out of business. Before you do this, you have to consider several things.
   1. Customers are interested in quality service at least as much as they are interested in price. They want to be sure that their service pro-

viders will do a quality job every time over a period of months and years. You have to remember that it will take years to develop a reputation in a business. It takes time before your customers trust you for quality work. If you are a newcomer to the market, it will take a long time before they will trust you to do a good job. Value is as much established by quality as by quantity or completion of a job. You may promise to cut the price of a window job from $5.00 to $1.00 per window, but will you supply the same quality as those companies that charge $5.00 per window? If the customers in a certain market are accustomed to a certain level of quality and they don't get it, they will be upset with you. Because you failed to meet the reasonable expectations of a given market, you will have stolen from them and broken the eighth commandment.

2. You will have to work about the same amount of time on a window as your competitors. Counting travel time and preparation time, the average window washer may clean the average window in ten minutes. He earns about $30 per hour. If you are cutting the cost for

Window washing

your customer down to $1.00 per window, you (and your employees) will be earning about $6.00 per hour. Are you willing to do this all year and into the following years?

New home construction

3. You might also overlook the unseen costs involved in a business. You will need to pay for insurance, travel to the work site, employment taxes, equipment costs, and so forth. Also, don't forget the added risk of climbing ladders to clean third-story windows—and all of that for only $1.00 per window.

The average cost of doing business and providing services has already been thought out carefully by the market. The only way you could beat the average market price would be by improving on the method or the tooling used to clean windows.

4. Most importantly however, before you undercut the market, consider the words of Jesus. Would this be an act of love for your neighbor to disrupt the market in this way? In some cases, the competition you introduce to the market is healthy, and it stirs everybody up to produce a better product or service for a good price. But, in other cases, the competition is unhealthy and undermines already existing, healthy business relationships.

> "Therefore, whatever you want men to do to you, do also to them, for this is the Law and the Prophets." (Matt. 7:12)

SUPPLY AND PRICE

While there will always be a limited supply of everything in the world, the supply can change quickly. Sometimes changes in supply and demand determine pricing. For example, if a wildfire burns down 300 houses out of 3,000 homes in a town, the price of renting a house would increase immediately. That's because the demand for houses increased suddenly, and the supply is low. The price of apples would come down if lots more apple trees were planted where you live. Water may be plentiful where you live. But people who live in the desert have to pay more for their water. Perhaps somebody would haul water to the desert town using a large tanker truck. Or another businessman might drill very deep wells and draw up the water using electric pumps. All of that calls for money and effort. The water is not readily accessible in the desert, so people will have to pay more for it.

Various shoes

THE LAW OF SUPPLY FOR PRODUCERS

Most of the time, the price that people are willing to pay for products will drive the supply. Suppose that young men and women were willing to pay $50 for a certain special kind of tennis shoe during a certain year. But the following year, quite a few of these young folks were willing to pay $100 for the same pair of tennis shoes because their favorite sports stars were favoring these shoes. What do you think the manufacturer would do when they realized the market is willing to pay $100 for these tennis shoes? Then, on the second year of production, it turned out that the market was willing to pay $200 for the same tennis shoes because the product had become "all the rage." Now how many tennis shoes will the manufacturer supply to the market? As the price goes up, of course the manufacturer will increase the supply. That's because they suspect the market is growing, and they want to make as much profit as possible. *The law of supply states that the quantity of goods supplied will increase as the price of a good increases in the free market.* The following graph illustrates this trend.

THE LAW OF DEMAND GOVERNING CONSUMERS

However, as the price goes up, what happens to the demand for these tennis shoes? Poor families have a harder time paying $200 for tennis shoes. Most young people don't have a lot of money, so the rising price weakens the demand for the shoes. Thus, the demand for the shoes starts to drop. The following graph illustrates this trend. *The law of demand states that as the price of a good increases, the demand for it decreases in the free market.*

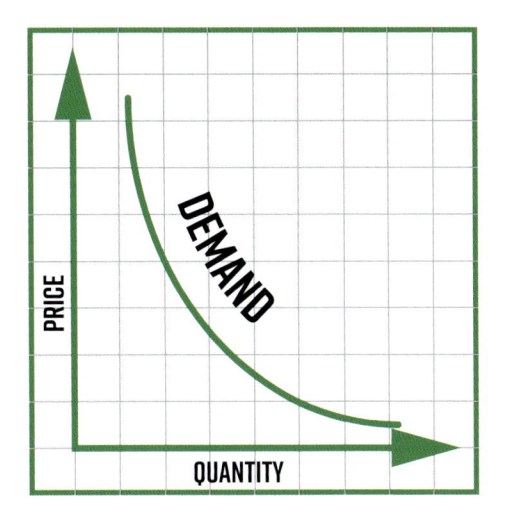

HOW SUPPLY AND DEMAND SET THE MARKET PRICE

Suppose there is a strong demand for lemonade on hot afternoons in your town. People are willing to pay quite a bit of money for a glass of lemonade. Several kids open up lemonade stands along the streets. How does supply from the lemonade stands and the demand set the price of lemonade? Here's how it works.

1. If the supply increases (more kids are making lemonade) and demand stays the same, the price for a glass of lemonade will have to go down.
2. If the supply decreases (fewer kids are making lemonade) and demand stays the same, the price will need to go up.
3. If the supply stays the same and demand for lemonade increases during the hot summer months, the price for lemonade will increase.
4. If the supply stays the same and demand for lemonade decreases, the price for lemonade will drop.

MARKET EQUILIBRIUM

Market equilibrium is the point at which the supply or the quantity of the product provided by companies meets the demand for the product in the market. This should work its way out naturally in a market as companies do their best to meet the demand at the price people are willing to pay.

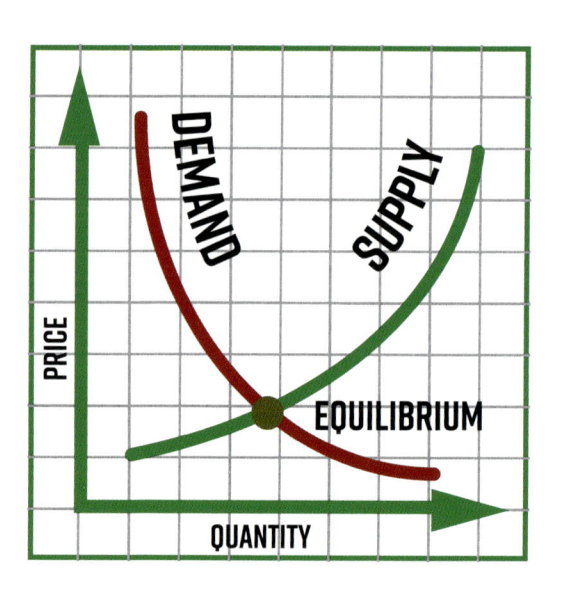

PRICE ELASTICITY

When setting prices for the products you sell, whether it is lemonade or lawn service, you want to know how a change in price might effect the demand. For example, let us suppose a young man opens a lemonade stand

and sets a price of $1.00 for a 16-ounce cup of lemonade. He is selling 100 cups a day. But then, he decides to up the price to $1.20. Will he lose any customers? **Elasticity of Demand** is the ratio of the change in demand to the change in price.

If the response to a 20% rise in the price of lemonade results in a 10% drop in demand, elasticity is calculated this way:

Elasticity = 10%/20% = 0.5

If the response to a 20% rise in the price of lemonade results in a 50% drop in demand, the elasticity would be:

Elasticity = 50%/10% = 5.0

This would indicate that people who buy lemonade are pretty sensitive to the price of it. They are less likely to buy the lemonade if the price goes up too much.

GOD'S GOODNESS SUPPLIES FOR THE WORLD'S NEEDS

Thomas Malthus (1766-1834) introduced the idea that world population would outpace the food supply. Since then, increasing numbers of people worry about running out of natural resources like food and water. Should the world's population exceed 10 billion, they are afraid we will run out of farmland, oil and gas, or other important resources. What Malthus and others forgot is that God is good. They do not believe that God's provision on this earth is sufficient to sustain a very large population. But what if God gave farmers special insight into better farming methods? What if there were still undiscovered farmlands somewhere on earth where certain crops would grow exceedingly well? By God's grace, He can lead us to ways in which we can increase the size of the pie so more supply is available to the increased demands (as more children are born into this world).

Thomas Malthus (1766-1834)

WHERE DOES SUPPLY COME FROM?

> "Therefore I say to you, do not worry about your life, what you will eat or what you will drink; nor about your body, what you will put on. Is not life more than food and the body more than clothing? Look at the birds of the air, for they neither sow nor reap nor gather into barns; yet your heavenly Father feeds them. Are you not of more value than they? Which of you by worrying can add one cubit to his stature? So why do you worry about clothing? Consider the lilies of the field, how they grow: they neither toil nor spin; and yet I say to you that even Solomon in all his glory was not arrayed like one of these. Now if God so clothes the grass of the field, which today is, and tomorrow is thrown into the oven, will He not much more clothe you, O you of little faith?" (Matt. 6:25-30)

Increased supply of a certain product in a certain market (where the population or demand remains the same) will reduce the cost of that product.

In order to supply a product, you need any of the following:

1. God's Resources

You need natural resources—or, better put, God's resources. The discovery, provision, or availability of God's resources enable the flow of materials into the market. Apple trees produce apples. While man plants the apple seed and waters the tree, God brings forth the increase.

Cattle herd

God supplies rain to water the earth and grow grass for herd animals. God's carbon dioxide and water grows the grass. God provides minerals, coal, oil, iron ore, and other raw materials hidden in the crust of the earth. To build houses, carpenters need iron ore for nails, limestone and silica sand for concrete, and God's trees for the lumber.

2. Labor

You need labor to find the materials, to mine the materials, and to cultivate the materials. Farmers work hard to plant seeds, water their plants, kill bugs, and harvest crops. Manufacturers take the raw materials and turn them into useful things for the consumer. All of this takes hard work, time, energy, brain-work, and cooperation.

To build an average 2,000 square foot house requires about 2,400 man hours. That's one man working for almost a whole year.

3. Tools and Capital

You need capital to build machines and to buy tools to get the work done. Capital (or investment money) is used to hire employees, build buildings, and buy the machines needed to do the work. For example, if a carpenter is going to build a house, he will need capital to buy nail guns, saws, levels, and other tools. He will need to buy the wood, nails and screws, concrete, glass windows, asphalt shingles for the roof, PVC pipes for the plumbing, and copper wiring for the electrical system.

4. Creativity, Daring, Risk, and Entrepreneurship

> In the beginning God created the heavens and the earth. (Gen. 1:1)

God is the ultimate Creator, and the ultimate economic Contributor. At the beginning, God started out with nothing and made everything out of nothing. His profit was infinite, and His creativity was original, exceedingly beneficial, and awe-inspiring to the ultimate degree.

The final ingredient needed to supply human needs is this creativity. Every job requires a degree of daring, risk, and entrepreneurship to make it happen. This includes marketing and sales work. Somebody has to start up the business. Somebody has to drive the process. Somebody has to put the capital to work, contract with people to do the work, and oversee the process of business. Every house built by a carpenter will present its own unique challenges. Somebody has to risk time or capital to initiate the project or to pay the subcontractors. Somebody has to file permits with the local government. Farmers have to risk investment in seeds, land rental, fencing, fertilizer, and other expenses to get a crop. Yet the harvest still depends on weather and other factors under God's control.

In the ultimate sense, then, the harvest and the supply for the market still comes by the blessing of God. After all that man puts into it, God brings forth the increase.

> I planted, Apollos watered, but God gave the increase. So then neither he who plants is anything, nor he who waters, but God who gives the increase. (1 Cor. 3:6-7)

Tools are necessary to get certain kinds of work done.

3

WEALTH INEQUALITY— WHY SOME NATIONS ARE RICH AND OTHERS ARE POOR

Now it shall come to pass, if you diligently obey the voice of the Lord your God, to observe carefully all His commandments which I command you today, that the Lord your God will set you high above all nations of the earth...And the Lord will grant you plenty of goods, in the fruit of your body, in the increase of your livestock, and in the produce of your ground, in the land of which the Lord swore to your fathers to give you. (Deuteronomy 28:1, 11)

To better understand how the world runs, first you must understand economics on the broad scale. This will help you to discover how you can play a part in it. *Economics is the study of producing wealth, consuming wealth, and transferring wealth.* It is the study of work, making things, and buying things. But, we want to be successful in the economic effort. We want to do economics properly. Therefore, biblical economics is done in obedience to God's law order. It is the application of God's moral principles to marketplace activity and relationships.

The **macroeconomy** is all the work, all the buying and selling, and all the useful things made by a whole nation of people working together. The **microeconomy** is one individual's or one household's participation in the economy.

To better understand macroeconomics, it would be good to know why some nations are poor and others rich. The wisdom of God's Word gives several clear answers to this question.

THE NUMBER ONE FACTOR IS GOD'S BLESSING

> "And you shall remember the LORD your God, for it is He who gives you power to get wealth." (Deut. 8:18)

Only God can provide the power and ability for any nation to make wealth. Ultimately, the motivation to work in the minds and hearts of 300 million people is determined by God. Only our all-wise and all-powerful Creator can provide the insight for making technological inventions and scientific breakthroughs. We have seen these economic blessings come almost exclusively to scientists and inventors of Christian faith over the last 600 years in Europe and America. These inventions have brought unprecedented economic blessings upon the whole world just since 1800.

Yet, when nations turn towards immorality, they subject themselves to the threat of God's judgment. In fact, Deuteronomy

28:15-19 says a nation will be cursed materially when the people as a whole refuse to obey God's commandments.

> "But it shall come to pass, if you do not obey the voice of the LORD your God, to observe carefully all His commandments and His statutes which I command you today, that all these curses will come upon you and overtake you: Cursed shall you be in the city, and cursed shall you be in the country. Cursed shall be your basket and your kneading bowl. Cursed shall be the fruit of your body and the produce of your land, the increase of your cattle and the offspring of your flocks. Cursed shall you be when you come in, and cursed shall you be when you go out." (Deut. 28:15-19)

THE SECOND REASON FOR GOOD ECONOMIES IS HARD WORK

> He who has a slack hand becomes poor,
> But the hand of the diligent makes rich. (Prov. 10:4)

> Remember the Sabbath day, to keep it holy. Six days you shall labor and do all your work, but the seventh day is the Sabbath of the LORD your God. In it you shall do no work: you, nor your son, nor your daughter, nor your male servant, nor your female servant, nor your cattle, nor your stranger who is within your gates. For in six days the LORD made the heavens and the earth, the sea, and all that is in them, and rested the seventh day. Therefore the LORD blessed the Sabbath day and hallowed it. (Ex. 20:8-11)

As part of the Ten Commandments (God's basic law), we are told to work six days a week and rest one day a week. This is what God wants for everybody—Christian and non-Christian alike. People cannot get along without rest. They would burn out quickly and fail to maximize their usefulness in the economy if they didn't get a day off every week. Here then

WEALTH INEQUALITY—WHY SOME NATIONS ARE RICH AND OTHERS ARE POOR

is the ratio of work to rest that will produce the most productive economy. Work six days, and rest a seventh.

From a human perspective, an economy is the grand total (or aggregate) of all the work that is getting done in a community or a nation. Lots of *hard work* produces a booming economy. When everybody in a society is *hardly working* and everybody lays around on the couch all day, there won't be many goods or services for people to purchase at low prices and enjoy. That should be obvious.

The following little anecdote illustrates this principle in a humorous tone.

> For a couple years I've been blaming my tiredness on low iron in my blood, lack of vitamins, and autoimmune disease. But now I think I have found out the real reason. I'm actually overworked. After doing a little research, I have learned that the population of this country is 237 million, of which 104 million are retired. That leaves 133 million to do the work. There are 85 million in school, which leaves 48 million to do the work. Out of these, there are 29 million employed by the federal government. That leaves 19 million to do the work. Four million are in the Armed Forces, which leaves 15 million to do the work. Take from this total the 14,800,000 people who work for state and city governments and that leaves 200,000 to do the work. There are 188,000 in hospitals, so that leaves 12,000 to do the work. Now, there are 11,998 people in prisons. That leaves just two people to do the work, you and me, and I'm tired of doing it all by myself!

A nail gun increases efficiency by 100x compared with a hammer.

Of course this is only a joke, and a strong economy can't be built on one person doing all the work. What we want is most of the people in the community working hard. Nonetheless, an economy must include more than just physical effort. If everybody in an economy were building large pyramids as burial places for presidents or pharaohs, we would not consider this to be wise and productive labor. If everybody designed computer games so that everybody else could play computer games, we would all starve to death. We still need wisdom to determine what are the good and needful projects to be done. We want to work "smart." This means that we want to work efficiently. We want to discover creative technological solutions to speed up the process of big projects. For example, the nail gun (invented by Morris Pynoos in 1944) can pound three big nails in one second. That's about one hundred times faster than using a hammer. To build an average house, a carpenter will use about 24,000 nails. Using manual hammers, the carpenter would be nailing for 200 hours. The nail gun cuts the total nailing time for the full home construction down to two hours. Do you see how a carpenter can build quite a few more houses per year if he uses a nail gun?

Lack of proper tools is another hindrance to work. An auto mechanic might work on a bolt for three hours because he isn't using the proper tool. Instead of getting the right tool to make the job easier (and remove a screw in thirty seconds), he wastes hours on it using the wrong tool.

Sometimes poor planning results in a lot of wasted time. When working on a project like building a deck, some guys will have to take six trips to the hardware store to get more materials. If these do-it-yourselfers had spent fifteen minutes making a list of everything they needed for the project, they wouldn't have wasted two hours on extra trips to the store.

Civil governments of poor nations are notorious for building up bureaucracy and slowing down progress. They slow everything down by red tape, bribery, and regulations. The best and brightest of the college graduates end up working for the government and doing nothing very productive. Governments don't produce useful things like cars and food. Most of the time, they just slow down production and economy.

A good economy will find ways to make efficient use of time and resources.

> The lazy man does not roast what he took in hunting,
> But diligence is man's precious possession. (Prov. 12:27)
>
> He who is slothful in his work
> Is a brother to him who is a great destroyer. (Prov. 18:9)
>
> See then that you walk circumspectly, not as fools but as wise, redeeming the time, because the days are evil. (Eph. 5:15-16)

A society that gives way to leisure and lives for entertainment will be wasteful. Slothful people are usually wasteful. Some people check their email and text messages a hundred times a day. They could save three hours if they would only check these communications once a day.

So, the hard work required for a good economy must include some hard *brain work*. There is one more basic characteristic needed for a good economy produced by work, and that is *honest work*. Cheating and stealing undermines trust and discourages the hard workers in a society. Sadly, the civil government usually contributes to this cheating and stealing more than anybody else. And this is what destroys economies.

Illustration of Cyrus McCormick's reaper

ANOTHER REASON FOR STRONG ECONOMIES IS DIVISION OF LABOR

When almost everybody worked as a farmer, there wasn't anybody making big plows and equipment to farm large pieces of land. There were few carpenters to build houses. There wasn't anybody who could take the time to invent automobiles, dishwashers, and refrigerators to make life easier on everybody. There was no division of labor, so everybody just planted a few seeds on a small piece of land. Everybody just barely survived, and they had very few conveniences. Several very important inventions helped with the division of labor.

- Improvements on the plow, which enabled farmers to cultivate larger pieces of land.
- The knitting machine or weaving machine, speeding up the process of producing cloth, was developed in the 1600s.
- Cyrus McCormick's reaper, automating the process of reaping grains, came in the 1800s.
- The nail gun and other power equipment that made the construction of homes go much faster.

Equipment that provided a quicker access to the necessities of life (food, clothing, and housing) freed up a lot of people who used to be farmers and hand weavers to do other work.

Mass production also enabled cheaper products as well as a division of labor in manufacturing. For example, the Carron Ironworks Company developed a method for making a lot of nails by dividing the process into several different tasks. Previous to this, blacksmiths would make nails one at a time, and the price was about 2 cents a nail. By forming a long iron bar, cutting nails from the bar, and bending part of it over to form a head, the Carron Ironworks Company was able to mass-produce nails for the first time (beginning in the 1750s). By 1900, this brought the price of nails down to about 0.2 cents per nail.

In summary, poor countries are poor for any of the following reasons:
1. People don't work hard for six days a week.
2. People are dishonest, and they cheat each other in business.

3. Civil governments introduce a lot of taxes, regulation, and bribes into the system, slowing everything down and discouraging hard work.
4. People waste a lot of time, and they don't work efficiently using innovative methods to do their work.
5. There isn't enough division of labor in the economy.
6. The nation is immoral, and God does not bless it.

GOD'S ECONOMIC PRINCIPLES MATTER MOST

There is a lot to learn about the economy and your part in it. But the most important principles of all are God's principles and the wisdom He put in the book of Proverbs. More will be said about these principles throughout the remainder of this course. What follows are the most basic principles for God's system of economics.

Principle #1. God owns the world, and we are stewards of it.

This is the most basic economic principle of all. Everything belongs to God, and no individual person or government can claim ultimate ownership of anything. God owns all the dirt, all the trees, and everything else. God created each of us, and He owns us too.

> The earth is the LORD's, and all its fullness,
> The world and those who dwell therein. (Ps. 24:1)

God owns the whole world.

> If I were hungry, I would not tell you;
> For the world is Mine, and all its fullness. (Ps. 50:12)
>
> Who has preceded Me, that I should pay him?
> Everything under heaven is Mine. (Job 41:11)

When God created man, He put him in a garden "to tend and keep it" (Gen. 2:15). He expects man to rule over this creation; God has appointed him for that purpose. In this sense, everybody works for God. However, most of the world continues in rebellion against God. They pretend they are working for themselves or for their human social unit. They have rebelled against their Master, and they do their work for themselves with no intent of serving God. In this sense, they have stolen God's resources and are using them entirely for themselves.

> Then the LORD God took the man and put him in the garden of Eden to tend and keep it. (Gen. 2:15)
>
> What is man that You are mindful of him,
> And the son of man that You visit him?
> For You have made him a little lower than the angels,
> And You have crowned him with glory and honor.
> You have made him to have dominion over the works of Your hands;
> You have put all things under his feet. (Ps. 8:4-6)

God has placed man over all His creation, to cultivate the fields, to care for the animals, to make good use of the oil in the ground, and to be sure that there will be more trees and crops each year. Every one of us has been given a little bit of God's wealth to look after. Some of us own pets. Some of us own property. Some of us have twenty dollars to our name. Some of us are given a bed and a little closet for our clothes. But all of us have some little part of God's stuff to take care of.

According to His gracious purposes, God gives each of us talents and tools. Money is a tool or a means of blessing others and producing more goods and services. Our talents, intelligence, skills, training, and capital are all gifts from God to be used for profitable ends.

We are stewards of God's creation.

Every Christian, whether he be a lowly slave or a powerful business owner, must realize that he works for God. He is a servant of Jesus Christ in every aspect of his work. Therefore, in whatever we do, we must work with all our heart, knowing that we are laboring every minute for our Lord who gave Himself for us on the cross.

> Bondservants, obey in all things your masters according to the flesh, not with eyeservice, as men-pleasers, but in sincerity of heart, fearing God. And whatever you do, do it heartily, as to the Lord and not to men, knowing that from the Lord you will receive the reward of the inheritance; for you serve the Lord Christ. (Col. 3:22-24)

Principle #2. God assigns to each of us some property and wealth.

As previously stated, God owns everything. "The earth is the LORD's, and all its fullness" (Ps. 24:1). Therefore, private property ownership is property that is on loan from God. We are stewards of God's things, and He reserves the right to take them away from us (especially if we are not stewarding His gifts well). All wealth comes from God, the ultimate source of all blessings.

> The blessing of the LORD makes one rich,
> And He adds no sorrow with it. (Prov. 10:22)

Some people think the civil government owns everything and that it's supposed to lend some of it to each person in the community. Some believe that the whole community is supposed to share all the wealth. No single person should own anything for themselves, they say. Although the govern-

Civil government is not God.

ment may at times grab everything and pretend like it owns everything, this is a lie. The government isn't a god. Our Creator God owns everything, and when government grabs everything for itself, the government has turned into a robber. God gives the civil government some things to look after. Governments are supposed to take dominion over criminals who rob banks and kill people. They rightfully own courtrooms, jails, and a few guns. But they do not own everything. When they take the things that don't belong to them (as determined by God's law), they act like mobsters and robbers. They set a bad example for everybody else in society.

It is wrong to steal your friend's things. It is wrong because God gave those things to your friend, not to you. To steal them from your friend is to take something that God did not give you. That's why stealing from your friend is disobedience to God. And, in fact, it is stealing from God.

> You shall not steal. (Ex. 20:15)

> Let him who stole steal no longer, but rather let him labor, working with his hands what is good, that he may have something to give him who has need. (Eph. 4:28)

This is the basis for the ownership of private property. Within a society, there should be clear definitions as to who owns what or who has the responsibility to care for any particular property, wealth, or assets. Otherwise, evil men will take advantage of the lack of clarity and collect wealth that doesn't belong to them. And nothing will stop them from doing that.

Some people will attempt to gain wealth illegitimately by robbing others. Of course, the Lord God will see to it that this wealth will quickly dissipate. He will add nothing but sorrow to such wealth.

> Wealth gained by dishonesty will be diminished,
> But he who gathers by labor will increase. (Prov. 13:11)

> One who increases his possessions by usury and extortion
> Gathers it for him who will pity the poor. (Prov. 28:8)

There are many wrong responses to handling wealth, including greed, covetousness, idolatry, and so forth. But the two right responses to wealth are gratitude and wise stewardship. The more wealth we receive, the more God expects us to handle this wealth responsibly. Therefore, when just starting out in life, you want to be faithful in small things. If you are faithful with handling $100, some day you may receive $1,000. If you are responsible with that, some day you may receive $10,000, and so forth. Above all, God has given us our daily needs, and we should receive these with thanksgiving.

> For every creature of God is good, and nothing is to be refused if it is received with thanksgiving. (1 Tim. 4:4)

We must be good stewards of God's blessings by cleaning and maintaining our possessions such as a house.

Before you seek after more money, more business, more capital, or more stuff, consider whether you are able to steward it. Consider this before you buy anything. Every vehicle or piece of electronic equipment you purchase will require care and maintenance. A 1,000 square foot home requires cleaning, maintenance, and upkeep. A 10,000 square foot house requires ten times the work of that required of a 1,000 square foot home. A 100,000 square foot house requires 100 times the work of a 1,000 square foot home.

You would have to hire at least thirty people to maintain a home that large.

> Be diligent to know the state of your flocks,
> And attend to your herds;
> For riches are not forever,
> Nor does a crown endure to all generations. (Prov. 27:23-24)

Capital investments tend towards disorder and chaos unless people put work into them and take good care of them. Herd animals die. Houses are eaten by carpenter ants or termites. Businesses disintegrate without careful management. Some people think they can invest in stocks or build a business that gives them residual (automatic) income with the hopes that they can coast on this investment. But that's only an illusion. When God turns capital over to a steward, He expects that money to be well-managed.

Principle #3. Economic blessings are not the highest blessings.

While we are thankful for material blessings, the Christian will consider other blessings to be of higher value than these. For example, receiving God's Word and living it out is of more value than gold.

The Word of God is of more value than gold.

> I have treasured the words of His mouth
> More than my necessary food. (Job 23:12)
>
> The statutes of the LORD are right, rejoicing the heart;
> The commandment of the LORD is pure, enlightening the eyes;
> The fear of the LORD is clean, enduring forever;
> The judgments of the LORD are true and righteous altogether.
> More to be desired are they than gold,
> Yea, than much fine gold;
> Sweeter also than honey and the honeycomb.
> Moreover by them Your servant is warned,
> And in keeping them there is great reward.
> (Ps. 19:8-11)

What could be better than an increase in riches? Godliness with contentment. To be loving God and worshiping God is the highest fulfillment of a person's life. To be at peace and rest when circumstances change—even when going through trials—is the best life to live here on earth. That's Paul's assessment in 1 Timothy 6.

> Now godliness with contentment is great gain. For we brought nothing into this world, and it is certain we can carry nothing out. And having food and clothing, with these we shall be content. (1 Tim. 6:6-7)

Rich people are often the most miserable people of all. Wealthy nations are known for their complaining. In fact, recent surveys found that the whiniest people in the world live in Sweden, the UK, Australia, Canada, and the US—some of the richest nations on earth. The least whiny nations turn out to be poorer countries.

In the Parable of the Rich Fool, Jesus commended those who are "rich toward God," as opposed to those who store up wealth for themselves here on earth (Luke 12:21). This wealth comes by giving to the poor (Luke 12:33) and caring for Jesus' servants or His missionaries (Luke 12:42). Treasures in heaven are much more valuable than treasures on earth "where moth and rust destroy and where thieves break in and steal" (Matt. 6:19).

Storing up treasures in heaven is much more important than storing up treasures on earth.

> Riches do not profit in the day of wrath,
> But righteousness delivers from death. (Prov. 11:4)
>
> There is one who makes himself rich, yet has nothing;
> And one who makes himself poor, yet has great riches. (Prov. 13:7)
>
> A good name is to be chosen rather than great riches,
> Loving favor rather than silver and gold. (Prov. 22:1)
>
> Better is the poor who walks in his integrity
> Than one perverse in his ways, though he be rich. (Prov. 28:6)

Principle #4. Slothfulness is miserable, and this is the cursed thing that ruins big and small economies.

The New Testament is more concerned about spiritual slothfulness and sleepiness, but the root of this spiritual sin can sometimes be found in physical sluggardliness. There are various kinds of slothfulness as well.

Some sloths won't work. Some will work until they confront a "lion in the street"—an obstacle of some sort (Prov. 22:13). They quickly give up. Some sloths lack a conscientiousness in their work. They do not carefully take all the meat from an animal they have killed in hunting (Prov. 12:27). That level of detail and care is just too hard for them. Basically, the sluggard hates work.

> The way of the lazy man is like a hedge of thorns,
> But the way of the upright is a highway. (Prov. 15:19)
>
> He who is slothful in his work
> Is a brother to him who is a great destroyer. (Prov. 18:9)
>
> As vinegar to the teeth and smoke to the eyes,
> So is the lazy man to those who send him. (Prov. 10:26)

One sluggard can destroy a small start-up business. The sluggard is intimidated by every job, and every effort becomes torturous. Economic blessings for everybody come when everybody works hard six days a week (both physically and mentally).

Those that will not work should not eat, according to 2 Thessalonians 3:10. And those men who will not provide the necessities for their own families are to be considered as unbelievers (1 Tim. 5:8).

Principle #5. The Lord wants us to serve the needs of others. Giving is a very important priority for Christians.

And those who are wealthier are instructed to be more willing to share their wealth with those in need.

> Command those who are rich in this present age not to be haughty, nor to trust in uncertain riches but in the living God, who gives us richly all things to enjoy. Let them do good, that they be rich in good works, ready to give, willing to share, storing up for themselves a good foundation for the time to come, that they may lay hold on eternal life. (1 Tim. 6:17–19)

When the Israelites refused to give at least ten percent of their income for the public worship and service of God, Malachi accused them of stealing from God (Mal. 3:8). If God rightly owns all things and demands a certain amount of His resources dedicated to His worship, then that is owed to God. To neglect to pay what is owed Him would amount to robbing Him.

The Bible commands we give resources for the Lord's worship and mission.

Principle #6. God wants us to use a system of honest money and honest exchange.

> Diverse weights and diverse measures,
> They are both alike, an abomination to the LORD. (Prov. 20:10)

This means that merchants should not change the perceived value of what people are getting in the exchange of goods and services. When an exchange happens, somebody trades a silver coin (for example) for a box of apples weighing twenty-five pounds. But, if the fellow who sells the apples puts a finger on the scale and the buyer only gets twenty pounds (while he thinks he's getting twenty-five pounds), this is an abomination to the Lord. Then, if the buyer shaves a little of the silver off the coin to keep for himself, he cheats the apple merchant. He purposefully devalues the coin, collects the silver shavings from quite a few coins, and mints another coin. This also is an abomination to the Lord.

The value of the silver coin or the price of apples might change according to the natural shifts happening with supply and demand. But individuals should not purposefully change the value to benefit themselves or their friends. In the wealthy nations of today, governments are most guilty of these crimes.

This also applies to the quality of the product offered in the exchange. For the merchant to hide bruises and rotting portions of the apples by only displaying the nicer-looking sides of their apples is another example of intentional cheating.

Principle #7. Love of money is the root of all kinds of evil. Greed is a sin.

All investment and business motivated by greed and the love of money are eventually corrupting. Sin is corrupting. When the stock investors are more interested in making a quick profit than they are in the annual earnings of the company they are investing in, the market is turning to greed. The love of money ruins relationships, marriages, churches, and nations.

> He who loves silver will not be satisfied with silver;
> Nor he who loves abundance, with increase.
> This also is vanity. (Eccl. 5:10)
>
> He who is greedy for gain troubles his own house,
> But he who hates bribes will live. (Prov. 15:27)

Principle #8. God blesses hard work, honesty, humility, the fear of God, wisdom, and faith.

Honest, God-fearing countries are profitable countries.

> By humility and the fear of the LORD
> Are riches and honor and life. (Prov. 22:4)

> He who has a slack hand becomes poor,
> But the hand of the diligent makes rich.
> He who gathers in summer is a wise son;
> He who sleeps in harvest is a son who causes shame. (Prov. 10:4-5)

According to His general rules by which He governs economies, God honors faithful work, modest work, and gradual increase of capital. He does not honor get-rich-quick approaches.

> An inheritance gained hastily at the beginning
> Will not be blessed at the end. (Prov. 20:21)

> A man with an evil eye hastens after riches,
> And does not consider that poverty will come upon him. (Prov. 28:22)

Hearts filled with greed almost always rush into get-rich-quick schemes. These takes many forms. Some businessmen will continually borrow money to build their "empires." Some will gamble on the stock market, buying and selling quickly in hopes that the markets will rise and fall in their favor. Others will gamble their money in card games and casinos.

There are several things that lead to poverty. For example, some will talk big plans and exaggerate about money they've made in the past, but they don't really like to work. Foolish people cannot possibly produce genuine wealth, which includes sustainable financial wealth.

> In all labor there is profit,
> But idle chatter leads only to poverty.
> The crown of the wise is their riches,
> But the foolishness of fools is folly. (Prov. 14:23-24)

> He who tills his land will be satisfied with bread, but he who follows frivolity is devoid of understanding. (Prov. 12:11)

As God would have it, the faithful, steady-as-you-go farmer is guaranteed to be satisfied with his bread. There is nothing spectacular about farming. It is hard work, but it's basic work.

Hard work is rewarding.

Proverbs 12:11 compares the humble, hard-working, salt-of-the-earth sort of person to the man devoid of understanding. Texans speak of the big talker who is "all hat and no cattle." A person is a fool if he follows big talkers, people who just want to have fun, and people who only have the trappings of success. These frivolous fellows usually tout a magnetic personality and draw many young people into their wake.

Principle #9. God commands rest. Even as the Lord commands a six-day work week for us all, He has assigned one day a week for rest. Too much work without rest leads to burnout and longer-term inefficiencies. But the most important reason for rest is to dedicate a day for worship and thanksgiving. When we cease from working for ourselves, even for a day, we testify to our faith that God is the One who is ultimately providing for us.

> For he who has entered [God's] rest has himself also ceased from his works as God did from His. Let us therefore be diligent to enter that rest. (Heb. 4:10-11)

Principle #10. Slavery and debt are negative consequences of man's fall into sin.

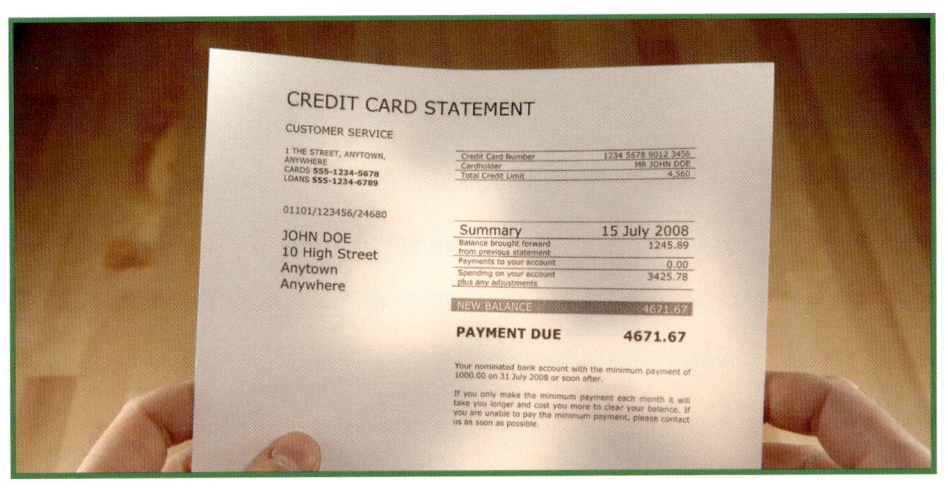

Debt is a form of slavery.

Thus, these are undesirable conditions. Debt is an indication of impoverishment (Deut. 15:7-8). With God's people, we want to limit debt (and, ideally, eliminate it).

Nations in deep debt are plainly under the judgment of God. This is the clear lesson of Deuteronomy 28:

> The alien who is among you shall rise higher and higher above you, and you shall come down lower and lower. He shall lend to you, but you shall not lend to him; he shall be the head, and you shall be the tail. Moreover all these curses shall come upon you and pursue and overtake you, until you are destroyed, because you did not obey the voice of

> the LORD your God, to keep His commandments and His statutes which He commanded you. (Deut. 28:43-45)
>
> The rich rules over the poor,
> And the borrower is servant to the lender. (Prov. 22:7)

CONCLUSION

These biblical principles must frame the Christian mind and life in the field of economics. Certainly, the Christian student should understand the world and the principles according to which worldly people live their lives and run their systems. Yet it is still more crucial that Christians be grounded in the principles by which God runs the world and the principles by which He wants us to operate. Worldly principles offer short-term success, and they do not take eternity into consideration. It would be wrong for Christians to study economics without considering eternal values.

So, when we consider how the world runs, we should be concerned with three things:
1. How God runs the world,
2. How people try to run the world,
3. How we should run the world by God's principles.

That is the thrust of this manual.

I, PENCIL *By Leonard E. Read*

Used by permission of the Foundation for Economic Education (www.fee.org).

I am a lead pencil—the ordinary wooden pencil familiar to all boys and girls and adults who can read and write. Writing is both my vocation and my avocation; that's all I do. You may wonder why I should write a genealogy. Well, to begin with, my story is interesting. And, next, I am a mystery—more so than a tree or a sunset or even a flash of lightning. But, sadly, I am taken for granted by those who use me, as if I were a mere incident and without background. This supercilious attitude relegates me to the level of the commonplace. This is a species of the grievous error in which mankind cannot too long persist without peril. For, the wise G. K. Chesterton observed, "We are perishing for want of wonder, not for want of wonders."

I, Pencil, simple though I appear to be, merit your wonder and awe, a claim I shall attempt to prove. In fact, if you can understand me—no, that's too much to ask of anyone—if you can become aware of the miraculousness which I symbolize, you can help save the freedom mankind is so unhappily losing. I have a profound lesson to teach. And I can teach this lesson better than can an automobile or an airplane or a mechanical dishwasher because—well, because I am seemingly so simple.

Simple? Yet not a single person on the face of this earth knows how to make me. This sounds fantastic, doesn't it? Especially when it is realized that there are about one and one-half billion of my kind produced in the U.S.A. each year.

Pick me up and look me over. What do you see? Not much meets the eye—there's some wood, lacquer, the printed labeling, graphite lead, a bit of metal, and an eraser.

Innumerable Antecedents

Just as you cannot trace your family tree back very far, so is it impossible for me to name and explain all my antecedents. But I would like to suggest enough of them to impress upon you the richness and complexity of my background.

My family tree begins with what in fact is a tree, a cedar of straight grain that grows in Northern California and Oregon. Now contemplate all the saws and trucks and rope and the countless other gear used in harvesting and carting the cedar logs to the railroad siding. Think of all the persons and the numberless skills that went into their fabrication: the mining of ore, the making of steel and its refinement into saws, axes, motors; the growing of hemp and bringing it through all the stages to heavy and strong rope; the logging camps with their beds and mess halls, the cookery and the raising of all the foods. Why, untold thousands of persons had a hand in every cup of coffee the loggers drink!

The logs are shipped to a mill in San Leandro, California. Can you imagine the individuals who make flat cars and rails and railroad engines and who construct and install the communication systems incidental thereto? These legions are among my antecedents.

Consider the millwork in San Leandro. The cedar logs are cut into small, pencil-length slats less than one-fourth of an inch in thickness. These are kiln dried and then tinted for the same reason women put rouge on their faces. People prefer that I look pretty, not a pallid white. The slats are waxed and kiln dried again. How many skills went into the making of the tint and the kilns, into supplying the heat, the light and power, the belts, motors, and all the other things a mill requires? Sweepers in the mill among my ancestors? Yes, and included are the men who poured the concrete for the dam of a Pacific Gas & Electric Company hydroplant which supplies the mill's power!

Don't overlook the ancestors present and distant who have a hand in transporting sixty carloads of slats across the nation.

Once in the pencil factory—$4,000,000 in machinery and building, all capital accumulated by thrifty and saving parents of mine—each slat is given eight grooves by a complex machine, after which another machine lays leads in every other slat, applies glue, and places another slat atop—a lead sandwich, so to speak. Seven brothers and I are mechanically carved from this "wood-clinched" sandwich.

My "lead" itself—it contains no lead at all—is complex. The graphite is mined in Ceylon [Sri Lanka]. Consider these miners and those who make their many tools and the makers of the paper sacks in which the graphite is shipped and those who make the string that ties the sacks and those who put them aboard ships and those who make the ships. Even the lighthouse keepers along the way assisted in my birth—and the harbor pilots.

The graphite is mixed with clay from Mississippi in which ammonium hydroxide is used in the refining process. Then wetting agents are added such as sulfonated tallow—animal fats chemically reacted with sulfuric acid. After passing through numerous machines, the mixture finally appears as endless extrusions—as from a sausage grinder—cut to size, dried, and baked for several hours at 1,850 degrees Fahrenheit. To increase their strength and smoothness the leads are then treated with a hot mixture which includes candelilla wax from Mexico, paraffin wax, and hydrogenated natural fats.

My cedar receives six coats of lacquer. Do you know all the ingredients of lacquer? Who would think that the growers of castor beans and the refiners of castor oil are a part of it? They are. Why, even the processes by which the lacquer is made a beautiful yellow involve the skills of more persons than one can enumerate!

Observe the labeling. That's a film formed by applying heat to carbon black mixed with resins. How do you make resins and what, pray, is carbon black?

My bit of metal—the ferrule—is brass. Think of all the persons who mine zinc and copper and those who have the skills to make shiny sheet brass from these products of nature. Those black rings on my ferrule are black nickel. What is black nickel and how is it applied? The complete story of why the center of my ferrule has no black nickel on it would take pages to explain.

Then there's my crowning glory, inelegantly referred to in the trade as "the plug," the part man uses to erase the errors he makes with me. An ingredient called "factice" is what does the erasing. It is a rubber-like product made by reacting rapeseed oil from the Dutch East Indies [Indonesia] with sulfur chloride. Rubber, contrary to the common notion, is only for binding purposes. Then, too, there are numerous vulcanizing and accelerating agents. The pumice comes from Italy; and the pigment which gives "the plug" its color is cadmium sulfide.

No One Knows

Does anyone wish to challenge my earlier assertion that no single person on the face of this earth knows how to make me?

Actually, millions of human beings have had a hand in my creation, no one of whom even knows more than a very few of the others. Now, you may say that I go too far in relating the picker of a coffee berry in far-off Brazil and food growers elsewhere to my creation; that this is an extreme position. I shall stand by my claim. There isn't a single person in all these millions, including the president of the pencil company, who contributes more than a tiny, infinitesimal bit of know-how. From the standpoint of know-how the only difference between the miner of graphite in Ceylon and the logger in Oregon is in the type of know-how. Neither the miner nor the logger can be dispensed with, any more than can the chemist at the factory or the worker in the oil field—paraffin being a by-product of petroleum.

Here is an astounding fact: Neither the worker in the oil field nor the chemist nor the digger of graphite or clay nor any who mans or makes the ships or trains or trucks nor the one who runs the machine that does the knurling on my bit of metal nor the president of the company performs his singular task because he wants me. Each one wants me less, perhaps, than does a child in the first grade. Indeed, there are some among this vast multitude who never saw a pencil nor would they know how to use one. Their motivation is other than me. Perhaps it is something like this: Each of these millions sees that he can thus exchange his tiny know-how for the goods and services he needs or wants. I may or may not be among these items.

No Master Mind

There is a fact still more astounding: The absence of a master mind, of anyone dictating or forcibly directing these countless actions which bring me into being. No trace of such a person can be found. Instead, we find the Invisible Hand at work. This is the mystery to which I earlier referred.

It has been said that "only God can make a tree." Why do we agree with this? Isn't it because we realize that we ourselves could not make one? Indeed, can we even describe a tree? We cannot, except in superficial terms. We can say, for instance, that a certain molecular configuration manifests itself as a tree. But what mind is there among men that could even record, let alone direct, the constant changes in molecules that transpire in the life span of a tree? Such a feat is utterly unthinkable!

I, Pencil, am a complex combination of miracles: a tree, zinc, copper, graphite, and so on. But to these miracles which manifest themselves in Nature an even more extraordinary miracle has been added: the configuration of creative human energies—millions of tiny know-hows configurating naturally and spontaneously in response to human necessity and desire and in the absence of any human masterminding! Since only God can make a tree, I insist that only God could make me. Man can no more direct these millions of know-hows to bring me into being than he can put molecules together to create a tree.

The above is what I meant when writing, "If you can become aware of the miraculousness which I symbolize, you can help save the freedom mankind is so unhappily losing." For, if one is aware that these know-hows will naturally, yes, automatically, arrange themselves into creative and productive patterns in response to human necessity and demand—that is, in the absence of governmental or any other coercive master-minding—then one will possess an absolutely essential ingredient for freedom: a faith in free people. Freedom is impossible without this faith.

Once government has had a monopoly of a creative activity such, for instance, as the delivery of the mails, most individuals will believe that the mails could not be efficiently delivered by men acting freely. And here is the reason: Each one acknowledges that he himself doesn't know how to do all the things incident to mail delivery. He also recognizes that no other individual could do it. These assumptions are correct. No individual possesses enough know-how to perform a nation's mail delivery any more than any individual possesses enough know-how to make a pencil. Now, in the absence of faith in free people—in the unawareness that millions of tiny know-hows would naturally and miraculously form and cooperate to satisfy this necessity—the individual cannot help but reach the erroneous conclusion that mail can be delivered only by governmental "masterminding."

Testimony Galore

If I, Pencil, were the only item that could offer testimony on what men and women can accomplish when free to try, then those with little faith would have a fair case. However, there is testimony galore; it's all about us and on every hand. Mail delivery is exceedingly simple when compared, for instance, to the making of an automobile or a calculating machine or a grain combine or a milling machine or to tens of thousands of other things. Delivery? Why, in this area where men have been left free to try, they deliver the human voice around the world in less than one second; they deliver an event visually and in motion to any person's home when it is happening; they deliver 150 passengers from Seattle to Baltimore in less than four hours; they deliver gas from Texas to one's range or furnace in New York at unbelievably low rates and without subsidy; they deliver each four pounds of oil from the Persian Gulf to our Eastern Seaboard—halfway around the world—for less money than the government charges for delivering a one-ounce letter across the street!

The lesson I have to teach is this: Leave all creative energies uninhibited. Merely organize society to act in harmony with this lesson. Let society's legal apparatus remove all obstacles the best it can. Permit these creative know-hows freely to flow. Have faith that free men and women will respond to the Invisible Hand. This faith will be confirmed. I, Pencil, seemingly simple though I am, offer the miracle of my creation as testimony that this is a practical faith, as practical as the sun, the rain, a cedar tree, the good earth.

4

THORNS AND THISTLES— THE REALITY OF SIN, THE EFFECTS OF SIN, AND JUDGMENT

Then to Adam He said, "Because you have heeded the voice of your wife,
and have eaten from the tree of which I commanded you, saying,
'You shall not eat of it':
Cursed is the ground for your sake;
In toil you shall eat of it all the days of your life.
Both thorns and thistles it shall bring forth for you,
And you shall eat the herb of the field.
In the sweat of your face you shall eat bread
Till you return to the ground,
For out of it you were taken; For dust you are,
And to dust you shall return."
(Gen. 3:17-19)

At the creation, the Lord God assigned to Adam the responsibility of tending and keeping the Garden of Eden. Then man fell into sin, and came under the curse. This introduced serious personal and economic problems for himself and his children. Life would be tough from here on out. The ground would not yield its increase as easily as it had before.

Let's consider how much time it takes to cultivate a garden. One gardener estimated that it takes 100 hours per year to tend 400 square feet of a garden. To yield a full acre of vegetables (about 20 tons), a gardener would have to invest about 10,000 hours per year. That would require the work of four persons working full time. Before the fall, far less effort would have been required. Think about yielding 20 tons of vegetables with only 1,000 hours per year—the part-time work of a single farmer. That was the blessing of the Garden of Eden. There was work to do but less weeds, less sweat, and less effort overall.

And so, after the fall, we would expect more "lions in the street." There would be more challenges hindering us from getting work done. As already mentioned, **entropy** set in after the fall. This is the tendency for gardens and economies to decay or descend into disorder. What would happen to a house if nobody lived in it, or main-

The effects of entropy upon an abandoned house

tained it or cleaned it? Assuming the house was left without any care whatsoever for five or ten years, it would disintegrate into a ramshackle condition—spiderwebs, dust and dirt, dead insects, and animal droppings would be everywhere. Water damage would doubtless rot out the floors, and the paint would fade on the siding and internal walls.

Without labor and God's blessing of the fruit of labor, humans will starve to death. Incredibly, despite the improvements in technology over the past hundred years, the world still experiences famines.

Most of the recent famines were caused by evil civil governments and their perverse policies. These tyrannies confiscated the profits of hardworking peoples, stole their properties, and generally discouraged production and hard work. They implemented economic policies that opposed the laws of God. That is what happened with the North Korean, Ethiopian, Communist Chinese, and Soviet famines. When nations oppose Christ and His rule, the hand of God's judgment is usually close to follow.

Years	Famine	Populace Starved to Death (estimated)
1921-1922	Soviet Union Famine	9,000,000
1932-1933	Soviet Union/Ukrainian Famine	7,000,000
1942-1943	Bengal Indian Famines	2,000,000
1959-1961	Communist Chinese Famine	20,000,000 – 50,000,000
1983-1985	Ethiopian Famine	250,000
1994-1998	North Korean Famine	3,000,000
1998	Sudanese Famine	75,000
2005-2011	East African Famines	100,000

Why do the nations rage,
And the people plot a vain thing?
The kings of the earth set themselves,
And the rulers take counsel together,
Against the LORD and against His Anointed, saying,
"Let us break Their bonds in pieces

> And cast away Their cords from us." . . .
> Now therefore, be wise, O kings;
> Be instructed, you judges of the earth.
> Serve the LORD with fear,
> And rejoice with trembling.
> Kiss the Son, lest He be angry,
> And you perish in the way,
> When His wrath is kindled but a little.
> Blessed are all those who put their trust in Him. (Ps. 2:1-4, 10-12)

In large part, the African famines were due to droughts and poor economies. Most African communities rely on **"subsistence" farming**. These people farm only as much as they need, barely getting by from year to year. And they save little or no surplus for a bad year. In these countries, corrupt governments and a thieving populace also make it hard for an entrepreneurial farmer to get ahead. Class envy, socialist policies, red tape, and bribery keep farming from developing. This destroys any possibility for division of labor and consigns the entire nation to severe poverty. The influence of Christ and His transforming gospel have yet to transform these countries in significant ways. (Some African countries have a more sustainable economy and good surpluses. These countries include Tunisia, Morocco, Egypt, and Algeria in the north and South Africa and Namibia in the south.)

Farmer planting manioc in Malawi

Yet the nations most impacted by the Christian faith over the previous thousand years have avoided mass starvations. Most of these are Western nations. While their governments still have problems, God has preserved them from more severe consequences of man's fall. For example, the US consumes 355 million metric tons of grain each year and maintains about 600 million metric tons in storage.[1] Those reserves should be enough to feed the country for a period of two years, should a nationwide famine occur.

Government-imposed famines killed many in the 20th century.

COMMON GRACE

> Be sons of your Father in heaven; for He makes His sun rise on the evil and on the good, and sends rain on the just and on the unjust. (Matt. 5:45)

During the 20th century, between 42 and 72 million people died of starvation. But during the same period there were almost 13 billion people who did not die of starvation. We should be thankful that 99.7% of the world's population had enough food to eat during the last century. Taking out the famines caused by cruel and incompetent governments, that number would be closer to 100.0%. Well then, how did 99.7% of the people in the world get enough food to eat? The short answer is that God is still gracious to the world even though much of the world lives in rebellion and ingratitude towards Him.

Why do so few people starve to death? God is merciful, and He continues to send His rain and sunshine upon the just and the unjust. He preserves the world by His **common grace**. Often He protects nations from terrible communist tyrants who would destroy these nations. The Proverbs call these dictators "a roaring lion and a charging bear" (Prov. 28:15).

God is merciful to provide the world with an abundance of food.

SLAVERY AND DEBT

There are still more negative consequences that come as a result of man's fall into sin. Divorce, disease, debt, and slavery are some of the worst outward effects of this fall. While none of these are desirable conditions, they are inevitable conditions at certain times throughout mankind's existence. Slavery and debt are economic evils that sometimes affect certain families and communities over time.

The first record of slavery in the Bible is found in Genesis 9. After Ham had sinned against his father, Noah passed a curse on to Ham's son, Canaan.

> Cursed be Canaan;
> A servant of servants
> He shall be to his brethren. (Gen. 9:25)

Slavery is seen here as an evil consequence of sin. In the modern world, slavery or bondservanthood is usually limited to criminals serving time in prison. Sometimes, slavery results from wars between nations. During periods of famine and impoverishment, people would sell themselves or their children into slavery.

From the Genesis account, we learn that Egyptians maintained a slave-based economy, where Abram and Sarai obtained an Egyptian slave named Hagar (Gen. 16:1-2).

Slavery is an Evil Effect of the Fall - Slaves in the Roman Empire (200 AD).

Just as God established laws to control divorce, the Mosaic law instituted controls on slavery. Israelites were forbidden to hold slaves for more than six years. Then, every fiftieth year, the Israelites were commanded to have a special year of Jubilee in which all Israelite slaves were to be set free. This included all slaves who were forced to sell themselves to their fellow Israelites. If a poor Israelite was forced to sell off his land due to financial needs, the land would revert back to his family in the year of Jubilee.

> And if one of your brethren who dwells by you becomes poor, and sells himself to you, you shall not compel him to serve as a slave. As a hired servant and a sojourner he shall be with you, and shall serve you until the Year of Jubilee. And then he shall depart from you—he and his children with him—and shall return to his own family. He shall

> return to the possession of his fathers. For they are My servants, whom I brought out of the land of Egypt; they shall not be sold as slaves. (Lev. 25:39-42)

When Jesus Christ entered our world, He came with a proclamation of liberty for the captives (Luke 4:18-19). Although Christ was mainly speaking of liberty from the bondage of sin and the devil, the Apostle Paul in 1 Corinthians 7:21-23 extended this liberty to those who were actual bondslaves:

> Were you called while a slave? Do not be concerned about it; but if you can be made free, rather use it. For he who is called in the Lord while a slave is the Lord's freedman. Likewise he who is called while free is Christ's slave. You were bought at a price; do not become slaves of men. (1 Cor. 7:21-23)

Thus, slavery is considered a substandard or undesirable condition for God's people in the New Testament. The Apostle also encouraged Philemon to voluntarily free his slave Onesimus and to treat him no longer as a slave but as a beloved brother in Christ.

> For perhaps [Onesimus] departed for a while for this purpose, that you might receive him forever, no longer as a slave but more than a slave—a beloved brother, especially to me but how much more to you, both in the flesh and in the Lord. (Philem. 1:15-16)

Christians in the early church sought to provide manumission to redeem slaves. Patrick of Ireland is known for his fierce opposition to the Irish slave trade, especially evident in his letter to Coroticus. In the 7th century, the Christian King Clovis II of the Franks (633-657) married a slave. And, after his death, his redeemed slave-wife, Bathilda, dedicated the remainder of her life to redeeming slaves. Finally, in AD 1102, an English church council put an end to the slave trade entirely.

However, while the Christians were fighting hard to eliminate slavery, the Muslims continued the practice. Throughout the 8th, 9th, 10th, and 11th centuries, the African Moors enslaved Europeans while taking over

Spain and Portugal on the Iberian Peninsula. These African Muslims kidnapped slaves as far north as Norway and Sweden.

During the Italian (humanist) Renaissance in the 1400s, a very corrupt Roman church revived the slave trade. Pope Nicholas V issued the infamous *Dum Diversas*, initiating the modern system of slavery. Pope Nicholas' proclamation read in part:

> We grant you by these present documents, with our Apostolic Authority, full and free permission to invade, search out, capture, and subjugate the Saracens and pagans and any other unbelievers and enemies of Christ wherever they may be, as well as their kingdoms, duchies, counties, principalities, and other property, . . . and to reduce their persons into perpetual servitude.

Charles II and James II (both Roman Catholic kings) introduced slavery into North America in the 1670s and 1680s. Practically single-handedly, these English kings built up the slave-based economy in the colonies of America which continued until the US Civil War of 1861.

The slave trade was finally stopped largely through the efforts of William Wilberforce, a Christian evangelical from England. However, new forms of tyranny formed in the humanist era of the 1900s and 2000s.

Pope Nicholas V

Since the 1860s, the entire world has come under the heavy hand of tyrannical governments. These federal and state governments are twenty times more powerful than they were back then. Whereas they only controlled about 1% of the economy in the 1860s, now they control 30-50% of the economy.

Slowly but surely, most of the "democratic" nations in the West have accepted totalitarian forms of government. It wasn't just the communist governments in China, Cuba, and Russia. It was Sweden, Germany, England, and America.

Thus, Christians will resist all forms of slavery. But at the same time we have to put up with some consequences of sin in this world. Surely debt, tyrannical governments, and varying forms of enslavement are as inevitable as divorce and disease in this world of sin. But we are not content to leave it there. We continue to value and believe in the power of the blood redemption of Christ. We cling to His promise: "If the Son will set you free, you will be free indeed." Where Jesus Christ works His redemption, He will make thorough work of it. He will set the captives free in more ways than one. He will help us to bring political and economic freedoms to our countries.

William Wilberforce

We will not take one form of slavery in exchange for another. Should the federal government attempt to enslave a nation in exchange for abolishing fiefdoms in the southern states, we will not settle for it. We want an end to all forms of slavery, by legitimate means. We want an end to government tyranny, but by legitimate means. We don't rely on revolution and war to bring this about. We must rely on God's work of regeneration in the hearts of men. We cannot change the world by taking up guns and overturning our governments. We are primarily interested in the preaching of the Christian Gospel.

Lamentably, so much of human history is sunk in the dreary malaise of slavery resulting from the harsh constraints of regulative governments, despotic tyrannies, local fiefdoms, corporate institutions, and creditors of all stripes. Though tyranny may be the default in a sinful world, there have been significant moments in history in which Christian liberty catalyzed within certain nations, and the world was better for it.

DEBT

> The rich rules over the poor,
> And the borrower is servant to the lender. (Prov. 22:7)

Scripture treats debt as another form of servitude much like slavery. The

Hebrew word used for "servant" in Proverbs 22:7 is the same word used for "slave" in Leviticus 25.

> Owe no one anything except to love one another, for he who loves another has fulfilled the law. (Rom. 13:8)

God's law allows for debt to assist those who fall into poverty. If a man became so poor that his children were going to starve to death or go without shoes, he would borrow money. Or he would enslave himself to a rich landowner. Clearly (from a biblical perspective), only the poor should borrow money.

> If there is among you a poor man of your brethren, within any of the gates in your land which the LORD your God is giving you, you shall not harden your heart nor shut your hand from your poor brother, but you shall open your hand wide to him and willingly lend him sufficient for his need, whatever he needs. (Deut. 15:7-8)

Certainly, there are situations in which debt is called for. For example, many young families at present cannot afford to buy their first home. Every family, at the very least, needs a roof over their heads. They don't need a mansion, but they do need 400-800 square feet of living space. In such cases, these poor families may need to borrow money to get a place to live. However, the Bible also limits this debt to seven years. While this principle did not apply to unbelievers as the Lord intended it for His people, we see from this that He always prefers liberty rather than debt.

> At the end of every seven years you shall grant a release of debts. . . . Of a foreigner you may require it; but you shall give up your claim to what is owed by your brother, except when there may be no poor among you; for the LORD will greatly bless you in the land which the LORD your God is giving you to possess as an inheritance—only if you carefully obey the voice of the LORD your God, to observe with care all these commandments which I command you today. (Deut. 15:1, 3-5)

The modern businessman thinks he will get rich if he goes into more debt. This is the wrong thinking of a world that abandons common sense and God's principles. Homeowners will often think this way too. They will count on inflation to benefit them when they go into debt. Inflation is the devaluation of money, where things go up in price because the value of money has diminished.

Here is the way the scheme works. A businessman buys five houses worth $100,000 each. But he borrows $90,000 for each house, paying only $10,000 each out of his own pocket. Because the value of money is decreasing, he expects the homes to be worth $120,000 in two years. Altogether, he has paid $50,000 for five houses. When he sells the homes, he walks away with five times $20,000, because each house went up in value by $20,000. He walks away with an additional $100,000 to add to his original $50,000. Now he has $150,000, a gain of $100,000 in two years. This is how modern businessmen try to get rich by using debt. Of course such get-rich-quick approaches are attractive, but they run counter to biblical principle and wisdom.

UNEMPLOYMENT, RECESSIONS, AND DEPRESSIONS

There are other economic consequences of a fallen world, including times of recessions and depressions. A **recession** is a period of economic decline, where there is less demand for products and less production of goods and services. This usually means loss of jobs and high rates of unemployment.

The **Gross Domestic Product** or GDP is a measurement of the productivity of a nation. How much food, homes, and cars are being produced? And how much buying and selling goes on in a year? When economies contract (or get smaller), the Gross Domestic Product goes down. There is less economic activity going on and there's less food, cars, and homes being produced. Officially, a nation goes through a recession when the productivity of the nation (as measured by the gross domestic product or GDP) goes down for two quarters in a row (or half of a year). A **depression** will

A bank run during the Great Depression

continue for years. For example, the Great Depression in America lasted from 1929 to 1934. The productivity of the nation dropped about 30%, and about 25% of American workers lost their jobs. Farmers who had no debt were not affected much by the bad economy. These small farms usually kept large vegetable gardens. They had plenty of milk, butter, and cream from their milk cows, and chickens provided plenty of eggs and meat.

Despite all the impoverishment that came out of the 1930s, American death rates were not affected by the Depression. Amazingly, there are no records of anybody starving to death during these years. God was still good to America. The death rate actually fell from 196 (per 100,000) in 1929 to 148 (per 100,000) in 1932. Here is another example of the mercy of God upon this country.

> Or do you despise the riches of His goodness, forbearance, and longsuffering, not knowing that the goodness of God leads you to repentance? But in accordance with your hardness and your impenitent

> heart you are treasuring up for yourself wrath in the day of wrath and revelation of the righteous judgment of God. (Rom. 2:4-5)

Usually, recessions are caused by sin and sinful habits among the peoples of a nation. Some of these sins include:
1. Too much greed and too many people getting into debt.
2. Too much stealing, cheating, and greed on the part of bankers.
3. Too much government involvement in the economy, especially when governments try to adjust the value of money.

At the least, recessions result in higher unemployment (at least in certain sectors). For example, the Covid-19 recession of 2020 impacted the hospitality and leisure industries. By the end of 2020, about 15% of these employees were without jobs.

Unemployment can come about by an oversupply of certain kinds of workers (and products) and/or a reduced demand. Or a certain product or service might become obsolete. After passenger airlines became popular, the passenger train lines didn't need as many conductors and other workers anymore.

Many restaurants temporarily or permanently closed during the COVID-19 recession.

Since unemployment means that there are certain sectors of the economy doing badly, one can always assume there are other sectors still healthy and strong. There is always work to do. The faithful, hardworking Christian will search out these new opportunities. These transitions from one field to another may be a little stressful. It usually takes a few months or even a year before the worker is trained and ready to go in a new field of work.

TYRANNY

> Like a roaring lion and a charging bear
> Is a wicked ruler over poor people. (Prov. 28:15)

As already mentioned, the biggest threats to a healthy economy are politicians, dictators, legislators, and political governors. More than anything, it is the wicked ruler that tears up an economy like a lion or a bear tears up its victim. The wicked ruler is the man who does not fear God and has no respect for God's commandments. He can do a lot of damage.

How do these wicked rulers come to reign? The Bible is clear. God raises up kings and brings them down. But if a nation is cursed with tyrants who are hurtful to the people, this has happened because God brought this judgment upon them. In fact, Proverbs 28:2 is quite clear:

> Because of the transgression of a land, many are its princes;
> But by a man of understanding and knowledge right will be prolonged.

Princes (or rulers) are expensive, and they take a lot of money from the people to support their lifestyles. With democracies, these princes are usually bureaucrats that don't do anything productive. But how do these bureaucracies grow so much? First, the people in a country or nation become very sinful. They break down the family by divorce. Men refuse to provide for their own households. Men and women break God's commandments everywhere. Businessmen cheat each other. Officials take bribes. These nations will suffer terrible decline. Then tyranny rises, and powerful government leaders kill the people and steal their belongings. This Scripture plainly says it is a sinful people that open the door to bad government and tyrants. As the immorality in a nation rises, civil governments will impose more regulation, more taxation, and more controls upon the citizens. They will hire more bureaucrats to do the job for them.

HOW TO BRING BLESSINGS UPON A NATION

> Then the men turned away from there and went toward Sodom, but Abraham still stood before the LORD. And Abraham came near and said, "Would You also destroy the righteous with the wicked? Suppose there were fifty righteous within the city; would You also destroy the place and not spare it for the fifty righteous that were in it? Far be it from You to do such a thing as this, to slay the righteous with the wicked, so that the righteous should be as the wicked; far be it from You! Shall not the Judge of all the earth do right?" So the LORD said, "If I find in Sodom fifty righteous within the city, then I will spare all the place for their sakes." . . . Then [Abraham] said, "Let not the LORD be angry, and I will speak but once more: Suppose ten should be found there?" And He said, "I will not destroy it for the sake of ten." (Gen. 18:22-26, 32)

What can you do to bless the community or the country where you live? Just a few Christians can do a lot of good. If there had only been ten righteous men left in Sodom and Gomorrah, God would not have destroyed those wicked cities. As it turned out, there was only one man in those cities who feared God and cared for the ways of God.

Using the same ratio that would have saved Sodom and Gomorrah, we would conclude that God would not destroy the city of Seattle if there were 700-1,000 righteous people living there. Just a small minority of faithful Christians in a business market or a city government could preserve the nation. Perhaps God would not destroy Los Angeles if there were 4,000 faithful Christians there. A few Christians can provide quite a lot of salt. These are humble people who trust in God. They don't idolize money. They care for the poor, without turning the poor over to the government. They fear God, and they are honest in their dealings. The children honor their parents and work hard.

> Praise the LORD!
> Blessed is the man who fears the LORD,
> Who delights greatly in His commandments.
> His descendants will be mighty on earth;
> The generation of the upright will be blessed.
> Wealth and riches will be in his house,
> And his righteousness endures forever.
> Unto the upright there arises light in the darkness;
> He is gracious, and full of compassion, and righteous.
> A good man deals graciously and lends;
> He will guide his affairs with discretion.
> Surely he will never be shaken;
> The righteous will be in everlasting remembrance.
> He will not be afraid of evil tidings;
> His heart is steadfast, trusting in the LORD.
> His heart is established;
> He will not be afraid,
> Until he sees his desire upon his enemies.
> He has dispersed abroad,
> He has given to the poor;
> His righteousness endures forever;
> His horn will be exalted with honor.
> The wicked will see it and be grieved;
> He will gnash his teeth and melt away;
> The desire of the wicked shall perish. (Ps. 112:1-10)

While sin brings destruction upon human society, there are two things that preserve human society: God's common grace and Christian salt.

God sends rain on the just and the unjust, and sometimes He favors a country with a wise and benevolent ruler. While this leader may not be a Christian, he could still make good decisions that benefit the country. This is common grace.

Sometimes Christians provide a preserving and blessed influence upon a nation as well. This is what we have seen in Protestant nations since the Reformation. Since the 16th century, these reformed Christians have produced the strongest economies in the world, including those of America, England, the Netherlands, and Switzerland. Transparency International conducts its Corruption Perception Index each year to determine what is the most honest nations in the world (and what are the most dishonest nations in the world). Of the sixteen least-corrupt nations, thirteen were predominantly Protestant nations, one was half Catholic and half Protestant, and the other two were nations colonized by Protestants.[2] These nations were founded by men and women who were taught the Christian faith and the commandments of God (Rev. 14:12). By God's grace, and by careful discipleship in all that Jesus has commanded, they learned to keep the eighth and tenth commandments. The freeman will be an honest man, maintaining a high degree of integrity in his business dealings. Nations like

God is merciful to send rain upon the just and the unjust.

Somalia, Venezuela, Yemen, Mexico, Haiti, and Congo are still impoverished because these nations have yet to be discipled in the things Jesus has commanded. They have yet to hear the Gospel of Christ that will set them free (from breaking the eighth and tenth commandments). Free enterprise systems are corrupted when greed comes to dominate in the hearts of men and they begin to cheat, lie, and steal. This is the story of capitalism in the 20th century. Labor-management relations broke down by oppression, envy, mistrust, lying, sexual intimidation, and economic inequities. The principles of the Bible are basic to the maintenance of free enterprise: "Masters, give your bondservants what is just and fair, knowing that you also have a Master in heaven" (Col. 4:1).

When Jesus came, He brought His redemption to the world. He came to "reconcile all things to Himself" (Col. 1:20). The blessings of this redemption are already evident everywhere around the world. As the Christmas carol puts it, He came to make His blessings known "as far as the curse is found!"

An impoverished family during the Great Depression (1935).

ADDENDUM
How People Survived America's Great Depression
1. Folks sold apples and other fruits grown in their backyard.
2. Some families relied on hunting, fishing, and gathering, supplementing their diets with blackberries, raspberries, wild nuts, wild asparagus, dandelions, and wild game in the countryside.
3. For protein, families relied on beans, peanut butter, eggs, fish, etc.
4. Many would find extra work to supplement their income—shoveling snow, mowing lawns, baby-sitting, shoe-shining, selling door-to-door, mining, etc.
5. Some repaired clothes and lined coats with blankets for extra warmth.
6. Some gave up their telephone or shared it with others.
7. Doctors and dentists reverted to home visits to save on rental costs for their businesses.
8. Some left the city for a self-sustainable lifestyle in the country.
9. Some sold their car and used a bicycle or motorcycle instead.
10. Some relied on neighbors for trading clothes or sharing water sources.
11. Some families moved in with extended family members.
12. Some pawned belongings.
13. Folks would use socks for gloves.
14. Some traded work for food.
15. Some families moved to where work was available.
16. Folks sewed and repaired their own clothing.
17. During heat waves, families slept on lawns, in basements, or in cellars.
18. Some lived out of cars and trucks. Some lived in tents.
19. Some grew their own vegetables in a garden. A cow and a garden made all the difference in the world.
20. Some used rubber tires as suitable replacements for shoe soles.
21. Migrant farm work became a staple for some.
22. Driftwood was collected and sold for firewood. Just about anything was collected and sold to somebody who could use it.
23. Some folks relied more on saving cash and gold or silver in the home than keeping money in banks.

24. Neighbors connected more with neighbors—neighbors helping neighbors (sharing ideas, providing help where needed).
25. Churches and missions scraped together extra funds to feed the hungry.
26. Everybody worked, kids included. Wherever neighbors could find odd jobs to be done, they would hire neighbors for them.
27. Nobody wanted welfare. People still had self-respect enough to work for food, and everybody shunned the entitlement attitude.
28. Nobody retired.
29. Stores and city governments loaned money, expecting repayment.
30. Strange foods came about from whatever was on hand—codfish gravy and bean sandwiches. Just about everything could go into a soup.
31. Families would shop for vegetables and fruits going bad in the grocery stores (for the better price).
32. Housewives learned to can goods and keep a well-stocked pantry.
33. Families would trade produce from their gardens.
34. Without electricity or refrigerators, families would learn to eat all that was cooked.
35. Garden plots would take up empty lots, sometimes shared with the community.
36. Some women would prepare meals to sell to workers during the workday.
37. To cool down during the hot summer months, families would hang wet sheets in the windows and doorways.
38. Fabric feed sacks were used to make clothing. Just about anything was reconstructed into chairs and couches. The motto coined during the Depression was: Use it up. Wear it out. Make it do or do without.

5

ECONOMIC THEORIES— BIBLICAL ECONOMICS AND THE ECONOMIC SYSTEMS OF MEN

> You desire and do not have, so you murder.
> You covet and cannot obtain, so you fight and quarrel.
> (Jas. 4:2 ESV)

ECONOMIC THEORIES—BIBLICAL ECONOMICS AND THE ECONOMIC SYSTEMS OF MEN

For much of human history, the desires that have fueled economies can be summed up as *conquest* and *plunder*. Not long after Adam and Eve left the Garden, we find accounts of murder and violence in the Bible. Man's sinful and covetous nature drove his increasing lust for power and possessions until "the earth also was corrupt before God, and the earth was filled with violence" (Gen. 6:11).

Throughout the ancient world, conquest, plunder, and enslavement of neighboring peoples served as the primary means of empire-building and accumulating wealth. The Egyptians, Babylonians, Persians, Greeks, and Romans all used conquest and plunder to increase their revenues. They conquered and enslaved neighboring kingdoms until they ran out of kingdoms to conquer or until they were conquered themselves.

The fall of Babylon to Cyrus the Great, 539 BC

The world seeks prosperity through conquest and plunder, but God has a different plan for prosperity. It begins with understanding that He alone is the source of all wealth: "You shall remember the LORD your God, for it is He who gives you power to get wealth, that He may establish His covenant which He swore to your fathers, as it is this day" (Deut. 8:18). This is God's way. But, apart from God, men will always fall into corruption, violence, and plunder.

Following the collapse of Rome, a new order arose in the West. This was a civilization rooted in the teachings of the Man from Galilee, the Son of God. His teaching and His redemptive work transformed the world. In time, the biblical principles of law, liberty, property, and industriousness would lay the foundations for an economic prosperity the ancient world had never known.

WHAT IS AN ECONOMIC SYSTEM?

An **economic system** is the way in which a society works. It is a description of how the world runs–how nations organize the economic activity among the peoples. Economic activities include buying and selling, earning income from a job, paying taxes on that income, starting a new business, or investing in other businesses. Virtually everything we do has some direct impact on the economy. And the type of economic system a society embraces has a profound impact on the well-being of its people.

In this chapter we will examine the dominant economic systems that have played out in Western civilization over the last thousand years. They include **feudalism**, **capitalism**, **socialism**, and **communism**. We will compare and contrast these economic systems against the standard of God's Word. We will also examine newer theories like **distributism**. Lastly, we will look at the **family economy**, which is God's original plan for economic stewardship of His creation. This chapter will give you a basic understanding of the powerful economic theories that govern our world today. You will understand how these theories measure up to God's standards, and you'll be able to discern the good and evil aspects of these traditions of men.

Now, let's begin by stepping back 1,000 years.

"FOR KING AND COUNTRY": FEUDALISM IN THE MIDDLE AGES

After the fall of the Roman Empire, a new economic system took shape in Medieval Europe. The people could no longer depend on Roman infrastructure—Roman roads, aqueducts, building materials and methods—to hold their civilization together. They couldn't exchange goods for Roman currency. They couldn't buy products from distant parts of the Empire. Most significantly, they could no longer depend on the Roman armies to defend their borders. The city states and tribes were now on their own.

Roman aqueduct

Without Rome to protect them, people banded together in small settlements known as manors for mutual aid and defense. Under the supervision of landlords or "lords," peasants worked the land and tended their flocks. They gave part of their produce to the lord, and he in return protected them from raiders and barbarians. The lord also acted as a judge in civil matters, settling disputes among his people. The peasants (or serfs, as they were called) were taxed no more than twenty-five percent of their income. But they gave up many freedoms in exchange for this security. Most notably, serfs were "tied to the land" and could not leave the manor without the lord's permission. But serfs were not slaves; they often owned property and spent most of their time farming their own land. They were free as long as they assisted the lord with his harvest and other duties. This societal arrangement came to be known as feudalism. This was the predominant economic system in mainland Europe from the 9th to the 15th century.

Medieval King invests or presents the honor of knighthood.

This was also the era of armored knights and fair maidens, of castles and crusades. The Knight's Code of Chivalry, which pervaded European

Medieval castle

thought during the Middle Ages, established a standard of conduct for noblemen. They were to fear God, protect the weak, provide for widows and orphans, live honorably, love their country, and fight for their king. Above all, they were to be "everywhere and always the champion of the Right and the Good against Injustice and Evil."[3]

Lords of very large estates awarded "fiefs" or tracts of land to other noblemen. These noblemen pledged their military allegiance and support to the lord. Noblemen and lords served the kingdom under the rule of a monarch. This was a form of representative government. The noblemen and lords protected their own people and lands and looked out for their interests. This system of shared power was the basis for the *Magna Carta* and representative forms of government practiced today.

Feudalism survived as a stable way of life for more than six centuries. It replaced the old slave-based systems, and provided more freedom for the

King John signing the *Magna Carta*.

poorer class in society. The present systems of capitalism or socialism have only been around for about 200 years, and they are not doing well. Feudalism arose naturally and everywhere, without top-down coordination. It sprang up after the collapse of the large world empires and the breakdown of centralized authority. If the large world empires of the modern world were to collapse, feudalism can be seen as a proven and stable alternative.

THE WEALTH OF NATIONS: FREE MARKETS AND CAPITALISM

The same year that American colonists declared independence from Great Britain and began their struggle for freedom, another revolution was underway. In 1776, a Scottish philosopher named Adam Smith published *The Wealth of Nations*. This book was the first and the most widely read treatise on the subject of wealth accumulation in free markets and free nations.

Adam Smith

Adam Smith claimed that it was self-interest, not central planning, that gradually built a nation's wealth over time. People work because they receive benefits from their work. This inspires them to work harder and more efficiently to receive greater benefits. They also work at what they are good at because this allows them to make more money than working at a job they aren't good at. He went on to say that nations don't need to start wars or conquer other nations to increase their wealth. Division of labor, productivity, and individual self-interest are all ingredients that could grow a nation's wealth from within: "It is not from the benevolence of the butcher, the brewer, or the baker that we expect our dinner, but from their regard to their own self-interest."[4] In other words, the butcher doesn't sell you meat because he thinks everyone deserves to eat meat. Instead, he sells you meat because he thinks he can make a profit doing this. This inspires him to work harder, which means that there is more meat available for people to buy. This helps you as well as the butcher.

Smith wrote of an "invisible hand" which benefits society as a whole, if only its people are free to pursue their own interests. He said,

> The study of his own advantage ... leads him to prefer that employment which is most advantageous to the society.... And by directing that industry in such a manner as its produce may be of the greatest value, he intends only his own gain, and he is in this, as in many other cases, led by an invisible hand to promote an end which was no part of his intention.[5]

In other words, people naturally desire to perform work that pays the best wages, and they work harder at those jobs. They may be thinking only about themselves, but when society as a whole works harder, more goods are produced. This benefits society as a whole.

Smith's observations about free trade and free markets became the foundation for classical economic theory and modern socioeconomic systems like capitalism. Under feudalism, a relatively small number of lords owned the castles and the serfs either owned their land or rented it from the lord. Kings ruled over their kingdoms, but the lords and serfs could claim ownership of the land. With the disappearance of kings and the rise of democracies (or republics), the people were empowered to vote for their leaders. The farms and businesses were either owned and controlled by the citizen-elected governments or by individuals and corporations. Most of the time, private individuals started up businesses, or groups of private individuals banded together as owners and operators of businesses. "Capitalism" is that form of economy where private individuals own the businesses (or the means of production). A capitalist economy will minimize government intrusion in the marketplace. People are free to buy and sell as they think best. Capitalist societies try to avoid onerous regulations, high taxes, or special protections that would inhibit people's ability to produce, consume, and transact freely with one another. The farms and businesses (the **means of production**) are not owned and controlled by the government, but by private individuals and groups of investors who form corporations. As a result, the manufacture of goods and services is not organized according to any centralized plan; production is allowed to organize itself according to the needs and desires of the market. Prices and wages are not set by a king's edict or government legislation. Buyers and sellers decide the prices by what both deem is fair. Employers and employees agree on wages by what each finds acceptable.

Gas prices fluctuate with supply and demand.

THE INDUSTRIAL REVOLUTION

The desires of men and women are a dangerous foundation upon which to build an empire. "The heart is deceitful above all things, and desperately wicked; who can know it?" (Jer. 17:9).

During the 18th and 19th centuries, many people were driven by a pursuit of wealth. This sparked a revolution in industry and commerce. Following the economic theory that developed from Smith's *Wealth of Nations*, the Industrial Revolution reorganized society around efficiency. For the first time in history, the factory replaced the family as the primary means

In capitalist economies, prices fluctuate based on supply and demand. When an oil tanker runs aground or negotiations with oil-producing nations are disrupted, the price of gasoline will also rise even if demand remains constant. This is because the supply of gasoline is reduced.

But the opposite is also true: When the supply of a product increases, its price drops. When gasoline prices increase, there is an incentive for oil companies to produce more gasoline and collect the profits from higher prices. As new oil fields are discovered and refineries come online, the supply of gasoline will increase, and its price will begin to fall.

This is part of the self-regulating nature of free markets, and this explains the inverse relationship between supply and demand which is essential to understanding price fluctuations in capitalist economies.

of production. Products which had been hand-crafted in homes for millennia started being mass-produced in factories with the aid of machines.

Increasingly, the ownership of the farms and businesses fell into the hands of fewer individuals or corporations. Between 1920 and 2020, the number of farms in the US fell off from 6.5 million to 2 million. The average size of the farm increased from 150 acres to 450 acres. More recently, big factory farms have taken over the majority of US agricultural output. Small family farms were producing about half of agricultural production in 1990. Thirty years later they were only producing about a quarter of it.[6]

The Industrial Revolution changed world economies.

But this disruption of the family farm began as early as the 18th century. The industrial revolution brought huge upheaval to the nuclear family. Thousands of years of social customs were set aside in a single generation. Much of the advance was welcome, however. Families enjoyed financial abundance like they had never known before as individual members found profitable employment in factories. Women and even children could work for wages with little or no prior skill due to the specialization of labor and the standardization of parts.

For others, the changes were most unwelcome. Mass production depressed prices of commodities everywhere, forcing subsistence farmers and artisans into factories simply to survive. Farms ceased to operate as they had for centuries. Parents who left the home to find work in factory labor no longer educated and mentored their children at home. Dependence on the family and community was replaced with dependence on the employer.[7]

Box making at a watch factory in the late 1800s, USA

Without moral restraints as prescribed by the Bible, self-interest and the unbridled pursuit of financial gain yielded abuses on an industrial scale. Working conditions during this period were notoriously bad, and families who separated to work in factories faced many hardships. Shifts extended twelve to fourteen hours per day, six days per week. And children were not excluded. "It was not until 1842 that the hours of labor for children under twelve years of age were limited to ten per day."[8]

Conquest had returned, but this time it was the family who was being plundered.

IS CAPITALISM BIBLICAL?

Many aspects of capitalism as an economic system are supported by the Bible. Private ownership of enterprise, property rights, freedom to trade, and keeping the rewards of one's labor are biblical concepts (Gen. 1:28; Ex. 20:15; Deut. 30:9; Prov. 22:28; Eph. 4:28). Scripture calls us to live as free people (1 Pet. 2:16). This applies to economic situations as well as matters of conscience.

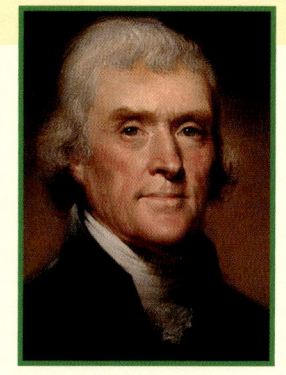

Thomas Jefferson

But capitalism as an economic system makes no underlying claims about morality. It doesn't recognize God as the source of all law and order in society. By failing to do this, it falls short of God's standards. Capitalism is primarily concerned with maximizing efficiency. Economist John Ikerd writes, "Under the enterprise belief system, a person's worth is fully reflected in his or her ability to contribute economic value to society, and a person's highest social responsibility is to maximize his or her productivity and personal wealth."[9]

Furthermore, organizing society around economic incentives has contributed to the breakdown of moral and ethical limits that have governed the Christian West for centuries. Godless entertainment, pornography, narcotics and child prostitution are all enterprises that flourish in capitalist economies around the world. When the heart of man is desperately wicked, freedom itself is not the highest virtue. Personal profit and wealth take the place of freedom under God.

The Ten Commandments place restrictions on our "freedoms": You shall not murder, commit adultery, steal, lie, worship idols, or profane God's name. Economies which operate within the boundaries of biblical law can enjoy maximum freedom without compromising individual morality. But economic activity divorced from God's standards will always yield death and judgment. This is a concept that the founders of the United States understood well.

> Can the liberties of a nation be secure when we have removed a conviction that these liberties are the gift of God? Indeed I tremble for my country when I reflect that God is just, that His justice cannot sleep forever. — Thomas Jefferson[10]

"WORKERS OF THE WORLD, UNITE!": SOCIALISM AND COMMUNISM

In response to the gross abuses of the Industrial Revolution, a new economic theory gained traction in the mid-19th century. Seeking to unite the working classes and overthrow capitalism, Karl Marx and Friedrich Engels published their utopian vision for a fair and equal society in *The Communist Manifesto* in 1848.

Marx and Engels argued that workers would be better off if the civil government eliminated property rights. They recommended placing the control of production into the hands of democratically-elected officials. They believed workers would find fair treatment and economic equality through this means. Instead of individuals, families, and corporations owning property and manufacturing goods, everything from land to factories would be owned by "the people" and operated according to government dictates. A communist society, Marx claimed, would have neither rich nor poor people. There would be no need for money because every product would be free, and everyone would share equally in the work.

> From each according to his ability, to each according to his needs.
> — Karl Marx

CAPITALISM AROUND THE WORLD

Where can capitalism and communism be found in the world today? Examples of capitalist countries today include the United States, Canada, Ireland, Singapore, and Australia. Examples of communist countries include China, North Korea, Cuba, Laos, and Vietnam. Most of the world's nations are **mixed economies**, which means they combine aspects of both capitalism and socialism in differing degrees. For example, in the United States, there is a great deal of economic freedom (capitalism), but there is also high taxation and redistribution of wealth through government welfare programs (socialism).

The resulting material abundance, Marx argued, would far surpass anything to be found in capitalist economies, and class distinctions and conflicts would cease to exist.

This promise of economic equality and material abundance found a ready audience in impoverished nations like Russia, China, Cuba, Vietnam, and North Korea, where bloody revolutions were fought to overthrow the existing order. By the mid-1980s, less than 140 years after the publication of *The Communist Manifesto*, "one-third of the world's people lived under this form of government."[11]

Socialism is similar to **communism**. While differing in degree, they are the same in kind. Both come from Marxist ideas and both share the goal of equally distributing wealth within a society. A key distinction is that socialism seeks to achieve equality through gradual reforms whereas communism is typically associated with violent revolutions. As Karl Marx stated it, "*The Communists everywhere support every revolutionary movement against the existing social and political order of things. . . . They openly declare that their ends can be attained only by the forcible overthrow of all existing social conditions.*"[12]

Karl Marx

Friedrich Engels

In socialism, the means of production is owned by the state. In communism, the means of production is owned by "the people." But it's a distinction without a difference; decisions on behalf of "the people" are always made by a privileged few. Vladimir Lenin, the first chairman of the Communist Party in Soviet Russia, put it plainly: "The goal of socialism is communism."

Marx said, "The theory of the Communists may be summed up in the single sentence: Abolition of private property."[13] Marx wanted economic equality. In order to realize this vision, he intended that government would become the highest authority in all of life. He claimed "human self-consciousness as the highest divinity."¹⁴ He wanted to make civil government into a god. This, of course, directly contradicts the Bible, which states: "The LORD is our Judge, the LORD is our Lawgiver, the LORD is our King; He will save us" (Isa. 33:22). And, "You shall have no other gods before Me" (Ex. 20:3).

God alone is the judge and arbiter of man. He has ordained government to operate in a very limited capacity. He has given it the task of defending its citizens in war, protecting private property, and punishing the evildoer (Ex. 20:15; Ps. 144:1; Rom. 13:4).

The underlying error of socialism is the belief that man is innately good. Socialism believes that people will do good things if given the chance. Freedom, equality, and abundance would result, the thinking goes, if only society was more fairly organized. But the Bible teaches that, because of sin, man is innately evil: "There is none righteous, no, not one" (Rom. 3:10). Instead of doing good for others, people will tend toward selfishness when given the chance to do so. Any economic system which does not recognize and restrain this central sin of human nature will always destroy wealth rather than create it.

Karl Marx himself was a good example of innate evil. For he would testify that, "My object in life is to dethrone God and destroy capitalism." Despite

Statue of Vladimir Lenin in St. Petersburg, Russia (formerly Leningrad, Soviet Union)

his ambitions for the New Socialist Man, Marx showed little regard or concern for others in his own life. To the contrary, his life was marked by selfishness and a complete disregard for other people. Marx refused to earn a living himself. Instead, he lived off contributions and inheritances from his parents and colleagues while he labored on his philosophical treatises. His family lived in squalid conditions. They were frequently evicted from their home. As a raging alcoholic, Marx would often spend what little amount he had on drinking binges while his family starved. Three of his children died as infants from malnutrition. Another died before reaching adolescence. Of his three children that survived to adulthood, two committed suicide. Marx fathered another child out of wedlock and went to great lengths to cover it up, giving the infant away to a working-class family and never providing financial support or allowing his son to see him. When his wife of thirty-eight years died in 1881, Marx did not attend the funeral.[15]

Mao Tse-Tung

Though Karl Marx did not wield enough power or live long enough to see his social experiment enacted, his adherents did. "In due course, Lenin, Stalin, and Mao Tse-Tung practiced, on an enormous scale, what Marx felt in his heart and which his works exude."[16] Marxist philosophies decimated economies in the 20th century, resulting in the deaths of 80 to 200 million people, mostly by mass starvation.

It is important to note that socialism and communism are not abstract theories relegated to the minds of a few 19th-century philosophers. Neither is it true that they have never been properly practiced, as some proponents claim. There are nearly two centuries worth of evidence to prove that these belief systems bring chaos and disaster on any society. Both socialism and communism, rooted in envy and theft, will result in tyranny, bondage, and death.

| By their fruits you will know them. (Matt. 7:20)

WHICH SOCIETY WOULD YOU RATHER LIVE IN?

Would you like to live in an "equal" society where everyone has the same amount of money? Or would you prefer a "free" society where there are both the rich and the poor together? When illustrated on a chart, the two societies might look like the chart on the left (see below):

On the surface, an equal society certainly seems fairer—unless you are lucky enough to be rich in the free society, right? But let's add some real-world numbers to the chart and ask the question again.

Cuba is the purest example of socialism in the world today. "Apart from some governmental and military officials, the highest salaries in the country are only four times the amount of the lowest salaries."[17] In Cuba, doctors, engineers, and professors earn barely any more than street sweepers.[18]

Socialism wants everyone to make the same amount of money. When incomes are equalized in society, a person's pay is no longer based on experience, education, quality, or quantity of work. Thus, the incentive to work is removed, resulting in less overall production of goods and services in that economy. In other words, people do not work as hard or start as many businesses in socialist economies, so there's less wealth to share.

Before Fidel Castro took over in 1959 with his communist regime, Cuba had a higher per capita income than Europe. Cubans ranked eighth in the world for salaries paid to industrial workers and seventh in the world for agricultural workers. Sixty years later, the average wage in Cuba is twenty dollars per month—fifty times lower than the poverty line in the US.[19]

> The inherent vice of capitalism is the unequal sharing of blessings; the inherent virtue of socialism is the equal sharing of miseries. —Winston Churchill

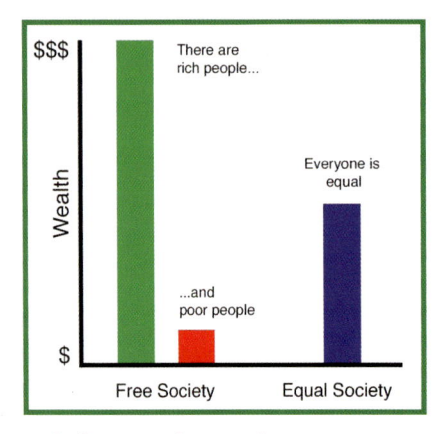

A theoretical example

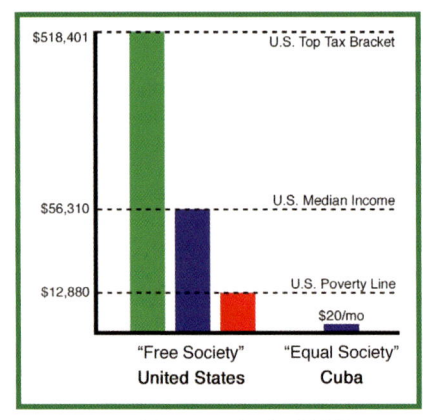

A real-world example (c. 2000)
Source: BLS; HHS; Republic of Cuba

Havana, Cuba

"THREE ACRES AND A COW": DISTRIBUTISM AND AGRARIAN ECONOMICS

Around the turn of the 20th century, another economic theory emerged. By this time, many had noticed both the abuses of factory production and the dangers of socialist governments. To fix this, some proposed a return to agrarian economics or family economy—an economic theory called distributism. This social theory rejected the idea that economic control should be centralized through state socialism or corporate monopolies. Could man create for himself a socially responsible free enterprise system, accompanied by a wide ownership of assets (land and otherwise)? This would mainly involve the distribution of productive farmland. One of the earliest and strongest proponents of distributism was G. K. Chesterton, who was fond of summarizing his theory as "three acres and a cow." He used this phrase to refer to widespread ownership of small family farms.

G. K. Chesterton

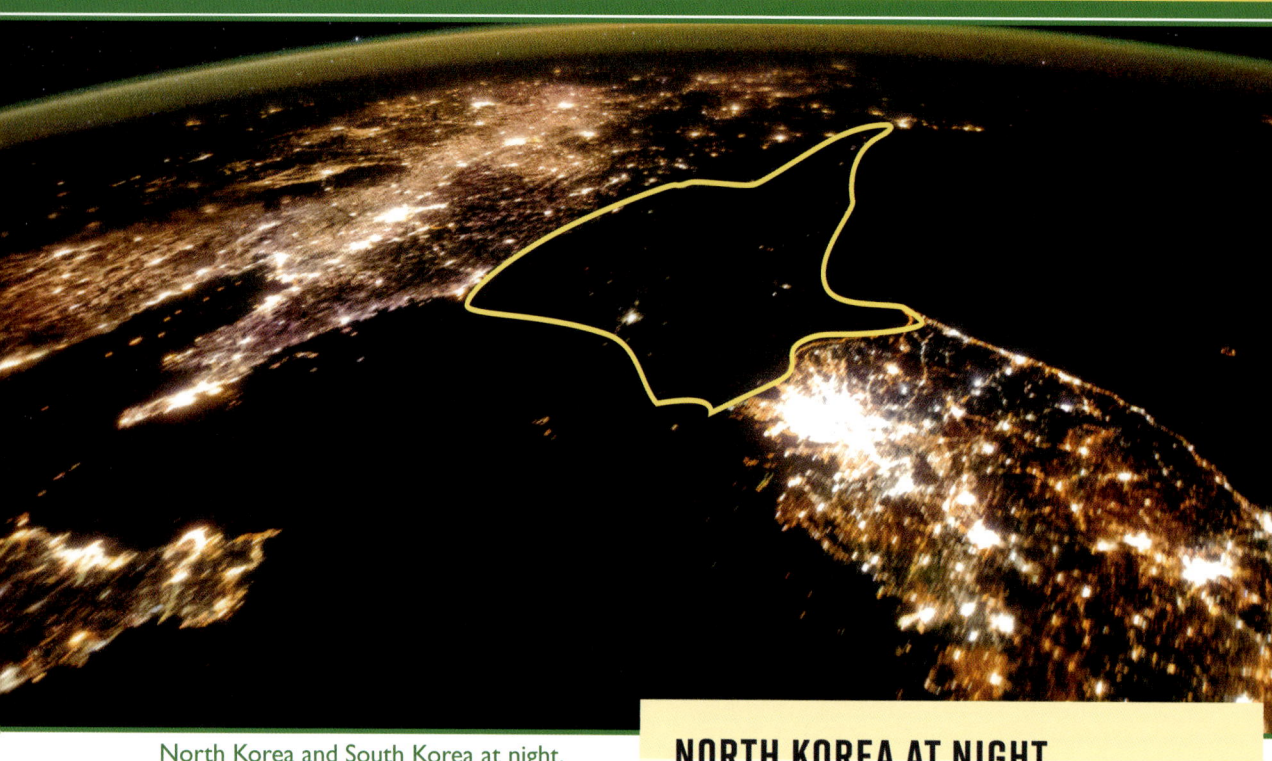

North Korea and South Korea at night.

NORTH KOREA AT NIGHT

Does economics matter? Korea used to be a single nation but divided in 1945 when communists took over the northern provinces. For seventy years, the world has watched as two very different economic systems played out in this peninsula. Today, South Korea is a bustling center of commerce and industry, as evidenced by the lights in the above photograph. North Korea, an impoverished shell of a nation, is barely visible.

Author and historian Allan C. Carlson writes: "Distributism is an economic system that celebrates the small and the human. It rests on strong home economies and seeks the widest possible distribution and ownership of productive property, particularly farm land. For necessarily larger enterprises and machines, it favors worker ownership through cooperatives."[20]

Although not clearly defined as an economic system until the early 20th century, distributist ideas can be found earlier in history. Thomas Jefferson, the third president of the United States, spoke fondly of family farmers in 1785: "They are the most vigorous, the most independent, the most virtuous, and they are tied to their country and wedded to its liberty and interests by the most lasting bands."[21] Until the Industrial Revolution, most Americans lived the distributist ideal. The United States was full of small family-run farms and cooperative businesses. The US Homesteading Act of 1862 awarded more than 270 million acres of land to homesteaders in return for settling and improving the land. This law allowed millions of Americans to become landowners instead of tenant farmers or factory workers.

G. K. Chesterton and Hilaire Belloc were staunch supporters of distributism. Chesterton devoted the latter portion of his life to promoting this "third way" economics through numerous books and periodicals. In *The Servile State*, Belloc showed that capitalist economies tend to concentrate power in the civil government because the government can provide protections to "Big Business" that free-market competition cannot. In the end, Belloc argued, the government serves the interests of the corporations rather than the people.

In the United States, a band of Americans known as the Southern Agrarians (publishers of a periodical named *Free America*) promoted distributism in the 1930s and 40s. "They favored a land of family farms, small shops, decentralized industry, and the freedom which the ownership of productive property begets. They also described themselves as 'equally opposed' to fascism, communism, and finance capitalism."[22]

Often criticized as idealistic, distributism was never fully realized as an economic system, and it fell out of favor with the rise of mechanized farming. By the end of World War II, it was all but forgotten as a viable economic alternative. But, following the environmental movement of the 1970s and farm crisis of the 1980s, agrarian economics was revived in the hearts and minds of a public wary of inflation, recession, and globalization. Writers like Wendell Berry, Gene Logsdon, and Allan Carlson generated renewed interest in a return to local economies, ecological stewardship, and traditional values. This interest continues today.

A BIBLICAL ALTERNATIVE: THE FAMILY ECONOMY

Long before human governments and economic systems existed, before

WAS JESUS A COMMUNIST?

Some Christians have made the erroneous claim that Jesus was a communist. They base this assertion on New Testament passages that identify the early church as having all things in common. They quote from Acts:

> Now all who believed were together, and had all things in common, and sold their possessions and goods, and divided them among all, as anyone had need. (Acts 2:44-45)

Since a key tenet of socialism is the equal redistribution of wealth, it might appear that the early church was functioning according to socialist principles. But this is where the similarities end. The early church was not socialist. The distinction between socialism and the New Testament example is that the believers' actions were voluntary. These believers *chose* to give their goods to members of the church. They weren't forced to do this. The Bible forbids stealing from one's neighbor no matter how noble the purpose or significant the need: "You shall not steal." (Ex. 20:15).

Believers in the early church were not coerced by human governments to redistribute their property; they gave voluntarily. They were not rejecting property rights but publicly witnessing to God's grace in their lives through charitable and sacrificial giving.

kings and corporations, God instituted the family and entrusted creation to its care. "Then God blessed them, and God said to them, 'Be fruitful and multiply; fill the earth and subdue it; have dominion over the fish of the sea, over the birds of the air, and over every living thing that moves on the earth'" (Gen. 1:28).

The family existed before all political structures and economic theories. The family precedes and supersedes all man-made institutions and traditions. In a biblical economy, the family is central.

In a family economy, all members work together to provide the things the family needs. They do not rely on bloated governments or multinational corporations. They value self-reliance and interdependence. That is, they rely on each other and on other families in their community.

The term *economy* comes from the Greek word *oikonomia*. This word means *household management* or *household law*. "In the beginning, it was all in the house—the whole economy," writes C. R. Wiley. "The economy was the law of the house; and it was overseen by the *paterfamilias*—the father of the family."[23]

As created by God originally, the basic economic unit is not an individual nor is it the corporation or the government. The basic economic unit is the family. When God-given talents and abilities of family members are combined into a shared mission, the results are multiplied. The husband and wife may be thought of as an ax head on an ax handle. By itself, an ax head is of little use to take down trees. Place an ax head on an ax handle, and the capability for useful work has increased a hundred-fold. Here is God's design for the economy. The Lord God provided Adam with a wife as a helper in the dominion task.

> And the LORD God said, "It is not good that man should be alone; I will make him a helper comparable to him." (Gen. 2:18)

The family economy is about more than family-owned enterprises. Business and work does form an essential part of the family, but that isn't all.

Friedrich Engels, co-author of *The Communist Manifesto*, agrees. "If some few passages of the Bible may be favorable to communism, the general spirit of its doctrines is, nevertheless, totally opposed to it."[24]

Jesus is neither a communist nor a capitalist. He is King of kings and Lord of lords, the Creator through Whom all things were made, "and without Him nothing was made that was made" (John 1:3). We are all His servants, and everything we own belongs to Him.

> For every beast of the forest is Mine, and the cattle on a thousand hills. I know all the birds of the mountains, and the wild beasts of the field are Mine. If I were hungry, I would not tell you; for the world is Mine, and all its fullness. (Ps. 50:10-12)

Caring for chickens on a family farm.

The family economy includes all the elements of a biblical household: education, discipleship, apprenticeship, work, hospitality, charity, recreation, and care for one another. In the family, individual desires and dreams are formed into a common purpose, a shared family vision.

FRACTURED FAMILIES

The ideal of a family working together contrasts greatly with the typical household in which dad spends most of his day laboring apart from his family, mom works outside the home for a boss who is not her husband, children are left to the care of strangers, and siblings are separated into age-segregated classrooms.

The historic understanding of the family as a "work unit" has disappeared. It has been replaced by the idea of the "recreational household," where families serve merely as a source for emotional fulfillment. Husband and wife no longer need each other in order to survive, so marriage is reduced to a lifestyle choice. Children are no longer integral to a shared family vision, so they are seen as burdens, and families have fewer of them.[25]

As a result, the modern family has abandoned nearly all the functions historically practiced at home. Education, work, worship, childcare, and eldercare have been parceled out to institutions, government, and corporations. Even our entertainment is age-oriented and consumed apart more frequently than together. The home, which for millenniums was a "self-producing and self-sustaining community," has turned into an "overnight parking place."[26]

This is not the model God had in mind when He instituted the family. With the destruction of the family comes the destruction of the economy. It is not surprising, then, to find a mammoth breakdown of social order in the present generation. We see a mass exodus from the Christian faith. This faith has been passed down primarily through families for the last fifty generations.[27] As the Christian faith disappears, the morals of a nation are destroyed. Societal collapse will follow.

INDIVIDUALISM, COLLECTIVISM, AND THE ECONOMY OF GOD

The family economy has existed and persisted under all economic systems. But how does it stack up against the powerful economic systems that dominate our world today? Of those discussed here, distributism is most favorable to the family economy. Socialism is the most hostile. Capitalism may be beneficial, but it also has problems.

Distributism identifies the family as the basic economic unit of society. It aims to reinforce the nuclear bonds of the family. Socialism and communism, by contrast, are directly opposed to the family economy. They seek to remove individual and family authority. They make all economic decisions based on what is best for "society," which is why these economic systems are also known as **collectivism**.

> With the transfer of the means of production into common ownership, the single family ceases to be the economic unit of society.
> — Friedrich Engels[28]
>
> Blessed is he who has no family.
> — Karl Marx[29]

Capitalism maintains that the basic economic unit of society is the individual, which is why it has been labeled **individualism**. Capitalism brings profound opportunities for families in terms of wealth accumulation. But it also favors a materialist approach to life that has proven particularly destructive to the bonds of family life. In pursuit of maximum efficiency and endless affluence, modern industrial economies demand that all able-bodied adults work full-time outside the home. Economist John Ikerd writes, "Capitalistic economies gain their efficient advantage by using people to do work, while doing nothing to restore the social capital needed to sustain positive personal relationships within society. There is no economic incentive for capitalists to invest in families, communities, or society for the benefit of future generations."[30]

THE PROBLEM OF CARE

> Now there stood by the cross of Jesus His mother, and His mother's sister, Mary the wife of Clopas, and Mary Magdalene. When Jesus therefore saw His mother, and the disciple whom He loved standing by, He said to His mother, "Woman, behold your son!" Then He said to the disciple, "Behold your mother!" And from that hour that disciple took her to his own home. (John 19:25-27)

The individualistic approach to wealth-creation in capitalist economies presents a serious challenge for the family unit. Sociologists refer to this issue as "the dependency problem." When mother and father are absent, "who will care for the very young, the very old, the weak and the infirm? How shall the rewards given to productive adults be shared with those who are not or cannot be productive?"[31]

Instead of placing unproductive members of society in institutional care facilities, the family economy provides care at the most basic level: at home. Such arrangements should not be strange, given that the Lord Jesus, the Son of God, provided care for His mother in His dying moments. "In the natural human order, these tasks fall on kin networks, where spouses care for each other 'in sickness or in health,' where parents nurture, train, and protect their offspring until they are able to create marriages of their own, where the aged enjoy care, purpose, and respect around the hearth of their grown children, and where kin ensure that no family member falls through the family's safety net."[32]

Capitalism seeks efficiency, and socialism seeks equality. But the Bible stresses the primacy of human relationships in economic dealings. Our desire for material gain must be subordinate to the principle of loving our neighbor. God's Word never allows us to neglect those who are too young, too old, too weak, too sick, or too unplanned to be productive members of society. Scripture teaches that relationships are always the priority, not problems to be avoided on the pathway to prosperity.

> Let nothing be done through selfish ambition or conceit, but in lowliness of mind let each esteem others better than himself. Let each

> of you look out not only for his own interests, but also for the interests of others. (Phil. 2:3-4)

THE DISCIPLESHIP OF WORK

In addition to caring for "the least of these," the family economy also affords more opportunity for intergenerational mentorship and discipleship. This is something sorely lacking in modern economies. A few centuries ago, as factories replaced the home as centers of production, it became

Father and son working together.

economically impractical for families to work together. Women went to work in textile mills. Men and boys left the farm to work in coal mines. As families divided into factories, they no longer spent most of their time together, which meant less time for mentorship and discipleship. The division of labor was more efficient at producing goods, but it came at the cost of broken relationships.

In the pre-industrial way of life, "the apprentice system was in vogue, and all parts of a trade were then taught where it is now usual and needful to teach but a single branch. The youth who aspired to become a shoemaker might, for instance, during his period of apprenticeship, acquire knowledge of every step from the tanning of the leather to its embodiment in the finished shoe.... The system permitted a more intimate relation between employer and employee than is usual today."[33]

Work is not just about making things. The Bible teaches that we are to be discipling our families *while* we work:

> And these words which I command you today shall be in your heart. You shall teach them diligently to your children, and shall talk of them when you sit in your house, when you walk by the way, when you lie down, and when you rise up. (Deut, 6:6-7)

When parents work alongside their children, they are not only teaching skills. They are also passing their values, faith, and culture on to the next generation.

> It is at work that true discipleship takes place, more so than at church or in the classroom. Work is where the real person resides. The true nature of a man is revealed when he is swinging a hammer, felling a tree, or negotiating a contract. For good or ill, we speak loudest to those around us when we are at work. Integrity, perseverance, and faith in divine providence cannot be transmitted in a lecture hall. They must be modeled.[34]

THE BULWARK OF LIBERTY

Finally, families who work together have a measure of independence that wage-earners do not. A home-based family economy does not depend on employers to sign their paychecks. Households that own and manage productive property (which could be anything from gardens to farmland to garage workshops) are more insulated from shocks to the global economy and changing winds of political sentiment. Cancel culture and vaccine mandates do not threaten the vibrant home economy.

During the Great Depression in the United States, some families who owned farms reported that they did not even know they were in a depression. Their pantries were stocked. Their homes were heated. They still had jobs. Their wealth was not at the mercy of Wall Street speculators. Their wealth was standing in the fields or in their barns. During this time, people left the city to find jobs on farms.

Unemployed men outside a soup kitchen in Chicago during the Great Depression

At that time, around 20% of Americans were farmers, and 50% of the US population lived in cities. Today, only 2% of Americans are involved in agriculture, and more than 80% live in cities. Ponder that for a moment. Two percent of the people in the US are responsible for feeding the other 98%.

Would Americans have ever won a War for Independence if 98% of the population was dependent on the British Empire for its basic needs? Doubtful. It is unlikely that they would have even declared their independence, let alone win a war, if the young colonies resembled 21st-century America.

Liberty and independence come from self-government and responsibility. Liberty cannot be sustained when men will not work with their hands and when men look to the government to take care of them. Liberty cannot survive where there is a lack of character with the emerging generations. If we will have stable societies and free countries for the future, we must restore the family economy. In previous centuries, families didn't depend on the civil government to help them make a living. They were self-governing. Tyrannical governments were easily restrained because families and communities governed themselves and families took care of their own.

Passing more legislation will not in itself restore liberty. Neither will electing the "right person" to a political office. Liberty can only come by the redemptive work of Christ, by hard work and personal responsibility, and by healthy families building robust economies within their homes.

"THE CONCLUSION OF THE WHOLE MATTER"

In this chapter, we examined several economic systems that have dominated the last thousand years of Western civilization. There are advantages and disadvantages to every system. Some promote freedom. Others seek equality at the expense of freedom. Some recognize and reinforce family bonds. Others work against the family or prioritize money over relationships.

Jesus said that the teachings and traditions of men should be judged by their fruit. We must judge economic systems by what they produce, not by their intentions.

> Beware of false prophets, who come to you in sheep's clothing, but inwardly they are ravenous wolves. You will know them by their fruits. Do men gather grapes from thornbushes or figs from

> thistles? Even so, every good tree bears good fruit, but a bad tree bears bad fruit. A good tree cannot bear bad fruit, nor can a bad tree bear good fruit. Every tree that does not bear good fruit is cut down and thrown into the fire. Therefore by their fruits you will know them. (Matt. 7:15-20)

Economic systems and the governments that enforce them exert significant influence over the lives of their people. Therefore it is important for Christians to understand the origins of these systems. We need to recognize the "fruits" they are producing and the philosophical "roots" that are feeding them.

In all matters, the Bible gives us standards by which we must live in any economic system. Solomon said: "Let us hear the conclusion of the whole matter: Fear God and keep His commandments, for this is man's all" (Eccl. 12:13).

Let us first love and fear God, trusting Him for our provision. We must never allow envy or greed to guide our economic decisions. We must be generous at all times, regarding the widow, the orphan, and "the least of these." We must provide for our own families. And we must work diligently in all things, to the glory of God.

> And whatever you do, do it heartily, as to the Lord and not to men, knowing that from the Lord you will receive the reward of the inheritance; for you serve the Lord Christ. (Col. 3:23-24)

As we work together in God's economy, we will invest much of our time and energy into discipling the next generation to love God, to fear God, and to love others.

6

GETTING YOUR JOB— WORK IN THE ECONOMY

Bondservants, obey in all things your masters according to the flesh, not with eyeservice, as men-pleasers, but in sincerity of heart, fearing God. And whatever you do, do it heartily, as to the Lord and not to men, knowing that from the Lord you will receive the reward of the inheritance; for you serve the Lord Christ. (Col. 3:22-24)

Landing of the pilgrims in 1620.

When the Pilgrims came to America in 1620, there weren't any high-paying jobs waiting for them. But there was a lot of work to do. This means that each family had to get busy clearing land, planting gardens, and building homes. They relied on self-employment to get the work done.

A large part of the world is still self-employed. Overall, about 43% of adult workers do not work for employers.[35] Today, the highest percentage of self-employed persons live in sub-Sahara Africa and Southeast Asia. There is much less manufacturing and division of labor in these parts of the world. They try to survive by farming small plots. About 6% of American workers are self-employed in the 2020s, leaving the other 94% working for an employer or company.

As mentioned in previous chapters, economies are built on work. When people are not working, nothing gets done and there isn't much supply available. Only the richest people can afford to buy whatever is available to buy. If we want a good economy, people need to start working.

Moving bricks involves lots of hard work.

> But we urge you, brethren, that you increase more and more; that you also aspire to lead a quiet life, to mind your own business, and to work with your own hands, as we commanded you, that you may walk properly toward those who are outside, and that you may lack nothing. (1 Thess. 4:10-12)

> For even when we were with you, we commanded you this: If anyone will not work, neither shall he eat. (2 Thess. 3:10)

Plainly, God wants His people to work. He doesn't want us mooching off others. This is so fundamental to being a Christian that Paul tells us in

1 Timothy 5:8 that a man who will not provide for his own family's needs is worse than an unbeliever. Work is an integral part of our lives. Although most of the world has turned to a five-day work week, God wants us working six days out of seven. We are not supposed to overwork ourselves by working over 6 days in a row. At Creation, the Lord mercifully provided a Sabbath day (or rest day) for man as a break from work for each seven-day period.

> Remember the Sabbath day, to keep it holy. Six days you shall labor and do all your work, but the seventh day is the Sabbath of the LORD your God. In it you shall do no work: you, nor your son, nor your daughter, nor your male servant, nor your female servant, nor your cattle, nor your stranger who is within your gates. For in six days the LORD made the heavens and the earth, the sea, and all that is in them, and rested the seventh day. Therefore the LORD blessed the Sabbath day and hallowed it. (Ex. 20:8-11)

WHAT IS WORK?

> The LORD God planted a garden eastward in Eden, and there He put the man whom He had formed. And out of the ground the LORD God made every tree grow that is pleasant to the sight and good for food.... Then the LORD God took the man and put him in the garden of Eden to tend and keep it. (Gen. 2:8,9,15)

Economists define work as the necessary labor to keep people alive in a community. From a biblical perspective, work is the necessary cultivation and care of God's material creation for the benefit of one's family and community. Work is required in order to provide shelter, food, and clothing for our families. At the beginning, Adam was created to work, and he was assigned to "tend and keep" the Garden of Eden. God wants us to work. When we take dominion over the animals and take care of God's resources by honest labor, we do this in obedience to God.

Making sandwiches

Good work seeks to produce both quality and quantity at the same time. For example, the fellow who works in a sandwich shop should do his best to make a high-quality sandwich. But he shouldn't take a full hour to make one sandwich. If that were the case, his employer would get rid of him. For the sandwich business to be a worthwhile enterprise, the employer needs the worker to assemble at least twenty quality sandwiches in an hour.

At the end of the day, the employee should seek to make his employer happy with his work. The employer wants to be sure the customers are happy with his company's products and services. There is a certain level of quality that is expected and appreciated by the customer. That quality of service and product will bring the customer back to do more business. The company wants to be sure that this level of quality is maintained. If that quality is produced at the highest level of efficiency, the company will probably compete well in the marketplace and make money. If the company is too inefficient (and wastes a lot of time and money), it won't make money; and companies that don't make money go out of business.

WASTING TIME

> See then that you walk circumspectly, not as fools but as wise, redeeming the time, because the days are evil. (Eph. 5:15-16)

God doesn't want us to waste our time. As Ephesians 5 instructs, we are to manage our time well. When working, we are looking for efficiency and productivity. Usually, we are inefficient because we are distracted or unfocused. According to one survey, here are some of the biggest time wasters in the workplace:[36]

1. Smartphone and internet surfing is the most notorious time bandit. The average person wastes 145 minutes a day on social media like Facebook and Snapchat.[37] Altogether, the average person spends six and a half hours on the internet every day. That's about a quarter of their lives.[38] Most of that time is wasted.

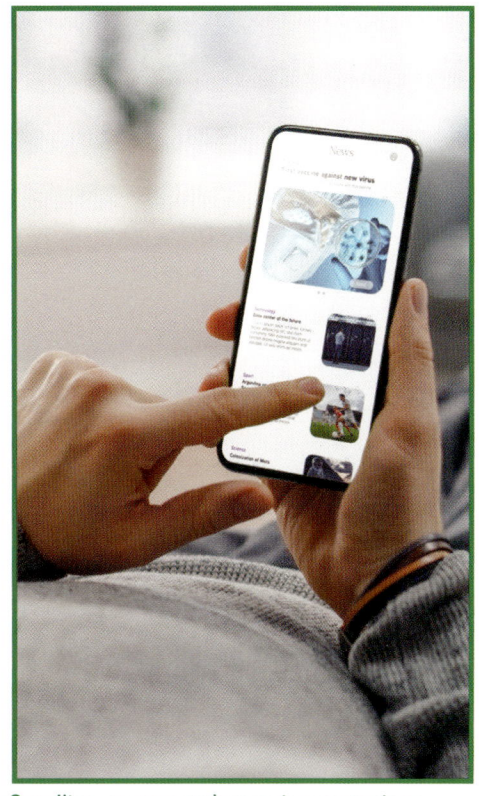

Scrolling on smartphones is a notorious time bandit.

2. The second most common form of time wasting is gossip. Instead of focusing on work, company workers will fill the time with mindless chatter, usually sharing information about others which they should not be sharing. Appropriately, the Apostle Paul warns about this very thing in 2 Thessalonians 3:

> For we hear that there are some who walk among you in a disorderly manner, not working at all, but are busybodies. Now those who are such we command and exhort through our Lord Jesus Christ that they work in quietness and eat their own bread. (2 Thess. 3:11-12)

3. The third big time waster is meetings. That's when people in a company get together to talk about doing work instead of actually doing the work. Sometimes team meetings can provide excuses for people not taking responsibility for their own tasks. When done right, team meetings can help with communication between team members and an efficient delegation of tasks. But these meetings can also be a way to shirk work and avoid getting our jobs done.

Team meetings can be useful, but they can also waste time.

> In all labor there is profit,
> But idle chatter leads only to poverty.
> (Prov. 14:23)

4. Finally, daydreaming and lack of focus can also be a time waster.

Few people have the self-control to govern their time and avoid these time-wasting traps. These things can be minimized if a manager is watching the employees most of the time. Ideally, the Christian workers shouldn't need that constant supervision. Within God's animal creation, the ant serves as a good example of one who needs little supervision.

> Go to the ant, you sluggard!
> Consider her ways and be wise,
> Which, having no captain,
> Overseer or ruler,
> Provides her supplies in the summer,
> And gathers her food in the harvest. (Prov. 6:6-8)

DIFFERENT KINDS OF WORK

God has provided different kinds of work for different kinds of people in the world. Everybody has received a set of gifts, talents, and abilities from God. Some people are especially gifted to work in some tasks, and other people are gifted to work in other tasks. The following summarizes these different kinds of work made available to us.

> Let the elders who rule well be counted worthy of double honor, especially those who labor in the word and doctrine. For the Scripture says, "You shall not muzzle an ox while it treads out the grain," and, "The laborer is worthy of his wages." (1 Tim. 5:17-18)

First, there is a difference between ministry work and business work. The verses above tell us that pastors who work hard with preaching and teaching should receive wages for it. This is ministry work. Some are called to full-time ministry in the church, while others are not. The "double honor" mentioned in 1 Timothy 5 is full-time wages for full-time work.

But sometimes ministers are paid for ministry work, and sometimes they are not. The Apostle Paul worked as a tentmaker, and he didn't require compensation from the Corinthian church (1 Cor. 9:12). But he still told them: "Who ever goes to war at his own expense? Who plants a vineyard and does not eat of its fruit? Or who tends a flock and does not drink of the milk of the flock?" If you do the work, you should expect to be paid for it. But sometimes people do their work voluntarily, and they forgo the pay. This is called volunteer ministry work.

Church ministry work is primarily concerned with feeding the souls of men, not their bodies. Pastors are not growing corn, building houses, or selling clothing in the marketplace. Pastors are mainly concerned about spreading the gospel message, saving souls, and making disciples for Jesus Christ. Their work is mainly in the Word and prayer.

Ministry work may also include caring for the poor, feeding the orphans, seeking to relieve persecuted Christians, and opening your home to visitors. All Christians are called to some hospitality and charity in Hebrews 13:

> Let brotherly love continue. Do not forget to entertain strangers, for by so doing some have unwittingly entertained angels. Remember the prisoners as if chained with them—those who are mistreated—since you yourselves are in the body also. (Heb. 13:1-3)

Motherhood is another form of ministry work. Typically, mothers are not paid for their work. But their sacrificial labors to raise the next generation should be recognized and greatly appreciated. Moms do a lot of work. While they may not gain a lot of wealth and worldly honor to show for their hard work, families, churches, and communities would fall apart without them. The character of each new generation is very much dependent on the work that moms put into it.

Motherhood involves a lot of hard work.

The world experimented with motherless children between 1960 and 2020. Mothers left home for the workplace. Children spent most of their time watching television or hanging out with friends. The end results were terrible. The character of the millennial generation of young people in the 2020s was far worse than previous generations. Self-centered narcissism among the younger generation was three times higher than it was among their grandparents.[39] That means the younger generation was more selfish. They were living for themselves, not others. They weren't getting married. They weren't having children. Back in 1968, over 80% of twenty-five to thirty-seven-year-old men and women were married. That percentage has dropped off to about 42% in 2019.[40] Millennials are making 20% less on average than the older generations did at the same age, and they have eight times more debt than young people in the 1980s and 1990s. While the younger generation received more schooling and 39% have bachelor's degrees, college did not help them make more money. In contrast, only 25% of their parents' generation had a bachelor's degree."[41] But college didn't help them make more money. Character is what matters most, and that is lacking in the millennial generation. Character is a function of healthy parenting.

BUSINESS WORK

Throughout the world's marketplaces, you will find various kinds of business work. These break down into bond slavery, hired servanthood, apprenticeships, and business ownership. There is part-time labor, temporary labor, and full-time labor. There is entrepreneurial work, trade business work, franchise work, government work, and corporate work. Depending on each individual's gifts and calling, everybody in the world will find themselves laboring in one or more of these categories of business.

TYPES OF WORKERS

Bond slavery or **forced slavery** is the state in which a person is committed to working for somebody else without regular pay and without the ability to leave that condition. The slave master is responsible to provide housing and food for his slaves. This terrible condition of bondage was covered in chapter two. Most people work as **hired servants**, which means they are employees of a master in a small business or a large business. **Apprenticeships** may or may not be paid positions. But the apprentice is able to learn a trade, a skill, or a business model from a master in the field. This is an extremely valuable opportunity for a young person who wishes to succeed in the economy.

TYPES OF WORK

A lemonade stand is a good example of entrepreneurship.

Some work is temporary, and therefore the workers are hired on a temporary basis. About 16 million people work temporary or **contract labor** in any given year in the US. That's about 10% of the labor market. Contract labor is when a person does a particular job that is limited in scope and time frame. It might take one week or six months to accomplish the task. The job is agreed upon by the person hired and those hiring through a verbal or written contract.

Some people are self-employed, which means they own their own businesses. There are four main types of business ownership.

1. **Entrepreneurs** start their own businesses, providing a unique product or service. Any business started by one person who is investing money, hiring other people, and providing a product or service is an entrepreneurial endeavor. When a child opens a lemonade stand in front of his house, he is an entrepreneur. A young man's yard maintenance business or lawn mowing work is entrepreneurial work.

    There are 6.1 million businesses in the US that hire employees. There are another 26.5 million small family businesses. In all, about 20% of Americans are business owners. About 96% of all these businesses have less than ten employees. And businesses with 500 or less employees employ about half of the workers in the country.[42] So, a very large part of American productivity comes through small family businesses.

    Entrepreneurs build small businesses which sometimes turn into large businesses. A business might begin as a small family business. Then it might grow into a large corporation with a thousand employees. Walmart is the largest family-owned business in the world. The Sam Walton family business has 2.3 million employees and does $520 billion

Largest Family Businesses in the World	Annual Sales (2021)
Walmart (Family owns about 49% of company)	$520 billion
Volkswagen	$290 billion
Berkshire Hathaway (Dairy Queen, Geico)	$246 billion
Ford (Family still owns 2% of company)	$157 billion

of business every year.

2. **Trade businesses** are owned and operated by individuals, but it doesn't take an entrepreneur to create them. These businesses offer certain trade skills to supply a common demand in a given market. It is the most common type of self-employment. Trades would include dental businesses, plumbing businesses, electrical businesses, chiropractic businesses, building contracting, etc. While this work requires special training in certain skills, they don't usually require a high level of marketing. People who own these types of businesses not only obtain the skill required, but they love the trade itself. They dedicate their lives to the trade, and they don't really need to be that good at selling. Their skills and reputation in the market is what makes the difference.

A McDonalds restaurant in Orlando, Florida.

3. **Franchises** are slightly different from entrepreneurial businesses.

When you buy into a franchise, you will borrow from somebody else's business model. You own the business, but the franchise organization tells you what to do. Franchising does not really call for much creativity on your part. You need to build your own customer base, and you hire your own employees. But, every part of the business is controlled by the franchising organization, and they will train you in all aspects of the business. You still need to be willing to work long hours, motivate your staff, and follow the rules. Examples of franchises include Chick-fil-A, McDonalds, Kentucky Fried Chicken, Burger King, 7-Eleven, Domino's Pizza, and Ace Hardware. There are about 800,000 franchises in America.

4. Publicly-owned **corporations** are the fourth type of business ownership. The owners of these businesses are people who buy stock in the company. These large corporations hire hundreds and thousands of employees. The day-to-day operations are run by executive officers and managers.

THE BHOPAL INDIA INDUSTRIAL DISASTER

On December 3, 1984, the worst industrial accident in history occurred in Bhopal, India. A pesticide plant developed a gas leak, and 30 tons of poisonous chemicals poured out over villages surrounding the plant. As many as 16,000 people were killed, and 600,000 were injured. Previously, the plant had experienced leaks, putting 24 people in the hospital. Safety devices were not working. An American company called Union Carbide had majority ownership in the company, but the India plant was operated by an Indian-owned company. Although the American corporation held no individual liable for the accident, eight senior employees of the Indian-owned company were convicted of gross negligence in 2010 – 26 years after the accident occurred. As it turned out the Indian government was part owner in the Indian-owned side of the business; and previous to the accident had prevented oversight from the American company.[43] Too often bad government policies are also to blame for disasters like this.

Memorial for the 1984 disaster

PARTNERSHIPS AND CORPORATIONS

Some businesses are formed by **partnerships**, where two or more persons will team up to build a business. This spreads the risk a little and allows a sharing of talents. Some people have a knack for business and sales, while others are innovative and can develop products. The most successful partnerships are those involving fathers and sons or members of families who remain loyal to each other. With partnerships, the owners and operators are responsible for debts and actions taken by the business.

The corporation is a business shared by multiple partners, but it is created as a separate legal entity. The largest corporations are funded by thousands of investors. When something goes wrong, the owners are not held responsible for debts. Instead, the corporation is held liable. This is unbiblical. Suppose that the operators of a nuclear power plant or a chemical plant make bad decisions, ignore warnings, and precipitate a huge explosion or disaster. According to current law, the men who made the decisions are not held personally liable for their actions. Usually, the corporation will have to pay millions of dollars to compensate the community for the accident. However, biblical law would hold the individuals responsible for fires and other disasters.

> If fire break out, and catch in thorns, so that the stacks of corn, or the standing corn, or the field, be consumed therewith; he that kindled the fire shall surely make restitution. (Ex. 22:6 KJV)

Ownership in a corporation is decided either through private contracts or by a public offering of stock in the open market. There are two kinds of stock available for purchase: common and preferred. Common stockholders have a vote on company matters, while preferred stockholders do not. Also, preferred stockholders usually receive a pre-determined dividend at a set interest rate. Common stockholders get a variable amount depending on how well the company did in a given year.

The beginnings of the American stock market can be traced back to the 1790s when investors began buying shares in the First Bank of the United States. If there was a profit realized by the end of the year, the company would pay the stockholders with dividends or interest payments. However, this investment money worked more like a loan because the stockholders did not (for the most part) have any control over the operation of the business. God's book of Proverbs is not very supportive of long-term contracts and debt, both of which are important in a modern capitalist society.

> Be not thou one of them that strike hands, or of them that are sureties for debts. If thou hast nothing to pay, why should he take away thy bed from under thee? (Prov. 22:26-27 KJV)

Corporations started in Europe in the 16th century. As they increased wealth, these businesses quickly gained political power with kings and princes. They were first used for the slave trade out of Africa. It wasn't long before greedy corporations used government power to create an exclusive market. For example, English tea merchants would use the government to force the American colonists to purchase tea from them at a higher price. They tried to ban tea imports into the colonies from all other sources. This was a government-enforced monopoly called **mercantilism**-another example of government favoring one business over another. When some businesses grow to be big, rich, and powerful, they will contribute to elec-

A French seaport during the age of mercantilism

tion campaigns and push for government favors. This violates the biblical principle that forbids partiality when making judgments.

> Thou shalt not wrest judgment; thou shalt not respect persons, neither take a gift: for a gift doth blind the eyes of the wise, and pervert the words of the righteous. (Deut. 16:19 KJV)

The Bible foresees eventual problems with systems that are built on debt. And, over time, modern nations would run into extreme troubles with government debt and corporate debt. While the Word of God discourages debt, it still supports the free market in every way possible. God's law does not allow governments to favor the poor (Ex. 23:3; 30:15). At the same time, God's law forbids government subsidies or special favors for wealthy men and big corporations (Lev. 19:15; Jas. 2:1-4). Such favorable treatment is stealing. It is what the Scriptures refer to as "the respect of persons."

By borrowing money and selling stock, corporations could expand quickly. This instant capital and quick growth was sometimes used to edge out other competitors early on in the game. In some cases, this would accommodate the operation of temporary monopolies-exclusive control of the supply of a product or service. Startup competitors would need more time to save money, invest, innovate, and compete. Given this quick access to capital then, the big industrialists could squeeze out the smaller competitors, and make a lot of money in the process.

> John D. Rockefeller (1839-1937) became the wealthiest American of all time, with an estimated worth of $336 billion. He started out in 1867 by developing a better way to refine oil into something usable (especially for household lighting). Rockefeller's Standard Oil Company found highly efficient ways to process oil. In 1870, the company controlled 4% of the refined oil business. By 1880, Rockefeller had secured about 85% of the market. As his company dropped the price of oil, Americans replaced their whale oil lights with kerosene fuel. Because Rockefeller was able to capture such a high percentage of the oil market, some political leaders in the country cried, "Foul!" The concern was that Rockefeller had created an unfair monopoly over the oil industry.

John D. Rockefeller

To better understand the nature of the corporation, consider yourself a young entrepreneur who wants to succeed in the lemonade business. You want to control the lemonade stands in the city, so you decide to open thirty-five stands in thirty-five separate neighborhoods. The goal is to make a lot of money and put all the other kids out of business.

First, you develop a recipe that everybody likes, and you use fresh-squeezed lemons. However, each stand will cost $500 to cover the lemonade-squeezing machine, the dispensing unit, a table, and a chair. To cover all thirty-five stands, you'll need $17,500. On top of this, you'll have to buy enough sugar and lemons for each stand beforehand. Hiring thirty-five friends to run the stands for the first month will cost about $35,000. Altogether, you'll need about $60,000 to get going. But you only have $500 in your bank account. So you start up a corporation and find sixty investors who agree to give you $1,000 each. Then you issue 60,000 stock certificates worth $1.00 apiece.

If you sell each cup of lemonade for $4.00, and each stand sells about thirty cups a day, you'll earn $4,200 per day, for a total of about $400,000 all summer long. Your expenses will run about $100,000, which means you'll have $300,000 in profit. After paying yourself $100,000, you split the remaining $200,000 with your sixty investors. Each investor will receive $3,333, and that's a pretty good profit for the first year. Incorporation and business debt can make it so you get rich quick, but there are still risks involved with that.

THE WICKED BORROWS AND DOES NOT REPAY

> The wicked borrows and does not repay,
> But the righteous shows mercy and gives. (Ps. 37:21)

There are at least two ways in which the wicked borrows and evades repayment of debts. A wicked man starts up a corporation, runs up the debt, and then walks away from his corporation. He is not liable for the debts. Others will evade debt by filing **bankruptcy**. The laws relating to bankruptcy vary between countries. Some nations, such as the UK, Hong Kong, Hungary, and Singapore, maintain a more honest system, generally requiring the payment of debts. On the other end of the scale, the US, Canada, and Australia are the most lenient with irresponsible debtors. There are several different "legal" routes for filing bankruptcy in the US.

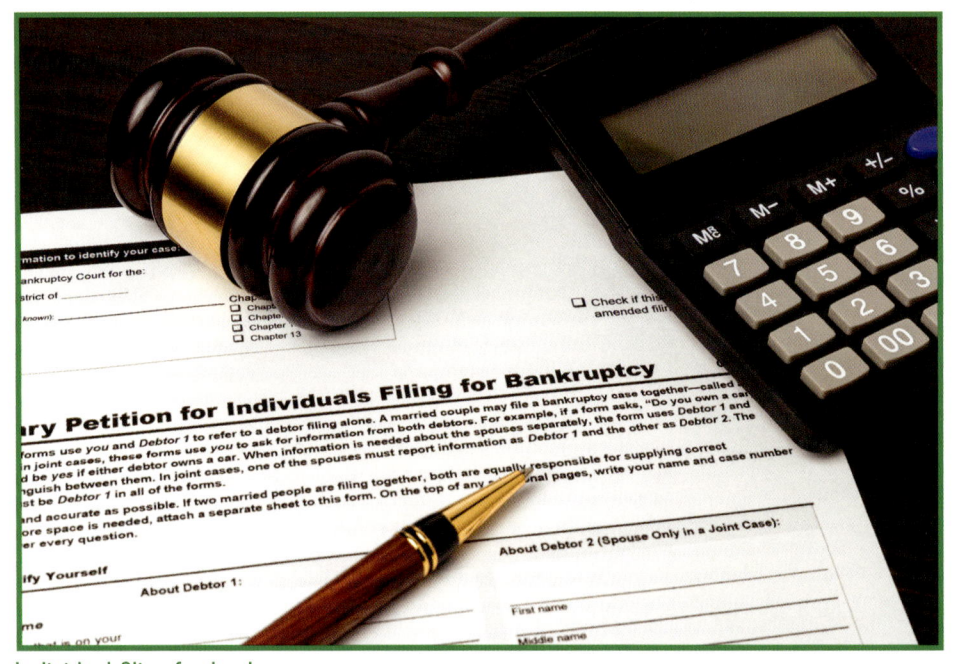

Individual filing for bankruptcy.

- Chapter 7 bankruptcy only requires you to liquidate certain assets, and then you are relieved from paying all other debts. This usually requires the surrendering of a home.
- Chapter 11 bankruptcy allows large businesses to keep repaying their lenders, but at a slower pace.
- Chapter 13 bankruptcy is for individuals who want to save their homes but pay off other debts such as credit card balances, medical bills, and personal loans. The repayment plan reduces the debts sometimes to 5-20% of the original loan, and the debtor is allowed a three-to-five-year period for payment.

In the past, a man would have to work off his debts by indenturing himself as a servant to a productive business or employer. It might take him a long time to pay off his debts, but this is a way he could do it honesty. The modern world has created "legal" means for avoiding the payment of debts. However, these approaches are dishonest, and they will always and eventually undermine the integrity of an economy.

ARE YOU AN ENTREPRENEUR?

Starting up businesses can be thrilling and rewarding for the entrepreneur. There is an excitement in taking risks, and a personal sense of accomplishment when you build something that helps other people. Those who own their own businesses or work for themselves also experience a sense of freedom. However, most people are not entrepreneurs. If you are not gifted in this area, it would be a waste of time for you to pursue it. Here are a few questions to answer before putting time into developing your own businesses.

- Are you a self-starter? Do you like to do things your own way? Are you self-motivated enough that you don't need anybody to tell you what to do each day?
- Are you able to motivate others to follow you? Do people like to follow your ideas?
- Are you the kind of person who likes to take charge? Do you want to make sure that the project gets completed? Or do you get discouraged and just walk away?
- Can you keep going when the going gets tough? Are you a super-hard worker even when work is difficult? Will you make sure the job gets done no matter how hard it might be?
- Can you make quick decisions with wise input from others?
- Are you able to take risks and make mistakes without worrying too much about failure?
- Are you careful not to get bogged down or distracted by unimportant things?
- Are you able to handle a wide variety of tasks in the business?

- Can you pay attention to a lot of different things at the same time without stressing out?

If you answer yes to most of these questions, you are probably an entrepreneur.

EMPLOYEES

If only 20% of Americans are business owners, then the other 80% will be employees. Some business owners work for others on a part-time basis, because they don't earn enough money with their business to make ends meet. Most people will work for others as hired servants. When you are hired by a company, you are given a certain job to do. Sometimes, there is a written job description for that position. Typically, you will work under a manager who will assign you tasks and monitor your work.

HOW TO GET A GOOD JOB

The best way to get a good job is to become acquainted with the business ahead of time. Mentorships (or apprenticeships) are the best way to introduce yourself to the marketplace. This allows you to get to know people in the business. And when you get to know people, you build trust and increase your opportunities.

HOW TO DO WELL IN AN INTERVIEW

One of the most important parts of getting a job is the interview. Here are some points to remember when you go for your first interview.
1. Maintain a high degree of energy. Will you exhibit motivation to do the job? That depends on whether you display an interest in the company, a confidence that you can do it (assuming you have the gifts), and your energy in the interview.
2. Be informed on the business. Read up as much as you can about it before the interview. Who are the competitors for this business? What are the advantages and disadvantages of this business?

3. Be sure to mention the areas of your gifts that would fit the job. Beforehand, jot down three to five strong points you can contribute to the job. But don't brag or exaggerate your accomplishments.

> For I say, through the grace given to me, to everyone who is among you, not to think of himself more highly than he ought to think, but to think soberly, as God has dealt to each one a measure of faith. (Rom. 12:3)

4. Identify ahead of time the things that interest you about the job. The interviewer needs to know that you are interested in the job.
5. Put yourself in the shoes of the interviewer. What would be the reason why they might be hesitant to hire you? They might think of you as too young. Or they might take notice of your lack of experience. How can you answer these concerns?
6. Familiarize yourself with the typical interview questions, and be ready with an honest answer.
    - What are your strong points?
    - What are your weak points?
    - How did you hear about this job?
    - Why did you leave previous jobs?
7. Many interviewers will start off by asking you to tell them about yourself. Instead of talking about your upbringing, your pet cat, and your favorite hobby, it would be better to outline the reasons why you are best fitted for the job. Remember, you don't have much time to make your point. Make the best of it.
8. Most interviewers will ask you if you have any questions. Be prepared ahead of time with a list of questions about the position, about the business, or about the future plans of the company. Here are some good questions you might ask.
    - What would the ideal candidate look like for this job?
    - How do your best employees succeed in their jobs?
    - Where are the current growth areas for the company?
    - What is the potential for personal growth in this company if I

were to receive a position?

- Do the managers provide mentorship? How do you gauge performance?

9. Practice for the interview beforehand. You might practice with a friend or in front of the mirror. Write down some of your answers and then memorize them. Repeat them aloud over and over again. Record your voice.

10. Consider your overall demeanor and attitude before walking into the interview. Are you trusting in God? Are you too proud? Are you too fearful? Have you prayed ahead of time for God's special direction in your life? Are you operating in faith?

Job interview

11. First impressions matter. You probably aren't going to get a second chance to make a good first impression. Think through what the first five minutes of the interview should look like. Do you look the interviewer in the eye, shake his or her hand? What are you going to say? "Thank you for taking this time with me today." Are you going

to wait until the interviewer motions you to take a seat before you sit down? Add energy to the conversation. You might say something complementary about the business, but don't be obsequious.

12. Your body language is important. Figure out ahead of time the appropriate dress code. For example, you shouldn't wear a suit and tie to an interview for a landscaping job. Sit straight up, and don't sit too far back in the chair. Lean forward slightly and listen carefully to everything the interviewer is saying.
13. Bring several copies of your resume to the interview.
14. Don't get into an argument with the interviewer. The interviewer may list reasons why you won't work for the position. Don't contradict him. Do your best to agree with certain factual points while adding some factor the interviewer may not have considered.

Having a resume for your interview is important.

15. Re-emphasize important points. Most people don't get the main point you are trying to make the first time around. A good rule of thumb is to come back to the main point three times. Why are you the right person for this job? Go over the major selling point

one more time.

16. Don't complain. Whatever you do, do not speak negatively of previous jobs, managers, or companies you've worked for in the past. Whiners usually don't get hired. Communicate gratefulness, respect for your managers, and loyalty. Turn a negative question or point made by the interviewer into something positive. Suppose that the interviewer asks about the thing you liked least about your previous job. You might say, "I was really challenged by some of the office politics, but we found ways to work together and get the job done."
17. End on a positive note of appreciation, enthusiasm, and confidence.
18. Follow up. You might send a thank you note or follow up with an email noting your continued interest in the position "as a good fit for you." Don't give in to discouraging thoughts. You've already invested time and energy to get you this far. Regardless of how the interview went, continue to follow up with the human resources department or the interviewer by phone or email.

WHAT IS A GOOD EMPLOYEE?

> Servants, be submissive to your masters with all fear, not only to the good and gentle, but also to the harsh. For this is commendable, if because of conscience toward God one endures grief, suffering wrongfully. For what credit is it if, when you are beaten for your faults, you take it patiently? But when you do good and suffer, if you take it patiently, this is commendable before God. For to this you were called, because Christ also suffered for us, leaving us an example, that you should follow His steps: "Who committed no sin, Nor was deceit found in His mouth;" who, when He was reviled, did not revile in return; when He suffered, He did not threaten, but committed Himself to Him who judges righteously; who Himself bore our sins in His own body on the tree, that we, having died to sins, might live for righteousness—by whose stripes you were healed. (1 Pet. 2:18-24)

Before you can be a leader or a manager, you must be a good student, a good apprentice, or a good employee. Therefore, you should learn the skills and virtues of a good worker.

Biblically, the principles are very simple, although they are not always easy to fulfill.

1. We should work hard and put our hearts into our work, as if we are doing it for the Lord. Be proactive in your work. Look for things that need to be done, and do them without being asked. Don't sit around while others are doing the work. That's a sure sign you will be fired.
2. We are called to honor our managers. We should never speak negatively of our managers or of fellow employees.
3. We are called to be honest. It may be difficult to report a problem to management. Some employees may be tempted to hide a problem, but it is far better to be open and honest about it. The sooner management knows the problem, the sooner they can work on a fix. Hiding problems just makes things worse.

> He who speaks truth declares righteousness,
> But a false witness, deceit. (Prov. 12:17)
>
> Lying lips are an abomination to the LORD,
> But those who deal truthfully are His delight. (Prov. 12:22)

4. We must not be people pleasers in the workplace, seeking approval and compliments from men (Col. 3:22). Rather, we are called to be faithful to the task. The workplace becomes very ugly and political when people are competing with each other for the favor of managers. But this is not what we as Christians should do. We are not trying to beat other employees for promotions and money. We want to do a good job because we're doing it for the Lord.
5. Be humble. Be a good listener. Ask questions. Don't be condescending to the managers. Follow through on a task until you get it done. Don't be self-willed, always introducing your own ideas to the

Be honest with management about issues that need to be resolved.

process. Respect and honor your managers in your heart, not just by outward conformance.

6. Do your best to make your customers and managers happy with your work. Always consider two things: Think about how you can be efficient in the work you do, and how you can do a good job. Managers are always concerned with both the quantity and the quality of your work. Double check your own work before you hand it off to your managers or the customers. Did you make a good sandwich? Did you do a good job mowing the lawn? How does it look? Examine the job a little more carefully than your customer would look at it.

Remember, your big goal in life is not to make money. Your ultimate goal is not to make your customers or managers happy. Your goal is to do everything with all your heart as unto the Lord Jesus Christ. Remember, in everything you do every day, you are a servant of Christ. You represent Him in your attitude, your work, your relationships, and the jobs you do.

THE BENEFITS OF SELF-EMPLOYMENT

In many cases, farmers, carpenters, plumbers, electricians, dentists, chiropractors, and auto mechanics are self-employed. Small businesses, small restaurants, retail outlets, gas stations, and internet businesses are often run by the self-employed. Families might team up to operate these businesses.

1. Family-owned businesses and small businesses provide the backbone of a free market economy. They tend to be more stable in difficult economic times. Those working the business are more loyal to the business, and they don't quit or change jobs as quickly.
2. More self-employment in an economy decentralizes power and wealth. This usually provides for more upward mobility. That means that poorer people have the opportunity to expand their wealth. And the wealth doesn't collect into the hands of a very few rich people.
3. Self-employment can increase freedom for those who get out from under corporate structures. The self-employed can make their own decisions for their own lives. Big businesses will sometimes force their employees to do things that would violate their consciences. They will oppose the principles of God's law. At times, these businesses will cheat their customers and break the eighth and ninth commandments. They will promote certain sexual sins and thereby break the seventh commandment.

    Businesses can also force a family to uproot and move to a different community, thereby abandoning their church relationships. In some cases, a father may have to work sixty to seventy-hour weeks away from his family. This makes it hard for dads to disciple their sons and daughters as they sit in the house, as they walk by the way, as they rise up, and as they lie down (Deut. 6:7-9).
4. Self-employment allows for the development of a family economy, where whole families can work together as a team. This provides work opportunities for both sons and daughters. Whereas eleven-year-old boys would have a hard time finding jobs in an adult workforce, the family economy can provide that much-needed work experience. Boys can start making money earlier in life. Instead

of filling their time with boring schoolwork and games, they can be doing something productive. This provides a needed context in which to grow character. Families need something to do together, and this could be just the thing.

Family-owned businesses enable families to work together.

In our society, marriage and family have become less and less important over the last fifty years. Dads and moms went to work. Children were shuffled off to schools. But a renewed family economy can re-establish the family as a relevant social entity. Our young daughters can also find an economic role in the context of the family instead of in a family-less, marriage-less world.

Also, too much schooling is irrelevant to life. When education is merely theoretical and there is no real-life experience, much of education becomes a waste of time. Life integration is a basic principle for all of learning. The family economy can provide opportunity for that.

THE CHALLENGES OF SELF-EMPLOYMENT

1. Most jobs provide a regular paycheck, and you can count on the money coming in every month. But self-employment usually doesn't give you that steady paycheck. The small business owner will enjoy good months with good income followed by bad months with less income. That means he has to be careful not to spend all the money he makes. He needs to save for a rainy day or for a rainy season.

    The self-employed need to trust in God for their daily bread and regular income. Of course, the employee can always lose his job and then lose his income even though he might find security in the company for a while. Ultimately, all our income comes from God, whether we're self-employed or not. Modern big companies and big governments give people the impression of security. But Christians know that these systems can fail too. So all of us (whether employee or self-employed) need to trust God to supply our needs.

> Look at the birds of the air, for they neither sow nor reap nor gather into barns; yet your heavenly Father feeds them. Are you not of more value than they? Which of you by worrying can add one cubit to his stature? So why do you worry about clothing? Consider the lilies

The self-employed must trust God for provision.

> of the field, how they grow: they neither toil nor spin; and yet I say to you that even Solomon in all his glory was not arrayed like one of these. Now if God so clothes the grass of the field, which today is, and tomorrow is thrown into the oven, will He not much more clothe you, O you of little faith? (Matt. 6:26-30)

2. Self-employed people can work themselves too hard out of sheer greed. The Bible requires one rest day in seven. But since the amount of money self-employed people make usually depends on how hard they work, they will sometimes work too many hours. This is not always the case. However, when dads don't spend enough time with their families, things can go badly.
3. Also, a self-employed person usually has to be a jack-of-all-trades. Because the business owner can't afford to hire specialists to do marketing, accounting, and other parts of the business, they have to do all of that themselves. If members of the family pitch in, that can relieve the sole owner of some of the responsibilities. But business startups do require excellence in many areas if they are going to succeed.
4. Most countries or states require a lot of paperwork from self-employed people. In some cases, small businesses have to withhold income taxes for their employees (including the owners) every month. This usually requires filing a form each month.

MENTAL WORK, TECHNICAL WORK, MANUAL LABOR

God has uniquely blessed each person with certain talents and abilities. Some are called to do one thing, and some another. Some will be employees and others will be self-employed. Another division of work (and talent) is in the type of work that is done. This may be divided into mental work, technical work, and manual labor. Know that all work is honorable, and all may be done equally for the glory of God. A humble garbageman may do his work joyfully as unto the Lord. At the same time, a president of a large company may fail at his job; and therein, he will be less honorable than the garbageman.

Mental work is usually required for jobs like these:
1) Pastoring (and other ministry work)
2) Engineering
3) Managing
4) Lawyering

Technical work is more hands-on yet requires an amount of mental work. This includes jobs like:
1) Electrical work
2) Technician and equipment repair work
3) Mechanical work
4) Dental, medical, and surgical work
5) Heavy equipment handling

Heavy equipment driver.

Manual labor requires physical skill and energy and less organizational skills/planning. Examples include:

1) Clerking in stores and offices
2) Manufacturing assembly work
3) Manual agricultural labor
4) Manual construction labor
5) Manual roadwork

WORKPLACE

Another category of work has to do with the workplace. Most moms work inside the home because their work involves raising children, preparing meals, and running home businesses.

More and more, corporate work can be done from the home as well. This is called **telecommuting**. A recent survey found 38% of workers could do their work from home.[44] At the peak of the COVID-19 crisis of 2020, about 70% of American workers did some or all of their work at home. That's up from 17% in 2019. Phones and computer technology have made it easier for professional work to be done at home. There are many benefits to this, one of which is that workers don't have to waste time commuting back and forth to a workplace.

WHAT ARE YOU CALLED TO DO IN THE ECONOMY?

> Trust in the LORD with all your heart,
> And lean not on your own understanding;
> In all your ways acknowledge Him,
> And He shall direct your paths. (Prov. 3:5-6)

As we conclude this chapter, it would be good for each young person to consider their own calling in life. This means that there are certain things God has called you to do. There are certain things He has prepared you to do.

Some young people bury their talents. This is not what God wants them to do. Some do unwise things with their time, and that is not according to the will of God. How then does a young person understand the best use of their time and talents? Here are a few basic guidelines:

1. The above verse from Proverbs explicitly tells us to seek to know God in our present situation. What are God's values? What are God's priorities for your situation? Based on everything you know from His Word, what would He say about how you spend your time? What would He say about your endeavors?
2. Pray for wisdom. If you pray in faith, God will give you wisdom. And wisdom enables you to "walk circumspectly, not as fools but as wise, redeeming the time, because the days are evil" (Eph. 5:15-16).

> If any of you lacks wisdom, let him ask of God, who gives to all liberally and without reproach, and it will be given to him. But let him ask in faith, with no doubting, for he who doubts is like a wave of the sea driven and tossed by the wind. For let not that man suppose that he will receive anything from the Lord; he is a double-minded man, unstable in all his ways. (Jas. 1:5-8)

3. Take into account God's requirements of you as a man or woman. Generally, God wants women to be ready to manage their homes (1 Tim. 5:14) and to serve as helpers for their husbands in his economic task (Gen. 2:18). Young men are called to be providers for the material needs of the home (1 Tim. 5:8) and to be spiritual leaders in the home and disciplers of their children (1 Cor. 14:34-35; Eph. 6:4).
4. Seek counsel. In the multitude of counselors is safety (Prov. 11:14).
5. Gain experience. Test your skills by working different jobs. Where have you been most effective, and what jobs have interested you most?

THE WORK ETHIC

> Laziness casts one into a deep sleep,
> And an idle person will suffer hunger. (Prov. 19:15)

Much of the book of Proverbs speaks to the curse of slothfulness. First, the Proverbs describe slothfulness as a sleepiness or dullness (Prov. 6:9-11; 19:15). Lack of activity usually results in a lack of vision and a lack of purpose. A lazy person lives in a dream state, usually resorting to endless diversions—games, novels, media, alcohol, and drugs.

The lazy person is easily intimidated by challenging situations (Prov. 22:13). He wastes time and resources up front, which causes more work for everybody later on (Prov. 12:27). He allows little inconveniences to prevent him from doing his work (Prov. 20:4). He thinks he's smart, but actually he is both ignorant and foolish (Prov. 26:16; 24:30). He just lets things go. He doesn't maintain his car. He doesn't change the oil in his car, and his engine goes bad. He doesn't paint his house, and the wood rots out. He doesn't pull weeds in his garden, and the weeds take over.

> I went by the field of the lazy man,
> And by the vineyard of the man devoid of understanding;
> And there it was, all overgrown with thorns;
> Its surface was covered with nettles;
> Its stone wall was broken down.
> When I saw it, I considered it well;
> I looked on it and received instruction. . . (Prov. 24:30-32)

There are different kinds of slothfulness. Some sluggards won't stick to a job until it's done. Some do sloppy jobs, and they won't pay attention to detail. Some sluggards work very slowly because they are easily distracted. And some are easily discouraged by imaginary or real obstacles.

Eventually, the curse of slothfulness always involves poverty. Not everybody who is poor is slothful. But those who are slothful will become increasingly poor. That poverty comes like an armed man. The slothful person is confronted with more obstacles than anybody else (Prov. 15:19). Problems stack up on him. Life becomes even more of a burden. Nothing goes easily for him. He is almost constantly frustrated (Prov. 21:25). In short, the slothful man is miserable.

Hard work and diligence are usually trained into a child by a mother or

Laziness produces poverty.

father. Once the habit of slothfulness has become well ingrained, it's pretty hard to root it out. Both Christians and non-Christians alike can learn the virtue of hard work. When children are rewarded for their diligence, they develop a taste for it. If they are chastised for slothfulness, sometimes that itself is sufficient motivation to work hard.

No follower of Christ should give way to a habit of slothfulness. We are His servants, and we have a billion reasons to serve Him with gladness. He served us. He washed our feet and all our souls with His blood. Love is the greatest motivator of all.

If a young person is hoping to discipline himself or herself to be industrious, the following tips will be helpful:

1. Ask the Holy Spirit for the gift of self-control.
2. Develop a long-term vision for your life. What are some goals you would like to accomplish, considering your talents and abilities?
3. Schedule each week ahead of time, laying out specific priorities and goals you would like to get done.
4. Take fifteen minutes each morning to lay out the priorities and goals you would like to get done for that day. Keep your list in front of you throughout the day.

5. Put your electronic devices and distractions away for long periods of time. If the internet is counter-productive for you, turn it off. Throw away your smartphone if it is hindering you from completing your work.
6. Eat healthily. Get sufficient sleep. With the exception of those who have to work night shifts, the most industrious persons will sleep when it gets dark. Those who stay up until midnight are usually not very efficient during the nighttime hours. Those who are in bed by 9:00 p.m. are usually up early. They find themselves most efficient at 5:30 a.m. when the sun rises. If you get sluggish throughout the day, go for a walk or take a short power nap.
7. Obey the fourth commandment, and establish a regular habit of resting one day in seven. God wants us to take this day for His worship, for thanksgiving, for communion with Him and His people, and for resting in His presence and provision. Be sure you have scheduled time for personal prayer and meditation on the Word of God. Don't let work get in the way of worship.

> Remember the Sabbath day, to keep it holy....For in six days the LORD made the heavens and the earth, the sea, and all that is in them, and rested the seventh day. Therefore the LORD blessed the Sabbath day and hallowed it. (Ex. 20:8,11)

We have just a few years on earth. Then we will enter eternity. We are stewards of the time and talents God has given us. Our lives do not belong to ourselves. Our time is not our own. Let us use what God has given us to achieve the highest purpose. Above all, let us always think of laying up treasures in heaven, investing in eternity with the time God has given us here on earth.

7

BANKING AND YOUR MONEY— HOW THE WORLD ROBS, CHEATS, AND STEALS

A feast is made for laughter,
And wine makes merry;
But money answers everything.
(Eccl. 10:19)

BANKING AND YOUR MONEY— HOW THE WORLD ROBS, CHEATS, AND STEALS

The Bible has a great deal to say about money because God cares about money and honest dealing. As already mentioned, much of Jesus' teaching dealt with the matter of money. At least three of the Ten Commandments deal with money and possessions. So this chapter will take up this subject of money.

Silver and gold coins

Money is a store of material value and a means to facilitate trade. Almost any material thing could be used for money, but some forms are better than others.

Remember that a free market trade occurs when one party gives up something to a second party to get something else he wants more than the thing he is giving up. Each party gives up something he considers less useful or important for something he finds more desirable. Now, one of the reasons a party in the trade might consider his commodity less useful to himself would be that he has too much of it. For instance, if the party has raised 1,000 chickens, there is no way his family would be able to consume that much chicken meat in a year. So he would be willing to trade some of his chickens for a kitchen table, for example. This farmer has plenty of chicken, but his wife is tired of the family eating on the kitchen floor. She wants a table. And, as it turns out, his neighbor is a woodworker who makes furniture and would be glad to trade a table for thirty chickens. He is so busy with his woodworking business that he has no time to raise chickens. Among earlier, more simple civilizations, people didn't use money. So they would trade one thing for another, such as chickens for tables. This is usually called a **barter economy**.

Now, suppose the woodworker who makes the furniture doesn't eat chicken meat. He would rather eat mutton. What does the chicken farmer do if he needs to buy the table? The sheep rancher doesn't want a table, and the chicken farmer doesn't like mutton. So, how does the chicken farmer get his table and the woodworker get his mutton? The solution to this problem is achieved using money. The chicken farmer sells his chickens to somebody else. He collects the money and uses that to pay for the table. Then the woodworker has the money to pay the sheep rancher for his mutton. Thus, you see money provides a convenient and flexible means of trade. Money enables us to buy something from just about anyone at any time.

WHAT MAKES FOR GOOD MONEY

As it turns out, some kinds of money are better than others. For example, some societies have used salt for money. But there are a number of drawbacks with salt.

1. Salt can't be contained in a wallet very well, and you have to take a lot of it with you to buy a car or a horse.
2. You have to weigh out the salt every time you make the exchange.
3. There's a lot of salt in the world, and the value of salt would change drastically if somebody brought a large amount of salt into a community all at once. If everyone has too much salt, no one will want to trade for more of it, so your salt wouldn't be worth anything. This would contribute to the instability of the value of salt.

Salt doesn't make for a good form of money.

4. Salt can be counterfeited pretty easily by coloring small grains of sand white and passing it off as salt.
5. Salt can dissolve easily into water and disappear, leaving you with nothing to trade.

So, what is the best thing to use for money? Economists define six necessary characteristics for something to qualify as money.

1. Durability. Paper or a basket of fresh fish would not be very durable, so these things wouldn't serve well as money.
2. Portability. Elephants are not very portable and thus wouldn't serve well as money.
3. Divisibility. Something used as money would have to be divisible into smaller parts. Pianos, for example, are not divisible, so you wouldn't use musical instruments as money.
4. Universal acceptance or desirability. Manure or fertilizer is not universally desired and therefore would make poor forms of money.

5. Scarcity (high value in relation to volume and weight). Beans and salt are too easily obtained and therefore are not scarce.
6. Stability and predictability of value. Air conditioners and patio furniture in Alaska would not be as desirable in the wintertime; therefore these things would lose value at certain times of year. Their value lacks stability, so they wouldn't serve well as money.

Salt is not very portable, durable, scarce, or stable in value. But it is recognizable, universally desired, and divisible. However, gold is durable, portable, divisible, recognizable and universally desired, scarce, and maintains stable value. Silver is more divisible than gold and a little less scarce. Therefore gold is usually considered a good place to hold your wealth, though it is a little less convenient for day-to-day exchanges.

But what about little sheets of paper with pictures of dictators and politicians on the faces of them? These are portable and divisible. But they are not very durable. Nor are they scarce or stable in value, and they are only sometimes universally desired.

Gold is durable, portable, and scarce.

A good way to think about money is to ask the question: What is the most desirable and marketable thing in a society? People do not want to use cows for money because not everybody owns cows or wants to take care of them. It's also hard to figure out how many cows to trade for a couch. People don't want to trade horseshoes because not everybody owns horses or finds horseshoes useful. And it's hard to figure out how many horseshoes you should trade for a loaf of bread. Horseshoes are not considered of equal value to everybody.

Moreover, people will not consider something of value if it won't be of some value in the future. When the Swiss Family Robinson left the sinking ship for the island, they took the knives, barrels, and rope with them. They probably left a chest of silver coins on the ship. After all, what good would this "money" do them on the island? There were no stores on the island; there was nothing to buy. The marooned family would have taken those things with them, which would be useful to them later on. Money is valuable to all of us because we believe it will hold its value. We believe that others will find it valuable too, so we can use it to make exchanges of goods or services.

THE FUNCTION OF MONEY

Having defined the qualities of good money or means of exchange, now consider the functions of money of which there are three.
— Money is a convenient medium of exchange for buying stuff.
— Money is a good way to measure value.
— Money provides a place to store wealth with the hope that it won't lose value over time.

When stores put a price on something using a standard unit of money (like the American dollar, the Japanese Yen, or the Chinese Yuan), you can compare how much one thing is valued against another. You can compare a $20,000 Toyota Camry with a $220,000 Lamborghini and decide which one you can afford. You can decide whether you want to purchase a $25 book or a $25 box of candy. Given these prices, you might choose the book over the candy. But, if the book was priced at $100, you might choose to buy the $25 box of candy instead.

Another good way to look at money is to see it as a tool. Suppose you owned a lot of money or a lot of gold and silver. Now what if you bought 100 power tools and buried them in the ground? What good would this investment do for anybody, buried in the ground? What would wisdom dictate you should do with $10,000 of power tools buried in the backyard? Naturally, it would be better if you built houses with them, sold the houses, and made more money. That way you could buy more power tools, hire more people, and build more houses.

To store value in money and keep it hidden under your bed for a long time is not a good idea. This is not a good use of the resources God has

Storing money under your bed indefinitely is not a good idea.

given you. To store up lots of money without actually using it for something profitable is called "miserliness." You can do three things with your money: buy things you need right now, give it away to the poor, or invest it in some profitable venture.

> The people will curse him who withholds grain,
> But blessing will be on the head of him who sells it. (Prov. 11:26)
>
> There is a severe evil which I have seen under the sun:
> Riches kept for their owner to his hurt. (Eccl. 5:13)
>
> Cast your bread upon the waters,
> For you will find it after many days. (Eccl. 11:1)
>
> So he who had received five talents came and brought five other talents, saying, "Lord, you delivered to me five talents; look, I have gained five more talents besides them." His lord said to him, "Well done, good and faithful servant; you were faithful over a few things, I will make you ruler over many things. Enter into the joy of your lord." (Matt. 25:20-21)

THE ORIGINS OF MONEY

> Now a river went out of Eden to water the garden, and from there it parted and became four riverheads. The name of the first is Pishon; it is the one which skirts the whole land of Havilah, where there is gold. And the gold of that land is good. Bdellium and the onyx stone are there. (Gen. 2:10-12)

Gold has long maintained its value in free marketplaces.

Who could certify value for any created substance better than the Creator Himself? While humans may find this or that of value for a time, only God can establish value for all time. Here in Genesis 2, God's Word tells us about the pre-fall creation—the gold was good. Although the bdellium and onyx were found in the same place as the gold, these were not described or qualified as good by God's declaration. Sure enough, gold has been desirable and marketable in every country, in every place around the world, and in every era of human existence.

Remarkably, gold has maintained a constant value in the free marketplace over a long period of time. Back in 1880, the rental of a four-room flat (apartment) would run about $6.00 (or one third of an ounce of gold) per month. In today's dollars, that would amount to about $600 per month based on the price of an ounce of gold today. In 2020, you could rent a four-room flat in Wichita, Kansas for between $600 and $1,000. Monthly house rent in England in 1768 would have cost a little less than half an ounce of gold, which would amount to about $850 today. For hundreds of years, you could pay a monthly rent for a home in the average-sized town using gold. It would cost you between one third and one half an ounce.

As early as 2100 BC, private parties were using silver to purchase land. Abraham paid Ephron 400 shekels of silver for the cave of Machpelah (Gen. 23:16). There were no governments officially approving certain coinage or issuing paper money at the time. No one needed governments to do this. Silver and gold were universally accepted money everywhere around the world.

Ancient Roman coins

The civil government did not invent money. God did. People didn't need governments to tell them how to develop money. It wasn't until 600 BC that emperors and kings began minting coins, usually with their faces prominently displayed on the money.

WHO CAN ISSUE MONEY?

Throughout history, virtually anybody could issue money as long as people recognized the money having value. The first American money was manufactured by a silversmith named John Hull of Boston in 1652. He was commissioned by the Massachusetts General Court to produce a silver coin. It was named "the pine shilling" because of the pine tree imprinted on the back of it.

Pine shilling, minted in Boston

At the formation of the nation in 1789, the US Constitution allowed the federal government to issue coins but not paper money. Nonetheless, this did not limit the states and other private groups from issuing their own money. Between 1837 and 1866, privately produced currencies popped up everywhere in the US. At least 8,000 different types were produced by states, cities, private banks, railroad and construction companies, stores, restaurants, churches, and individuals. Private coining of money was banned by Congress in 1864.

American Gold Eagle, minted in 1907

HONEST MONEY

> You shall do no injustice in judgment, in measurement of length, weight, or volume. You shall have honest scales, honest weights, an honest ephah, and an honest hin: I am the LORD your God, who brought you out of the land of Egypt. Therefore you shall observe all My statutes and all My judgments, and perform them: I am the LORD. (Lev. 19:35-37)

Historically, there were three major ways to cheat in transactions. Almost everything in a trade had to be weighed on scales, from sheep and cows to vegetables and gold. If the same scale was used to weigh both items in the transaction, then there wouldn't be a problem. Nobody could cheat. But suppose that a certain scale is used to weigh the vegetables, and a different (more precise) scale was used to weigh the gold for the exchange. For this trade however, suppose someone would adjust the scale used to weigh the gold just a little bit in his own favor. Then the one receiving the gold in the transaction would believe he was getting more gold than he really was.

The second way to cheat was to take a known coin of a certain value and shave off a little piece of it (after it had been weighed). When dishonest persons would shave a little bit off of 100 silver coins, they could make another coin about the size of the others. For this reason, some coins were made with a serrated (or milled) edge. Then, if someone were to shave some of the silver or gold off the coin edge, those receiving the coin in a trade would notice somebody was cheating.

The third way to cheat was to change the quality of the substance itself. Back in the 1800s, a slimy rancher named Dan Grew would skimp on feeding his cattle. Just before selling the cows, he would have them drink large amounts of water. So when the buyer weighed the cattle, he thought

Serrated edge on a coin keeps cheaters from shaving off pieces of it.

he was getting more meat. He didn't realize he was actually paying for water instead.

For thousands of years, the preferred way of devaluing money was to mix lower quality substances like tin, lead, or copper into the silver or gold. The prophet Isaiah condemned Judah for mixing dross with silver. This was easy for smelters to do, and few people could figure it out. It's hard for the average person to tell the difference between 90% silver and 99% silver in a coin. After kings and emperors began minting silver coins with their images stamped on them, it wasn't long before they were debauching the money. After manufacturing cheaper coins, they would make their people trade in the old coins for the new. This would enrich the kings and emperors at the expense of the people. Around the time Christ was born, the Augustus denarius was made of 95% silver. By the reign of Trajan (AD 117), the coin had been debased to a silver content of 85%. A century later, the coin held only 50% of its original value. By AD 268, the coin had fallen out of use, and at that point only 0.5% silver content was left in the coin.

> How the faithful city has become a harlot!
> It was full of justice;
> Righteousness lodged in it,
> But now murderers.
> Your silver has become dross,
> Your wine mixed with water.
> Your princes are rebellious,
> And companions of thieves;
> Everyone loves bribes,
> And follows after rewards.
> They do not defend the fatherless,
> Nor does the cause of the widow come before them. (Isa. 1:21-23)

Now, what would happen to an economy full of greedy, cheating silver smelters? These guys mix tin into the silver, and they use the debased coins to buy things in the market. After a while, when all the cheating smelters start introducing a lot of new cheap coins into the market, there's more of this money flooding into the economy. That means the prices of everything goes up, and you have to spend more money to buy stuff. But who gets rich in this situation? The first cheaters who spend the first cheap coins (while prices are low) get the most stuff. The first person to be robbed is the seller who receives the cheapened coins for his products. Those who are hurt the most are those who collect the debased coins and keep them in savings. These are usually widows who live off their savings. God has some harsh words for people who cheat widows and vulnerable members of society.

> You shall not afflict any widow or fatherless child. If you afflict them in any way, and they cry at all to Me, I will surely hear their cry; and My wrath will become hot, and I will kill you with the sword; your wives shall be widows, and your children fatherless. (Ex. 22:22–24)

PAPER MONEY

Most banks today offer checking accounts. When you write a check for $100, sign it, and give it to somebody, that person treats the check like money. They know they can take the check to a bank and trade it for $100. When they do so, the bank will take $100 out of your checking account. Suppose you had $500 in your account, and you wrote six $100 checks and gave them to six different people. This is usually referred to as "bouncing a check." It is illegal.

When paper money came into existence, banks and their customers would treat the paper money like a check. In this case, however, the money deposited in the bank was gold and silver. You could exchange the paper money for

British pound sterling, paper notes

gold or silver any time you wanted. If some bank issued $10,000 of paper money but didn't have $10,000 of gold and silver in storage, that would be fraud.

With paper money, however, thieves would have an easier time issuing counterfeits. It's a lot harder to create a counterfeit gold piece than it is to create a counterfeit dollar bill. So the institutions that issued bills began placing serial numbers on the bills. Or they found other ways to make it difficult for counterfeiters. As you can imagine, paper money is risky and provides an easy target for cheaters and counterfeiters.

King Louis XIV of France

God wanted governments to arrest counterfeiters, put them in jail, and provide restitution. This is one of the jobs He gave to the civil government. But this often doesn't happen. Highly sophisticated counterfeiters sometimes bribed government officials and kept themselves out of prison while stealing money from everybody else.

Eventually, the civil government took over the business of counterfeiting. This began somewhere around the year 1700, when a murderer named John Law escaped from Scotland and came to France. This man also happened to be an economist. And, since King Louis XIV was having a hard time paying his bills, he asked

John Law

John Law to fix the problem for him. This economist printed paper bills that were only partially backed by silver. When the people figured out what had happened, they rioted in the streets, and John Law barely escaped France with his life.

The second attempt to print paper money like this came with Abraham Lincoln during the US Civil War. He printed "greenbacks" without the backing of silver or gold. Later, President Rutherford Hayes attempted to restore value to this paper money by exchanging it for silver or gold.

Greenbacks, issued in 1862

Franklin Delano Roosevelt adjusted the value of gold to $35.00 per ounce in 1934, and the US Congress removed the gold standard completely in 1974. That ended 1,700 years of honest money in the Christian world (in Europe and America). Now there was no limit to the amount of paper money the government could issue into the economy.

CRYPTOCURRENCY

In the 2000s, computer programmers came up with the idea of **cryptocurrencies**. This was supposed to be money, but only about 13% of the US population held this make-believe digital money. At least 10,000 different kinds of this digital currency were created. Because the cryptocurrencies limited the number of the coins issued, and a market developed for the digital coins, they would increase in value. For example, programmers for "Bitcoin" limited total issuance to 21 million units. These coins were computer-generated money, and there was nothing tangible about them.

Now, suppose that I painted 100 little stones using red, yellow, and blue colors in a very particular design. Then I buried the stones inside of 100 square miles of earth. I buried the first ten stones in such a way that it would take about a year to find each one. The second set of ten stones would take about 100 years to unbury. The third set of ten stones would take about 1,000 years to discover, and so on. The last set of ten stones would take about 50,000 years to find. Each of these stones would be valued at $2,500,000, given that the average person earning $50,000 per year would have to search for the stone over a period of 50,000 years. My intent is to use these stones as a form of money. The stone has no real intrinsic value to it except that I made it difficult to find. Once somebody mines the stone, I issue a certificate to them, and they can trade the stone for other items of value. So, as investors dig up the stones, they begin selling shares in them. Would you invest $2,500,000 in one of these stones before the stone is mined, or even after the stone is mined?

Your investment in the stone depends on the strength of the sales job, and the value placed on them by a limited number of investors. Ongoing trade of the stones would also assume the market would continue to value them. This also assumes that the whole world would value these little stones. Suppose you could only talk twenty of your friends into investing in the stones as if they were worth millions of dollars. But what if the rest of the world thought your little scheme was stupid? Such an investment would be highly risky and would be unfruitful in the end.

Should we think of these stones as an investment (like owning rental houses), or should they be considered money? Well, if these little stones were treated as an investment, it would be a bad investment. Who would invest in something as useless as little red, yellow, and blue-colored stones? After all, anybody could make something that looks like these little stones in five minutes. And what use could anybody make of them? If the stones are supposed to be money, then all or most stores should be willing to accept them as money. And this probably wouldn't happen.

Let's look at the basic requirement for money once more. Are these little stones the most desirable and marketable thing in the economy? That was the question that should have been asked about cryptocurrency. It cannot be considered a currency until

Cryptocurrency wallet on a mobile phone

everybody in the economy is convinced it is valuable and worth owning. To be money, it must turn into the most universally desirable thing to use as a means of trade. Moreover, the money must prove to be stable over a long period of time, even as gold has proven its stability over 6,000 years. Compare the stability of "bitcoin" to "gold" over many years.

STABILITY OF GOLD VS. BITCOIN (CRYPTOCURRENCY OVER 300 YEARS)		
	Gold to Rent a Flat for One Month	Bitcoin to Rent a Flat for One Month
1700	½ ounce	N/A
1800	½ ounce	N/A
1900	½ ounce	N/A
2000	½ ounce	N/A
2015	½ ounce	N/A
2016	½ ounce	1 Bitcoin (est.)
2017	½ ounce	1/2 Bitcoin (est.)
2018	½ ounce	1/5 Bitcoin (est.)
2019	½ ounce	1/16 Bitcoin (est.)
2020	½ ounce	1/20 Bitcoin (est.)
2021	½ ounce	1/80 Bitcoin (est.)

WHAT ESTABLISHES THE VALUE OF THIS THING CALLED CRYPTOCURRENCY?

Mainly, the value is guaranteed by the trust people put in the new currency. This trust is established by a universal acceptance of it as a means of exchange for goods and services. Trust is maintained with long-term stability in value.

BANKING, DEBT, AND INTEREST

> Then he who had received the one talent came and said, "Lord, I knew you to be a hard man, reaping where you have not sown, and gathering where you have not scattered seed. And I was afraid, and went and hid your talent in the ground. Look, there you have what is yours." But his lord answered and said to him, "You wicked and lazy servant, you knew that I reap where I have not sown, and gather where I have not scattered seed. So you ought to have deposited my money with the bankers, and at my coming I would have received back my own with interest. So take the talent from him, and give it to him who has ten talents." (Matt. 25:24–28)

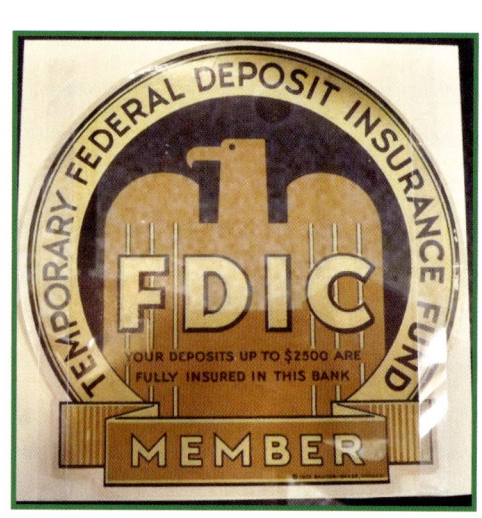

The FDIC insures deposits up to $2,500 in 1934.

Banks have been around for a long time. In Jesus' parable of the talents, the master was looking for an increase on the money that he turned over to his servants. Typically, banks have been money lenders who looked for interest from those who borrowed their money.

The main function of banks is to keep your money safe and to find uses for it. Investors want to use money, like making use of the power tools in the example used above. Where should you invest your money? You could partner with somebody to buy materials and build houses. Or you could invest the money in a business project yourself. But most people don't have the time or the expertise to figure out how best to use their money. So they put the money in a bank, and the bank uses it. Usually, the bank lends it out to others, so they can build houses and live in them or rent them

The main function of banks is to keep your money safe and to find uses for it.

out. Sometimes people borrow money from banks to build businesses. As already mentioned, banks also issued paper money or certificates for the gold and silver they held in deposit.

Now, when a bank lends out your money to somebody else, the bank will charge interest. So each month, the lender will have to pay a certain amount of money (interest) so he can continue to use the money for his home or investment. Many families will borrow money from the bank for their homes. Since they can't afford to buy a house, they will borrow the money to pay for the house. The interest rates for house mortgages (loans) vary from 4% to 10% per year. That means if somebody borrows $200,000 for a house, they would have to pay between $8,000 and $20,000 per year in interest, depending on the interest rate. The banks are happy to collect the interest. But they are using your savings or money deposited in your bank account to do this. What does the saver get out of it? Usually, the depositor will get between 1% and 3% interest on the money deposited in the bank. So, if you put $200,000 into the bank and the borrower is paying 10% interest, you'll get about $6,000 a year in interest, and the bank gets about $14,000 a year. The bank takes the biggest risk when it lends out the money, though. If the borrower doesn't pay on the loan, the bank could lose some amount of the money it lent to the borrower. You'll still get your money back, which means the bank will have to pay for the loss of money (unless the bank goes bankrupt). However, governments began insuring deposits back in the 1930s. The US Federal Deposit Insurance Corporation was formed in 1934 to guarantee payment should banks run out of money to pay depositors making withdrawals. The FDIC records 561 bank failures occurring between 2001 and 2021.[45]

A RECENT HISTORY OF BANKING

For thousands of years, private banks operated without a lot of government control, except when they cheated people. Shortly after the establishment of the United States, Alexander Hamilton championed the formation of the First National Bank. Although it was privately owned and operated, the bank was given special privileges. It was immune from state-based taxation, and its major client was the US federal government. This gave it an edge over other private banks. Within twenty years, the national bank got a little too greedy and proceeded to lend out more money than it held in deposits (in gold and silver coins). When the depositors got wind of this, they all tried to pull out their money at the same time. This produced a bank run known as the Panic of 1819.

President Andrew Jackson ended the US National Bank on July 10, 1832. But the bank came back with the National Banking Act signed by President Abraham Lincoln in 1863.

Alexander Hamilton

Between 1863 and 1913, the national bank became something of a financial monopoly in America. The member banks developed a uniform currency accepted by all member banks. By 1870, there were 1,638 national bank locations (and only 325 state banks). Just over the last century, government control over banking came slowly but surely to America and most other countries around the world.

Finally, in 1913, the US Congress approved the Federal Reserve Act. This introduced complete centralized control over banking. The president of the United States appoints the Federal Reserve board members who are responsible for the oversight of twelve regional banks.

The Federal Reserve system was put in place to control the money supply and the whole US economy. This very powerful, centralized control was supposed to protect the nation from financial ruin and depressions. However, this is nothing but a pretense. Human beings don't make a very good god. They cannot maintain control over this world and protect it from disaster. When men gain a great deal of power, they will inevitably use it for corrupt purposes. They will not play fair. They will make big mistakes. They will pretend to be upright and judicious and intelligent. But they cannot possibly solve the basic problems in a society. Only Jesus Christ can do that. Only the gospel can reach the hearts of men and form true character in a nation.

The Federal Reserve Building in Washington, D.C.

From this time forward, neither the US nor any other modern nation issued money on the basis of the amount of gold and silver held in bank vaults.

For a while, the Federal Reserve appeared to be issuing honest money. They issued paper money (or bank notes), which they said was transferable to gold they held in reserve. The first notes issued in 1914 included $5, $10, $20, $50, and $100 bills. And each note included an important printed byline: *"Redeemable in gold on demand at the United States Treasury, or in gold or lawful money at any Federal Reserve Bank."*

Then, quietly, while very few people would notice, the Federal Reserve removed this byline, and this is how the nation transitioned to dishonest money. The following table illustrates how this happened over seventy-five years.

Year Currency Issued	Byline
1914-1927	"This note is receivable by all national and member banks and Federal Reserve Banks and for all taxes, customs and other public dues. It is redeemable in gold on demand at the Treasury Department of the United States in the city of Washington, District of Columbia or in gold or lawful money at any Federal Reserve Bank."
1928-1949	"Redeemable in gold on demand at the United States Treasury, or in gold or lawful money at any Federal Reserve Bank"
1950-1962	"This note is legal tender for all debts, public and private, and is redeemable in lawful money at the United States Treasury, or at any Federal Reserve Bank"
1963-Present	"This note is legal tender for all debts, public and private"

Evidently, the final switchover to dishonest money happened in 1950. But first, in 1933, President Franklin D. Roosevelt issued an executive order banning the private ownership of gold, punishable by a very severe ten-year prison sentence. This ban continued until 1974. This provided anes-

Franklin D. Roosevelt

thesia for the transition, allowing for a quiet and uneventful severance of the gold standard.

The abandonment of silver as a means of exchange occurred about the same time. In 1878, the US Treasury began issuing silver certificates (which you could redeem at any time for silver). Between 1878 and 1898, these were issued in $1 to $1,000 denominations. Between 1898 and 1964, the silver certificates were issued in $1, $5, and $10 denominations. For instance, each $1 certificate was printed with the guarantee that $1 in silver was always available to every person who wished to exchange the dollar for silver. This ended on June 24, 1968. From this point forward, this money would no longer be exchangeable for real silver.

The American public hardly noticed the sneaky changes coming about with their money. As the pictures of this paper money bear out, the new dollar bills issued by the Federal Reserve looked almost exactly like the old silver certificates issued by the US Treasury. Henceforth, the paper money was worthless and its value relative only to the public trust in the Federal Reserve Board.

> I will sing a new song to You, O God;
> On a harp of ten strings I will sing praises to You,
> The One who gives salvation to kings,
> Who delivers David His servant
> From the deadly sword.
> Rescue me and deliver me from the hand of foreigners,
> Whose mouth speaks lying words,
> And whose right hand is a right hand of falsehood—
> That our sons may be as plants grown up in their youth;
> That our daughters may be as pillars,
> Sculptured in palace style;
> That our barns may be full,
> Supplying all kinds of produce;

> That our sheep may bring forth thousands
> And ten thousands in our fields;
> That our oxen may be well laden;
> That there be no breaking in or going out;
> That there be no outcry in our streets.
> Happy are the people who are in such a state;
> Happy are the people whose God is the LORD! (Ps. 144:9-15)

At its formation in 1913, the US Federal Reserve Board was given power to increase or decrease the amount of money in circulation. This powerful institution has three tools at its disposal to make this happen.

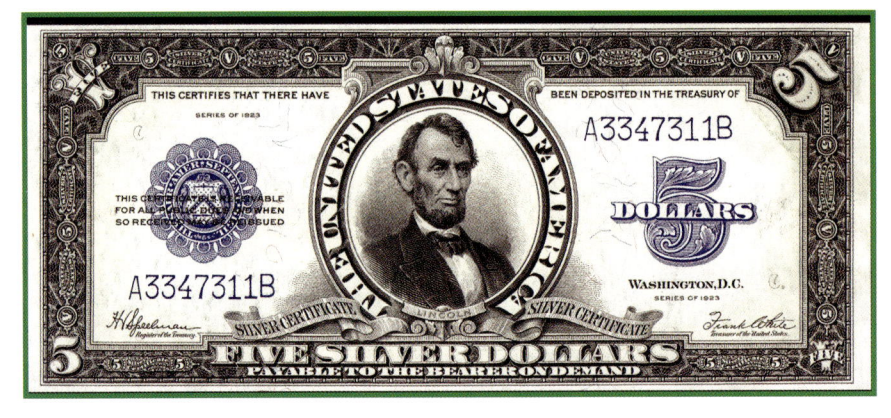

Silver Certificate, 1935 series, redeemable by silver coin until 1968

1. The US Federal Reserve could issue money by buying federal government debt (bonds). At first, this happened by printing more $20 and $100 bills. But the Federal Reserve doesn't need to print money anymore. Nowadays, the money is issued by just adding money into bank accounts on a computer ledger. Now, these board members of the Federal Reserve do not issue the money in order to put it directly into their own personal savings accounts. That sort of robbery is still illegal. But, the board is actually issuing new money in order to purchase the government bonds. When the federal government increased its debt from $50 billion in 1960 to $21 trillion in 2021, some of the bonds

Federal Reserve Note, not backed by silver

were bought by other countries, some by private citizens, and some by various other banks and corporations. But a lot of it was purchased by the Federal Reserve. That's how more money is introduced into the economy. Sometimes, the Federal Reserve will sell the government bonds it holds to other people or institutions. When this happens, the money turned into the Federal Reserve gets erased from its books.

2. The Federal Reserve Board has also been given the power to control every bank in the country by setting the **Reserve Requirement Ratio**. Believe it or not, banks are allowed to lend out five to ten times the amount of money people deposit in the bank. While a bank might only have $1 million in deposits, the Federal Reserve allows it to lend $5 million to people who need to borrow the money. Initially, the Reserve Ratio was set at 20%, and later reduced to 10%, and then lowered to 0% on March 26, 2020. That was the point at which the nation's banks were allowed to lend out as much money as they wanted.

3. The US Federal Reserve also has huge control over the interest rates at which Americans borrow money. Commercial banks borrow money from the federal reserve when money is tight. And the federal reserve board is in charge of setting this **reserve rate.**

Lower interest rates or lower reserve rates mean easier borrowing. When interest payments are pretty low, more borrowing takes place, and government debt, corporate debt, and personal debt soar. When economies begin to slow down, the Federal Reserve Board will try to get more people into debt by lowering the interest rates. This is supposed to stimulate more investment, provide more jobs, and get people to spend more money. It is an artificial means to get the economy going again. While this strategy may work for a few bad economic seasons, eventually the strategy wears out. The nation becomes swamped in debt, and some parts of the economy default on the debt. That means they can't pay their debt. Eventually, interest rates are set close to zero, and they can't go any lower. Raising the interest rates would only make things worse for the debtors already in the system. So there comes a point at which the Federal Reserve Board can't do anything to save the national economy. This happened to the US monetary system in the 2020s. There was far too much debt everywhere. After the 2008 recession, the reserve interest rate hovered between 0.06% and 2.4%.[46] After 100 years of control over the economy, there wasn't much these powerful board members could do to stimulate the economy anymore.

The Gross Domestic Product (GDP) is the size of a country's economy in one year. During any given year, a lot of people were buying things and investing in things. Governments were spending money. Add all of that activity up, and you get the GDP.

Encouraged by the Federal Reserve and the US government, household debt increased from 43% of the GDP in 1980 to 80% of the GDP in 2020, according to the tradingeconomics.com. Business debt also expanded from 31% of the GDP in 1980 to 50% of the GDP in 2020 according to the Federal Reserve Bank of St. Louis. The same source reports that the US government debt increased from 32% to 133% of the GDP between 1980 and 2020.

The huge amounts of money released into the economy and the expansion of debt is a sneaky way to cheat and steal. The wealthiest billionaires profit the most from it. In 1980, the wealthiest .01% of United States families held 2% of the nation's wealth. These families increased their share of that wealth to 8% in 2008, and this number climbed to 18% by 2021 according to Financial Times' article: "The Billionaire Boom." Meanwhile, the condition of the poorest 50% of Americans remained about the same. The following table shows the disparity that grows while the Federal Reserve releases more money into the economy.

WEALTH DISPARITY IN US HOUSEHOLDS[47]

	Lowest 50%	Richest 1%
1990	$16,226	$5,380,000
2005	$23,134	$14,000,000
2015	$13,903	$20,000,000
2021	$47,900	$34,000,000

While the wealthiest 400 families increased their share of the nation's wealth by nine times, the richest 1% of American households increased their wealth by about seven-fold. Meanwhile the poorest 50% increased their wealth by only about two-and-a-half times.

Much of the increase in wealth came through the civil government funneling money into the economy, which increased the value of stocks. For example, a famous billionaire named Elon Musk increased his wealth from $25 billion to $125 billion in the year 2020, and then up to $300 billion the next year.[48] This huge increase in wealth comes by several means. First, certain big companies receive government subsidies, government bailouts, and special rebates—money handed out to these companies. Sometimes, the Federal Reserve (in cahoots with the federal government) puts money into stocks, which increases the value of these companies. As the government-controlled banks handed out all that debt money, the large corporations jumped into the mix. Instead of putting the money into tools and research and development, the companies bought back their own stock. When their stocks would drop in the market, the companies would artificially prop up the value of the stock by buying their own stock. As they invested in their own stock using easy debt money, the stock would rise. This would invite other investors to jump back into the market. Corporate debt ballooned from $4 trillion to $11 trillion between 2007 and 2020,[49] while companies put $5.5 trillion into buying back their own stock.[50] This inflated the stock market, making the companies look like they were worth more than they really were.

Elon Musk

Apple Computer made the most aggressive use of stock buybacks in the early 2020s, putting $85.5 billion in purchasing their own stock shares in 2021. In part, this is what contributed to an explosion of the company's stock value, from $38 in 2019 to $182 by the end of 2021—an almost 4-fold (400%) increase. But the company's sales increased only 40%, from $260 billion to $366 billion over the same time frame. Plainly, the 4-fold increase in stock value was unreasonable, largely stimulated by fake buybacks. That is how Apple Computer became the highest valued company in the world, capitalized at $3 trillion by the year 2022.[51]

To make matters even worse, companies began borrowing money to pay dividends to stockholders. These are supposed to be shares of the company's profit. If the company made a profit, why does the company have to borrow money to pay these dividends? As reported on February 19th, 2021 in the *New York Times*, companies were borrowing upwards of $100 billion per year to make these payments (up from $3 billion in 2003). Once again, this is how high finance swindles investors. Companies presented themselves as if they were more profitable and of greater value than they really were.

By these means, corporate owners would increase their wealth. And the rich get richer, and the poor get poorer. This is how the whole system becomes a den of thieves and a conspiracy of robbers.

Those people who are most hurt in all of this are those who are saving their money in the banks—the retirees, widows, savers, and pensioners. The value of their savings would only decrease because the interest they get from the bank could not keep up with inflation.

When the people discover that the powerful Federal Reserve Board members can't fix the economy, the nation's economy will collapse. The people no longer trust in the corrupt monetary system. Since the success of a fiat monetary system (that is not backed by gold and silver) depends on the trust of the people, the economy will crash. God will bring it down.

FRACTIONAL RESERVE BANKING

Here is a short allegory to help explain fractional reserve banking. There was once a little country called Deficit, in which there were several banks. People would put their money into these banks and receive 1%

interest. And the banks would lend out the money at 2% interest. One of these banks had only $1,000 in deposits, which meant that it was collecting just $10 per year from the interest. So the owner of the bank got a little greedy. He decided to lend out $10,000 even though he only had $1,000 in deposits. He printed more money, and he issued $10,000 to people who wanted to borrow money, even though he only had $1,000 in his bank. At 2% interest, now the bank earned $200 per year in interest payments, and the bank owner was very happy.

However, the king of this little realm found out about what the bank owner was doing. He was not happy that this banker was making $200 per year. So the king said, "I must control all the banks. I need more money to fight my wars and to build my castles. I will make all the rules for these banks, and I will appoint the board members of every bank in my little country. And these board members will do what I tell them to do."

The king then took control of the banks, and he let all of them lend out as much as $20,000 even though each of them only had $1,000 in deposits. Also he required the banks to lend himself large amounts of money without interest, for his projects.

So, each of the three banks lent the king $15,000, for a total of $45,000, even though the banks only had $3,000 in deposits. Now the king was happy. The bank owners were happy. And the people were happy to borrow more money from the banks.

Finally, on March 26, 2020, the board of these banks reduced the reserve requirement to 0%. This enabled each bank to lend out $500,000 or even more, while the deposits stayed at $1,000 per bank. The king happily received most of this money in lending, which he used for his favorite projects. Some of it was distributed to the citizenry, and everybody was happy at first. But prices began to rise because there was so much money floating around, until there was nothing money could buy. And then, the whole rotten system came tumbling down.

March 26, 2020 was the date that the US Federal Reserve reduced the reserve requirement to 0% for the first time. That meant the nation's banks could lend out as much money as they wanted to. Since interest rates were close to zero, they had to lend out a whole lot of money to make a decent profit. However, this huge increase of debt in an economy produces inflation and a breakdown of trust in the monetary system.

> Like a roaring lion and a charging bear
> Is a wicked ruler over poor people.
> A ruler who lacks understanding is a great oppressor,
> But he who hates covetousness will prolong his days.
> (Prov. 28:15-16)

This is how the world runs now. Modern nations are made up of sinners, but that has always been the case since the Garden of Eden. However, the Western world respected God's law for over a thousand years, especially when it came to honest money. Our colleges and schools respected the Scriptures. But that has all changed since the 1860s. Now, the great institutions running our systems ignore God's laws. We live in a post-Christian age, which means that those who run our institutions are not Christians. In fact, they are very much opposed to Christ. Since the schools and the universities have turned against the Scriptures, all our educational, economic, political, and cultural systems are increasingly hostile to Christian principles.

Yet, the robbing and stealing going on is not like that of primitive nations, where one man would steal another man's goat. The unbiblical, anti-Christian economies today are far more sophisticated and powerful in their cheating and robbing schemes. In fact, it may appear that these greedy banks and individuals will get away with their thefts. How could anybody stand against such powerful systems?

In all probability, government-sponsored systems of theft will last longer than when common thieves or gangsters counterfeit unlimited amounts of money. This happens for two reasons:
1. People trust governments. They trust governments more than they would trust counterfeiters and dishonest silver smelters. Incredibly,

quite a few people think government to be a good, wonderful, and righteous god who will never do wrong and will always take good care of everybody. And, for that reason they will turn a lot of power over to these governments. Of course, they believe a lie about the nature of man and powerful governments. This worldview results in the creation of an increasingly dangerous and evil state, and the demise of the nation and its economy.

2. Also, government officials don't go crazy making money all at once. They are very careful technicians. They devalue the money slowly over many years so that hardly anybody notices.

Ignoring God's laws is a bad idea. Those who ignore the law of gravity will do so to their own destruction, and the same thing applies to God's moral law. As sure as there is a God in the heavens, He will bring these governments and nations to account. It would be better for them if they repent now, before it is too late.

> Why do the nations rage,
> And the people plot a vain thing?
> The kings of the earth set themselves,
> And the rulers take counsel together,
> Against the LORD and against His Anointed, saying,
> "Let us break Their bonds in pieces
> And cast away Their cords from us."
> He who sits in the heavens shall laugh;
> The Lord shall hold them in derision. . . .
> Now therefore, be wise, O kings;
> Be instructed, you judges of the earth.
> Serve the LORD with fear,
> And rejoice with trembling.
> Kiss the Son, lest He be angry,
> And you perish in the way,
> When His wrath is kindled but a little.
> Blessed are all those who put their trust in Him. (Ps. 2:1-4, 10-12)

INFLATION

Inflation is a word economists use to describe the rise in prices due to a flood of money flowing into the economy.

There are localized, temporary rises in prices due to supply and demand issues. Demand-pull inflation happens when there is a sudden increase in a need for a product. Cost-push inflation happens when suppliers have a hard time getting raw materials to make their products. Farmers face this sort of problem when they get low crop yields due to droughts. This kind of inflation comes and goes. It's only temporary. Nevertheless, most modern inflation isn't caused by these issues. It is mainly caused by governments. In 1930 America, gas cost 20 cents a gallon, and milk cost 30 cents a gallon. In 2020, gas costs $3.50 per gallon, and milk costs about $2.50 a gallon. The increase is caused by inflation. However, people are making quite a bit more money today than they were in 1930.

When governments issue more money or print more currency they create inflation (and devalue the money already in circulation).

The average person earned about $1,400 per year in 1930, while the modern worker averages about $62,000 per year. Part of the increase is inflation, and the other part is due to an improved standard of living. Technology and automated manufacturing have improved the standard of living quite a lot since the early 1900s. As already covered, the main reason for inflation is that governments spend into a lot of debt. The government-controlled banks then must issue more and more money into the economy. This little story will help explain the relationship between quantitative easing (or money printing), government handouts, and inflation.

The Bank of England

Let us say that there were 1,000 people, and 1,000 one-dollar bills in a small community, and you were the king. Each person was in possession of one dollar. You decide to print 2,000 more one-dollar bills, and this would make each dollar bill in the community worth 33 cents. Then, from the

2,000 one-dollar bills you printed, you sent every person a one-dollar bill, which is worth 33 cents, and you keep the other $1,000 you printed for yourself (for administrative costs, of course). Now, everybody used to have $1 each in their savings accounts. But at this point, each of the citizens is in possession of two full dollars. But really, each person only has 66 cents in real value. And they are all very happy. "What a wonderful king!" they say. And they offer their thanksgivings to the king for giving them $1 (which is only worth 33 cents) and reducing their total savings to 66 cents in value. However, there was one little problem for the community. A loaf of bread used to cost 10 cents, but now a loaf of bread is priced at 30 cents. That means that everybody used to be able to afford ten loaves of bread with their savings of $1. But now they can only afford six loaves of bread with their $2. Yet very few of the citizens could figure out what happened.

Beginning around the 2008 recession, the United States Federal Reserve began a practice called **quantitative easing**. This is one way in which the Federal Reserve introduces more money into the economy (or prints more money, as it were). When the federal government wants to spend a

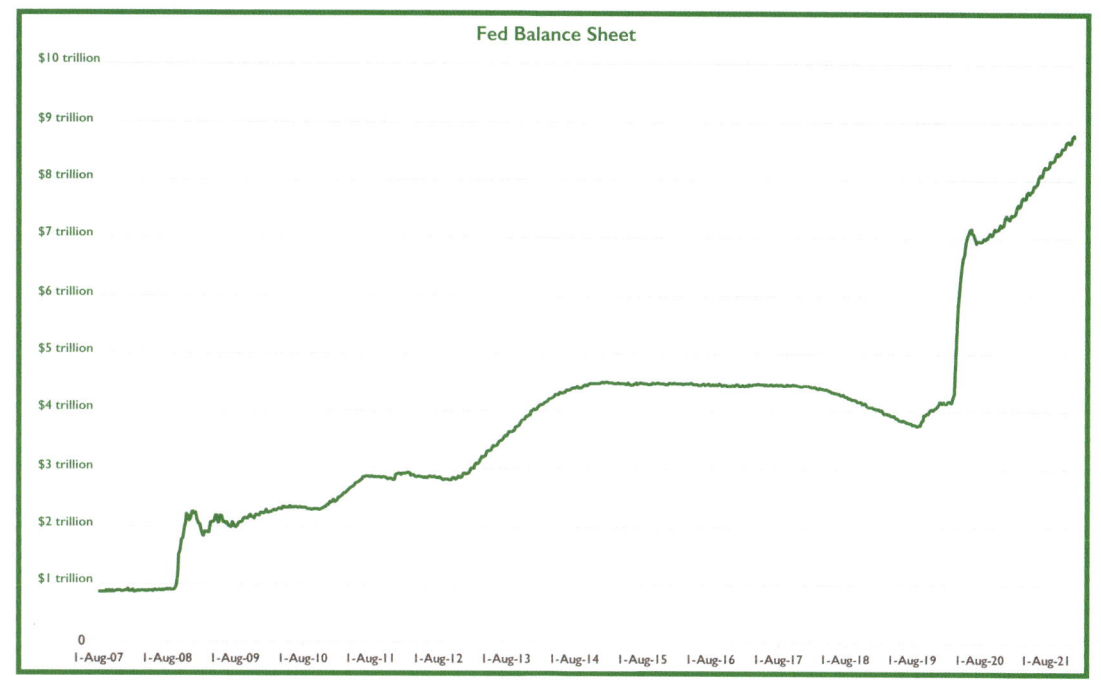

Fed Balance Sheet

The Federal Reserve issues money in quantitative easing between 2008 and 2021, increasing the balance from $1 Trillion to $10 Trillion. Source: Federal Reserve

huge amount of money all at once, who will lend it the money? President Donald Trump wanted to spend $3 trillion in the spring of 2020, but where would he find the money to borrow? The Federal Reserve bought the bonds through Quantitative Easing. But where did the Federal Reserve get the money to do this? They just added the money to their accounts… just like that! The word for this is stealing. Between 2008 and 2021, the Federal Reserve increased its QE from $500 billion to $9 trillion. The UK increased their QE to $1.4 trillion, the European Union increased their QE to $9 trillion, and Japan released up to $7 trillion.[52]

Presidents Donald Trump and Joe Biden softened the impact of this stealing by redistributing cash to American households. These were called stimulus packages. Every adult received $3,200 in three different checks between 2020 and 2021.

The point of the above story is that somebody is going to lose in this dishonest system, and in the end, everybody loses. The same powerful group of people that sneak inflation into the country by increasing the money supply are the people who calculate the inflation percentage each year. This is used for cost-of-living increases in paychecks for workers. Everybody knows that prices are going up. So they would expect to make a little more money from their employers to cover the increased costs. That's why the government produces official inflation numbers each year.

For example, the US official "consumer price index" is supposed to have been 2.48% per year. Based on official numbers, the median (average) household income increased about 20-30% between 1975 and 2021. But actually, the median income has been cut in half since 1975.

Look at how much these major household expenses have increased since 1975.

The median new house in 1975 cost $48,000. Based on a median income of $12,700, you could pay off that house in 3.78 years (if you saved every dime you earned). But, in 2021, the median new house price was $404,000. And based on a median household income of $67,500, it would take you 6.0 years to pay it off (if you saved every dime).

The average new car was priced at $3,800 in 1975, and you could pay it off in four months (based on a median income of $12,700). But in 2021, the average new car was priced at $41,000, and it would take 7.2 months to pay it off. A four-year public college education was valued at $7,276 in 1975 and would have required 57% of a median annual income to pay for it. By 2021, the same 4-year college education would require 112% of the current median annual income to pay it off. The other major household expense is medical care. Back in 1975, medical insurance and health costs would have only absorbed 4.7% of the household income. Forty-five years later, medical insurance for a family of four consumes 20.4% of the household income.

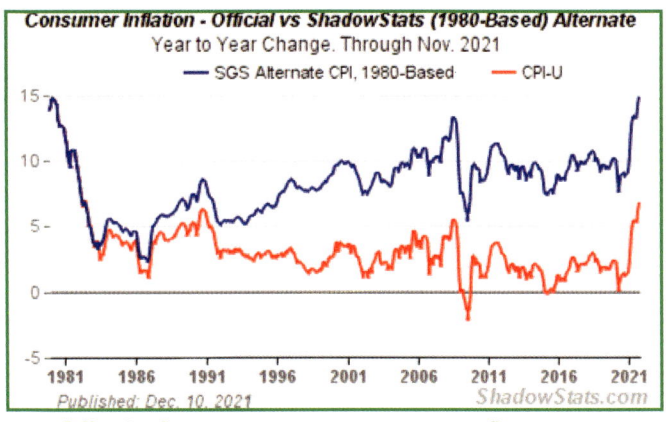

Official inflation rate vs. more accurate inflation rate in the US. Courtesy of ShadowStats.com

Of course, workers in 2020 thought they were making much more money with a median household income of $67,500 compared to the median income of $12,700 in 1975. But inflation has fooled them. They thought their income was keeping up with their expenses. Actually, they were earning about half of what they were in 1975 if you take into account these huge increases in household expenses brought on by inflation.

> Better is the poor who walks in his integrity
> Than one perverse in his ways, though he be rich. (Prov. 28:6)
>
> Getting treasures by a lying tongue
> Is the fleeting fantasy of those who seek death. (Prov. 21:6)

Slowly but surely, this inflationary strategy makes a few people very rich at the expense of the poor and the middle class. The system awards the debtors and punishes the savers. For example, Americans who invested in

Treasury bills (government securities) lost $4 trillion in twelve years of savings, adjusted for inflation by the CPI.[53] Another allegory might be helpful to better understand what is going on here.

Suppose you are a king in a small country, and you want to become very, very wealthy, and add to your net worth without directly taxing the people. What would you do? You could break into everybody's home and rob them at night, but then, you might be discovered. So the following approach is suggested.

The first thing you must do is establish a Private Money Printing Business, which is run by a board of thugs you appoint to the positions. These thugs begin printing money, which they are supposed to make available to people who wish to borrow it. They receive a small amount in interest, a rate which they set for the banks over which they have control. If there was $1 million of money available in the kingdom, these robbers will print up an extra $2 million.

Now, as a king you wish to spend more money, own more property, and control more of the assets of the kingdom. You would like to purchase the properties and businesses of the kingdom. But how might you do this? Well, you must issue bonds (I Owe U's. . .) and pay a small amount of interest (like 2%) to the people in your kingdom who will buy the bonds.

You can also borrow money from the Private Money Printing Business, run by the board of thugs you appointed, at a small amount of interest (like 2%).

Once you have collected about $1 million of debt, you can quickly buy up property and assets in the kingdom with all that money. The good news is that everything you bought just increased in value from $1 million to $3 million (because of all the money printing going on). And, everybody who lent you money just lost 67% of the value of their money (or the value of the bond). Anybody who bought one of your savings' bonds for $100, lost $67 dollars in value. The interest they get paid isn't even close to the value they have lost on their money.

Get your high-flying business friends involved in this too, and they can be part of the scam to impoverish all the rest of the "dumb" citizens of your kingdom. Now, if my reader can't figure this whole thing out, that's okay.

This is how scams work. Dishonest systems are set up so that hardly one in a hundred people can figure out what is going on.

WHEN INFLATION DESTROYS A NATION

What happens when the Federal Reserve pours more money into the economy? This huge increase in money to pay for government debt makes the government bigger and stronger, but it weakens national economies. When the king in the story or real governments issue more money into an economy, they will devalue money and inflate the price of products and services. That's exactly what happened in the history of the world economy, especially after 2020. When the US Federal Reserve issued $9 trillion of extra money into the economy where only about $21 trillion was exchanging hands each year, what do you think would happen? The value of products and services were on the rise in the US and Europe, going up at 8-10% per year by 2022. Now, people couldn't spend as much money. Their savings accounts lost value, and workers weren't getting paid raises big enough to pay for things. Their pay increases were 3-5% less than the inflation rate. To reduce inflation then, you would have to take money back out of the economy. The king in the allegory would have to collect and burn the money he already printed. The Federal Reserve tried to reduce the amount of money in the system by a little bit. Another way to reduce inflation is to raise interest rates, which would reduce debt spending in the economy.

So, the Federal Reserve was really stuck by 2022. The board had reduced interest rates from 6% to almost 0% (between 2000 and 2022) to drive up debt spending. To bring down inflation the board would need to raise interest rates upwards of 8-10%. Such severe measures though, would squelch debt spending and bring on a worldwide depression. But still, inflation was already a problem in that people could not spend as much as they could before. By this time, there wasn't much powerful banks and governments could do anymore to save the economy. Powerful governments were trying to fix economies by spending more and more money. They were trying to control the national economy by manipulating the interest rates. They had encouraged everybody into increasing levels of debt. They created inflation by issuing more money to pay for government debt. Rather than fixing economic problems then, they ended up ruining the world economy in the 2020s.

HOW MUCH MONEY IS IN THE ECONOMY?

Some national governments are honest about how much money they are releasing into the economy. Although, most people don't pay much attention to it, this is what drives prices up more than anything else. The **M1 money supply** includes all of the money in checking accounts, coins, and currency in the country put together.

The Gross Domestic Product (GDP) measures how much money is exchanging hands in a given year. People are buying things and investing in things throughout the year, and governments are spending money. Add up all these exchanges and you get the GDP. But, how much money in currency and coin is being used to make these transactions throughout the year? That's the money supply. The amount of money used to fund those exchanges should be pretty stable. But, you can see in the following chart that it increases every year. However, that has not been the case in the US between 1960 and 2021. The largest increase happened between 2020 and 2021.

M1 Money Supply (St. Louis Fed.)	GDP	M1/GDP
1960: $140 billion	$3 trillion	4.70%
1980: $400 billion	$7 trillion	5.70%
2000: $1.1 trillion	$13 trillion	8.50%
2020: $4 trillion	$19 trillion	21%
2021: $20 trillion	$19 trillion	105%

But where does all that extra money come from? In most countries today, the government or the government-controlled banks issue the money into the economy. According to the economic theories of John Maynard Keynes, increased debt was supposed to jump start a slow economy. But there comes a point at which this does not work anymore. All that debt creates a host of problems. Here is how these ideas ruin the economy. Nations get addicted to debt, and the payments required for the debts run too high. There comes a point at which the most irresponsible borrowers and lenders ruin the system. The borrowers have no intent to pay back debt, but only to increase their debt load as long as possible. Depositors are less and less interested in saving their money in banks. The interest rates offered savers cannot keep up with inflation. Depositors realize they would lose money if they left it in the banks. Companies and individuals are given the legal right to file bankruptcy when they can't pay their debts. Company stocks are also overpriced due to government involvement and corporate buybacks, resulting in stock market crashes. Greed and get-rich-quick schemes produce slothfulness and a breakdown of character. Less and less people want to work, while more people rely on government handouts. Over 50% of the country receive a check from the government during these economic bad times. The most productive people then are saddled with paying the taxes to cover these welfare programs. Higher taxes result in less money for hiring productive workers for businesses. Lower employment means there will be less money to purchase goods and services, and thus less demand. This describes the breakdown of modern economies, especially in the West. All this comes about by foolishness, greed, deception, and, thievery. The biggest problem is that these economies ignore the principles laid down in God's Word.

> The borrower is servant to the lender. (Prov. 22:7)
>
> The wicked borrows and does not repay,
> But the righteous shows mercy and gives. (Ps. 37:21)
>
> You shall not steal. (Ex. 20:15)

Socialism advanced greatly in America after 2020. By this time, 70 million American elderly were supported by federal social security programs, and 59 million Americans were on welfare. The average poor family received $76,400 in benefits, which was about the same as the median income for middle income families. Under the Biden administration, the federal government began offering all families a $250-$300/child welfare check each month, covering 61 million children. That placed 82% of American families with children on welfare. Altogether, at least 75% of Americans were on welfare by 2021. Such actions would disintegrate the character of the nation, undermine the work motive, and further wreck the economy.[54]

Christians must beware of supporting these ungodly schemes fueled primarily by debt. As much as possible, Christians should not participate in wicked government programs, unrighteous banking, and dishonest companies. They must demand the most honest exchange of goods and services. They should avoid all get-rich-quick-by-debt schemes. They must insist on honest money. They should never file bankruptcy for any reason. And they should pay off their debts as soon as possible. Christian-run companies should never artificially inflate the value of their company by buying back stock. They should never look for special handouts or welfare from the government. When times are tough, they should always prefer private charity rather than government intervention. Let us watch out for those sins that underlie all of this corruption. There is too much love for money, which is the root of all evil (1 Tim. 6:10). Covetousness lurks in the heart. Self-centeredness prevails. And people want to get rich quickly.

Seek a proper view of money. It is a tool. These assets belong to the Lord, and we are merely stewards of what He has given us. Seek to grow these assets, not by debt, but by adding real value. Seek to bless more people with your assets by investing in more tools and hiring more people to get work done. And of course, give voluntarily in real charity to those really in need of food and clothing. As much as possible, do not support welfare recipients who are playing the system for more money from the government.

> My son, if sinners enrice you,
> Do not consent.
> If they say, "Come with us, . . .
> We shall find all kinds of precious possessions,
> We shall fill our houses with spoil;
> Cast in your lot among us,
> Let us all have one purse"—
> My son, do not walk in the way with them. (Prov. 1:10-11,13-15)

THE BLESSING OF WEALTH

> "And you shall remember the LORD your God, for it is He who gives you power to get wealth, that He may establish His covenant which He swore to your fathers, as it is this day." (Deut. 8:18)

Wealth is owning or possessing lots of things considered valuable to yourself and others. For example, money is considered valuable; thus, if you have lots of money, you are considered wealthy. Houses, cars, silver, and gold are considered valuable to us and to almost everybody else in the world. If you have lots of this stuff, you are considered wealthy. Wealth is usually gained by hard work, efficient work, and coordinating the work of a large number of persons. As already mentioned, material wealth is a value, although not the highest value in life. Jesus warned us to "beware of covetousness, for one's life does not consist in the abundance of the things he possesses" (Luke 12:15). Wealth comes from God. "The blessing of the LORD makes one rich" (Prov. 10:22).

Throughout the story of Abraham, we find God blessing him with substantial wealth (Gen. 13:1-2). Around the same time, God blessed Job with great possessions—and even greater possessions after his trials (Job 42:12-14). Nations obedient to God are promised material blessings in Deuteronomy 28. During his reign, Solomon was the wealthiest king in the world (2 Chron. 9:22).

Does the New Testament treat riches any differently than the Old Testament? Zacchaeus was a rich man who, after he met Jesus, gave half his goods to feed the poor. While there are warnings for those with wealth, there are also blessings. In 1 Timothy 6, Paul points out that the rich have more to share with others. Our Lord gives various gifts to His people, but He expects them to pass these gifts on to others as they have opportunity. Wealthy Christians have more to share in material blessings. It isn't wrong to be rich, but those with wealth have more responsibility to handle it as God desires them to handle it.

> Command those who are rich in this present age not to be haughty, nor to trust in uncertain riches but in the living God, who gives us richly all things to enjoy. Let them do good, that they be rich in good works, ready to give, willing to share, storing up for themselves a good foundation for the time to come, that they may lay hold on eternal life. (1 Tim. 6:17–19)

8

INVESTMENTS—DON'T BURY YOUR TALENTS IN THE GROUND!

Be diligent to know the state of your flocks, and attend to your herds; for riches are not forever, nor does a crown endure to all generations. When the hay is removed, and the tender grass shows itself, and the herbs of the mountains are gathered in, the lambs will provide your clothing, and the goats the price of a field; you shall have enough goats' milk for your food, for the food of your household, and the nourishment of your maidservants. (Prov. 27:23-27)

INVESTMENTS—DON'T BURY YOUR TALENTS IN THE GROUND!

Our Creator has given each of us a certain amount of time, talents, and money for this life. And He expects us to make good use of these resources. This will require diligence and hard work, as Proverbs 27:23-27 enjoins.

When God created this world He made sure systems were in place for much reproduction or fruit-bearing. Trees and plants yield thousands of seeds for the purpose of generating new vegetation each year. Likewise, in the spiritual realm, the Lord intends us to bear much fruit. Spiritual pruning is part of the process, as Jesus taught in John 15:2. The Father prunes or clips us back so as to yield even more fruit. Similarly, God expects productivity in our economic endeavors. Farmers grow more plants with the intent of yielding more fruit. Ranchers hope to see four to five calves come from each mama cow. Over a period of twenty years, one mama cow and her daughter cows might produce sixty cows (four generations). How many cows might four mama cows have produced in twenty years? This is an example of what is called **compounding increase**.

For us as well, having children and making disciples of these little ones is all part of the kingdom vision for Christians.

God expects productivity and fruitfulness in our endeavors.

> Then he who had received the one talent came and said, "Lord, I knew you to be a hard man, reaping where you have not sown, and gathering where you have not scattered seed. And I was afraid, and went and hid your talent in the ground. Look, there you have what is yours."
>
> But his lord answered and said to him, "You wicked and lazy servant, you knew that I reap where I have not sown, and gather where I have not scattered seed. So you ought to have deposited my money with the bankers, and at my coming I would have received back my own with interest." (Matt. 25:24–27)

CAPITAL INVESTMENT VERSUS CONSUMABLES AND RAW MATERIALS

There are several different ways to use the money God has given you. Suppose you held $3,000 in your bank account. What should you do with it?

You could spend $100 on bubble gum and another $200 on tennis shoes. That would mean you have put 10% of your savings into personal **consumables**. You aren't going to get any of that back. That's not really an investment. Sometimes consumables are needful. Everybody needs shoes, but maybe they don't need shoes that cost $200. And not everybody needs bubble gum.

Shoes are an example of a personal consumable. They don't make any money.

But then you decide to put the other $2,700 into building a lemonade stand. You build a mobile stand on wheels for $2,000 and purchase a commercial lemonade maker for $400. That's about $2,400 in a **capital investment**. Then, finally, you put the last $300 into sugar, lemons, and plastic cups. These are typically referred to as **raw materials** or **operating expenses**. Now, you have purchased bubble gum, tennis shoes, a lemonade stand, a commercial lemonade maker, and material expenses for your lemonade business—all for $3,000. You expect to sell about 500 cups of lemonade for $4 each, to yield $2,000. Now, how much are you worth? The tennis shoes and the bubble gum don't contribute to your net worth. You already used up the lemons, sugar, and plastic cups too. But you still have the value of your capital investment. In total, you are worth $4,400.

A capital investment of a lemonade stand gives you a resource to make money.

BANK SAVINGS, BANK CHECKING, AND CD ACCOUNTS

Year	Investing at a 6% Interest Rate		Investing at an Average CD Rate of 1%	
	Investment at 6% interest	Subtracting an inflation rate of 3%	Investment at 1%	Subtracting an inflation rate of 3%
0	$100.00	$100.00	$100.00	
1	$106.00	$103.00	$101.00	$98.00
2	$112.36	$106.09	$102.01	$96.04
3	$119.10	$109.27	$103.03	$94.12
4	$126.25	$112.55	$104.06	$92.24
5	$133.82	$115.93	$105.10	$90.39
6	$141.85	$119.41	$106.15	$88.58
7	$150.36	$122.99	$107.21	$86.81
8	$159.38	$126.68	$108.29	$85.08
9	$168.95	$130.48	$109.37	$83.37
10	$179.08	$134.39	$110.46	$81.71
11	$189.83	$138.42	$111.57	$80.07
12	$201.22	$142.58	$112.68	$78.47
13	$213.29	$146.85	$113.81	$76.90
14	$226.09	$151.26	$114.95	$75.36
15	$239.66	$155.80	$116.10	$73.86
16	$254.04	$160.47	$117.26	$72.38
17	$269.28	$165.28	$118.43	$70.93
18	$285.43	$170.24	$119.61	$69.51
19	$302.56	$175.35	$120.81	$68.12
20	$320.71	$180.61	$122.02	$66.76

Savings accounts and CDs rarely yield much growth of investment due to inflation.

When you invest money in banks or various businesses, you want to see an increase on your investment. Banks do not usually provide any increase on your money, mainly because of the effect of inflation on the value of your deposits. Normally, checking accounts and savings accounts won't provide any interest; if they do, usually the rate offered will be less than 1%. With a certificate of deposit (CD), the bank has a right to keep your money for a certain length of time, such as six months, one year, three years, or five years. Because banks hold these deposits for a more lengthy period of time, they will offer you a little more interest.

The adjoining chart shows the detrimental effect inflation has had on the value of savings accounts over the last ten years. Inflation has averaged 2.5%-3.0%, and even certificates of deposit have not exceeded 1% (for six month to one year CDs).

Rarely have investments yielded 6%, but the first two columns of the chart follows the growth of an investment collecting 6% interest (with and without the effect of inflation).

Adjusted for inflation, you can see that money saved in the bank is actually losing value. This includes certificates of deposit, which are supposed to be the best yield you can get out of the bank. After twenty years, the $100 deposited in the bank has lost a third of its value! A 6% yield on your investment would almost double your $100 deposit (to $180.61). But no certificate of deposit in the US provided that much interest between the year 2000 and the year 2020.

THE VALUE OF SAVING

Suppose there was a very wise and purposeful young man who studied hard and worked two jobs from the time he was sixteen years old. During the 102 hours of his waking hours of a week, the young man chose to make the most of it. He would work ten hours a week in one job for his spending money and tithe. Then he also worked twenty hours a week at a sandwich shop at $16 an hour, and continued this for ten years. He saved everything he made at the shop. Inflation averaged around 3%, and he received a 3% pay raise each year to compensate. Investing these earnings or savings, he set a goal of a 6% return on the money. His long-term objective for working these twenty hours every week was to pay off a house in full before getting married and settling down. Could he accomplish this at twenty-six years of age?

SAVINGS FROM 20 HOURS PER WEEK OVER 10 YEARS			
	Sandwich Shop Pay	Savings	6% interest
Year 1	$16,640.00	$16,640.00	$0.00
Year 2	$17,139.20	$33,779.20	$998.40
Year 3	$17,653.38	$52,430.98	$2,026.75
Year 4	$18,182.98	$72,640.71	$3,145.86
Year 5	$18,728.47	$94,515.04	$4,358.44
Year 6	$19,290.32	$118,163.80	$5,670.90
Year 7	$19,869.03	$143,703.73	$7,089.83
Year 8	$20,465.10	$171,258.66	$8,622.22

Year 9	$21,079.05	$200,959.93	$10,275.52
Year 10	$21,711.42	$232,946.87	$12,057.60
Total	**$190,758.95**		**$54,245.52**

Based on this table, you can see that the young man's total savings would reach almost $233,000 at the end of ten years. If he had not invested his savings at 6% interest, he would have only held $190,758.95. Investing everything at 6% each year yielded an additional $54,245.52. In 2021, the average house price in Texas was $247,210, or $233,661 in the state of Illinois. If house prices did not inflate, the young man could pay off the average house in these two states in ten years. Now, this does not consider the amount he has to pay in taxes. And it does not account for the increase of house prices by inflation. But this illustration does show how a young man can save quite a lot of money in ten years. What a difference it makes when a young man refuses to waste time playing games, and stops wasting his money on frivolous things!

The biggest challenge for any saver is still to beat inflation. The game is rigged against the saver, and it favors the big corporate debtors. The best investment is almost always to put money back into your own business, or better yet, to lay up treasures in heaven where moths and rust do not corrupt and where thieves do not break in and steal.

STOCKS AND BONDS

Bonds are another popular investment, especially with people who like to save money, and do not like to take risks. Sometimes called "notes," these are issued by governments and businesses as loans. You might call them "I.O.U.'s." If a government wanted to construct a school building costing $5 million, they would issue $5 million in bonds to lenders. Usually, they would give the investor a fixed interest rate. Typically, the rates will run from 2% to 5% on a ten to twenty-year bond. That means the lender has ten to twenty years to pay off the bond. Large institutions like city governments

Working hard and saving money pays off.

are supposed to be dependable and they are not likely to default on their loans. Governments usually don't go bankrupt because they can always increase taxes to make sure everything gets paid for. If you lent money to an irresponsible young man, you would probably charge higher interest because he might fail to make payments on his loan. The higher interest rate is charged because the loan is a higher risk. But bonds issued by large institutions and civil governments are considered a safer investment.

Treasury bonds or savings bonds are issued by the government, and the US ten-year T-bill rates averaged about 2% between 2010 and 2022. Over these twelve years, the interest rates didn't quite beat inflation. However, the ten years prior (2000-2010) yielded a positive inflation-adjusted interest averaging 1.8%. Who wanted to invest in government bonds in 2022 when the government was issuing more money causing inflation, and depreciated the bond values? People who invest in government bonds now were losing value on their investments. Interest on bonds may be variable or fixed. A variable rate can go up or down depending on the Federal Reserve's target

United States savings bonds

rate. The fixed interest rate will remain the same for the whole lifetime of the loan (or bond).

As already covered in the previous chapter, stocks are part ownership in companies. There are thirteen stock exchanges in the United States, of which the New York Stock Exchange and the Nasdaq are the largest. Other large stock exchanges around the world include the London Stock Exchange (England), the Tokyo Stock Exchange (Japan), the Shanghai Stock Exchange (China), and the Hong Kong Stock Exchange.

When buying or selling stocks (your ownership in companies), you have to sell through a broker. That's the purpose of the stock exchange.

There are also market indexes that keep track of how certain segments of business are doing in the country. For example, the Nasdaq Composite monitors how well technology companies are doing. When the Nasdaq moves up 5% in a week, that means that the total value of technology companies has increased by 5% (on average). Some technology companies within the group may have done better than 5%, and some may have come in lower for the week.

The most famous index in the world is the Dow Jones Industrial

Wall Street in New York City, the location of the New York Stock Exchange

Average, which monitors the most popular industrial (manufacturing) companies like Apple, Boeing, Microsoft, IBM, Walmart, Cisco, Johnson & Johnson, Visa, Nike, Home Depot, and Coca-Cola.

The Standard and Poor (S&P 500) index averages the value of 500 of America's largest companies (representing eleven sectors). It's probably the most accurate measurement of how American businesses are doing.

MUTUAL FUNDS AND INDEX FUNDS

Some people like to invest in a block of multiple companies at the same time. **Index funds** are provided for those who want to invest in all thirty companies included in the Dow Jones Industrial Average at the same time. There are also **mutual funds.** These funds collect a pool of money from investors and then allocate the funds to various stocks, which are supposed to be more profitable companies.

UNEQUAL YOKING AND EMPLOYMENT WITH UNBELIEVERS

> Do not be unequally yoked together with unbelievers. For what fellowship has righteousness with lawlessness? And what communion has light with darkness? And what accord has Christ with Belial? Or what part has a believer with an unbeliever? (2 Cor. 6:14–15)

As Christians, we find ourselves in various positions in life. Sometimes we may work for an unbelieving employer who may be very unprincipled or even criminal in his business practices. While we might prefer a better employment situation, at times we are pressed to continue under less than ideal conditions. The Apostle Peter still exhorts us to be subject to our masters with respect and fear. "Servants, be subject to your masters with all fear; not only to the good and gentle, but also to the froward" (1 Pet. 2:18 KJV).

However, the Christian employee must never violate his own conscience, or compromise on God's law, no matter the pressure placed on him. For example, Joseph in the Old Testament repelled the temptations of Potiphar's wife because he would not sin against God (Gen. 39:1-12). But what about investing in a company known for its ungodly policies and immoral actions? Should we do this? The Christian's commitment is not set entirely upon making money. Always, he is to be focused on seeking the kingdom of God and His righteousness. We are committed to the overall advancement of God's righteousness in the earth. We are called to be the salt and light of the earth. If a Christian, through his work and investments, fails to influence the economic community for the sake of righteousness, we must conclude that the salt has lost its flavor.

> Salt is good: but if the salt have lost his savour, wherewith shall it be seasoned? It is neither fit for the land, nor yet for the dunghill; but men cast it out. He that hath ears to hear, let him hear. (Luke 14:34–35 KJV)

GREED IN THE STOCK MARKET

> He that is greedy of gain troubleth his own house; but he that hateth gifts shall live. (Prov. 15:27 KJV)

Investors make money in stocks by two methods. They receive dividends at the end of the year (or at the end of a three-month period) as the company divides up its profit. Average dividends for the S&P 500 between 2016 and 2021 was about 1.9%. These dividends did not keep up with inflation. By 2021, average dividends had dropped to 1.3%, well under the "official" inflation rate of 6.2% for the same year.

The second way in which investors try to make money is by buying stock, and then selling it for a profit. Day traders will buy and sell many times throughout the day. A favorite technique used by these "investors" or gamblers is scalping. By this means, they will invest $25,000 in a $50 stock, watch the stock fluctuate ten cents, and sell right away for a $50 total gain. The day trader may only hold the stock for a few seconds before he sells it. If he repeats this ten to twenty times a day, he could increase his wealth by $1,000.

Two heart dispositions work side by side among those who play these games—fear of losing money and greed. The greedy hold the stock for longer as the stock rises in price. The fearful sell off the stock quickly when the price begins to drop. Neither of these controlling dispositions are spiritually healthy.

While all investment involves some risk, there is a point at which the investor gives way to the sinful habit of greed, gambling, or get-rich-quick schemes. No longer is the investor's focus on the wise and faithful use of God-given talents. Now the chief desire is to get rich and to get rich quickly.

Gambling makes money on other people's losses, whereas investing makes money by a company's gainful work and success. In an investment, everyone must win if you are going to make a gain. When you purchase something, you usually have a pretty good idea of what you are getting. For example, let's say that you and three friends decide to invest in a bulldozer. Surely, all four of you would want to know that the bulldozer works and

Some people day trade for a quick profit.

that it isn't overpriced compared to other bulldozers on the market. The same should apply to investing in the stock market. If you are going to own part of a company, you want to be sure that it's a good company and that it isn't overvalued compared to other companies like it. You would want to know how much profit the company made over the last five years before you invested in it.

Gamblers are not investors. Day traders don't care about the company they are investing in. They want a quick profit. Suppose when you and your friends purchased the bulldozer, you didn't care whether the bulldozer worked. All you cared about was whether you could sell it for a little more than you bought it for. You're hoping that another group of fools would pay a little more for it without even looking into the quality of the machine. That bulldozer might trade hands twenty times before anybody tested it and learned that it was a piece of junk.

Before the stock market crash of 2022, the **options market** was exploding in 2021. This was another type of gambling in the market. The gamblers actually bet on the future value of a stock. We can determine the present value of a stock based on the company's current situation—profit, income, debt, and so on. We can compare the health of businesses in the present, but we cannot know the future of any company a year from now. Only God knows the future.

When a trader buys a stock option, he doesn't own any stock yet. He only purchases the right to buy a stock at a certain price in the future. Purchasing a **call option** is to bet on the stock increasing in price sometime in the future. Suppose a trader buys a call option for 100 shares of ABC company's stock at $25. The stock is currently worth $15. He pays $150 for the option, betting on the stock value rising above $25 sometime in the future. The option expires in six months, so he watches the price of the stock. The stock rises to something above $25. As the expiration date finally arrives, the stock is valued at $35. The guy who bought the option purchases 100 shares of the stock at $25 and immediately sells the stock at $35. Then he walks away with $1,000. Subtracting the $150 he paid for the option, he has earned himself $850. But the guy who sold the option has lost $850 in the bet. He was betting the stock would not go higher than $25, and he was hoping he would make $150 on the deal.

Between 1973 (when options trading got started) and 2020, the stock market was still mostly based on investors who bought stock in companies with the hope of producing value. In a very real sense, the US stock market turned into a gambling casino in 2021. During the first nine months of 2021, $6.9 trillion of options exchanged hands, while only $5.8 trillion in stocks were traded. Elon Musk's company, Tesla Inc., became the favorite for market gamblers. About $80 billion of Tesla options were traded in 2021, compared to only $20 billion of Tesla stock.

WHEN THE WHOLE MARKET TURNS TO GREED

> Do you not know that the unrighteous will not inherit the kingdom of God? Do not be deceived. Neither fornicators, nor idolaters, nor adulterers, nor homosexuals, nor sodomites, nor thieves, nor covetous, nor drunkards, nor revilers, nor extortioners will inherit the kingdom of

> God. And such were some of you. But you were washed, but you were sanctified, but you were justified in the name of the Lord Jesus and by the Spirit of our God. (1 Cor. 6:9-11)

Because we live in a sinful world, there will always be greed operating in the markets. But sometimes greed takes over, and the whole market falls apart. The whole American stock market gave itself over to greed between 2000 and 2021.

Economists developed a **price to earnings ratio** for the Standard and Poor Index of 500 companies. This ratio compared the stock value of the companies to the productivity of these companies. It's a great way to determine if stocks are a good value, and you might think of it as a "Greed Ratio." For seventy years, the average P/E hovered around 13, exceeding 16 for the first time in 1985. Historically, companies were earning about 6% of the total value of their company in a single year. Between 1995 and 2021, the price to earnings ratio ramped up from 13 to 43. This meant that investors were now more interested in the price of the stock, than they were in the companies' productivity. As stock buyers rushed in to buy more stock hoping to make a quick buck on the sale, stock prices inflated, and companies became less productive. At the same time, companies were borrowing money to invest in their own stock. They hoped this would attract more buyers and raise the price of the stock even more.

INVESTING IN THE STOCK MARKET

The following provides a simple beginner's guide to investing in stocks:
1. Pay attention to the price to earnings ratio in any national stock market. For instance, you don't want to invest in the US stock market unless the P/E ratio has dipped under 15. If the P/E is above this, the market is too saturated in greed for judicious and honest persons to get into it.
2. The general rule of thumb is to buy low and sell high. Stocks experience ups and downs over days and weeks, and it's better to buy on a dip as the stock is headed for a trough.

3. Research the stock. Who are the heads of the companies in which you are looking to invest? By 2020, the largest companies in the US were led by men who were of questionable character. Jeff Bezos was divorced in 2020. Bill Gates was divorced in 2021. In the same year, Elon Musk was unmarried and loose, and the chief executive officer of Apple was a homosexual. The leadership of a company is by far the most important factor contributing to the success of the company. Before investing in a company's stock, you should also consider the following:

    - What is the past performance of the company? What is the company's profitability trend over the previous five years? What is the dividend they've been handing out to their investors? How does it compare to other companies within the same business sector? (That is, you want to compare a manufacturing business with other manufacturing businesses.)

    - How much debt has the company taken on? Has the company used debt to buy back stocks?

    - What do thoughtful, judicious, and wise counselors say about the stock?

    - What is the competitive advantage this company has over others? Is there some unique feature about their products that puts them head and shoulders above their competitors?

4. Be ready to commit to the stock for a long time. The exception to this rule applies during market corrections and crashes. There have been some severe market corrections in which the value of all the stocks come crashing down. When the market crashes, you can lose about half of the value of your investment in a day or two. The 2008 crash took about five years to recover the loss. Among the US markets, crashes occurred in 1929, 1987, 2001, and 2008. It's hard to predict a crash, but the price to earnings ratio is probably the best rule of thumb (as provided above).

Running a small business is a great way to invest your money.

YOUR BEST INVESTMENT

Always be aware that the best place to invest your money is in your own business. Above and beyond anybody else, you will do the best possible job to make sure your business is successful. Generally, caretakers or hired stewards won't take the best care of other people's investments. The owner is more likely to look after his flocks and to know the state of his herds than a hired hand.

While you may work a job, you can always keep a part-time business going on the side. For example, you may want to take your savings of $5,000 and purchase 100 electronic devices to sell on eBay. If you sell each device for $75 (excluding postage), you would make 50% on the investment. That's a pretty good return on your investment compared to what you would get if you put the money in a bank. A project like this would still require a little work on your part (if you have to package the devices for shipment, for example).

Earthly treasures are subject to decay or theft.

YOUR VERY BEST INVESTMENT

> Lay not up for yourselves treasures upon earth, where moth and rust doth corrupt, and where thieves break through and steal: but lay up for yourselves treasures in heaven, where neither moth nor rust doth corrupt, and where thieves do not break through nor steal. (Matt. 6:19-20 KJV)

Before getting the rest of the investments available to us in this world, the words of Jesus should direct us towards the very best investments of all. What are these treasures?

Jesus clarifies this in Matthew 19:27-29. He points out that a heavenly investment is anything given up for the sake of Christ. "Everyone who has left houses or brothers or sisters or father or mother or wife or children or lands, for My name's sake, shall receive a hundredfold, and inherit eternal life."

Heavenly treasures have much to do with visiting the poor in their affliction. It is an investment of time, money, and energy into "the least of these," who follow Jesus. Proverbs 19:17 also promises that "He who has pity on the poor lends to the LORD, and He will pay back what he has given." Paul enjoins the rich in 1 Timothy 6 to be generous with the poor. By doing this, they will be "storing up for themselves a good foundation for the time to come, that they may lay hold on eternal life" (1 Tim. 6:19).

This is the major concern of Christ, as He speaks to the sheep and the goats on the final day of judgment.

> Then the King will say to those on His right hand, "Come, you blessed of My Father, inherit the kingdom prepared for you from the foundation of the world: for I was hungry and you gave Me food; I was thirsty and you gave Me drink; I was a stranger and you took Me in; I was naked and you clothed Me; I was sick and you visited Me; I was in prison and you came to Me."
> Then the righteous will answer Him, saying, "Lord, when did we see You hungry and feed You, or thirsty and give You drink? When did we see You a stranger and take You in, or naked and clothe You? Or when did we see You sick, or in prison, and come to You?"
> And the King will answer and say to them, "Assuredly, I say to you, inasmuch as you did it to one of the least of these My brethren, you did it to Me." (Matt. 25:34-40)

In the Old Testament, God laid out three requirements for helping the poor (or the teachers in the church):

1. Families and individuals were to provide a 10% tithe to the church.

> Then the LORD spoke to Moses, saying, "Speak thus to the Levites, and say to them: 'When you take from the children of Israel the tithes which I have given you from them as your inheritance, then you shall offer up a heave offering of it to the LORD, a tenth of the tithe. And your heave offering shall be reckoned to you as though it were the grain of the threshing floor and as the fullness of the winepress. Thus you shall also offer a heave offering to the LORD from all your tithes which you receive from the children of Israel, and you shall give

> the LORD's heave offering from it to Aaron the priest. Of all your gifts you shall offer up every heave offering due to the LORD, from all the best of them, the consecrated part of them.' Therefore you shall say to them: 'When you have lifted up the best of it, then the rest shall be accounted to the Levites as the produce of the threshing floor and as the produce of the winepress. You may eat it in any place, you and your households, for it is your reward for your work in the tabernacle of meeting.'" (Num. 18:25-31)

2. Families were to provide 3.33% of their yearly income to the poor in their local community.

> At the end of every third year you shall bring out the tithe of your produce of that year and store it up within your gates. And the Levite, because he has no portion nor inheritance with you, and the stranger and the fatherless and the widow who are within your gates, may come and eat and be satisfied, that the LORD your God may bless you in all the work of your hand which you do. (Deut. 14:28-29)

3. Farms and businesses were to allow some gleaning for the poor.

> When you reap your harvest in your field, and forget a sheaf in the field, you shall not go back to get it; it shall be for the stranger, the fatherless, and the widow, that the LORD your God may bless you in all the work of your hands. When you beat your olive trees, you shall not go over the boughs again; it shall be for the stranger, the fatherless, and the widow. When you gather the grapes of your vineyard, you shall not glean it afterward; it shall be for the stranger, the fatherless, and the widow. And you shall remember that you were a slave in the land of Egypt; therefore I command you to do this thing. (Deut. 24:19-22, see also Lev. 19:9-10)

But how does this apply now? Certainly, the Father will call us to even more generosity as we have been the recipients of God's grace by the great gift of His Son. Hopefully, the hearts of God's people are even warmer now

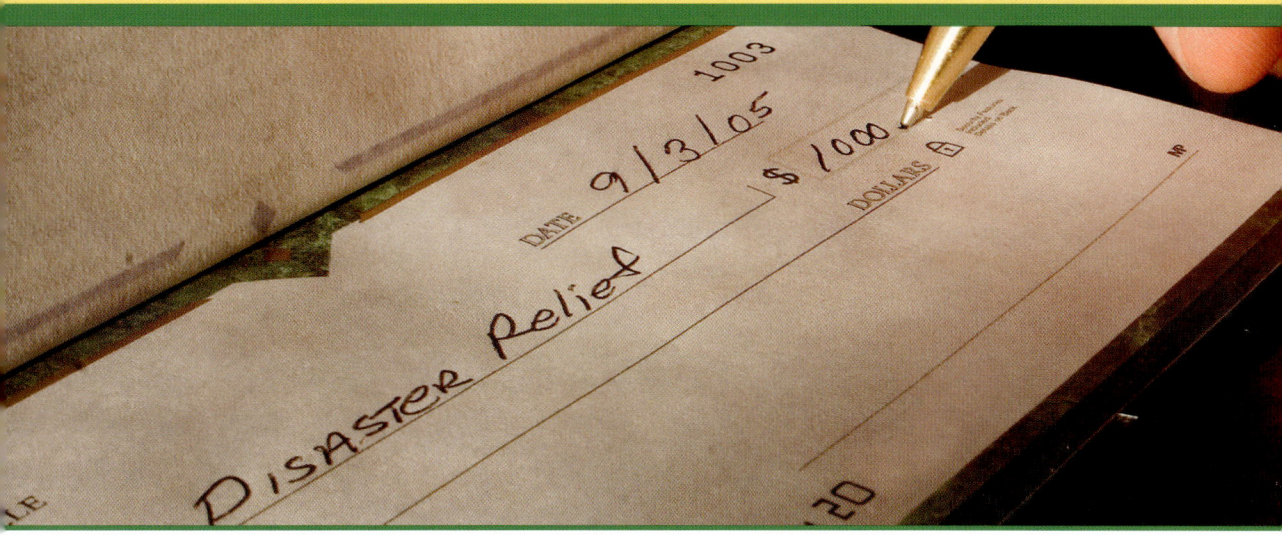

We are to be generous in helping those in need.

than they were among the Old Testament Jews.

> Cast thy bread upon the waters: for thou shalt find it after many days. Give a portion to seven and also to eight; for thou knowest not what evil shall be upon the earth. . . . In the morning sow thy seed, and in the evening withhold not thine hand: for thou knowest not whether shall prosper, either this or that, or whether they both shall be alike good. (Eccl. 11:1-2, 6 KJV)

This passage from the biblical wisdom literature is sometimes used to recommend a diversification in investments. But the same principle could apply to *every* form of investment, including charity to the poor. Would it be better to give a little here and a little there than to focus all your charitable contributions towards one source?

> Therefore I thought it necessary to exhort the brethren to go to you ahead of time, and prepare your generous gift beforehand, which you had previously promised, that it may be ready as a matter of generosity and not as a grudging obligation. But this I say: He who sows sparingly will also reap sparingly, and he who sows bountifully will also reap bountifully. So let each one give as he purposes in his heart, not grudgingly or of necessity; for God loves a cheerful giver. (2 Cor. 9:5-7)

Above all, God wants us to give freely and cheerfully, without the feeling of compulsion. All charity should come out of pure love for God and for our neighbor or brother in Christ.

The general principle for giving is not to pass up any opportunity that immediately presents itself to you. The Good Samaritan in the parable was not responsible to take care of every wayfaring stranger who was accosted by robbers everywhere in the world. In the providence of God, he encountered one man, and he took care of him. In the same way, we should not pass over a single needy case. The problem with the rich man in Jesus' parable was that he had the opportunity to help Lazarus every day for a long time, but he didn't help the single case that presented itself to him. Any help Lazarus received at the rich man's table was purely accidental—crumbs that fell from his table. Only the dogs helped the poor man, a little bit, by licking his sores.

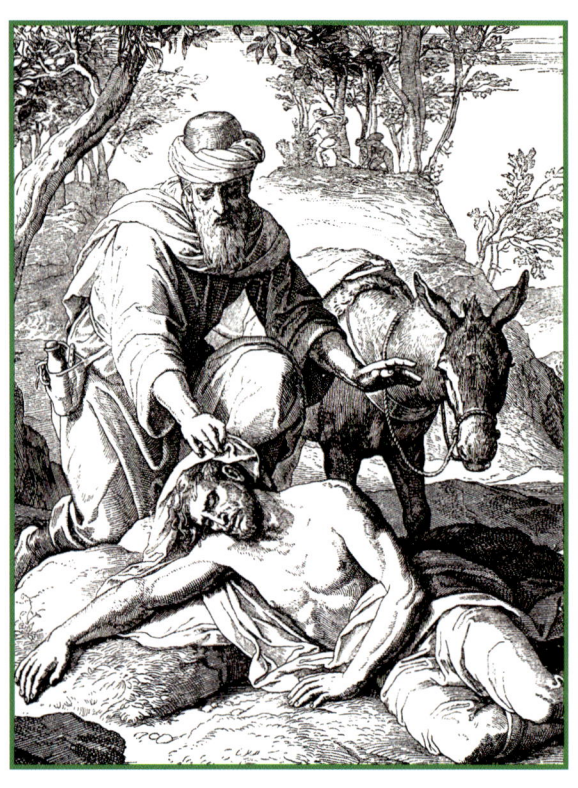

The Good Samaritan did not pass up the opportunity to serve someone in need.

> There was a certain rich man, which was clothed in purple and fine linen, and fared sumptuously every day; and there was a certain beggar named Lazarus, which was laid at his gate, full of sores, and desiring to be fed with the crumbs which fell from the rich man's table; moreover the dogs came and licked his sores. And it came to pass, that the beggar died, and was carried by the angels into Abraham's bosom; the rich man also died, and was buried; and in hell he lift up his eyes, being in torments, and seeth Abraham afar off, and Lazarus in his bosom. And he

cried and said, Father Abraham, have mercy on me, and send Lazarus, that he may dip the tip of his finger in water, and cool my tongue; for I am tormented in this flame. But Abraham said, Son, remember that thou in thy lifetime receivedst thy good things, and likewise Lazarus evil things: but now he is comforted and thou art tormented.
(Luke 16:19–25 KJV)

Real estate is often a good investment.

REAL ESTATE, COMMODITIES, AND GOLD AND SILVER

Now, what else is there to invest in besides your business and other people's businesses? Well, look around you. What do you see? Dirt. Land. Trees. Houses. Animals. Metal. These don't exactly produce things like businesses do. But you can trade your money for these sorts of things.

Real estate is just dirt and rock until improvements are made on the land. This includes houses, barns, fencing, or other improvements. Unless the real estate is overpriced because of an increase in debt spending and greed, this is usually a pretty good investment. Fenced pastureland can provide good grazing for animals. And houses and other buildings can be rented, which provides some interest on your investment. Usually, the value of the property increases with inflation rates, so you don't lose value when buying real estate.

There are risks with all investments. For real estate, you might run into maintenance problems on your buildings, or you might have to deal with irresponsible tenants who won't pay their rent. Let's say you saved up $200,000 to put into a small rental. The monthly rent amounts to $1,200 per month. Don't forget the average property tax in the US is about 1.1% per year on the value of the home. Here is what your budget would look like:

Annual Rental Income	$14,400
Property Taxes Expense	-$2,200
Insurance Expense	-$1,500
Maintenance Expense	-$2,000
Your Profit	$8,700

Subtracting your expenses, your profit would be $8,700 per year, which is about 4.3% of your investment. That's not bad, as long as the value of your home increases to compensate for inflation. Rentals do require some work on your part. You have to find good renters. You want to make sure the property is properly maintained, and you have to deposit the rent checks every month.

HOME COST-TO-RENT RATIOS

Be strategic when looking at the rental business. To get the best deal, you want to consider the price-to-annual rental ratio. The very best ratio scores run under 15, while the worst run as high as 25 to 30. That means that if you pay $200,000 for a rental house, a ratio of 15 would get you $13,333 per year in rent.

Excellent Rental Markets in 2021[55]			
City	Average Price per Home	Average Annual Rental	Ratio
Charlotte, North Carolina	$265,000	$21,000	12.6
Orlando, Florida	$215,000	$18,000	12
Atlanta, Georgia	$200,000	$17,450	11.5
Albuquerque, New Mexico	$150,000	$15,400	10
Dallas, Texas	$165,000	$16,800	10
Cincinnati, Ohio	$180,000	$21,060	9
Birmingham, Alabama	$119,600	$13,200	9

One of the worst cities for landlords is San Francisco, where the median price-to-rent ratio is 50. Also very high are Los Angeles, California at 39, Seattle, Washington at 36, Portland, Oregon at 29, and Miami, Florida at 23. Generally, the largest cities and the most liberal (or sinful) areas of the country are terrible places to invest in real estate.

OTHER COMMODITIES

Other stuff available for purchase with your savings includes commodities like grains, steel, cloth, and animals. Some people buy commodities when they expect the market to improve for them some time in the near future.

Animals can be a good investment just about any time because they grow bigger and reproduce. And there is value to their meat. Cows, pigs, chickens, and goats are usually good investments, especially if you live in farm country. You might lose money if they get sick and die or if they run out of food to eat. A $200 calf can grow into a large cow within a year or two, and the meat can sell for $600-$1,000. However, cows will need some land to graze on, and you will need to supplement their diet with nutrients (which will add expense to your investment).

Gold and silver can be a means of holding value.

People who don't want to lose value in their savings will often put their money into gold and silver. Technically, these hard metals are not investments as much as they are a means of holding value while money is losing its value. Investors will move their investments into gold and silver during economic downturns. But this is usually only temporary. When stocks and real estate are overpriced and bonds can't beat inflation, the only safe haven for investments are gold and silver.

TRAPS TO AVOID WHEN INVESTING OR PROVIDING CHARITY

> Let your conduct be without covetousness; be content with such

> things as you have. For He Himself has said, "I will never leave you nor forsake you." (Heb. 13:5)

There are several traps you must avoid when making investments. The first is obvious, because this is what the whole world has done since the turn of the 20th century. People want to get rich quick by using debt.

Previously (in chapter two), we looked at the temptation to use debt to increase your wealth. But let's apply this to a young investor who is just getting started. Suppose the young person decides to invest his savings in a rental house. Let's say that he can't afford the $200,000 home paid in full, but he does have the $10,000 needed for a down payment. So he borrows the remaining $190,000. Because real estate prices usually increase with inflation, he is counting on his investment increasing about 4% per year, or 20% in 5 years. That means the $200,000 home will be worth $240,000 in five years, but remember, he only put a $10,000 down payment into the home. However, there is one more factor to consider. He will have to pay the bank interest on the loan. His fixed rate (30-year) mortgage on the $190,000 borrowed was about 4% over 5 years. That means he will have to pay about $7,250 per year in interest on the investment. So here is the young investor's budget for the little rental business he started up, over a period of five years:

Annual Expenses for a Rental House	
Expense	**Amount**
Annual Rental Income	$14,400
Property Taxes	$2,200
Insurance	$1,500
Maintenance	$2,000
Interest Payments	$7,250
Total Annual Profit	$1,450

This would give the young investor about 15% return on his $10,000 investment. That's pretty good, especially if he can sell the property in five years and keep $50,000 in profit from the sale. Herein is the lure of debt. Adding up the $1,450 of profit taken each year from the rental income to the $40,000 gained in the increased value at the sale of the home, the investor would have made $47,250 on a $10,000 investment in five years. That's almost a 100% annual return on the investment. How can you beat that?

There is one little problem, however. What happens if the value of the property deflates (or drops)? That's the risk the debtor takes. If the property value drops from $200,000 to $180,000, then you will lose all your down payment, and the $7,250 you made in five years' rent won't quite pay off the reduction in the value of the home. This eventuality is hardly ever considered by big investors. Yet, prudent men and women would still allow for this possibility, depending on how God's providence determines the future.

Deflation may come about by recessions, high unemployment, an increase in interest rates, or high foreclosure rates (where a large number of people have to default on their mortgage loans).

A BIBLICAL VIEW OF DEBT

> If there is among you a poor man of your brethren, within any of the gates in your land which the LORD your God is giving you, you shall not harden your heart nor shut your hand from your poor brother, but you shall open your hand wide to him and willingly lend him sufficient for his need, whatever he needs. (Deut. 15:7-8)
>
> Owe no one anything except to love one another, for he who loves another has fulfilled the law. (Rom. 13:8)

The Bible is clear that debt is legitimate for the poor brother. Also, Deuteronomy 15 limits the length of a debt allowed for God's people to seven years (Deut. 15:1). This would require the debtor to establish a reasonable plan to pay off the debt in that time frame. Now most young families don't have a lot of money when they start out. They can't afford to pay $200,000 for a home. So they usually have to go into debt to purchase their first home. But will they be able to pay off the debt within seven years? That would depend on how fancy a home they purchase. The modern world encourages families to live beyond their means, and debt enables them to do that. Paupers are encouraged to live like kings. So they will borrow as much as they can. They run up credit card debt. They file for bankruptcy if they can't pay off their debts. They live high off the hog because they think they deserve it. It is the life of discontentment, covetousness, theft, and idolatry.

Just starting out, a young twenty-six-year-old professional might earn an annual income of $30,000 to $50,000 per year. He should be able to start off on a real estate investment of 1.25 times his annual salary. Within the US economy, that amounts to $40,000 to $62,000. This author paid off a home at twenty-six years of age valued at 1.0 - 1.25 times his annual salary. At the beginning, the home was a 1,000 square-foot trailer on acreage, complete with a well and septic system. After saving a little more money over the next three years, we had saved enough to purchase a 1,700 square foot home. This is how a family avoids living beyond their means, and living in perpetual debt slavery. Christians should carefully consider what God's Word says about getting rich quick. This will frame their approach to investments.

> An inheritance gained hastily at the beginning
> Will not be blessed at the end. (Prov. 20:21)

OTHER TRAPS

Another trap people fall into when making investments or providing charity, is the "paralysis of analysis." They don't do anything because they are perpetually analyzing the pluses and minuses of the decision. They just can't decide what to do. This may be due to fear of losing their money, miserliness, the idolatry of money, or an aversion to risk. Everything done in life involves risk and therefore must be done in faith. We must pray.

One more trap in these financial decisions is to move ahead without prayer and without acknowledging God. This is a form of autonomy or self-will. We need to seek God's will in all matters, especially the important matters, by honest and humble prayer before making investments.

> Trust in the LORD with all your heart,
> And lean not on your own understanding;
> In all your ways acknowledge Him,
> And He shall direct your paths. (Prov. 3:5-6)

THE QUESTION OF SAVING

Some societies will spend everything they have. Nations of the world with the lowest savings rates include most of the countries of Africa as well as the Bahamas, Belize, and El Salvador. Sometimes this reticence to save is due to extreme poverty. Some societies have troubles with laziness. And some cultures have little hope for the future so they won't plan for the future. Sometimes this failure to save comes because of the constant impulse to spend money. Some people want to avoid the problem of envy. For example, when friends and relatives see they have saved money, they will demand a share of it and nobody gets ahead.

Most of these problems have been avoided in Western nations, and

Manual labor jobs for young people provide a path to building some initial savings.

nations like Japan and South Korea. These countries have done just about everything possible to avoid the risk of poverty. Our institutions require auto insurance, medical insurance, fire insurance, and life insurance in case of catastrophic emergencies. They enforce savings for retirement. But what does the Scripture require of us? That is the most crucial question.

> Go to the ant, you sluggard!
> Consider her ways and be wise,
> Which, having no captain,
> Overseer or ruler,
> Provides her supplies in the summer,
> And gathers her food in the harvest. (Prov. 6:6-8)
>
> A prudent man foresees evil and hides himself,
> But the simple pass on and are punished. (Prov. 22:3)

The ant is our example. She gathers food for the wintertime. Saving is critical for future "rainy day" needs. Those who need to purchase something expensive that cannot be covered by one paycheck will have to save to make that happen. For example, every young fifteen-year-old person should know they need transportation to get to a job. In most economies, workers use motorcycles or cars to commute back and forth to work. (There are exceptions in places like Japan or China where public transportation is used almost exclusively, especially in larger cities.) So, if your first motorcycle will cost $1,500, you will need to save for it. This is much preferred over buying the motorcycle on credit (or debt). Most young teens (thirteen to fifteen years of age) can earn about $100 per month doing manual labor like cutting grass or painting houses. After fifteen months, you would have saved about $1,500 for that first motorcycle. Better transportation will give you more flexibility to get better jobs and more jobs further away from home. Then if you can save $400 per month (at sixteen years of age), you could purchase your first automobile for $4,800 after a year of work. By the time you are seventeen years old, you will have enough money to purchase your first car.

After transportation, shelter is your next major necessity. So to purchase a house you will have to work hard and save your money for a longer period of time. Based on Scripture's cautions concerning debt, it is better to save money than to go into debt for these necessities. Suppose you were to go into debt to buy your first car (at $4,800). The average interest rate on a loan for a used car runs around 8.5%. Your monthly payments over five years would be $98.48, and total interest payments would be $1,109. In total, then, you would pay $5,909 for the car. If you had saved ahead of time, you would have only paid $4,800. Debtors will always fall behind savers, although they may think they are getting ahead for a time.

> The plans of the diligent lead surely to plenty,
> But those of everyone who is hasty, surely to poverty. (Prov. 21:5)

Aesop's fable concerning the tortoise and the hare applies to financial success as well. In the end, careful savings and investment will produce more wealth than investing with debt, living beyond your means, and jumping into get-rich-quick schemes. It may appear that the hare is making progress. But, through all the ups and downs of market fluctuation, the tortoise will always win the race. Occasional use of debt when there are no other options may be alright for a short amount of time. But a get-rich-quick mentality or the hare-mentality will never win the race.

THE TORTOISE AND THE HARE

A hare met a tortoise one day and began making fun of him for being so slow. "Do you ever get anywhere?" the hare asked with a mocking laugh.

"Yes," replied the tortoise, "and I get there sooner than you think. I'll run you a race and prove it."

The hare was much amused at the idea of running a race with the tortoise, but for the fun of the thing he agreed. So the fox, who had consented to act as judge, marked the distance and started the runners off.

The hare was soon far out of sight, and to make the tortoise feel very deeply how ridiculous it was for him to try a race with a hare, he lay down beside the course to take a nap until the tortoise should catch up.

The tortoise meanwhile kept plodding along slowly but steadily. After a time, he passed the place where the hare was sleeping. But the hare slept peacefully

INVESTMENTS—DON'T BURY YOUR TALENTS IN THE GROUND! 234

The tortoise ("slow and steady") wins the race.

on. When at last he did wake up, the tortoise was near the goal. The hare now ran his swiftest, but he could not overtake the tortoise in time.

RETIREMENT

In Europe, America, Australia, and Asia, a high priority is placed on saving for retirement. Sometimes savings programs are forced upon workers in these societies.

That means the government forcibly takes money out of your paycheck to save for your retirement. In America, this is called **social security.** Japan's system is called "public pension," and the UK maintains a "National Insurance Scheme." In America, the government keeps back 12.4% of your

US Social Security cards.

income for social security and 2.9% for Medicare (which is medical insurance for elderly people). That means that the civil government takes 15.3% of your income received from working.

The problem with these systems is that they are not savings programs. While you are forced to put money into the system from your paycheck, the government uses that money right away to support other peoples' needs. The money is spent taking care of elderly people who have already retired. When these systems were put together in the 1930s and 1940s, there were more young people working and less older people retiring. Sadly, the nations that used these social security systems would kill most of their babies between the 1950s and the 2020s. That means there would be more older people retiring and less younger people to do the work. The following chart illustrates the problem. In the 1950s, there were plenty of workers providing for the older people (retirees). After these societies encouraged the use of abortions and chemicals to kill babies over the course of seventy years, everything changed. There were far less workers to take care of the elderly folk.

How many young workers for every retiree?[56]				
	1950	1990	2020	2050
Japan	10	5.1	2	1.6
United States	16.5	4.7	4.1	2.8
United Kingdom	8	3.7	3.1	2.1

You can see there were far more older people than younger people in these countries by 2020. Or put another way, there were far more workers putting money into social security between 1950 and 1990, and far more people receiving money from the social security program after 2020. To make matters worse, the retiring generations had two more problems. Family relationships were not in good condition, so children were less likely to want to care for their elderly parents and grandparents. And the older generation failed to save an inheritance for their children and grandchildren. They didn't have much of a spiritual heritage or a financial heritage to pass on to the next generation. Instead, they had a great amount of debt. The average debt for baby boomers in the US (people 57-75 years of age in 2021) was $229,000, but they had only saved an average of $138,000 for retirement.[57] That means the average elderly person was saddled with $91,000 in debt at retirement.

This is what a failed economic system looks like. Government programs like this will always fail because they are not based on God's principles contained in Scripture.

At this point, Christians should realize how much the system has broken down. This is the inevitable result of ignoring God's principles. What would Jesus tell us to do now?

1. First of all, relationships are important. God calls us to love our families, our aging parents, and our own children. Let us value our relationships and take the time to nurture them. Success in life has much to do with keeping the fifth commandment because God Himself attached that all-important promise to it.

> Honor your father and your mother, that your days may be long upon the land which the LORD your God is giving you. (Ex. 20:12)

2. This generation will be tasked with getting rid of socialist programs that are failing so badly now. We will have to replace government charity with real charity, where individuals and families voluntarily care for the poor in their communities.
3. The churches should also be well prepared to take care of the widows in their local assemblies. This has been the function of the Christian church from the beginning. For instance, the Apostle Paul places the responsibility of caring for widowed mothers and grandmothers with the sons and grandsons in 1 Timothy 5. But he also specifies the church's responsibilities provide physical support for widows over sixty years of age. This still applies to each elderly widow in local churches who have no sons or grandsons to take care of them.

> But if any widow has children or grandchildren, let them first learn to show piety at home and to repay their parents; for this is good and acceptable before God. Now she who is really a widow, and left alone, trusts in God and continues in supplications and prayers night and day. But she who lives in pleasure is dead while she lives. And these things command, that they may be blameless. But if anyone does not provide for his own, and especially for those of his household, he has denied the faith and is worse than an unbeliever. Do not let a widow under sixty years old be taken into the number, and not unless she has been the wife of one man, well reported for good works: if she has brought up children, if she has lodged strangers, if she has washed the saints' feet, if she has relieved the afflicted, if she has diligently followed every good work. (1 Tim. 5:4-10)

In Matthew 15, the Lord Jesus Christ condemned the Pharisees for refusing to take care of their parents in their old age. Then, in real and genuine conformance to the will of God in this matter, our Lord also made sure His own mother was taken care of when He was crucified on Calvary.

> He answered and said to them, "Why do you also transgress the commandment of God because of your tradition? For God commanded, saying, 'Honor your father and your mother'; and, 'He who curses father or mother, let him be put to death.' But you say, 'Whoever says to his father or mother, "Whatever profit you might have received from me is a gift to God"—then he need not honor his father or mother.' Thus you have made the commandment of God of no effect by your tradition." (Matt. 15:3-6)

> Now there stood by the cross of Jesus His mother, and His mother's sister, Mary the wife of Clopas, and Mary Magdalene. When Jesus therefore saw His mother, and the disciple whom He loved standing by, He said to His mother, "Woman, behold your son!" Then He said to the disciple, "Behold your mother!" And from that hour that disciple took her to his own home. (John 19:25-27)

Instead of saving to provide for yourself, the better mindset is to save for the purpose of taking care of your spouse, your mother, or your grandmother should you die before they do.

Another good reason to save is so that we can leave an inheritance for our children and grandchildren. This worldview is virtually absent in our world today, especially in the United States. A recent survey found that 90% of the baby boom generation are planning to spend all their savings on themselves before they die.[58]

> A good man leaves an inheritance to his children's children,
> But the wealth of the sinner is stored up for the righteous. (Prov. 13:22)

The Scriptures do not speak of saving for ourselves. We are rather called to serve others in this life. Children are called to care for their ailing elderly parents. Fathers and grandfathers are called to leave an inheritance for their children's children. The Bible offers no retirement plan for able-bodied men. If a man is able to work, he should continue to labor until he dies. That doesn't mean that everybody needs to keep working in some particular corporate job. Nor does it mean that an elderly man must keep working at the same pace or for the same number of hours each day as younger men work. Nonetheless, God calls all of us to work. The Apostle Paul continued to "fulfill his ministry" until the end of his life (2 Tim. 4:5-7). As long as we are here, we have a job to do for Christ, in whatever He has called us to do.

> And being in Bethany at the house of Simon the leper, as He sat at the table, a woman came having an alabaster flask of very costly oil of spikenard. Then she broke the flask and poured it on His head. But there were some who were indignant among themselves, and said, "Why was this fragrant oil wasted? For it might have been sold for more than three hundred denarii and given to the poor." And they criticized her sharply.
>
> But Jesus said, "Let her alone. Why do you trouble her? She has done a good work for Me. For you have the poor with you always, and

> whenever you wish you may do them good; but Me you do not have always. She has done what she could. She has come beforehand to anoint My body for burial. Assuredly, I say to you, wherever this gospel is preached in the whole world, what this woman has done will also be told as a memorial to her." (Mark 14:3-9)

From this remarkable narrative contained in Mark 14, we learn of a woman who had collected an amount of about $30,000 in today's currency value. Investing her money into this extremely expensive ointment, she poured it over the body of Jesus. Some called this extravagant gift a waste of money, but Christ disagreed. She did what she could for the Savior out of love for Him. And we are called to do nothing less than this. As much as we love Christ and want to bless Him, we will find opportunities to save and then to pour out blessings upon His body—the Church.

IRAs and 401(k) accounts provide a way to save for retirement with tax benefits.

TAX BREAKS FOR SAVING

Some governments provide extra tax breaks for savings if savers would commit to not spending the money until they are over sixty years of age. In the US, these savings plans are called Individualized Retirement Accounts (IRAs) or 401(k)s. With the IRA, each saver can save up to $6,000 (or thereabouts) each year without paying taxes on the money. They will have to pay taxes on the money later, if they spend money during retirement. The 401(k) plan is similar to the IRA except that an employer will deposit the money into the account. The company withholds a certain amount of savings from your pay every month. As of 2021, the maximum allotted 401(k) contribution was $19,500 per year. These are also tax-deferred savings.

If you save $6,000 every year beginning at twenty-one years of age, and continue to tuck away that amount into savings until you are sixty-five years old (at 6% interest), you will have saved $1,270,000. The following chart provides a comparison of various savings amounts over a period of forty-four years.

Would this savings be enough to provide for a couple, assuming that neither worked a job after they turned sixty-five? The average retired couple (aged 65-74) spends $53,000 per year. Some can get by on as little as $24,000. If the couple spent just $24,000 per year, they would probably consume $550,000 over twenty years.

Savings for Retirement at Various Interest Rates

Amount Saved Per Year	% Interest	Total Saved	Total Saved Adjusted for Inflation (3%)
IRA Savings			
$6,000	6%	$1,270,000	$550,000
$3,000	6%	$635,230	$275,000
$6,000	5%	$952,200	$425,000
$3,000	5%	$476,000	$213,000
401(k) Savings			
$12,000	6%	$2,487,000	$1,089,000
$12,000	5%	$1,871,000	$845,000

Yet, if aging parents lived with their children or grandchildren, they could still save an inheritance and avoid many of these expenses. Does God want children to abandon their aging parents, and leave them to take care of themselves? Is it wise to consume an inheritance during the retirement years? Christians must seriously consider these questions. Too often the traditions of men make the will of God of "none effect" in our lives. This was the charge the Lord brought against the Jewish system in Matthew 15.

SAVING FOR MARKET DOWNTURNS

As mentioned in chapter two, recessions and depressions are part of modern economies. There were thirty-five recessions and depressions over a period of about 200 years in American history. The longest economic depression in the last century lasted three and a half years. It was called the Great Depression.

Tradesmen and small business owners are familiar with the ups and downs of the market, and they need to have a little money reserved for the lean times. Some businesses are seasonal, such as HVAC, farming, landscaping, and some retail businesses. They may take in 80% of their income during a three-month period in the year. Because of this, the owners will have to save a portion of their income to live on throughout the rest of the year.

Employees will count on a regular paycheck, but what happens if they lose their job? That's why employees should also think about saving up some money for a "rainy day." The average length of unemployment in the 2020 recession was 16.5 weeks, or four months. Since 1937, the longest economic recession in the United States lasted only one and a half years. For married couples and families, therefore, it would be advisable to have enough savings to keep things going for eighteen months. Only about 8% of Americans have that much in savings. As many as 70% of Americans couldn't live for more than 1 to 3 months if they lost their jobs.

KEEPING TRACK OF YOUR FLOCKS AND HERDS

> Be diligent to know the state of your flocks,
> And attend to your herds;
> For riches are not forever,
> Nor does a crown endure to all generations. (Prov. 27:23-24)

Accounting is an important part of stewarding your resources.

Accounting is the word used for keeping numerical tabs on a business. Good accounting practices are needed to keep an honest and realistic assessment of the state of your "flocks and herds."

Life is made up of ups and downs, and everybody will have to receive bad news as well as good news at some point. Whether the news is good or bad, what is most important to persons of high integrity is that they know the truth of the matter. Those who are afraid of hearing the bad news will not want to know the state of their herds. They don't want to know if the animals are diseased, or if bad weather is going to affect their farms and ranches. But this isn't true of the diligent, faith-filled, and honest investor.

Every farmer and every businessperson will encounter bad news. What matters most is how quickly one receives the bad news and how effectively he responds to it. Thus, accounting for your business income, expenses, and capital is vital. Those men and women who fear God are not afraid of receiving the bad news because they trust in the Lord. Psalm 112 begins with "Blessed is the man who fears the LORD, who delights greatly in His commandments." And then we read:

> A good man deals graciously and lends;
> He will guide his affairs with discretion.
> Surely he will never be shaken;
> The righteous will be in everlasting remembrance.
> He will not be afraid of evil tidings;
> His heart is steadfast, trusting in the LORD. (Ps. 112:5-7)

ACCOUNTING PRINCIPLES

The basic requirement in accounting is to keep track of money coming in and money going out. Money coming in is called **income**. Money going out is called *expenses*. Accounting is best seen as a discipline governed by five principles.

1. The **revenue principle** requires an honest record of sales. At the point of sale, the income is recorded, and that income must be the result of honest trade.
2. The **expense principle** requires an honest record of expenses. At the point at which the business receives goods and services from another business, that expense must be recorded.
3. The **matching principle** requires that there be a reason for the expense, and that reason must have something to do with the income received by the business. For example, your purchase of tennis shoes or bubble gum has nothing to do with your lemonade business. However, your purchase of lemons and sugar have every-

thing to do with the lemonade you sell.
4. The **cost principle** requires that the original price you paid for an item be maintained on the books. If you paid ten cents per lemon, you cannot change the value of that lemon while it is in your possession (or inventory).
5. The **objectivity principle** requires that everything be valued by factual, verifiable data. You should not guess at the value of your raw materials in your inventory. This means you should keep your receipts.

REPORTING OF YOUR BUSINESS ACCOUNTS

There are two kinds of reports that you will need for your business. The first is the **income-and-expense report** or **profit-and-loss report**, and the second is your **balance sheet.** Your balance sheet provides the net worth of your business at any point in time. The profit and loss report gives you the business activity over a period of time.

Suppose that you operated a lemonade stand from June 1st through August 31st. Would it be helpful to know how much money you made with the business during those months? You might want to compare it with how your business did the previous summer.

The following provides an example of a profit-loss report:

Lemonade Business Profit-Loss Report	
Revenue (June-August 2021)	
Total Revenue	$3,246.00
Gross Profit	$3,246.00
Expenditures	
Raw Materials	
Lemons	$359.32
Sugar	$56.46
Ice	$100.00

Lemonade Business Profit-Loss Report	
Plastic Cups	$120.00
Total Raw Materials:	$635.78
Marketing	
Signs from office supply store	$50.00
Payroll Expenses	
Employee 1 (your sister)	$360.00
Total Expenditures	$1,045.78
Net Revenue	$2,200.22

The **net revenue** is your profit after subtracting your expenses from your total income. In this example, as the owner of the lemonade business you did not pay yourself anything for running the business and operating the stand. To be more accurate, you would want to calculate your hours, which would have been about 150 hours. At $10 per hour, that means you would have to subtract that from your profit, leaving you with $700.22 of profit for the business.

Now compare the profit and loss totals from the previous summer to this report.

	Second Year	First Year
Income	$3,246.00	$2,645.00
Expenses	$1,045.78	$823.24
Your Pay	$1,500.00	$1,300.00
Net Profit	$700.22	$521.76

These charts give insight into the performance of your business. Is the business doing better or worse than it did the year before? Are you losing money or making money on the business? If you have several lemonade stands in different locations, these reports will help you see which lemonade stands are the most profitable. These tools will help you make wise decisions for the future of the company.

Suppose you were to introduce a new product to your lemonade stands. You learned through market research that about half of the people in your neighborhood would prefer iced tea (or iced tea and lemonade mix) over lemonade. Furthermore, you learn that tea bags are far cheaper than fresh lemons—at $49 for 250 bags. This would only add about $200 to your expenses. Extra cups would cost another $100. During the third year, you sold $2,500 in iced tea and an additional $1,200 in iced tea-lemonade mix. At the end of the third summer, you compared your profit-and-loss reports, and this is what you found:

	Third Year	Second Year	First Year
Income	$6,946.00	$3,246.00	$2,645.00
Expenses	$1,345.78	$1,045.78	$823.24
Your Pay	$1,700.00	$1,500.00	$1,300.00
Net Profit	$3,900.22	$700.22	$521.76

Comparing the third-year profit with the first- and second-year profit, what do you find? Incredibly, your profit increased by five-fold simply by introducing iced tea into the business! What will you do for the fourth year in the business?

THE BALANCE SHEET

The second report that is used most often for businesses is the balance sheet. Suppose you would like to know the value of your lemonade business at the end of the summer. You gather up all the things that belong to the business. That would include the cart, the lemonade machine, the materials, the bank account, the cash, and the raw materials left after the summer. Then you must put a value on them. Because the last of your lemons will go bad before you use them again, you'll have to value them at $0.00 and note the loss to the business. All raw materials and products you count on the balance sheet are considered your **inventory**.

A balance sheet is typically broken down into assets and liabilities. Assets are everything of value owned by the business. Liabilities are debts you owe to others. Let's suppose that you plan to pay your sister what you owe her for working at your lemonade stand. She will be paid on September 8th, but you are creating a balance sheet on September 1. You will need to count her payroll as a liability.

Balance Sheet on September 1	
Lemonade Stand	
Assets	
Cart	$1,400.00
Lemonade Mixer	$210.00
Inventory	
Lemons	$0.00
Sugar	$95.00
Teabags	$65.00
Bank Account	$4,042.00
Total Assets	$5,812.00
Liabilities	
Your Sister's Payroll	($300.00)
Total Liabilities and Equity	$5,512.00

The "total liabilities and equity" is the bottom-line value of your business (as of September 1). You may recall that you originally paid $2,000 for the cart and $300 for the lemonade mixer. These were capital expenses. Notice that the cart is now valued at $1,400 and the mixer $210. That's because of depreciation. For this example, we have used a depreciation schedule of ten years. Because equipment wears out over time, your balance sheet needs to account for this. Here also, you may want to compare your business's bottom-line balance on September 1 of this year to the bottom-line balance registered on September 1 of the previous year. That will give you a sense for whether your business is increasing in value or decreasing in value.

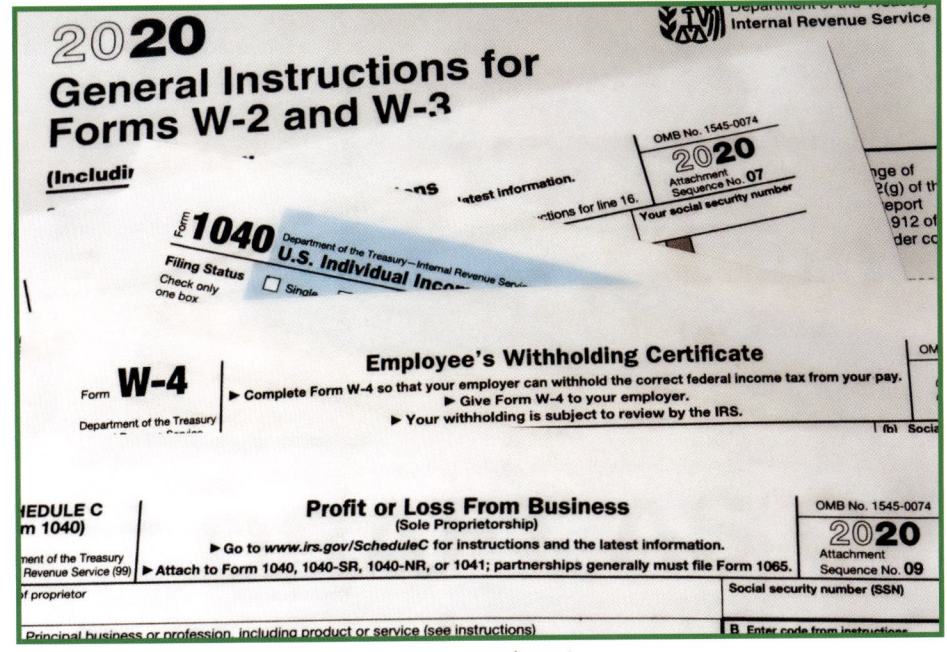

Keeping good records makes tax reporting much easier.

PERSONAL TAXES AND BUSINESS TAXES

Another reason responsible and wise people need to keep good records of accounts is for tax purposes. The government actually requires good records. Otherwise, business owners can go to jail or pay fines if they do not keep good records.

Through the ages, all the powerful empires and great nations have taxed their citizens and their businesses. Even the ancient Egyptians building the pyramids needed accountants to keep everything straight. When businesses don't keep careful track of their income and expenses, government officials usually find out about it. They will audit business records, and issue fines for mistakes. Those who don't pay their taxes or lie about their financial situation are sometimes put in prison. Most national tax systems are very complicated, and politicians change the rules every year. Big businesses use trained accountants to file their taxes for them. This important topic will be covered more fully in the next chapter.

9

SEEKING GOOD GOVERNMENT —HOW GOVERNMENTS RUIN ECONOMIES

> Let every soul be subject to the governing authorities. For there is no authority except from God, and the authorities that exist are appointed by God. Therefore whoever resists the authority resists the ordinance of God, and those who resist will bring judgment on themselves. For rulers are not a terror to good works, but to evil. Do you want to be unafraid of the authority? Do what is good, and you will have praise from the same. For he is God's minister to you for good. But if you do evil, be afraid; for he does not bear the sword in vain; for he is God's minister, an avenger to execute wrath on him who practices evil.
> (Rom. 13:1-4)

Civil governments cannot do much to help economies. However, they are quite capable of *hurting* economies, especially if they are given too much power. The best thing governments can do to help the free market is to stay out of the way. To the extent that a government keeps its hands off the businesses and keeps taxes at a minimum, the nation will be economically prosperous. This is usually not the case when it comes to human governments. With the exception of the founding leaders of the United States, there have been very few wise, righteous, and truly beneficent government officials to be found in the modern world. If righteousness is defined by God (and not by Karl Marx), and true wisdom is found in God's Word, then righteous governments will be very rare in this world. Not many leaders will pay attention to what the Bible says about government.

Since God's established purpose for governments is to use the sword on the person who commits criminal deeds (as defined by God's law), what should governments do? According to the Romans 13 injunction, rulers must limit themselves to providing defense and justice. But that is not what we find today. The following table provides the breakdown of the US government's expenses during the 2020s:

US Federal and State Government Expenditures Breakdown[59]	
Welfare/Social Security	33%
Health Care	21%
Education	13%
Defense	10%
Transportation	10%
Regulating Departments	8%
Justice	5%

Comparing this data to a biblical view of government's rightful functions, almost 85% of what governments do today is outside of

US Federal and State Governments Expenditures
Office of Management and Budget, 2019

- Welfare/Social Security: 33
- Health Care: 21
- Education: 13
- Defense: 10
- Transportation: 10
- Regulatory Departments: 8
- Justice: 5

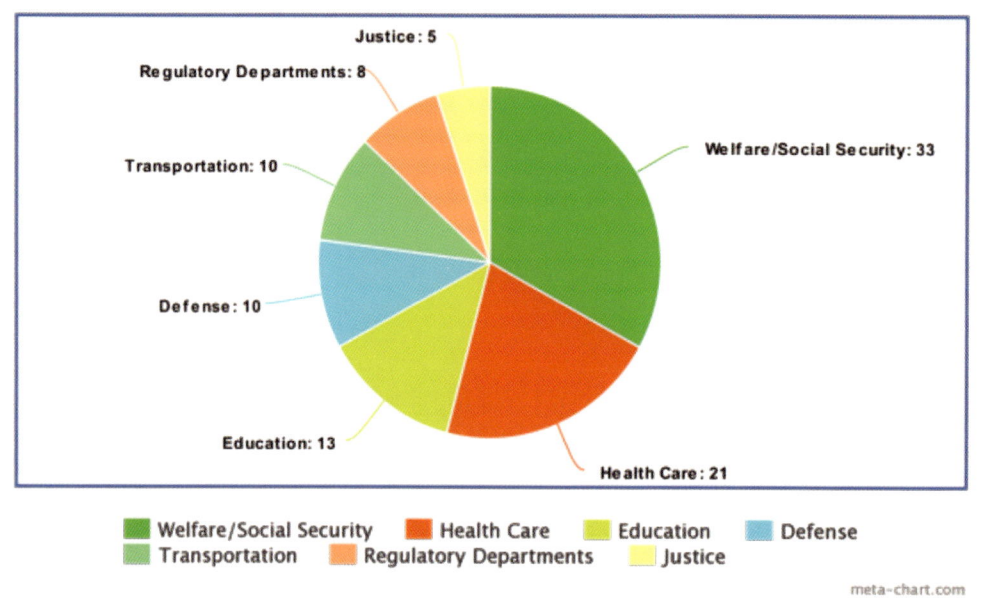

meta-chart.com

their God-assigned jurisdictional authority. As much as governments get involved in medical care and education, they will drive up the costs, undermine healthy competition, and provide poor services. While those who enjoy government benefits may think such services are free, these expenses impoverish the nation. The citizens still pay for the services and the government agencies that control these services by way of taxation.

Another way governments handicap a free economy is by playing favorites in the market. This usually happens through campaign donations or bribery. In certain countries, government employees and police officers will provide special favors to people who pay them a bribe.

The best and worst nations in the world for blatant bribery are listed in the following table. Listed with each country is the dominant religion or worldview that controls the minds of the people.

US Department of Education headquarters in Washington, DC.

Most Corrupt Nations in the World[60]	
Nation	**Dominant Worldview or Religion**
North Korea	Communist
Turkmenistan	Muslim (89%)
South Sudan	Roman Catholic (37%), Anglican (18%)
Venezuela	Roman Catholic (96%)
Eritrea	Eritrean Orthodox (35%), Muslim (37%)
Cambodia	Communist
Somalia	Muslim (90%)
Equatorial Guinea	Roman Catholic
Yemen	Muslim (99%)
Syria	Muslim (87%)

Pyongyang, capital of North Korea, among the most corrupt nations in the world.

Most Honest Nations in the World	
Nation	**Dominant Worldview or Religion**
Denmark	Protestant (75%)
Norway	Protestant (69%)
Finland	Protestant (69%)
New Zealand	Protestant (46%)
Sweden	Protestant (60%)
United Kingdom	Protestant (60%)
Netherlands	Roman Catholic/Protestant Mix
Germany	Protestant/Roman Catholic Mix

The most corrupt nations in the world are primarily Muslim, Communist, and Roman Catholic nations, and the most honest nations in the world are primarily Protestant.

Also, it turns out that God materially blesses those nations that stay true

Copenhagen, Denmark, among the most honest nations in the world.

to His Word to some extent. The most honest nations in the world are often the most prosperous.

Some corruption is blatant and obvious. But other forms of corruption take on a more sophisticated approach. As governments began to control more money in Western Protestant countries, the temptation to cheat was constant, and the abuse of power was the inevitable consequence. This came in the form of campaign donations.

> To show partiality is not good, because for a piece of bread a man will transgress. (Prov. 28:21)
>
> You shall not show partiality in judgment; you shall hear the small as well as the great; you shall not be afraid in any man's presence, for the judgment is God's. (Deut. 1:17)
>
> My brethren, do not hold the faith of our Lord Jesus Christ, the Lord of glory, with partiality. For if there should come into your assembly a man

> with gold rings, in fine apparel, and there should also come in a poor man in filthy clothes, and you pay attention to the one wearing the fine clothes and say to him, "You sit here in a good place," and say to the poor man, "You stand there," or, "Sit here at my footstool," have you not shown partiality among yourselves, and become judges with evil thoughts? (Jas. 2:1-4)

Donations for US presidential campaigns
in billions of dollars

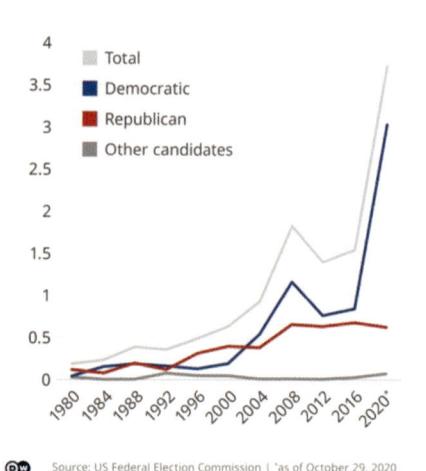

Source: US Federal Election Commission | *as of October 29, 2020

God's Word consistently warns about the vice of partiality. This is especially common with political leaders. God's law forbids the favoring of one person over another, or one private company over another. Nor should government officials take bribes or campaign donations from people who will benefit from their governmental policies.

The US has not taken God's advice on this matter. After the year 2000, corruption increased exponentially in American politics. Campaign donations also multiplied in similar fashion.

While running for election in 2004, George W. Bush received large donations from banking institutions for his presidential campaign. Individual people and political action committees associated with these same banks contributed the money. These entities afterward received billions of dollars from the federal government during the banking crisis of 2007-2008.

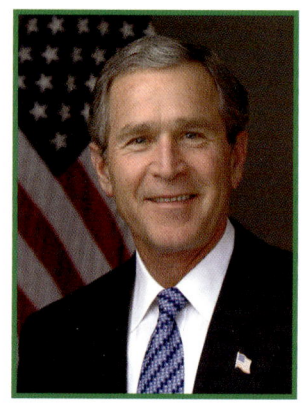

George W. Bush, 43rd President of the United States from 2001-2009

Major Campaign Donations to President George W. Bush in 2004[61]	
Morgan Stanley	$604,280
Goldman Sachs	$396,350
Citigroup	$317,375
Bank of America	$258,361
JP Morgan	$228,005

Company	Money Received from Bailout of 2008
Wells Fargo	$25 billion
Citigroup	$25 billion
JP Morgan	$25 billion
Bank of America	$15 billion
Morgan Stanley	$10 billion
Goldman Sachs	$10 billion
US Bancorp	$7 billion

Most of the time private companies who contract with the US military benefit the most from the huge federal budget each year. They are usually the largest campaign donors for national elections.

Company	Money Received in 2020[62]	Campaign Donations in 2020[63]
Lockheed Martin	$74 billion	$6,040,824
Boeing	$28 billion	$426,511
General Dynamics	$23 billion	$3,369,196
Raytheon	$26 billion	$5,817,521
Northrop	$16 billion	$5,266,270

With the growth of governmental involvement in the medical industry at the turn of the 21st Century, the big pharmaceutical companies became extremely rich and powerful. These companies produced the vaccines and medicines paid for or mandated by the federal government. Unlike any other economic sector, these companies enjoyed massive growth in the 2000s. Between 1985 and 2021, the pharmaceutical business increased from $20 billion per year to $550 billion per year – a thirty-fold increase![64] By 2020, the most successful companies were Pfizer, Merck, and Johnson & Johnson. During the 2020 elections, individuals and committees connected to the big pharmaceuticals contributed $14,000,000 in campaign donations. This money went to seventy-two senators and 302 members of the House of Representatives.[65] Add to that $13,000,000 spent by Pfizer on lobbying the politicians, and you realize political favors are a very big deal to these companies. Such large donations are a small price to pay when you consider that Pfizer raked in a cool $33 billion on the production of the government-mandated Covid-19 shot in 2021.[66] The other major Covid-19 mRNA shot manufacturer, Moderna, would walk away with $19 billion in the same year.[67]

Other large companies receive special government favors as well. For example, the Microsoft corporation has received subsidies or special favors from federal and state governments amounting to $807,000,000,[68] and Amazon received another $4.2 billion.[69] Then, it should come as no surprise that Microsoft contributed $17 million to political candidates in the 2020 election, and

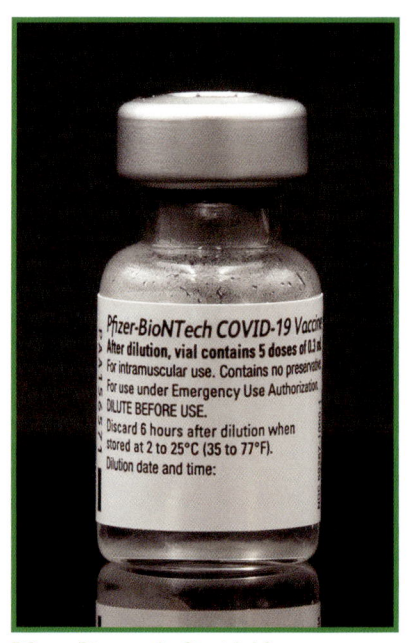

Pfizer-Biontech Covid-19.

Amazon contributed another $9 million.[70] These special subsidies favor the big corporation over the little mom and pop shops that are trying to compete for business.

Amazon fulfillment center in Macon, Georgia.

> You shall not pervert the judgment of your poor in his dispute. Keep yourself far from a false matter; do not kill the innocent and righteous. For I will not justify the wicked. And you shall take no bribe, for a bribe blinds the discerning and perverts the words of the righteous. (Ex. 23:6-8)
>
> You shall do no injustice in judgment. You shall not be partial to the poor, nor honor the person of the mighty. In righteousness you shall judge your neighbor. (Lev. 19:15)

God's law does not allow for special treatment and subsidies for rich and powerful companies, whether by state or federal governments. Hoping to improve local economies, states think they will attract businesses by offering special subsidies. However, this does not allow for a level playing field, and these are just more examples of corruption at the highest levels.

THE REGULATORY STATE

Karl Marx pushed for government ownership of businesses and the means of production. But other socialists like Adolf Hitler took a different approach. Hitler said, "Let them own land or factories as much as they please. The decisive factor is that the State, through

Adolf Hitler (1889-1945)

the party, is supreme over them, regardless whether they are owners or workers. Our socialism goes far deeper. It establishes the relation of the individual to the State, the national community."

While allowing private interests to own property, Hitler could achieve his own ends by imposing controls over all business and telling them what to do. And that is what most of the governments of the world decided to do after World War II. The following chart indicates the growth of the US federal government bureaucracy between 1826 and 2020. Most of the growth occurred after the 1940s.

US Federal Employees (including contract)[71]

Year	Number of Employees	Percentage of Population
1826[72]	10,415	0.10%
1933	500,000	0.40%
1940	1,800,000	1.40%
1950	3,600,000	2.30%
1960	4,400,000	2.40%
1970	5,400,000	2.50%
1980	5,300,000	2.40%
2020	11,000,000	3.30%

Following the course of the rest of the world, the United States became a socialist nation under the presidency of Franklin D. Roosevelt (in the 1930s). As is clear from the above chart, the 1930s and 1940s witnessed a huge increase in the percentage of Americans working for the federal government. State governments experienced similar increases between 1940 and 2020.

What do all these government workers do throughout the year? Most of them work at desks, and they do not produce anything useful. They are not producing cars, food, clothing, houses to live in, glasses, medicines, or helpful services. With a few exceptions, these government employees regulate the free market, and cripple the economy.

These government employees impose ever-increasing rules and regulations for private persons and businesses. The chart below shows the total number of pages of rules issued by the federal government from 1950 to 2018. With the exception of a slight decrease under Presidents Reagan and Clinton, the trend has always been more regulation. Imagine trying to run your business while paying attention to 185,000 pages of regulations!

Bill Clinton, 42nd President of the United States from 1993 to 2001

Beginning in 1938, the government began imposing a minimum wage law on US businesses. Instead of allowing the market to determine the price for low-end labor, the federal requirement set the minimum wage at 25 cents per hour.

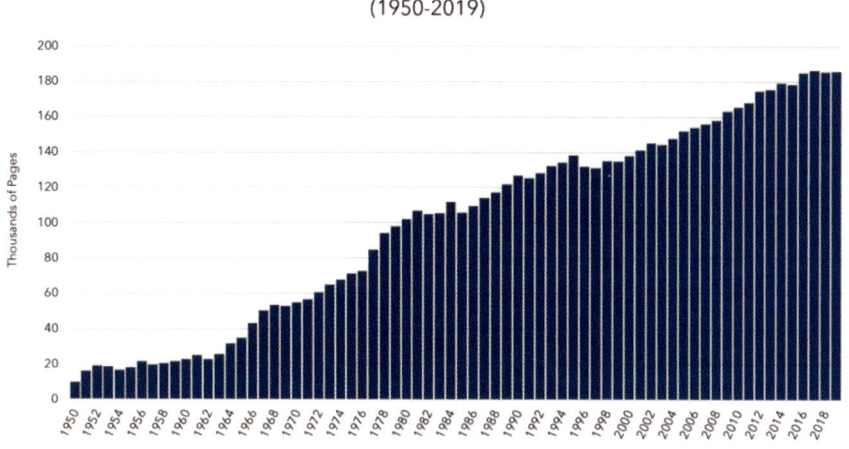

Total Pages Published in the Code of Federal Regulations (1950-2019)

This was raised to $7.25 per hour by 2020, at which some states like California had set the minimum wage at $14.00 per hour.

The problem with the Minimum Wage is that it artificially cuts out lower paying jobs. People who would have worked for less pay would eventually turn to the government for free handouts. Before 1930, barely 1-2%

of Americans received any government assistance. But by 1980, 30% of American households received some form of government aid, and then in 2011, 49.1% of American households were on government aid.[73]

Another example of what is usually called "price controls" are rent controls. Some big cities like San Francisco and New York City limit the amount of rent landlords can charge for their apartments. Of course, this doesn't do people any good. Such practices limit the number of apartments available for people in the cities. What landlord would want to buy an expensive apartment and then rent it out for a lower price?

"Electronic Benefit Transfer" cards issued by states to supply food and other goods via welfare programs.

From 1933, the US government began providing subsidies for farmers, and at the same time, would try to control the prices of agricultural products. In the US, agricultural subsidies have been around since the Great Depression. If farmers didn't quite get the crop yield they expected, the government would give them money to make up the difference. Farmers received the money for the crops that did not grow regardless of market prices. In 2005, the government handed out $25 billion in agricultural subsidies.

Sometimes governments offer tax credits and vouchers for people who want to use private education or use alternative energy resources for their cars and homes. Often, this is another way to play favorites. But, there is usually an ideological agenda at work in these programs. That is, the government wants to encourage a certain approach to education or energy use.

The difference between a tax credit and a voucher may be understood by this analogy. Suppose the government wanted to provide tennis shoes for every teenager in America. So an agency of the federal government issued

Headquarters of the United States Department of Agriculture in Washington, DC.

a voucher program. Families would pay $400 into a tennis shoe each year through taxes. At the end of the year, each family would receive a $280 voucher to cover the cost of tennis shoes for the kids. However, the agency would attach a few regulations to the program. You could only purchase the shoes from a few certified manufacturers, and no tennis shoe must have any Christian insignia associated with it. Now, a tax credit is much different from a voucher. With a tax credit, the family keeps the $400 and just purchases their own tennis shoes. They can buy any tennis shoes they desire, and the $400 is subtracted from the taxes they would ordinarily pay at the end of the year.

By the 21st century, this government control over the nation's businesses was almost total. During the Covid-19 crisis of 2020 and 2021, national governments shut down most of the businesses in the world. Only the nation of Nicaragua avoided most regulations during this period. In March and April of 2020, at least half of the world was under lockdown by government enforcement. Buenos Aires, Argentina, and Melbourne, Australia were under lockdown for 9-10 months. Only six of the states within the United

THE NOT-RAISING HOGS BUSINESS

Upon discovering there were subsidies for farmers who were not raising hogs, one clever farmer wrote this letter to the US Department of Agriculture.

Dear Sir,

My friends, Wayne and Janelle, over at Wichita Falls, Texas, received a check the other day for $1,000 from the government for not raising hogs. So, I want to go into the "not raising hogs" business myself next year.

What I want to know is, in your opinion, what is the best type of farm not to raise hogs on, and what is the best breed of hogs not to raise? I want to be sure that I approach this endeavor in keeping with all government policies. I would prefer not to raise Razor Back hogs, but if that is not a good breed not to raise, then I can just as easily not raise Yorkshires or Durocs.

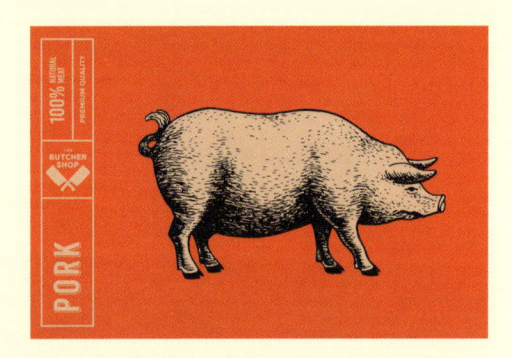

As I see it, the hardest part of this program will be keeping an accurate inventory of how many hogs I haven't raised.

My friend Wayne is very excited about the future of this business. He has been raising hogs for 20 years and the most he ever made was $420 in 1978, until this year, when he got your check for $1,000 for not raising hogs. If I can get $1,000 for not raising 50 hogs, will I get $2,000 for not raising 100 hogs? I plan to operate on a small scale at first, holding myself down to about 4,000 "not raised" hogs, which will give me $80,000 income the first year. Then I can buy an airplane.

Now another thing: these hogs I will not raise will not eat 100,000 bushels of corn. I understand that you also pay farmers for not raising corn and wheat. Will I qualify for payments for not raising wheat and corn not to feed the 4,000 hogs I am not going to raise?

I want to get started not feeding as soon as possible, as this seems to be a good time of the year to not raise hogs and grain.

I am also considering the "not milking cows" business, so please send me any information on that also.

Sincerely yours,
Joe Farmer

States did not enforce the lockdowns. This decision resulted in a 3.1% drop in the gross world product,[74] the largest drop in world productivity since the 1800s. Such interference with the world economy by civil governments was devastating. Well into the year 2022, emerging markets like Latin America had not recovered from this government-imposed recession.

REGULATING PROPERTY

Empty streets in Chinatown, New York City, during government imposed lockdown in 2020.

For thousands of years, property owners had control over their own real estate. That all changed in the United States around 1908 when Los Angeles became the first city in America to introduce zoning and planning commissions. The first building codes had been introduced in Baltimore, Maryland four years earlier. For the next hundred years, government experts would tell property owners what they could and could not do with their property. Some of these regulations prohibited certain ethnic groups from buying property in certain neighborhoods. This was the nature of big government control over property.

> Is it not lawful for me to do what I wish with my own property? Or is your eye evil because I am good? (Matt. 20:15)

While biblical law requires certain safety measures to be put in place where there is a high risk of loss of life, there is no allowance for enforcement of the regulation by regulators. If, however, someone should get killed because of negligence on the part of the property owner, God's law would prosecute the owner for that negligence. On the basis of such wise standards then, the civil government need not hassle 320,000,000 people every day with regulations and inspections. Only when somebody is killed due to negligence should the government get involved. Around 5,000 workers are killed on the job each year in the US.[75] Only about 350 of these cases involve gross negligence requiring prosecution.[76] Would it be a wiser use of government resources to prosecute 350 people a year or regulate the lives and businesses of 320,000,000 people every day of the year? That is the question facing all governments around the world. The biblical approach endorses the former option.

> When you build a new house, then you shall make a parapet for your roof, that you may not bring guilt of bloodshed on your household if anyone falls from it. (Deut. 22:8)

> If an ox gores a man or a woman to death, then the ox shall surely be stoned, and its flesh shall not be eaten; but the owner of the ox shall be acquitted. But if the ox tended to thrust with its horn in times past, and it has been made known to his owner, and he has not kept it confined, so that it has killed a man or a woman, the ox shall be stoned and its owner also shall be put to death. (Ex. 21:28-29)

Governments profit from these regulatory agencies by issuing fines. The US federal government collects $20 billion in fines each year. This annual collection has increased about five-fold since 2002.[77] State and local governments are collecting $15 billion, up from $1.2 billion in 1980. These trends demonstrate the increasing chokehold big government has on private industry.

Total hours spent by U.S. adults in 2014

Shopping, except groceries, food and gas	20.2 bn hours
Laundry	16.1 bn hours
Kitchen and food clean-up	11.7 bn hours
Government Paperwork	**11.5 bn hours**
Grocery shopping	10.6 bn hours
Attending religious services	7.6 bn hours
Walking	4.7 bn hours
Participation in religious practices	4.6 bn hours

Interstate highway in St. Louis, Missouri.

Regulations also increase the amount of paperwork the average person has to complete. Based on one assessment, the average person spends more time filling out paperwork required by state and federal governments than the time taken in religious services and grocery shopping.[78]

HEAVY TAXATION ON BUSINESSES AND CAPITAL

The biggest negative impact on private investment is always government taxation. You will have less money to invest in your own business or other ventures if you are giving it to the government. Remember, the government doesn't produce anything except roads, which is only 2.3% of federal and state spending.[79] Governments don't make cars, food, clothing, homes, or electronic goods. They regulate private enterprise. At the same time, they have worked to displace private charity with welfare, which usually only makes things worse.

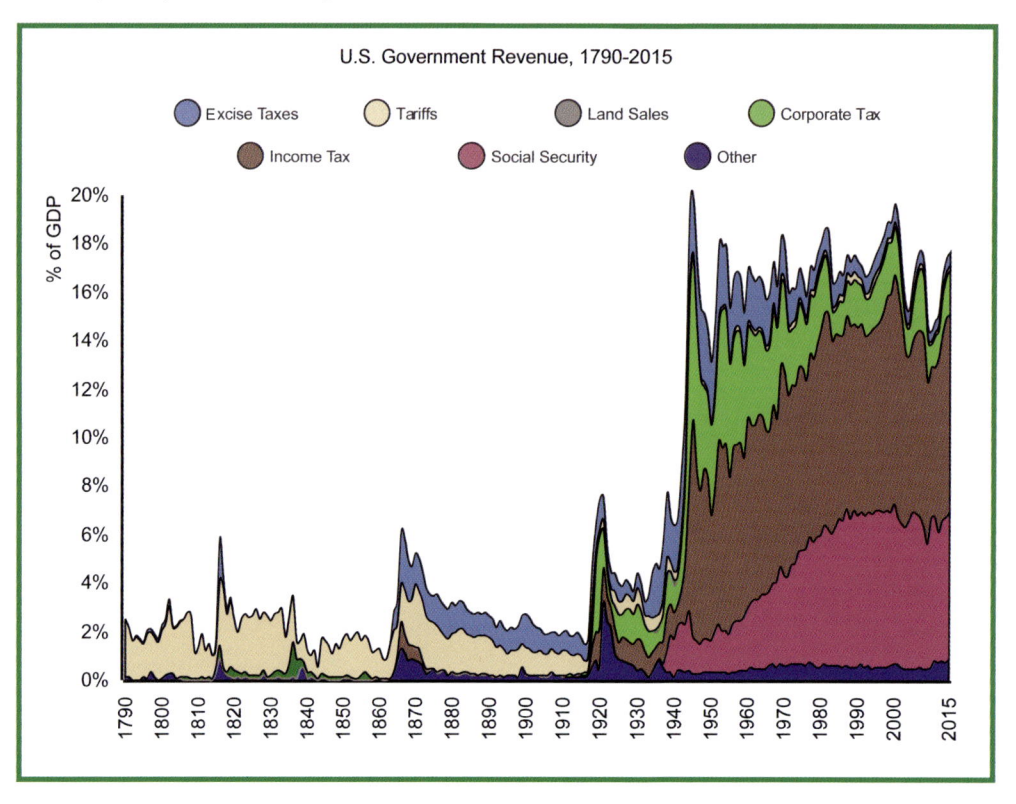

U.S. Government Revenue, 1790-2015

The following chart helpfully demonstrates how US taxation changed over the years. Initially, modern democratic governments taxed other nations through tariffs. Later, in the 20th century, governments collected money by taxing corporations and individuals through the income tax and social security tax. This chart does not include sales tax and property tax which are usually assessed by state and local governments.

Free enterprise explodes and blessings multiply for nations that are not saddled with a 20-30% tax rate by federal governments and an additional 15-20% tax rate at the hands of state and local governments. America witnessed this explosion of free enterprise and its manifold blessings until Woodrow Wilson took the presidency around 1915. Presidents Wilson and Franklin Delano Roosevelt are the most responsible for the rise of big government in the US. This represented a worldview shift from freedom to big government tyranny, and the rest of the world was soon to follow. This visual depiction of the rise of big government illustrates very well how much socialism and "democracy have changed the world since the 1910s.

What follows is a summary of the taxes you will have to be concerned with as you begin to earn money and do business in the world economy. Depending on where you live, taxes will vary in kind and percentages. For example, Bermuda and the Bahamas do not have an income tax. Within the United States, only Wyoming, Washington, Texas, South Dakota, Nevada, Florida, and Alaska do not require an income tax. Oregon, New Hampshire, and Montana do not impose a sales tax.

National Income Tax: Typically, income taxes are graduated according to your income level. This means that people with higher income will pay a

Woodrow Wilson (1856-1924)

higher tax rate, upwards of 30-40% of their income. Those earning less income will pay 5-15%. The highest income tax rates in the world are found in Japan and Finland, upwards of 56%. The United States income tax rates have varied over time. To illustrate how this works, take an example of a poor person who has earned $10,000 and a rich person who has earned $400,000 in the United States in 2021. The poor person's tax rate is 10% (the lowest tax bracket). Not counting deductions, the person earning $10,000 would pay $1,000 in taxes.

The rich person's tax rate is 32%, but he doesn't pay 32% on all $400,000. That would amount to $128,000. Instead, the taxes for $400,000 of income is calculated at a **graduated rate**, as follows:

He pays 10% on the first $19,900. That would amount to...$1,990.
He pays 12% on his income from $19,900 to $81,050.
That would amount to...$7,338.
He pays 22% on his income from $81,050 to $172,750.
That would amount to...$21,362.
He pays 32% on his income from $172,750 to $400,000.
That would amount to...$72,720.

Adding these four numbers together, the total tax bill turns out to be $103,410. You can see that this is less than $128,000. Actually, the rich person's tax rate comes out to 26% of his total income of $400,000. Thus, you can see that the rich guy is being taxed at a higher rate than the poor guy.

State/Local Income Tax: Similar to Federal Income Tax, most states in America will tax income. But state and local income tax rates are much lower than national taxes, usually ranging between 2% and 6%.

Social Security Tax: As already mentioned, social security tax rates run at 12.4%, with an additional 2.9% for Medicare.

Sales Tax: This tax is collected by stores and businesses at the point where a customer makes a purchase. Some countries like India, Hungary, Denmark, Norway, and Sweden have very high sales tax rates running up to 25-30%. The average sales tax in the United States is 5%. The highest sales tax in the US are found in some cities in Alabama and Tennessee, running upwards of 11-13%. Those interested in personal privacy usually prefer a

Receipts indicating sales tax amounts.

sales tax over income tax because sales tax is more anonymous. That is, the government doesn't get to review your personal financial records, as it does with income tax.

Excise Tax: This is basically a sales tax, except that the government only taxes a particular product like gasoline, tobacco, or certain luxury goods.

Capital Gains Tax: Not only do governments want to tax your income (what you earn from your work), but they also will tax your profit when you sell something like real estate. Suppose you were to purchase a piece of property for $100,000 and sell it five years later for $120,000. Governments will tax you on the $20,000 increase you received in the sale. Regrettably, they do not adjust for inflation. Given the average inflation rate of 3%, the property adjusted for inflation should be worth $115,000. However, the government does not tax you on the $5,000 difference. It will tax you on the $20,000 difference, and the taxes will consume almost all your profit. Capital gains taxes will run between 15% and 25%. If the government levies a tax of 25% on your capital gains of $20,000, your tax bill would amount to $5,000.

Property Tax: This is among the worst forms of taxation because it turns private property ownership over to the state. Regardless of whether you have paid for a home or other real estate, the state claims ultimate ownership. The property tax is a rental fee charged by the state for the right to live there or to make use of the property. If you are unable to pay this tax, the government will seize the property. A few nations (like Monaco, Malta, Israel, and Fiji) have no property tax, although these governments find other ways to bring in tax money. None of the states in the US are property tax free. However, Hawaii, Louisiana, Wyoming, and Alabama have the lowest rates (under 0.5%). Thankfully, there are at least ten states that exempt elderly people from paying property tax. These include South Dakota, Washington, Florida, Alabama, Alaska, Georgia, Hawaii, Mississippi, South Carolina, and Texas.

Inheritance and Estate Taxes: When a person dies, some governments will tax the money he or she has managed to save in a lifetime. Japan, South Korea, and France have the highest estate tax rates in the world at 45-55%. In the United States (as of 2021), anything over $12 million is taxed at a whopping 40%. Only about 1 in 1,000 persons dying every year would be affected by this tax. About twenty US states also have instituted their own inheritance and estate taxes.

WHAT DOES THE BIBLE SAY ABOUT TAXES?

> The rich shall not give more and the poor shall not give less than half a shekel, when you give an offering to the LORD, to make atonement for yourselves. (Ex. 30:15)

While the world of socialists seeks to eliminate poverty and to make it so everybody earns the same amount of money, Jesus told us, "You will always have the poor with you." Marxism encourages class envy, in which poor people hate rich people because of their riches. Hence, the Communist Manifesto included "A Heavy Progressive or Graduated Income Tax" as the second plank for its agenda.

When producing a public works project (like the tabernacle or a temple), Exodus 30:15 recommended that everybody pay a flat amount of money. So, if the US government needed $725 billion to fund its military (in 2021), then every person in America should pay $2,070. A family of four would have to pay about $8,000 per year to keep the military going. That comes out to about 12% of the average family income in America (assuming the median household income is $68,000 per year).

Of course, governments fund far more than the military these days. The state and local governments collect sales tax, income tax, and property tax as well. But if governments were focused on their God-given roles, they would not need to take much more money from their citizens. The rich would not have to pay more than $2,070. And the poor would not have to pay less than $2,070.

> There were also some who said, "We have mortgaged our lands and vineyards and houses, that we might buy grain because of the famine." There were also those who said, "We have borrowed money for the

The prophet Samuel before King Saul.

> king's tax on our lands and vineyards. Yet now our flesh is as the flesh of our brethren, our children as their children; and indeed we are forcing our sons and our daughters to be slaves, and some of our daughters have been brought into slavery. It is not in our power to redeem them, for other men have our lands and vineyards." And I became very angry when I heard their outcry and these words. (Neh. 5:3-6)

The Scriptures give descriptions of tyranny in which governments are very cruel towards their people. Nehemiah offers this example of tyranny where children were made slaves of the state in order to pay property taxes. First Samuel 8 also describes tyranny as requiring people to pay more than 10% of their increase to the king in taxation (1 Sam. 8:15). Sadly, most modern "democratic" governments take far more than 10% of the people's income.

How Much Did Governments Take from the People's Income?	
(Government Expenditures per GDP)[80]	
Roman sales tax (30 AD)	1.00%
Roman sales tax (444 AD)	4.50%
King Henry VIII (1550 AD England)	1.60%
United States including States (1780)	2%
United States including States (1880)	3%
United States including States (2020)	50%
France (2020)	62%
Norway (2020)	58%
Costa Rica (2020)	55%
Sweden (2020)	53%
Germany (2020)	51%
Japan (2020)	47%
Saudi Arabia (2020)	40%
Russia (2020)	39%

How Much Did Governments Take from the People's Income?	
(Government Expenditures per GDP)[80]	
China (2020)	37%
Chile (2020)	29%
Indonesia (2020)	18%
Guatemala (2020)	16%

From this chart, you can see that Guatemala, Indonesia, and Chile come much closer to a biblical standard for government taxation than nations in the West. Also, you can see that government expenses did not go beyond the 10% mark until the modern "democracies" beginning in the 20th century. In the history of human civilization, these big governments taking over most of the world economy is a new phenomenon. It came about by people voting for their leaders and handing over extraordinary amounts of power to them. The people trusted in government more than they trusted in God. The problem is far worse today than what Samuel predicted for Israel in 1 Samuel 8.

> So Samuel told all the words of the LORD to the people who asked him for a king. And he said, "This will be the behavior of the king who will reign over you: He will take your sons and appoint them for his own chariots and to be his horsemen, and some will run before his chariots. . . . He will take a tenth of your grain and your vintage, and give it to his officers and servants. And he will take your male servants, your female servants, your finest young men, and your donkeys, and put them to his work. He will take a tenth of your sheep. And you will be his servants. And you will cry out in that day because of your king whom you have chosen for yourselves, and the LORD will not hear you in that day." (1 Sam. 8:10-18)

The New Testament also reveals the attitude of Christ and His apostles toward taxation. In Matthew 17:24-27, Jesus tells His disciples to pay a tax even if it is excessive or tyrannical. While wisdom would dictate that governments should prefer freedom for their citizens, Christ still submits to paying this tax. The Lord does not recommend we fight every tax or avoid paying the taxes. In Matthew 5:41, He instructs His disciples to walk the extra mile should some bureaucrat force them to walk one mile. Furthermore, in verse 25 He encourages us to agree with our adversary (which may include a tax collector) quickly before he puts us in prison.

> When they had come to Capernaum, those who received the temple tax came to Peter and said, "Does your Teacher not pay the temple tax?" He said, "Yes."
>
> And when he had come into the house, Jesus anticipated him, saying, "What do you think, Simon? From whom do the kings of the earth take customs or taxes, from their sons or from strangers?"
>
> Peter said to Him, "From strangers."
>
> Jesus said to him, "Then the sons are free. Nevertheless, lest we offend them, go to the sea, cast in a hook, and take the fish that comes up first. And when you have opened its mouth, you will find a piece of money; take that and give it to them for Me and you." (Matt. 17:24-27)

Christ taught obedience to the civil government. Yet the Apostle Paul did not hesitate to assert his rights as a Roman citizen several times during his ministry career. He also urges the Corinthians to take advantage of opportunities for freedom when these are available. We should prefer freedom from unnecessary and optional constraints placed upon us by governments and powers.

> Were you called while a slave? Do not be concerned about it; but if you can be made free, rather use it. For he who is called in the Lord while a slave is the Lord's freedman. Likewise he who is called while free is Christ's slave. You were bought at a price; do not become slaves of men. (1 Cor. 7:21-23)

Finally, Romans 13 requires paying taxes "to whom taxes are due." The question of jurisdiction comes into play. If a foreign country or another state in which we do not reside should levy a tax upon us, would we be bound to pay it? At times, we must determine whether the tax authority has legitimate jurisdiction. While there are legal ways to push for lower taxes, the Christian is still bound to pay the taxes required

The Apostle Paul in Rome.

of him by the government. For the last one hundred years, the people have voted for leaders who would raise their taxes. The tyrants running for office promised the taxpayers many wonderful benefits. But the trade of liberty for security is always a bad deal. Christians should work hard to reduce the size of government from taxing and spending as much as 40-50% of the people's income down to below 10%. The government should never demand more than God requires in the tithe.

In summary, biblical principles would recommend the following conditions for government taxation.

1. Maintain the overall ratio of the people's income dedicated to taxation (at all levels of government) at well under 10%.
2. Incorporate a flat tax in amount (not percentage). If a poor man earning $15,000 per year pays $1,000 per year in taxes, a rich man earning $1,000,000 per year should pay the same amount of money.
3. Prefer forms of taxation that are not attached to income or property. These are the worst forms of taxation. Sales tax and poll taxes (in which one has to pay a tax to vote), would be preferred.
4. Eliminate all inheritance taxation and property taxation.

> Do not remove the ancient landmark
> Which your fathers have set. (Prov. 22:28)
>
> They covet fields and take them by violence, Also houses, and seize them. So they oppress a man and his house, A man and his inheritance. (Micah 2:2)

THE EFFECTS OF GOVERNMENT CONTROLLED ECONOMIES

Every year since the early 1990s, the Heritage Foundation has kept track of the influence of government control on economies. Does high regulation really work? Does it provide economic blessings to a nation?

These regulated economies are pretty new in the world (except for attempts by the Chinese Legalists who failed at it 2,000 years ago). So, the last hundred years have served as something of an experiment. The studies produced by the Heritage Foundation have been helpful. This organization looked at the following criteria and ranked each nation from 0 to 100 for these factors.

1. Rule of Law (property rights, government integrity, judicial effectiveness)
2. Government Size (government spending, tax burden, fiscal health)
3. Regulatory Efficiency (business freedom, labor freedom, monetary freedom)
4. Open Markets (trade freedom, investment freedom, financial freedom)

Let's look at the results, comparing freedom with the economic prosperity of these nations. The following tables compare the freedom ranking with the amount each person in the country earned (on average) in one year. Be aware that most of these rankings were established before the Covid-19 crisis took its toll on economic liberty worldwide.

Singapore, one of the most economically free and prosperous nations in Asia.

The Best Nations in the World (Most Free from Government Control)

Nation	Freedom Ranking[81]	GDP per Capita (2021 IMF Data)
1. Singapore	89.7	$64,103 (#1 best economy in Asia)
2. New Zealand	83.9	$47,499 (#22 best economy in the world)
3. Australia	82.4	$62,723 (#10 best economy in the world)
4. Switzerland	81.9	$94,696 (#1 best economy in Western Europe)
5. Ireland	81.4	$94,556 (#1 best economy in Northern Europe)
6. Taiwan	78.6	$32,123 (#3 best economy in Asia)
7. United Kingdom	78.4	$46,344 (#23 best economy in the world)
8. Estonia	78.2	$27,101 (#1 best economy in Eastern Europe)
9. Canada	77.9	$49,222 (#2 best economy in North America)
10. Denmark	77.8	$67,218 (#3 best economy in Northern Europe)
20. United States	74.8	$68,309 (#1 best economy in North America)

Venezuela, one of the least free nations in the Americas.

Ten Worst Nations in the World (Most Subject to Government Control)		
Nation	Freedom Ranking[82]	GDP per Capita (2021 IMF Data)
1. North Korea	5.2	$692 (#1 worst economy in Eastern Asia)
2. Venezuela	24.7	$1,522 (#1 worst economy in South America)
3. Cuba	28.1	$6,816 (#3 worst economy in Caribbean)
4. Sudan	39.1	$787 (#1 worst economy in Northern Africa)
5. Zimbabwe	39.5	$1,684 (#1 worst economy in South Africa)
6. Eritrea	42.3	$625 (#6 worst economy in East Africa)
7. Bolivia	42.7	$3,624 (#2 worst economy in South America)
8. Timor Leste	44.7	$1,285 (#1 worst economy in Asia)
9. Suriname	46.4	$4,030 (#3 worst economy in South America)
10. Iran	47.2	$12,730 (#11 worst economy in West Asia)

From this you can see that the most oppressed and government-regulated nations in the world are also the most impoverished nations. They have the worst economies. Imagine trying to live on just $700-$4,000 per year! Groceries usually cost about $200 per month, and really cheap housing would cost about $400 per month.

The South American nations provide the best example of this pattern. The three most regulated economies in South America are the three worst economies by GDP per capita. Then on the other hand, the two freest economies in South America are Chile (75.2) and Uruguay (69.3). And, as it turns out, the best economies in South America are Uruguay (with an average GDP per capita of $15,653) and Chile with a GDP per capita of $15,617. Wouldn't you rather live in Chile and Uruguay than Venezuela (where you would only earn $1,522 per year)?

Santiago, Chile

When politicians add more regulations and more taxation, they create more oppression for individuals and businesses, and they ruin the nation's economy. This has been the legacy of socialism and communism for the last hundred years.

Actually, all the nations which were once very free are losing ground. Once in the top ten, the United States came in at the miserable ranking of #20 on the 2021 Heritage Foundation report.

ECONOMIC FREEDOM DISAPPEARING WORLDWIDE

After monitoring political freedom worldwide for seventy years, Freedom House recently concludes that freedom is disappearing worldwide. While occasionally there are improvements in some nations, more countries are losing their freedoms. This is mostly because of the decline of Christian influence in national governments.

In 2021, Myanmar, Belarus, Azerbaijan, and Krygystan were the nations losing freedoms at the fastest pace. Also losing freedoms in 2021 were the United States, Australia, Germany, Columbia, India, Indonesia, Libya, Nigeria, and Mexico. Generally, freedom was gaining ground around the world until 2006. That was the year Freedom House reported three nations losing freedom for every one gaining. By 2020, there were 46 more nations losing freedoms than gaining freedom.[83] Will freedom disappear from off the earth, or will Christians who stand for liberty preserve the world from worldwide tyranny? Will Christians retain their salt? Will Christians light up this world, as the Lord Jesus would have it?

> You are the salt of the earth; but if the salt loses its flavor, how shall it be seasoned? It is then good for nothing but to be thrown out and trampled underfoot by men. You are the light of the world. A city that is set on a hill cannot be hidden. Nor do they light a lamp and put it under a basket, but on a lampstand, and it gives light to all who are in the house. Let your light so shine before men, that they may see your good works and glorify your Father in heaven. (Matt. 5:13-16)

INTERNATIONAL ECONOMIC MEDDLING

When it was formed in 1945, the stated purpose of the United Nations was to advocate for world peace and worldwide economic prosperity. To that end, the United Nations established the Economic and Social Council as well as the World Bank. The International Monetary Fund is another agency connected with the United Nations.

The purpose of the World Bank is to loan money to poor countries over which a world government might extend its control. Combining the $25 billion of zero-interest loans and all the foreign aid given to poor countries, the annual amount of financial assistance given by the World Bank is just under $200 billion. Nations receiving the most foreign aid include Ethiopia, Kenya, India, Bangladesh, Congo, and Uganda.[84] The top governments offering this free money are the United States, the UK, France, and the European Union.[85] The stated goal of this aid is to reduce poverty.

This money usually comes with strings attached, which means that the powerful nations are controlling the weaker. The rich will direct the poor.

> The rich rules over the poor,
> And the borrower is servant to the lender. (Prov. 22:7)

A total of $1.2 trillion has flowed from Western countries into Sub-Saharan Africa (Uganda, Malawi, Ethiopia, etc.) over the last forty years. This funding usually comes with an agenda. For example, between 2000 and 2021, the United States contributed $15 billion in foreign aid for abortions and abortifacient drugs to bring down birth rates in African and Asian countries.[86] The United Nations and other powerful countries contributed another $15 billion. This money encouraged the killing of babies in their mothers' wombs even among countries that might have been more reluctant to kill their little ones.

> Many entreat the favor of the nobility,
> And every man is a friend to one who gives gifts.
> All the brothers of the poor hate him;
> How much more do his friends go far from him!
> He may pursue them with words, yet they abandon him. (Prov. 19:6-7)

Whether the generosity of the powerful nations actually contributes to the betterment of the poor nations is hard to say. Since material success has a lot to do with the character of a people, distributing money usually isn't

World Bank building in Washington, DC.

going to fix that. Only the gospel of Jesus Christ will make any real fundamental change to the heart and character of a nation.

FREE TRADE

From the beginning of the world, nations and small city states have controlled trade by tariffs. Governments like to charge taxes on goods coming into the country. Jesus said that most nations would rather collect taxes from foreigners than from their own citizens (Matt. 17:25). If governments are going to receive taxes, this method is typically considered the least bothersome to taxpayers.

Many international organizations and trade agreements have come about with the caveat that nations will trade freely, without having to pay tariffs. However, this doesn't always work out. These agreements create new multi-national bureaucracies to oversee trading. For example, NAFTA (the North American Free Trade Agreement) was supposed to help establish free trade between Mexico, the United States, and Canada. While it reduced tariffs on goods flowing across borders, this treaty of some 1,200 pages added many regulations and associated fines for those who didn't abide by the rules. Such agreements give up national control in exchange for control maintained by an international body.

Generally, the freer the trade between countries, the better the situation for consumers. Also, free trade tends to cultivate good relations and prevent countries from going to war.

Tensions rose between the US and China during the Trump Administration over the trade deficit. China was gaining more world power and wealth, and America was struggling to keep up. Before the trade war got going around 2018, the US had an average 3.1% tariff on Chinese goods. Meanwhile, China was taxing American goods at 8%. By the end of the Trump administration, the average US tariff on Chinese goods was 19.3%, and China's average tariff on US goods was 20.7%.[87] However, it turned out that American importers were paying 90% of the taxes that should have

Cargo port in Shanghai, China.

saddled the Chinese companies. In the end, the American consumer were forced to pay higher prices for the Chinese goods.

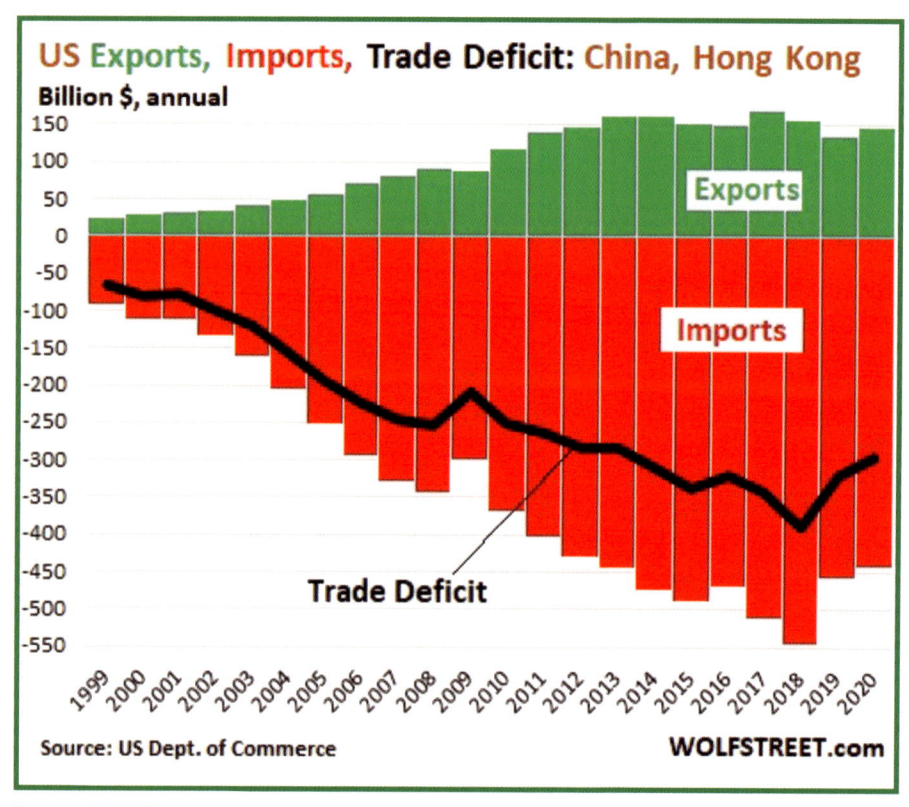

US Exports, Imports, Trade Deficit: China, Hong Kong
Billion $, annual

Source: US Dept. of Commerce — WOLFSTREET.com

Source: WolfStreet.com. Used by permission.

HOW GOVERNMENTS MAY LEGITIMATELY INVOLVE THEMSELVES IN THE ECONOMY

There are legitimate reasons for the civil government to get involved in the economy, or in the free exchange of goods and services. As mentioned at the beginning of this chapter, the government is responsible for prosecuting criminals. Here are some examples of how the government may legitimately get involved in private enterprise:

1. When a business is aiding an enemy government with military trade secrets or armaments. This especially applies to wartime.
2. When a business deceives its customers in advertising and contracts,

and does not fulfill its commitments.
3. When a business tries to ruin another business by violence or robbery.
4. When a business knowingly avoids safety measures, and employees get hurt and or killed.
5. When a business provides unfair access to critical information about the business to some investors but not to others. All investors should have equal access to information about the business that appears positive (and would increase the stock price) or negative (that would decrease the stock price). The U. S. Securities and Exchange Commission (SEC) will investigate companies that are not providing fair access to information for their investors.

THE MOST INSIDIOUS TAX OF ALL

The most insidious tax is debt spending. When governments go into debt to pay for things each year, this is really a hidden taxation. Either the debt is passed on to future taxpayers, or, the value of the debt is reduced by the government printing more money (inflation). Deceitful politicians (very often conservatives) would boast of lowering taxes while increasing

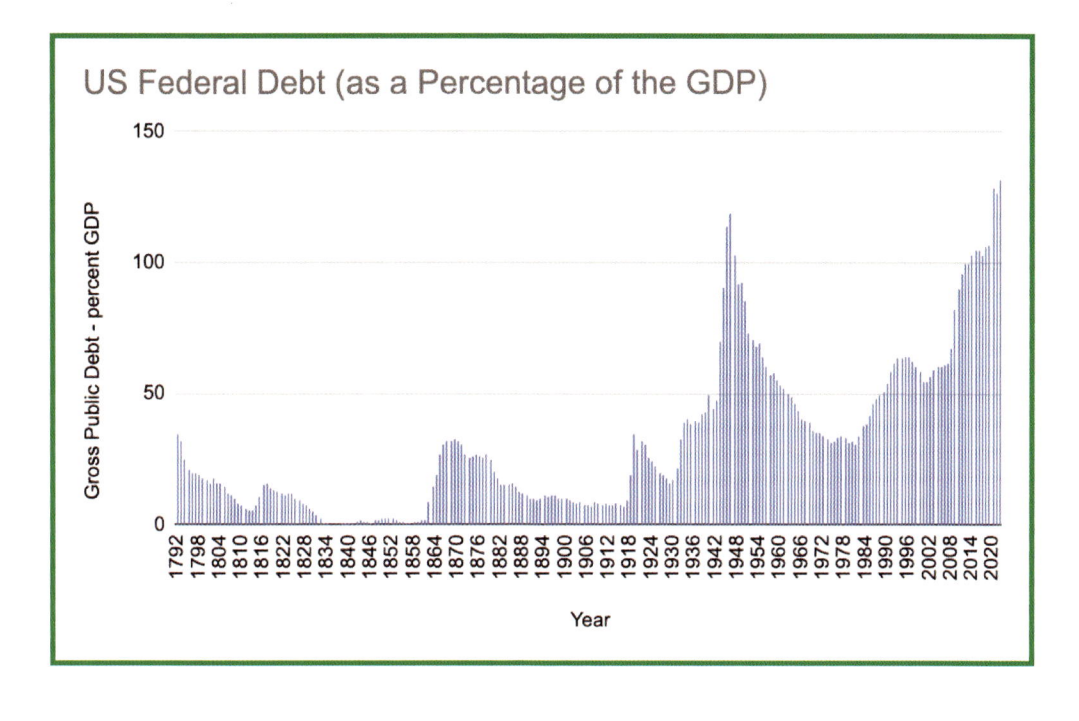

US Federal Debt (as a Percentage of the GDP)

government spending. How can you spend more money, while getting less money in taxes? The difference has to be covered by debt. This deceitful form of taxation came hard and fast in the US between 1980 and 2020 (see chart above).

Which presidential administrations contributed to this insidious form of taxation? Here is a historical summary, listing the average debt (deficit) as a percentage of their annual budgets.

President	Party	Annual Deficit Spending (%)
Richard Nixon	Republican	1.1%
Gerald Ford	Republican	3.6%
Jimmy Carter	Democrat	2.3%
Ronald Reagan	Republican	4.1%
George Bush	Republican	4.1%
Bill Clinton	Democrat	1.6%
George W. Bush	Republican	3.3%
Barack Obama	Democrat	4.9%
Donald Trump	Republican	7.4%

Over these fifty years, the average deficit spending for Republican administrations was 3.9%, and the average deficit spending for Democrat administrations was 2.9%. At the same time, the whole world followed the US into high levels of debt. For centuries, during periods of relative peace, world debt would hover between 20% and 30% of the Gross World Product. Between 1970 and 2020, this ratio increased from 30% to 100%. The national governments with the highest debt in the world (as a percentage of the GDP) were Japan, Greece, Lebanon, Italy, Portugal, and the United States (in 2022).

WHAT DOES THIS MEAN FOR YOU?

No doubt at this point, the reader would hope that something might stem the loss of freedoms somewhere in the world. The obvious solution would be for the citizens to stop voting for tyrants who increase taxes and government spending. But the matter is more complicated than that, and worth considering in more depth. The voters always tend to rely on governments to fix their problems for them, and that for several reasons:

1. People do not trust in God to take care of them. They worry about their money and daily provision, and they look to the government to provide for their needs.

> Therefore do not worry, saying, "What shall we eat?" or "What shall we drink?" or "What shall we wear?" For after all these things the Gentiles seek. For your heavenly Father knows that you need all these things. But seek first the kingdom of God and His righteousness, and

Garbage abandoned on a road. More faithful self-government will reduce government tyranny.

Zurich, Switzerland. Those nations most influenced by a biblical faith are among the most honest nations.

> all these things shall be added to you. Therefore do not worry about tomorrow, for tomorrow will worry about its own things. Sufficient for the day is its own trouble. (Matt. 6:31-34)

As Christ teaches us here, we need to trust in our heavenly Father to provide everything we need. Otherwise, we will look for security elsewhere—and most people put their trust in government.

2. People do not govern themselves. They get divorces. Their families break down. Fathers won't take care of their own children, and young men refuse to provide for their elderly parents and grandparents. That's why the government feels the need to create welfare programs and social security programs.

3. Voters who vote for big government are asking the all-powerful state to regulate their lives. That's because they are not governing their own lives. There is a steady disappearance of character with each successive generation. Recently, researchers dropped 17,000

wallets in the largest cities in various countries around the world. They wanted to see who would return them.[88] The most dishonest country in the world turned out to be communist China.

Also among the most dishonest nations were the Muslim countries of Morocco, Kazakhstan, United Arab Emirates, Indonesia, and Malaysia. The Roman Catholic countries of Mexico and Peru also ranked among the most dishonest. Only 5-15% of the citizens of these countries were honest. Once again, the most honest nations in the world were those most influenced by a Bible-based Christian Faith in the 1700s, 1800s, and 1900s. Switzerland, Norway, Denmark, Netherlands, and Sweden were the most honest countries, registering the highest percentage of wallets returned. Among these nations, about 70-80% of the people were found to be honest.

But how did these nations become so honest? By nature, we are all lying, thieving, and covetous people. Certainly, only the transforming grace of God working in the hearts of the people, as the Christian gospel is preached, could make a difference in the character of a nation.

> If you meet your enemy's ox or his donkey going astray, you shall surely bring it back to him again. If you see the donkey of one who hates you lying under its burden, and you would refrain from helping it, you shall surely help him with it. (Ex. 23:4-5)
>
> You shall not see your brother's ox or his sheep going astray, and hide yourself from them; you shall certainly bring them back to your brother. And if your brother is not near you, or if you do not know him, then you shall bring it to your own house, and it shall remain with you until your brother seeks it; then you shall restore it to him. You shall do the same with his donkey, and so shall you do with his garment; with any lost thing of your brother's, which he has lost and you have found, you shall do likewise; you must not hide yourself. You shall not see your brother's donkey or his ox fall down along the road, and hide yourself from them; you shall surely help him lift them up again. (Deut. 22:1-4)

SELF-GOVERNMENT IS THE ANSWER

Would you return a wallet if you found it lying on a park bench in your hometown?

Naturally, those nations that are mostly dishonest will have to submit to more regulations, more government inspections, and more government controls. They will be poor.

Drive through many of these dishonest nations and you will find garbage strewn everywhere. The roadways are lined with litter. These same people who would steal somebody else's wallet don't care about other people's property. This is a violation of the 8th commandment. We must respect the property of others. To toss our garbage on to other people's property is to do harm to their property. If I burned tires on my property, and soot from the burn pile floats into my neighbor's property, I have damaged his goods. I owe him reparations.

> If fire breaks out and catches in thorns, so that stacked grain, standing grain, or the field is consumed, he who kindled the fire shall surely make restitution. (Ex. 22:6)

If this sort of behavior becomes too common within a community, governments will act. They will issue regulations and will send inspectors into our homes and businesses to make sure we are doing the right thing. Fines and regulations are intended to keep people from doing something irresponsible and damaging the goods of their neighbors. Actually, fines and regulations don't work very well. But governments are merely trying to limit the damage that can be done by an irresponsible, careless, selfish, and unloving society.

However, a Christian society and Christian citizens should be much more careful to govern themselves. They should think twice before they make a gigantic fire in their yard that might cause ash to fall on their neighbor's home and property. They should be very careful never to litter or to allow debris to blow off their pickup truck as they drive down the road.

They would be careful to place coverings over deep holes in their yard so people won't fall into them. They would put fences around a swimming pool so a two-year-old neighbor doesn't fall into it and drown. They would build their homes using safety standards such that the second floor doesn't collapse when twenty people are congregating there. And they work to ensure that the house will stand through the earthquakes or hurricanes that are common in the area. This means that they will insist on engineering designs for their home that consider these things. They do not rely on planning commissions to tell them what to do.

When operating their lemonade stands, they will be sure that the lemons don't spoil. They will verify there is sufficient ice to keep everything cold before they set up for the day. They do not need the Food and Drug Administration to tell them what to do.

> Because of the transgression of a land, many are its princes;
> But by a man of understanding and knowledge right will be prolonged
> (Prov. 28:2)

RESOLVING PROBLEMS WITHOUT APPEALING TO THE GOVERNMENT

Suppose your neighbor decides to raise pigs on his five acres—a whole lot of the stinky, filthy, boisterous creatures. On top of this, his dogs bark all night long, keeping you awake. The noise and the stink of the farm is too much for you to endure, so you complain about it to your local government. The other neighbors join in, and you press for more laws and regulations governing animals, smells, and loud noises. To whom does the blame fall for the increase in tyrannical laws in your town or county? The neighbor who does not do to others as he would have them do to him is first at fault. On the other hand, he may be quite unaware of the effect his hogs and dogs are having upon his neighbors until somebody gently informs him of the issue. So, the fault may lie with both those who complained to the authorities and the neighbor issuing the hog smells and dog yells.

Now, of course the better approach is to find ways to work things out between you and your neighbor privately. You should speak with him and work on a peaceful resolution to the problem. This is another example of self-government. In the long run, such personal engagement will preserve freedom more than anything else.

> Agree with your adversary quickly, while you are on the way with him, lest your adversary deliver you to the judge, the judge hand you over to the officer, and you be thrown into prison. Assuredly, I say to you, you will by no means get out of there till you have paid the last penny. (Matt. 5:25-26)

10

HOW TO BE SUCCESSFUL IN BUSINESS

*Through wisdom a house is built,
And by understanding it is established;
By knowledge the rooms are filled
With all precious and pleasant riches.
(Prov. 24:3-4)*

Building a business is a lot like building a house. It takes a lot of wisdom and knowledge.

Building a business is a lot like building a house. It takes a lot of wisdom and knowledge to put a house together, especially if it will stay intact through storms – a house that won't fall down. It also takes much wisdom to raise a family to be fruitful, both in an economic and spiritual sense. Similarly, it takes knowledge and wisdom to establish a fruitful business, while avoiding big mistakes that could blow the whole thing up. God has given us time to do things in this life. We want to make good use of this time. We would like to be successful in our endeavors and produce good fruit.

Nobody wants to fail in business. We surely don't want to waste precious resources. To spend $1,000 on a lemonade stand and 500 lemons without using them to bless the neighborhood with lemonade would be a waste. What a disappointment to see 500 lemons rot in your pantry! But how does one achieve success?

God's Book of Wisdom (the Proverbs) gives a great deal of insight into success. First, wisdom (and the fear of God) is essential for building a home and a successful business. The right character, disposition, and outlook—which must be formed in humility and the fear of God—is key. Wisdom makes the right decisions, treats people in the right way, and retains the right perspective whether things are going well or not.

The world has borrowed some of this wisdom from the Book of Proverbs and from a Christian worldview. By God's common grace, varying amounts of this wisdom have been shared in the marketplace today. There are literally thousands of books published on how to be successful in business. Typically, an online bookstore like Amazon would feature 1,500-2,000 different books on the subject. The following briefly summarizes seven of the most popular books on business success.

Stephen Covey gave us *Seven Habits of Highly Effective People:*

- Successful people are more proactive than reactive.
- They work towards goals, with the end in mind.
- They prioritize thoughtfully, always putting first things first.
- They seek first to understand what others are saying and then to be understood by them. In all business relationships, they seek a win-win scenario (where both sides win in the deal).
- They synergize their efforts with others by identifying, and then working off the positive contributions of others.
- They identify their strongest assets and continually sharpen and improve them.

Dr. Thomas Stanley interviewed 733 millionaires in America and listed the top five factors for financial success in his book, *The Millionaire Mind.* **These included:**

1. Telling the truth
2. Hard work
3. Self-discipline
4. Getting along with others
5. Teaming up with a supportive spouse

Dale Carnegie inspired salesmen for generations with his *How to Win Friends and Influence People.*

Part 1: Fundamental Techniques in Handling People
Principle 1: Don't criticize, condemn, or complain.
Principle 2: Give honest and sincere appreciation.
Principle 3: Arouse in the other person a legitimate and enthusiastic sense of need.

Part 2: Six Ways to Make People Like You
Principle 1: Become genuinely interested in other people.
Principle 2: Smile.
Principle 3: Remember that a person's name is, to that person, the sweetest and most important sound in any language.
Principle 4: Be a good listener.
Principle 5: Talk in terms of the other person's interests.
Principle 6: Make the other person feel important—and do it sincerely.

Part 3: How to Win People to Your Way of Thinking
Principle 1: The only way to get the best of an argument is to avoid it.
Principle 2: Show respect for the other person's opinions. Never say, "You're wrong."
Principle 3: If you are wrong, admit it quickly and emphatically.
Principle 4: Begin your interactions in a friendly way.
Principle 5: Get the other person saying, "yes, yes" immediately.
Principle 6: Let the other person do a great deal of the talking.
Principle 7: Let the other person feel that the idea is his or hers.
Principle 8: Try honestly to see things from the other person's point of view.
Principle 9: Be sympathetic with the other person's ideas and desires.
Principle 10: Appeal to the nobler motives.
Principle 11: Dramatize your ideas.
Principle 12: Throw down a challenge.

Part 4: Be a Leader—How to Change People Without Giving Offense or Arousing Resentment
Principle 1: Begin with praise and honest appreciation.
Principle 2: Call attention to people's mistakes indirectly.
Principle 3: Talk about your own mistakes before criticizing the other person.
Principle 4: Ask questions instead of giving direct orders.

Principle 5: Let the other person save face.
Principle 6: Praise the slightest improvement and praise every improvement. Be "hearty in your approbation and lavish in your praise."
Principle 7: Give the other person a fine reputation to live up to.
Principle 8: Use encouragement. Make the fault seem easy to correct.
Principle 9: Make the other person happy about doing the thing you suggest.

George Clason's *The Richest Man in Babylon* taught that we should never confuse needs with desires.

Improve on your skills and seek a reliable income stream. And remember that procrastination is an enemy. You'll have to kill that bad habit.

Clason's seven rules for money management are simple:
1. Save money. If you are in debt, live on 70% of what you earn. Save 10% and use the remaining 20% to repay your debts.
2. Control your expenses: don't spend more than you need.
3. Make your gold multiply: invest wisely.
4. Guard your treasures from loss: avoid investments that sound too good to be true.
5. Make of your dwelling a profitable investment: own your home.
6. Ensure a future income. A man's wealth is in his regular income.
7. Improve your ability to earn: strive to become wiser and more knowledgeable.

Ken Blanchard's *One Minute Manager* focused on goals.

1. Your goals need to be clear and concise. Every worker should know what is expected of him. Make a list of your goals, and keep the list to 3-6 goals. Record the goals on one page. and be sure both the manager and the employee has the same list.
2. Follow up. Are the actions taken actually accomplishing the goals?
3. The manager should mark every time employees are making progress towards accomplishing the goals, and he should praise them. The manager tells the employee that they did right and commends him or her on the spot.

4. The manager also marks the thing that is done wrong and provides a one-minute reprimand. The correction is direct, describing exactly the thing that was done wrong. He may commend the employee as a person, but he corrects the wrong behavior. The correction is made, and we move on. No more discussion about it.

Manage by walking around

Tom Peter's *Passion for Excellence* provided wise pointers for managing businesses.

1. Manage by walking around and taking an interest in your employees. Find ways in which you can encourage them in their work. Learn about the problems they encounter and help them to fix these things. Get to know your customers, their needs, and expectations.
2. Learn about people's perceptions. They may have the wrong perceptions, but that is still how they look at your products and your business. You may have to adapt your business to their perceptions.
3. Always work for continual improvement in your product or ser-

vice. Look out for ways you can continually improve on the quality of your work.
4. Treat people with a high degree of courtesy. The companies that treat customers and employees the very best will usually do the very best financially.
5. Genuine appreciation for your employees and public accolades will be a higher value to them and more motivating than their regular paycheck.

Liz Wiseman's *Multipliers* investigated the gifts of good business leaders, whom she termed "Multipliers." Wiseman concluded the following:

Multipliers amplify or multiply the intelligence and the gifts of the people they work with. They multiply the energy in the room, and their teams are quick to solve problems and achieve goals. Multipliers are good motivators.

Teamwork and appreciation for one another's gifts is an important part of successful businesses.

Multipliers are also interested in multiplying other peoples' talents. These leaders focus on challenging their people. They expect great things from their people, and that's what they get. Five qualities mark these excellent leaders:

1. They attract good talent, people who want to be challenged, and they optimize on that talent. They aren't focused on building empires for themselves. They are more interested in seeing people excel with the talents God has given them.
2. They create an exciting, active organization that calls for the best thinking and aggressive problem solving.
3. They don't set directions for the organizations themselves. They encourage others to set directions, and they cheerlead the team to press forward in achieving goals.
4. They introduce debate on decisions and issues up front so there will be no surprise when the direction is set.
5. They are busy delegating responsibility or ownership instead of spending all their time micromanaging the team.

BIBLICAL WISDOM

While not all of this "wisdom" would find its roots in Scripture, much of it does. The underlying wisdom behind these success gurus' insights are to be found in more basic principles contained in the Bible.

> Love your neighbor as yourself. (Lev. 19:18)
>
> Therefore, whatever you want men to do to you, do also to them, for this is the Law and the Prophets. (Matt. 7:12)
>
> By humility and the fear of the LORD are riches and honor and life. (Prov. 22:4)

Tom Peters encourages courtesy, and calls for a vital interest in the needs of your employees and customers. This sounds a lot like loving your neighbor as yourself. Dr. Thomas Stanley's list of factors for success could have been found in the book of Proverbs. And, in accord with Proverbs 22:4, Liz Wiseman's multipliers are humble if their true intent is to maximize on the gifts of others. *But still, conspicuously absent in this worldly wisdom is the character trait of the fear of God.*

Dale Carnegie may not carefully distinguish between flattery and gratefulness. Biblically, the fundamental issue is to tell the truth. As we commend others for the work they do, we must still recognize that all gifts come from God. Thus, a man-centered view in gaining success in business still won't recognize God as the source of blessing or give Him the thanksgiving and praise for it. The foundation of all wisdom is the fear of God, and when that foundation is cracked, the entire building is doomed. Without God in the picture, without a love for God and a reverence for God, we will inevitably lose a respect for our fellowman created in His image. Godless wisdom like that found with Thomas Stanley, Liz Wiseman, Tom Peters, and Dale Carnegie will not sustain the kingdoms of men in the long run. These are fatal errors and would inevitably result in the breakdown of these economic systems.

Dale Carnegie

THE MOST ESSENTIAL CHARACTER ELEMENT CONTRIBUTING TO SUCCESS IN BUSINESS

> So Jesus answered and said to them, "Have faith in God. For assuredly, I say to you, whoever says to this mountain, 'Be removed and be cast into the sea,' and does not doubt in his heart, but believes that those things he says will be done, he will have whatever he says. Therefore I say to you, whatever things you ask when you pray, believe that you receive them, and you will have them." (Mark 11:22–24)

HOW TO BE SUCCESSFUL IN BUSINESS

It is the Lord that determines the size of our harvest, or the success of our business efforts.

> For we walk by faith, not by sight. (2 Cor. 5:7)

Turning to biblical wisdom, faith in God is primary. Confidence is basic to all human action. When people are discouraged and depressed, they aren't motivated to do anything. As Hebrews 12 encourages us, "Strengthen the hands which hang down, and the feeble knees, and make straight paths for your feet" (Heb. 12:12-13).

All successful business persons must act with forthright confidence in something. The people of the world understand this principle, and they put their faith in self, in man's raw ability to bring about a harvest. It's important to put our faith in something, but the object of faith matters very much. Man isn't much to trust.

> He who trusts in his own heart is a fool,
> But whoever walks wisely will be delivered. (Prov. 28:26)
>
> Thus says the LORD: "Cursed is the man who trusts in man and makes flesh his strength, whose heart departs from the LORD." (Jer. 17:5)

Therefore, Christians put their faith in that which is far more trustworthy—God Himself. We believe in God's goodness. We believe in God's calling on our lives and in the higher purpose God has placed on us—to seek His kingdom and His righteousness in all things. We approach the day with a strong sense of "This is what I am supposed to do today."

We trust in God to bring us the harvest. We cannot predetermine the precise reward, but we can be certain that God is good. He is an endless reservoir of strength when we are wearied, and He has ordered the following principles for reaping and sowing. We can work with confidence that He will be true to what He has promised us.

> Do not be deceived, God is not mocked; for whatever a man sows, that he will also reap. (Gal. 6:7)
>
> He who tills his land will be satisfied with bread,
> But he who follows frivolity is devoid of understanding. . . .
> A man will be satisfied with good by the fruit of his mouth,
> And the recompense of a man's hands will be rendered to him.
> (Prov. 12:11, 14)

This faith rejects all trepidation, irresolution, and apathy. Faith doesn't fear a negative outcome. Faith acts forthrightly with great expectations of eventual reward. Faith steps out and takes risks without concrete, empirical proof that the endeavor will be successful. Faith steps out of the boat and begins to walk on water—trusting God the whole way.

THE BIBLICAL SECRET TO SUCCESS IN LIFE

> Children, obey your parents in the Lord, for this is right. "Honor your father and mother," which is the first commandment with promise: "that it may be well with you and you may live long on the earth." (Eph. 6:1-3)

Here is the secret to success hardly ever mentioned in secular books on economics. Why are some families more successful than others? Why are some nations more fruitful than others? How many people have considered this principle from Ephesians 6 and Exodus 20? Children who honor their parents will have it better in their lives and live longer than if they behaved otherwise. Honor is respect and reverence. And honor is paid in the way we speak of our parents, the way we speak to them, and the way we take care of them in their old age.

The Lord promises blessings of fruitfulness and long life for those who honor their parents.

OTHER ESSENTIAL ELEMENTS

> There is one who scatters, yet increases more;
> And there is one who withholds more than is right,
> But it leads to poverty.
> The generous soul will be made rich,
> And he who waters will also be watered himself. (Prov. 11:24-25)
>
> The soul of a lazy man desires, and has nothing;
> But the soul of the diligent shall be made rich. (Prov. 13:4)
>
> The ransom of a man's life is his riches,
> But the poor does not hear rebuke. (Prov. 13:8)
>
> Poverty and shame will come to him who disdains correction,
> But he who regards a rebuke will be honored. (Prov. 13:18)

The Book of Proverbs offers several other key lessons. For example, Proverbs 11:24-25 describes success as the person who scatters, invests, and keeps the resources moving. Success comes with generosity, risk taking, and an insatiate desire to bless others.

Moreover, the slothful man has little to show, whereas the diligent will be fruitful in life. Importantly, the wisdom book doesn't define all profit as monetary. We will further explore the subject of profit later in this chapter.

Also, successful people always listen to rebuke and correction. This principle is sure. Though you may be poor at present, the more you listen to rebuke, the more success you will enjoy in the future. Successful people are humble, and they respond to correction from the wise. In fact, they will lean into it and repent. They will make corrections according to the rebukes they receive from those who have wisdom to share.

SUCCESSFUL PEOPLE DO NOT PROCRASTINATE

> Whatever your hand finds to do, do it with your might; for there is no work or device or knowledge or wisdom in the grave where you are going. (Eccl. 9:10)
>
> He who observes the wind will not sow,
> And he who regards the clouds will not reap. (Eccl. 11:4)
>
> The lazy man will not plow because of winter;
> He will beg during harvest and have nothing. (Prov. 20:4)
>
> But we urge you, brethren, that you increase more and more; that you also aspire to lead a quiet life, to mind your own business, and to work with your own hands, as we commanded you, that you may walk properly toward those who are outside, and that you may lack nothing. (1 Thess. 4:11-12)

Successful people do not have a procrastinating mindset. They don't put off until tomorrow what they can do today. They usually do the next thing, that is the next needful thing that presents itself immediately to them.

Successful people do not have a procrastinating mindset.

For example, after cooking scrambled eggs in a pan, you could take 20 seconds to soak the pan in water. Or, you could just leave it on the stove and scrub off the egg residue (which would take 3-5 minutes). The slothful man procrastinates. He doesn't do the thing in front of him that would save him time later on. If he cooks eggs twice a week, he is wasting an extra 300 minutes or 5 hours a year just scraping egg residue from frying pans at the kitchen sink. This is his life. He doesn't put things back into their place when he uses them, so he spends half his life looking for things. He doesn't wipe down the shower, so he will have to spend hours chipping away at calcium deposits later on. As the Proverbs puts it, his way is one long "hedge of thorns" (Prov. 15:19).

Successful people don't leave things for other people to do when they can easily do it themselves. They actually learn to enjoy working with their hands and finishing tasks they have set out to do. That's their mindset.

Successful people look out for ways to be more efficient. Larger clothes bins may help to keep things separated and organized for laundry day. They may purchase identical socks, so as not to have to waste an additional 10 minutes matching socks on laundry day. They buy non-perishables in bulk, so they don't have to waste an additional 30 minutes a month buying the same stuff over and over again. They buy presents when they come across something that would be nice for someone they love, instead of putting that off. They shop online. They keep busy with reading, writing, or researching when they are waiting for a meeting. They listen to the Bible or some other edifying book when driving in the car. They learn to group similar tasks together.

SUCCESSFUL PEOPLE PRIORITIZE ACCORDING TO THEIR VALUES

Successful people will plan out their days. They don't forget important appointments. They don't run through their days aimlessly doing this or that, and allowing themselves to be interrupted by endless diversions. They are intentional in the things they do. Slothful people tend to be mindless in their use of time. Some will waste time checking e-mail or watching endless short videos on the internet. Others are lost in daydreams.

> Now it happened as they went that He entered a certain village; and a certain woman named Martha welcomed Him into her house. And she had a sister called Mary, who also sat at Jesus' feet and heard His word. But Martha was distracted with much serving, and she approached Him and said, "Lord, do You not care that my sister has left me to serve alone? Therefore tell her to help me." And Jesus answered and said to her, "Martha, Martha, you are worried and troubled about many things. But one thing is needed, and Mary has chosen that good part, which will not be taken away from her." (Lk. 10:38-42)

Followers of Jesus will prioritize time in the Word and prayer each day. Like Mary in the Gospels, they receive grace from Christ first, before they share their time and energies with others. Yet, they still want to be obedient to the calling God has given them. If they will redeem the time, they will plan out their days and weeks according to the values Jesus sets for them.

Franklin-Covey recommends planning every week out ahead of time. A daily schedule will be prioritized thoughtfully according to the following basic structure:

1. Urgent and Important Duties
2. Not urgent, and Important Duties
3. Not Important, but Urgent Duties
4. Not Important, and Not Urgent Duties

Time for God's Word and prayer is essential for the Christian.

When listing out the things you will do in a given day, identify your top priorities with an "A," your secondary priorities with a "B," and your tertiary priorities with a "C." Some projects won't take very much time, and other projects will take more time. Address the big "A" projects, and then address the little "A"s. The same principle applies to the B projects and the C projects.

SUCCESSFUL BUSINESSES

> Now the days of David drew near that he should die, and he charged Solomon his son, saying: "I go the way of all the earth; be strong, therefore, and prove yourself a man. And keep the charge of the Lord your God: to walk in His ways, to keep His statutes, His commandments, His judgments, and His testimonies, as it is written in the Law of Moses, that you may prosper in all that you do and wherever you turn... (1 Kings 2:1-3)

God calls each of us to be faithful in our individual callings. Whether we own the company or just work for the company, we have a vested interest in the success of the company. While nothing can absolutely guarantee success except God's blessing, there are some general biblical principles which will often lead to success.

Success is sometimes monetary. It may also be measured in terms of the people who are blessed by our work. This success may come quickly, or it may come later. Of course, heavenly rewards are always preferred over earthly success.

The first principle of success given to Solomon in 1 Kings 2 is to walk in God's ways, according to His commandments. We are capable to live this life by the grace of God. It is the life of faith. Quite often businesses enjoy success and the blessing of God because they hire committed believers who walk with God – real men of faith like Joseph who worked for Potiphar's household.

> So it was, from the time that he had made him overseer of his house and all that he had, that the LORD blessed the Egyptian's house for Joseph's sake; and the blessing of the LORD was on all that he had in the house and in the field. (Gen. 39:5)

Joseph trusted God and was faithful even through many difficulties.

Joseph was an ideal employee. He trusted God. Throughout the Genesis story, we never see him complaining in spite of the terribleness of his circumstances. In every trying situation, Joseph is dependable, competent, and cooperative. His father trusted him with the sheep business. Potiphar trusted him with his agricultural businesses. The prison director trusted him with the prisoners. And the Pharaoh trusted him with running the entire national economy. Yet, the success of each enterprise was not so much the result of Joseph's work, but rather, God's blessing following this honest, hard-working, God-fearing man.

> And the keeper of the prison committed to Joseph's hand all the prisoners who were in the prison; whatever they did there, it was his doing. The keeper of the prison did not look into anything that was under Joseph's authority, because the LORD was with him; and whatever he did, the LORD made it prosper. (Gen. 39:22-23)

HOW TO BE A JOSEPH IN THE WORKPLACE

If the success of a company is tied to the presence of this believer, Joseph, what might we learn from his godly example? Two things. Never do we find this man of God worrying about his condition or grumbling over his trials. Joseph recognizes the hand of God in his life, and he is content with whatever happens to him for good or ill. He is confident that "all things work together for good" in God's good plans (Rom. 8:28, Gen. 50:20). Thus, we find an overall optimistic and hopeful attitude about Joseph. This optimism is crucial for success in whatever we are doing. Are we optimistic towards the outcome because we are in control of the effects of our efforts?

Or are we ultimately optimistic because we know God is in control of the outcome? For Joseph, it was the latter case. Joseph was also more concerned about sinning against God than he was about sinning against Potiphar. This is how he puts it to Potiphar's wife: "How then can I do this great wickedness, and sin against God?" The Christian employee is always aware that God is watching him, and that becomes the major controlling factor in his life.

As the biblical account plays out, Joseph refused to steal his employer's wife, in spite of the pressure from the woman, and the assurance that her husband wouldn't find out about it. The Christian employee is honest not because his manager is watching him but because God is watching him. This is the strongest motive for doing the right thing. If you ignore God and cast off His law, you will be more likely to cheat and steal when nobody else is watching. Your only hesitation would be the fear of getting caught by other people in the workplace. In contrast, those who fear God and retain a constant sense of His presence will hold consistent integrity in their business dealings.

Joseph was honest and faithful.

> The eyes of the LORD are in every place,
> Keeping watch on the evil and the good. (Prov. 15:3)

The 733 millionaires interviewed by Dr. Thomas Stanley concluded that honesty was the most important factor in their material success. Did God learn this from the millionaires, or did these millionaires somehow learn this lesson from God? Some of these successful business people may have been Christians, or at the very least they must have feared God. No doubt many learned the critical importance of honesty by hard lessons in their early career.

Honesty can be painful. When Joseph insisted on moral integrity in relation to Potiphar's wife, he paid for it by serving four to ten years in an Egyptian prison. If you tell the truth, you could lose your job, or miss out on a contract, or be forced to surrender something else of great value. In many instances, telling the truth will cost you something. But if you see these opportunities as God's tests, and if you are sure that God controls the outcome of every situation, then you will be more likely to do the right thing.

Dishonesty usually ends in failure anyway after a while. Used car salesmen who lie to their customers about the cars they sell will almost always see their reputation damaged eventually. They may be tempted to lie for a short-term gain. But it won't do them any good in the long run.

Honesty is the best policy, but mainly because God tells us this is the right thing to do. God is truth, and to lie runs contrary to His righteous character. Therefore, His world is designed to run according to the laws of honesty. Violation of these laws cannot possibly yield good results in the long run. Attempts to violate the law of gravity in the natural world would end badly. What happens when people make repeated violations of God's law in the market economy?

> You shall not steal, nor deal falsely, nor lie to one another… You shall not cheat your neighbor, nor rob him. The wages of him who is hired shall not remain with you all night until morning. (Lev. 19:11, 13)
>
> Woe to him who builds his house by unrighteousness
> And his chambers by injustice,
> Who uses his neighbor's service without wages
> And gives him nothing for his work. . . (Jer. 22:13)

These verses are focused on business dealings. If you have contracted to pay somebody for the work they have done, the sooner you pay up, the better. Companies often allow customers ninety days to pay their invoices or bills—the money owed for products or services. In many cases, businesses simply do not have the money in their accounts to pay these bills. But Christians should never operate this way. If they cannot afford to pay for a product or service, they should delay the purchase. Not surprisingly, small businesses are very negatively impacted by the problem of unpaid invoices. About 78% of business owners surveyed by the Fundbox polling organization said they can't write their own paychecks because of this problem. Another 23% can't buy needed equipment or hire new employees because their customers are so slow at paying invoices.[89] If you are a customer purchasing things or an employer hiring workers, you have an obligation to pay for the products and services people have rendered to you.

> A faithful witness does not lie, but a false witness will utter lies. (Prov. 14:5)

> Excellent speech is not becoming to a fool, much less lying lips to a prince. (Prov. 17:7)

Bearing false witness against others is especially condemned in Scripture—whether that witness be against your fellow employees, customers, or vendors. Though it may be tempting to cut down your competitors by underrating their products or calling their character into question, such behavior is unacceptable to followers of Jesus. Our first priority is not to monetary success or increasing our own business at the expense of others. First and foremost, in all of our business relationships, we will be directed by the fear of God and the command to love our neighbor as ourselves.

There is still nothing wrong with pointing out unique features characterizing your product, or particular qualitative differences between your products and a competitor's. But you take great risk of slandering your competitor when conveying wide-sweeping, negative reports about their work to others. To say, for example, "My competitor's products are *junk*.

They *always* do sloppy work. Their customer service is *worthless*," is akin to bearing false witness.

At times this slander can take on a more insidious tone. You might mention a weak element of your competitor's product or character and then forget to point out the strengths or benefits that outweigh the drawbacks. To compare yourself or your work with others is dangerous and verges on sin. Let your work speak for itself.

> For we dare not class ourselves or compare ourselves with those who commend themselves. But they, measuring themselves by themselves, and comparing themselves among themselves, are not wise. (2 Cor. 10:12)

Here are a few other ways in which Christians can maintain a high degree of integrity in the workforce.

- Tell the customer when you have made a mistake. Don't try to cover it up. The sooner you admit it, the better.
- Inform the store or supplier when they failed to collect all the money you owe. If you buy two coats and later discover on the receipt that they only charged you for one, what should you do? Of course, the honest person will return to the store, explain the mistake, and pay the difference.
- Be honest about bad news relating to your product or service. The question of how much to tell the customer is not always easy to answer. Are there certain things you might hold back on? Or, would it be better to tell the customer everything you know, good and bad, about your product or service? Keep in mind, honesty is always the best policy.

> Whoever secretly slanders his neighbor,
> Him I will destroy;
> The one who has a haughty look and a proud heart,
> Him I will not endure.
> My eyes shall be on the faithful of the land,
> That they may dwell with me;

> He who walks in a perfect way,
> He shall serve me.
> He who works deceit shall not dwell within my house;
> He who tells lies shall not continue in my presence. (Ps. 101:5-7)

WHAT'S A HUMBLE AND HONEST SALESMAN?

> Let another man praise you, and not your own mouth; a stranger, and not your own lips. (Prov. 27:2)

Is the act of selling legitimate at all? God's Word does not favor boasting, big talking, and hard selling. And all around us are to be found plenty of smooth-talking salesmen who know how to make an extra dollar by using a host of sales techniques. Most success programs emphasize sales as the big thing, and businesses are expected to talk up their products for better sales and income.

"Hard" salesmen have learned to keep pushing the product until the

A God-honoring salesman will follow God's commandments in helping a customer.

customer has said "no" three times. Or, they will play "good cop-bad cop" with the customer. First, they use flattery. Then they try to shame them. They also play on "the fear of missing out." Or they will tell the customer the price of the product is about to increase, within a day or two. They may pretend the product is scarce. Or, they may appeal to pity, or they may drag out the conversation to wear down the customer. How do we respond to these methods? And if we are going to compete with these hard-sell companies, must we take on their approach to sales? If Scripture forbids boasting about ourselves, our companies, and our products, how are we going to be successful with our sales? Here are several pointers to take into account when selling a product, with the intent towards building a company up on integrity and maintaining a God-honoring business.

1. Strive to understand the real need of the customer, and fill that need. Be sure that the sale and your profit is not your number one goal in the conversation. A good salesman isn't going to be talking the whole time. He's asking questions. He's attempting to provide needed expertise that would assist the customer. The goal of the company is to satisfy the customer but also to surprise the customer with a better product or service than the customer expected to receive.
2. Be truthful in the presentation of the product or service. To the extent that the product will not fulfill the customer's needs, he should know it. While it is okay to highlight the better features of your product, don't use the better features to cover up the worse.
3. Focus on quality. Instead of worrying about your competitors or hard selling your customers, just work on giving your customers the best product possible.

The Christian-owned Chick-fil-A fast food restaurant doesn't rely on advertising to push its products. If anything, they used humor to make the public aware of their product. Cartoon cows pushed people towards eating "mor chiken." But the company maintained unmatched quality of service for decades. The customer experience was always top notch. Chick-fil-A

In-N-Out Restaurant in Medford, Oregon

didn't need to advertise their quality. They demonstrated it. Their employees were upbeat, respectful, and attentive to every customer's needs. In 2021, this company pulled out the top American Customer Satisfaction Rating of 83, beating Domino's Pizza, Kentucky Fried Chicken, and Starbucks for first place.[90] This rating took into account cleanliness, accuracy, staff helpfulness, and reliability of mobile apps. By 2020, Chick-fil-A was the most profitable fast-food restaurant in America, averaging $5 million per store per year. Raising Cane's came in second place at $3.85 million, and What-a-Burger in third place at $3.85 million. The Christian-owned In-N-Out Burger took fourth place at $3.06 million,[91] and McDonald's came in fifth at $2.95 million.

From its first establishment in 1912, the L. L. Bean company created a sturdy reputation in the clothing and outdoor wear industry by insisting on quality and customer satisfaction. Mr. Bean's philosophy was: "Sell good merchandise at a reasonable profit, treat your customers like human beings, and they will always come back for more." The company insisted on 100% customer satisfaction. Their policy was, "Our products are guaranteed to give 100% satisfaction in every way. Return anything purchased from us at any time if it proves otherwise. We do not want you to have anything from L. L. Bean that is not completely satisfactory." Thus, customers could return a product five years after the purchase if it did not meet their expectations. To this day, L. L. Bean provides customer service response time by phone within 20 seconds, and by e-mail within 3 hours, and by chat within 7 seconds.

Assembling hamburgers

DEFINING QUALITY

Success in business has everything to do with quality work. But how does one define quality? There are both positive and negative descriptions of quality for products and services. Officially, *quality is the totality of features and characteristics of a product or service that bear on its ability to satisfy given needs*. At the least, quality products will conform to stated requirements or specifications. Negatively stated, quality seeks to produce products and services free from defects or any characteristic that may be disappointing to the customer.

Some work is very specific to a particular customer's needs, usually known as "custom work." A carpenter, for example, meets a particular customer's expectations when he does custom trim work on a house. He wants the job to meet the satisfaction of the customer by the way the job looks when he is finished. The standard will be visible appeal devoid of obvious defects and unsightly gaps.

High volume manufacturing and fast food restaurants will define quality a little differently. This is not custom production. These businesses produce the exact same product hundreds or thousands of times over in a work day. Their goal is to produce almost exactly the same standard of product every time. They do not want variation between the products or the food served. The customer expects a certain taste, a certain look, or a certain function with each product or meal purchased. They want the same hamburger in size, taste, and appearance, whether they purchase it in Denver, Colorado or Miami, Florida. They want the business to provide the same specifications in all the important features of the product, with minimal variation.

First, however, the company must identify the optimum design for each specification when they develop the product. Take, for example, the lemonade stand. You experiment with different amounts of lemon concentration and sugar. You conduct taste tests with ten friends and find just the right mix that everybody likes. And you discover that 2 tablespoons of sugar per glass is exactly the right amount. Now, if one of your employees (your sister, for example) begins to add 4 tablespoons of sugar per glass, or 1.5 tablespoons per glass, that would be a problem. Over several weeks, your repeat customers were satisfied with 2 tablespoons per glass. But when they purchase your lemonade with 4 tablespoons of sugar, they would find it much too sweet. If one of your employees added only 1.5 tablespoons, the

Making lemonade

lemonade would taste much too sour. This kind of variation in the production of your lemonade would result in you losing your customers.

In this example, the specification of 2 tablespoons is usually referred to as **the target**. A commitment to quality involves *reducing variation* as much as possible. When adding sugar to the mix, your employees should carefully measure the amounts. You don't want them tamping down the sugar in the measuring cup, and they should carefully level off the sugar in the measuring cup using the flat edge of a knife. This attention to detail will produce a quality product every time—just the right amount of sugar, no more and no less.

ACCURACY VS. PRECISION

When you are trying to produce the highest quality product, you want to come as close as possible to the specified target with everything produced. If the production is sloppy, the employees will miss the target by a lot, every time. If the employees are careful and conscientious, they will try to hit the target every time. **Accuracy** is the word used when the units manufactured are centered around the specified target. If the units produced are accurate and precise in terms of the specification, they will be centered close in to the target every time. The difference between accuracy and precision can be demonstrated with a bow and arrow or gunshots at a real target, as depicted in the diagrams.

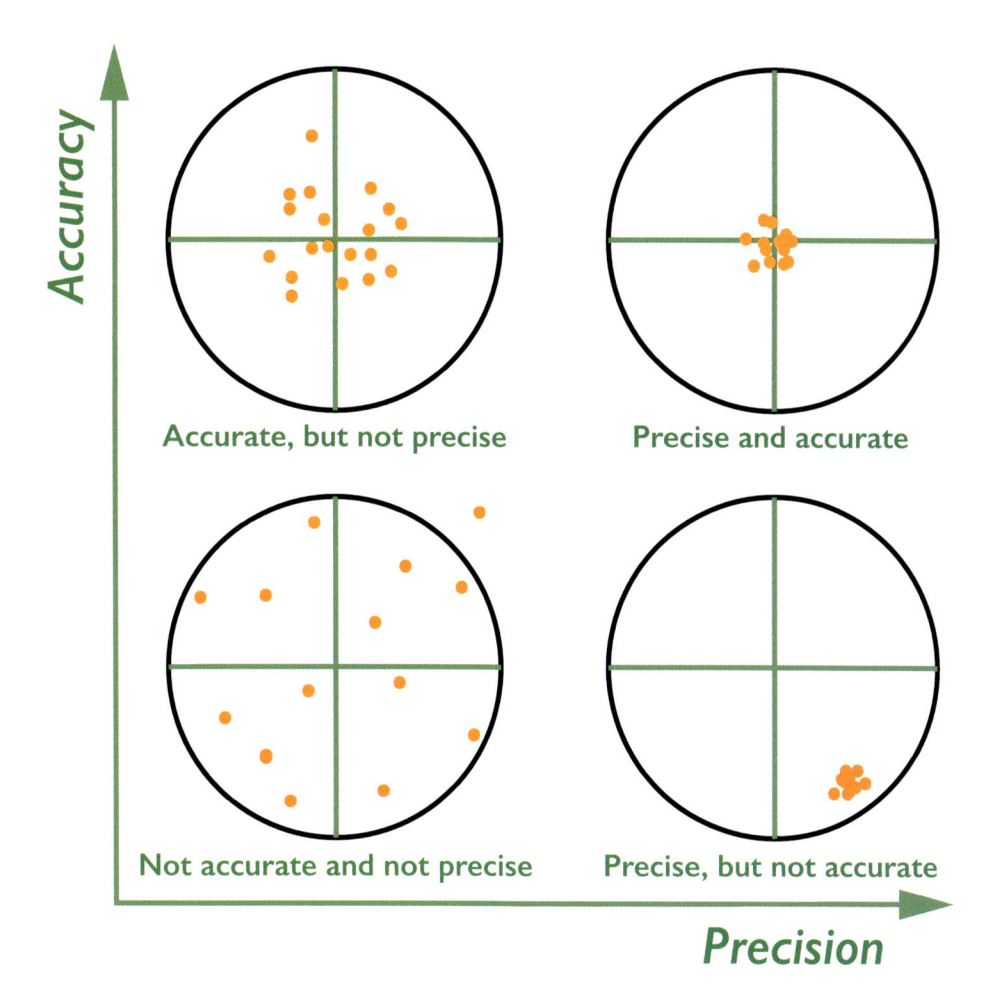

Accuracy

Accurate, but not precise

Precise and accurate

Not accurate and not precise

Precise, but not accurate

Precision

CONTINUOUS IMPROVEMENT

> And may the Lord make you increase and abound in love for one another and for all, as we do for you. (1 Thess. 3:12)
>
> And it is my prayer that your love may abound more and more, with knowledge and all discernment. (Phil. 1:9)
>
> Now may He who supplies seed to the sower, and bread for food, supply and multiply the seed you have sown and increase the fruits of your righteousness. (2 Cor. 9:10)

The entirety of a Christian life should be characterized by continuous improvement. That's what we find in these verses. Similarly, the pursuit of quality in our economic endeavors should also commit to continuous improvement. When the Lord gives us certain resources or businesses to manage, He expects us to improve on them.

When a writer publishes his first book, he may sell 1,000 copies in the first printing. Before releasing a second batch of 1,000 copies, he should correct the errors that showed up in the first printing. There are always

Making corrections on a book manuscript

improvements that could be made—spelling errors to correct and bad sentences to rewrite. We never achieve perfection in anything we do in life. But, with God's help, we work hard for improvement every year of our lives. In whatever business we are involved with, let us look for mistakes to correct and improve on our work.

INSPECTIONS

The quality department of an organization is usually tasked with inspecting the products. They will do a visual inspection to look for obvious defects. Or they will make measurements using scales, rulers, calipers, or other instruments. The company does not want to send bad stuff to the customers.

For the lemonade stand, you want to be sure that everybody is getting an equal amount of lemonade. If one person receives 8 ounces and another person receives 12 ounces, you are bound to disappoint some of your customers. An inspector might weigh 3 glasses of lemonade to be sure that everybody is getting the right amount. If the target is 12 ounces, then we want to be sure that everybody is getting about 12 ounces of lemonade.

BASIC STATISTICS

Everyone should know some basic statistics. This type of mathematics is used to analyze multiple data points. The **average** is a measurement of accuracy. The **standard deviation** is a measurement of precision. Let us say that an inspector weighs or measures three glasses of lemonade and obtains these measurements: 11 ounces, 12 ounces, and 13 ounces. Since the average of the three values is 12 ounces, the target has been achieved accurately. However, two of the glasses deviate from the average by a little bit.

Deviation 1 = 1 ounce
Deviation 2 = 0 ounces
Deviation 3 = 1 ounce

The **average deviation** is calculated by simply adding up the deviations and dividing by 3. The average deviation is 2/3 or .667. The standard deviation is a little more complicated, but it is obtained by measuring the average spread of the datapoint around the average. In this case, the standard deviation is 1.

Suppose you owned a business that manufactured baseballs. The specification for the diameter of the ball required by the Major League Baseball association is 73-75 mm. The target diameter would be 74 mm. A ball with a diameter of 72 mm would be too small, and a ball with a diameter of 76 mm would be too big. Now, suppose you have three machines making the balls, and your inspectors measure the diameter of ten balls, and this is what they find:

Machine 1	Machine 2	Machine 3
73	74	76
74	74	76
73	74	74
72	74	73
75	73	74
73	74	75
74	75	75
73	74	75
74	74	75
76	74	72

	Machine 1	Machine 2	Machine 3
Target	74	74	74
Average	73.7	74	74.5
Standard Deviation	1.155	0.471	1.269
How many bad balls?	2	0	3
Is this accurate?	Average is a little low	Yes	Average is a little high
Is this precise?	No	Yes	No

You can see that Machine #1 and Machine #3 made two and three bad balls respectively. These balls do not meet specification, so you will have to throw them away. Two or three bad baseballs out of ten is a very bad scrap rate. With such bad manufacturing, you would have to inspect every baseball and throw away the bad ones. To throw away 20%-30% of everything you made would be a terrible waste, and a company that made bad products like this would go out of business right away. With such lousy manufacturing, the inspectors would probably also miss some of the bad product and ship some of the defects to the customers.

Modern industry has worked hard to produce high levels of quality since the early 1980s. Companies will often shoot for what they call **6-sigma** or *6-standard deviation* production. This means that these companies are hoping to only produce three bad products out of a million. Given that kind of precision and accuracy, companies don't have to provide much inspection. Wouldn't it be nice if plumbers would get it right almost every time, by only rarely making a mistake? What if they made a leaky pipe junction only three times in a million? Wouldn't it be nice if there were only three bad baseballs produced per million? But how can you develop this kind of quality in your business?

PRODUCING HIGH LEVELS OF QUALITY (ACCURACY AND PRECISION)

> Then this Daniel distinguished himself above the governors and satraps, because an excellent spirit was in him; and the king gave thought to setting him over the whole realm. (Dan. 6:3)
>
> Do you see a man who excels in his work?
> He will stand before kings;
> He will not stand before unknown men. (Prov. 22:29)

Quality products and services are produced by quality work, which can only come from quality workers. The most important way to achieve quality in a business is to hire conscientious people. More than just hard working people, these workers excel in quality work. They are more conscientious about their work than others. They love their customers and fellow employees, as they love themselves. They obey the golden rule as a regular practice. They sincerely want to meet and exceed the expectations of their customers.

Consider the lawn care business for example. Typical complaints for lawn maintenance companies include the following – all of which can be traced to unconscientious employees.

1. The lawn guys left the gate open, and my dog ran off.
2. They don't answer the phone.
3. They break things and neglect to tell the customer. (Honesty really does pay off. If the lawn maintenance crews confess and offer to fix the thing they broke, they have a 99% chance they'll keep the job. If they don't, they have a 99% chance they'll lose the job.)
4. They are characteristically late to the job.
5. They missed a spot while cutting the lawn.
6. They leave a mess behind—debris on the sidewalk and the windowsills.
7. They are not clear with their prices, and they do not explain pre-

cisely what they will do for the customer.
8. They forget about special requests made by the client.
9. Their customer service is rude or condescending.
10. They don't respond to complaints right away.
11. They dilute the fertilizer to save money.
12. They don't improve the lawn by controlling crabgrass, dandelions, and other nuisances.

Now, this is just one example of a business that will lose business or win more business on the basis of quality. Conscientious workers will correct problems like these, and work hard to avoid making these mistakes.

Lawn care company

There are several other ways to improve the quality of your product or service.
1. Improve the original design or the recipe (if it is food), or the architectural blueprint (if it is a building). In many cases, the design itself is flawed. If that is improved upon, the company could get much higher quality and better customer satisfaction.

   Before taking a product to market, it's a good idea to put the first samples through rigorous testing. This is especially important for computer programs, for example. Manufactured products should be put through every possible environment in which they will be used. You might also test other comparable products and see how your product stands up to your competition. Rushing something to market before it has been tested is usually an indication of excessive pride or greed.

2. Improve on the construction, manufacturing, or cooking and serving process. Find ways to improve the consistency of the process. This may involve training the worker to do the same thing in the same way every time.

    This is the secret of success for the fast food industry. For example, every burger is cooked for the exact same length of time. Every bun is equally fresh. The chicken sandwich always gets three pickles. Every table is cleaned every thirty minutes whether it needs it or not. Every restroom is cleaned every two hours.

3. Provide and maintain good tooling for those who are producing the product or service. Keep an eye on the tools for any wear and tear or broken parts. For example, screw bits can wear down as you screw down a deck. This can result in a stripped screw head and a defective attachment.

4. Take every customer complaint seriously, no matter how minor it may appear to be. If somebody complains of a defective product (whether a toy or a sandwich or something else), a quality-minded business will go over it carefully. Sometimes, whole teams of people will study the customer complaints. They will try to fix the root problem for the complaints by adjusting and re-adjusting the design or the process.

Suppose that a customer returned his lemonade to your stand, complaining that it tasted rotten. You look into the bag of lemons and, sure enough, you discover that one of the stores selling lemons gave you rotten lemons. Of course, you must follow up on this. So you meet with the grocer and point out the problem. Finally, you decide to purchase lemons from another store, and this fixes the problem for your customers.

Faithful businesses are not afraid of evil reports. No matter how bad the report, Christians must be willing to hear about it. They are not afraid

Feedback from customers is valuable in improving your products and services.

of evil reports because they fear God and because they trust that God will help them through even the worst of situations.

> Praise the LORD!
> Blessed is the man who fears the LORD,
> Who delights greatly in His commandments.
> His descendants will be mighty on earth;
> The generation of the upright will be blessed.
>
> Wealth and riches will be in his house,
> And his righteousness endures forever. . . .
> He will not be afraid of evil tidings;
> His heart is steadfast, trusting in the LORD. (Ps. 112:1-3, 7)

PROFIT AND PROFITABILITY

A successful business will yield profit. If the lemonade business is spending $300 on lemons, sugar, and other supplies but only earns $290, the business is not successful.

Monetary profit is the amount of money made on a business venture. To calculate the amount of profit earned in a lemonade business, take the gross sales and subtract the cost of goods, which would include lemons, sugar, ice, cups, and anything you paid your employees. The profitability ratio is your profit divided by the amount of total sales. If you made $5,000 in sales and earned $1,000 in profit from these sales, your profitability ratio would be 20%.

Profitability = $1000/$5000 = 20%.

But, be careful. Profit and benefit in your business or ministry is not always measured by money. Some things yield eternal value. For example, consider a person who invests $100,000 in an evangelistic and discipleship outreach of a church. Five souls were saved after five years of work. Was this a good monetary investment? What is the eternal benefit of a single soul saved? Some things can't be measured by money.

In some cases the profit you get out of your work is an improvement for human life and the benefit of humanity here and now. At other times, the profit of our work will only be seen five or ten years from now, after a great deal of development and capital costs of time and money have been put into it. The anticipated long-term benefit of the development makes the long-term investment worthwhile.

For some risk takers or entrepreneurs, the profit comes by **"residual accounts"** or time savings in the future. Insurance salesmen, for example, will sell an account with the intent that people will keep buying insurance from them year after year.

> But his lord answered and said to him, "You wicked and lazy servant, you knew that I reap where I have not sown, and gather where I have not scattered seed. So you ought to have deposited my money with the bankers, and at my coming I would have received back my own with interest. So take the talent from him, and give it to him who has ten talents." (Matt. 25:26-28)

As a general principle, God blesses wise investors with monetary profit. This is the point made in the parable of the talents. The unwise investor lost his talent to the better investor. These wise risk takers walk away with profit. But this profit only increases the amount of money over which the investor is made responsible. When those who are proven to be wise investors earn a profit, the increase should be funneled into better and better investments. Productive producers are only using their resources to serve more people, to provide more charity where needed, and to hire more people into good jobs.

This principle is stated another way in the parable of the minas (Luke 19). Those who have been faithful with little are given more to manage. This parable applies to spiritual gifts, but the same general principle may be applied to physical gifts and capital holdings.

> Therefore He said: "A certain nobleman went into a far country to receive for himself a kingdom and to return. So he called ten of his servants, delivered to them ten minas, and said to them, 'Do business till I come.' But his citizens hated him, and sent a delegation after him, saying, 'We will not have this man to reign over us.'
>
> "And so it was that when he returned, having received the kingdom, he then commanded these servants, to whom he had given the money, to be called to him, that he might know how much every man had gained by trading. Then came the first, saying, 'Master, your mina has earned ten minas.' And he said to him, 'Well done, good servant; because you were faithful in a very little, have authority over ten cities.'" (Luke 19:12-17)

Successful people are tempted to use their money on themselves for their own pleasures. But profit is not to be "consumed on your pleasures." While we may enjoy the fruits of our labors with thanksgiving, these fruits must never become a means of stirring up our lusts, idolatry, and pride.

Profit should be put into more tools, more innovation, and more producing capabilities. Since the market is always changing, and since sales for one particular product may dry up, the risk taker/businessman must be ready to adapt. He will have to use his profit to develop new ideas, new tools, and new products to meet new customer needs. You can see that profit is necessary to pay for all these future investments. Profit keeps the economic ball rolling year to year and generation to generation.

> You lust and do not have. You murder and covet and cannot obtain. You fight and war. Yet you do not have because you do not ask. You ask and do not receive, because you ask amiss, that you may spend it on your pleasures. (Jas. 4:2-3)

EXPLOITATIVE CAPITALISM

> Now there was no bread in all the land; for the famine was very severe, so that the land of Egypt and the land of Canaan languished because of the famine. And Joseph gathered up all the money that was found in the land of Egypt and in the land of Canaan, for the grain which they bought; and Joseph brought the money into Pharaoh's house. So when the money failed in the land of Egypt and in the land of Canaan, all the Egyptians came to Joseph and said, "Give us bread, for why should we die in your presence? For the money has failed."
>
> Then Joseph said, "Give your livestock, and I will give you bread for your livestock, if the money is gone." So they brought their livestock to Joseph, and Joseph gave them bread in exchange for the horses, the flocks, the cattle of the herds, and for the donkeys. Thus he fed them with bread in exchange for all their livestock that year. When that year had ended, they came to him the next year and said to him, "We will not hide from my lord that our money is gone; my lord also has our herds of livestock. There is nothing left in the sight of my lord but our bodies and our lands. Why should we die before your eyes, both we and our land? Buy us and our land for bread, and we and our land will be servants of Pharaoh; give us seed, that we may live and not die, that the land may not be desolate."

> Then Joseph bought all the land of Egypt for Pharaoh; for every man of the Egyptians sold his field, because the famine was severe upon them. So the land became Pharaoh's. (Gen. 47:13-20)

Are there points at which people take too much profit in their business? This appears to be the case in this account of Joseph and the famine in Egypt. The lack of innovation and preparation on the part of others resulted in a monopoly of grain sales. A monopoly is defined as the "exclusive possession or control of the supply of or trade in a product" (like grains). In this case, the monopoly was held by the Pharaoh. The end result was that the Pharaoh owned all the property, and the Egyptians were all made slaves to him.

The Word of God does not condemn Joseph for this program. However, the Bible does condemn robbing the poor or taking undue advantage of them by deceit. As we have already pointed out, powerful companies can get the government on their side, obtain exorbitant debt or special government benefits, and squeeze out the little guy—the little businesses.

> "The people of the land have used oppressions, committed robbery, and mistreated the poor and needy; and they wrongfully oppress the stranger. So I sought for a man among them who would make a wall, and stand in the gap before Me on behalf of the land, that I should not destroy it; but I found no one. Therefore I have poured out My indignation on them; I have consumed them with the fire of My wrath; and I have recompensed their deeds on their own heads," says the Lord GOD. (Eze. 22:29-31)

> He who oppresses the poor to increase his riches,
> And he who gives to the rich, will surely come to poverty...
> Do not rob the poor because he is poor,
> Nor oppress the afflicted at the gate;
> For the LORD will plead their cause,
> And plunder the soul of those who plunder them. (Prov. 22:16, 22-23)

> The LORD stands up to plead,
> And stands to judge the people.
> The LORD will enter into judgment
> With the elders of His people and His princes:
> "For you have eaten up the vineyard;
> The plunder of the poor is in your houses.
> What do you mean by crushing My people
> And grinding the faces of the poor?"
> Says the Lord GOD of hosts. (Isa. 3:13-15)

Ezekiel and Isaiah condemned the princes for robbing the poor. These governors used their power of taxation to further impoverish the lower and middle classes of society. In some cases, greedy government officials like Ahab confiscated the property of others (like Naboth).

Yet the Bible warns us not to starve the poor or enslave the poor. Joseph's situation was unique in that the Egyptians were reduced to slavery. If the poor are unable to afford basic necessities like food and clothing, then Christian businessmen have a responsibility to care for them.

> If you extend your soul to the hungry
> And satisfy the afflicted soul,
> Then your light shall dawn in the darkness,
> And your darkness shall be as the noonday. (Isa. 58:10)

We obtain a better understanding of God's will for the poor in Nehemiah 5. Evidently, the Lord does not want rich people or government programs to force the poor into slavery. It was taxation and starvation (or the lack of grain) that was the problem. The government should never encourage debt or even mortgages on homes. Rich people should stop short of confiscating people's property in order to provide them with food. Before this happens, the wealthy among us have the responsibility to provide charitable donations to the poor.

> And there was a great outcry of the people and their wives against their Jewish brethren. For there were those who said, "We, our sons,

> and our daughters are many; therefore let us get grain, that we may eat and live." There were also some who said, "We have mortgaged our lands and vineyards and houses, that we might buy grain because of the famine."
>
> There were also those who said, "We have borrowed money for the king's tax on our lands and vineyards. Yet now our flesh is as the flesh of our brethren, our children as their children; and indeed we are forcing our sons and our daughters to be slaves, and some of our daughters have been brought into slavery. It is not in our power to redeem them, for other men have our lands and vineyards." . . .
>
> So I called a great assembly against them. And I said to them, "According to our ability we have redeemed our Jewish brethren who were sold to the nations. Now indeed, will you even sell your brethren? Or should they be sold to us?"
>
> Then they were silenced and found nothing to say. Then I said, "What you are doing is not good. Should you not walk in the fear of our God because of the reproach of the nations, our enemies? I also, with my brethren and my servants, am lending them money and grain. Please, let us stop this usury! Restore now to them, even this day, their lands, their vineyards, their olive groves, and their houses, also a hundredth of the money and the grain, the new wine and the oil, that you have charged them." (Neh. 5:1-11)

ENCOURAGING COMPETITION

Economies today include monopolies, oligopolies, and healthy competition. As far as a nation runs on government-favored monopolies, the poor will be oppressed, and the economy will suffer greatly.

We don't live in a perfect world. But, to the extent that an economy approaches high levels of competition, that nation will be blessed with prosperity. Optimum competition will have the following features:

1. A maximum number of independently owned and operated businesses.
2. A maximum number of independent buyers or consumers.
3. A relative ease of entering the market; a condition which occurs when there is minimal government regulation, red tape, big capital costs, or legal limitations due to patents.
4. All firms maintain an equally high level of quality, and there are almost no differences between the product offered. (A lemonade stand would qualify for this.)
5. Information concerning the product prices are easily accessible. (Gas stations would qualify for this, in that the prices are usually advertised prominently at the pumps. The internet has also helped with this by providing ready information concerning prices of goods and services.)

Price signs like gas station pricing enable open competition between different businesses.

A MONOPOLY ON OIL

The Bible would not have condemned John D. Rockefeller's monopoly on oil processing in the 19th century. For millennia, people had used whale oil, fish oil, or olive oil for their lamps. With the rise of the automobile and the need for oil and gas, John D. Rockefeller (1839-1937) brought together innovation and business skills to provide cheap oil for everyday use. He started out in 1867 by developing a better way to refine oil into something usable (especially for household lighting). Rockefeller was a faithful member and sometimes Sunday school teacher at Erie Street Baptist Mission Church in Chicago, Illinois.

John D. Rockefeller's Standard Oil Company found highly efficient ways to process oil. In 1870, the company controlled 4% of the refined oil business. But by 1880, Rockefeller was able to take 85% of the market.[92] As Rockefeller's company dropped the price of oil, Americans replaced their whale oil lights with kerosene fuel. As Rockefeller secured a high percentage of the oil market, some political leaders in the country cried "foul!"

John D. Rockefeller (1839-1937)

Robert Fulton (1765-1815)

The concern was that Rockefeller had created an unfair monopoly over the oil industry. But was this an unfair monopoly? Or was the monopoly caused by Rockefeller's innovations and his exceptional business methods? If Rockefeller's company had been involved in predatory pricing or withholding production, these would have been a violation of biblical principle. But this was not found to be the case. By the time the US Supreme Court forced Standard Oil to break up in 1911, the company's control over oil had already subsided from 90% to 65% of the industry.

Not all monopolies are ethical. In some cases, governments created monopolies out of private companies. For example, New York State gave **Robert Fulton** a thirty-year monopoly on steamboat traffic. **Cornelius Vanderbilt** forced his way into the steamboat traffic business in 1817 and broke the monopoly. In 1847, another steamboat company president, Edward K. Collins, asked for subsidies from the US Congress for a cross-Atlantic transport.

Cornelius Vanderbilt (1794-1877)

Congress agreed, and for a while Collins enjoyed a monopoly. Vanderbilt broke the monopoly again with his own private line of ships, and Collins was out of business by 1858. Much of the railroad industry was also built on government-sponsored monopolies. For the nation's first cross-continental railroad, the United States Congress subsidized two companies: the Union Pacific and the Central Pacific. The two companies building the railroad joined the tracks on May 10th, 1869. With government subsidies, of course, came government regulations. And this resulted in terrible inefficiencies and a breakdown in quality of service and production.

However, the railroads were not all built on government programs. An entrepreneur named **James J. Hill** built his own railroads, including the Great Northern Railway, without government assistance (completed in 1893). His railroads came to be known as the "best constructed and most profitable of all the world's major railroads."[93] Hill supplied the farmers along his route with seed. In turn, the farmers used his trains to transport their goods.

When a product or service is first developed by some creative inventor, a monopoly on that particular resource may continue for a while. That was the case with Rockefeller's Standard Oil. The concern with monopolies is that the company might price their product too high. However, Rockefeller was still faced with competition from whale oil or olive oil. Also, other companies were fast developing their own creative solutions for processing oil. It was just a matter of time before somebody would identify a better way to process oil.

Moreover, it doesn't always make sense to drive the price too high. Suppose that Joe was the only guitar teacher in town. At first, he charged $30 per lesson for 15 students, producing about $450 per week. But Joe figured out that if he charged $20 per lesson, he could increase his clientele to 40 and thereby earn $800 per week. Lowering the price per lesson increased his gross income each month and gave him enough to live on.

OLIGOPOLIES

Another economic mode, the oligopoly is a market dominated by only a few producers. This scarcity of businesses is usually due to the many barriers that prevent entrepreneurs from entering into business. These could be legal barriers limiting entry due to patents. For example, the first X-ray or

Boeing 747

MRI machines would have secured a patent. A patent is an official government license giving the inventor the exclusive right to provide the invention to a market for a period of time. The patent provides financial reward to the inventor for his research and development of the product.

There are also expensive tooling requirements for some products, and there are government regulations that make it difficult to get into business.

Automobile and jet manufacturing are good examples of oligopolies. Anybody can open a lemonade stand. Not many people can start producing automobiles and jets. There are only five major producers of commercial jets in the world—Airbus, Boeing, Bombardier, Embraer, and Tupoloev.

CONCLUSION

> If a man steals an ox or a sheep, and slaughters it or sells it, he shall restore five oxen for an ox and four sheep for a sheep. If the thief is found breaking in, and he is struck so that he dies, there shall be no guilt for his bloodshed. If the sun has risen on him, there shall be guilt for his bloodshed. He should make full restitution; if he has nothing, then he shall be sold for his theft. If the theft is certainly found alive in his hand, whether it is an ox or donkey or sheep, he shall restore double. (Ex. 22:1-4)

When it comes to the free market, the more competition the merrier. Governments should stay out of the way and minimize all regulation of business. The government's role is to act as a referee. If a business breaks God's rules and gets involved in criminal activity, the government is called to prosecute the evildoer (Rom. 13:1-4). Actually, the Bible does not recommend sending these criminals to jail, where the taxpayers have to pay for their room and board. Instead, God's law requires those who steal to pay restitution to those whom they have robbed. The state should compensate the victims instead of forcing the victims and other taxpayers to pay more money for the room and board of the criminals who broke the law.

Individuals, colleges, and governments may arrive at their own conclusions as to what is fair and what isn't fair in economics, and they will defend their position with great vehemence. Is it fair that John D. Rockefeller turned into the richest man in the world, with a net worth of $420 billion? Was his monopoly over oil processing legitimate and fair? People will argue these matters a great deal. But only the Word of God could possibly give a definitive answer to these questions. God's law must provide the final determination as to what is fair and what is not fair. As Christians, we are called to keep the commandments of God (Rev. 14:12). This is the standard by which we will regulate our businesses and civil governments. We are called to judge all things by God's law, as has been exemplified in this study.

The law of the LORD is perfect, converting the soul;
The testimony of the LORD is sure, making wise the simple;
The statutes of the LORD are right, rejoicing the heart;
The commandment of the LORD is pure, enlightening the eyes;
The fear of the LORD is clean, enduring forever;
The judgments of the LORD are true and righteous altogether.
More to be desired are they than gold,
Yea, than much fine gold;
Sweeter also than honey and the honeycomb.
Moreover by them Your servant is warned,
And in keeping them there is great reward. (Ps. 19:7-11)

11

MAKING WISE PURCHASING CHOICES

> Who can find a virtuous wife?
> For her worth is far above rubies.
> The heart of her husband safely trusts her;
> So he will have no lack of gain.
> She does him good and not evil
> All the days of her life.
> She seeks wool and flax,
> And willingly works with her hands.
> She is like the merchant ships,
> She brings her food from afar.
> She also rises while it is yet night,
> And provides food for her household,
> And a portion for her maidservants.
> She considers a field and buys it;
> From her profits she plants a vineyard. (Prov. 31:10-16)

Spending money is as important as earning money. Here again, God calls us to faithful stewardship. Earning money is a matter of stewarding time, while spending involves stewarding money. God gives us time to work and money to spend. All of this we must handle wisely. The virtuous wife described in Proverbs 31 is wise in her assessment of value. "She considers a field and buys it, and from her profits she plants a vineyard." She knows where to purchase good food, and she finds the raw materials necessary to knit cloth and make a sweater.

God calls us to be good stewards, but He also calls us to give generously and to diligently provide for those in our care. A young man who gets married is responsible for taking care of the material well-being of his family. If he neglects that responsibility, he has "denied the faith and he is worse than an unbeliever" (1 Tim. 5:8). We don't want to be spendthrifts. But we also want to avoid becoming miserly and ungenerous with our money and falling into the opposite ditch.

> No one can serve two masters, for either he will hate the one and love the other, or he will be devoted to the one and despise the other. You cannot serve God and money. (Matt. 6:24)

> Therefore, my beloved, flee from idolatry. (1 Cor. 10:14)

The person who values money more than God, and proceeds to break God's laws to get more of it, has turned money into an idol. Some folks prioritize money over relationships. Often, marriages are torn apart by arguments over money. Husbands and wives may have different priorities in mind for the household budget. The husband may wish to spend $3,000 on a nice vacation, while the wife would rather spend it on clothes and shoes for the children, for example. Money can be an implement of destruction. But genuine love for God and sacrificial love for one another will put money in its right place. Seeking God's will first in prayer is critical before

Budgeting is an important part of financial stewardship.

considering the spending priorities in the household budget.

What does a family do if they are not earning enough money to pay the bills? Or what does a young couple do if they are unable to save for something important like a car or a home? There are only two ways to save more money. Either they can earn more money or just spend less. Some husbands may have to take on a second job to make a little more income. But a more careful handling of money and expenses can help tremendously, and that is the subject of this chapter.

AVERAGE EXPENSES

Your average expenses will vary depending on whether you are married or not. The average monthly household budget in America is offered below. The biggest ticket items are housing, transportation, and insurance.

AVERAGE MONTHLY HOUSEHOLD BUDGET
US Average Household Budget Itemized

Item	Monthly cost	Percentage of spending
Housing	$1,674	32.8%
Transportation	$813	15.9%
Personal insurance and pensions	$608	11.9%
Healthcare	$414	8.1%
Groceries	$372	7.3%
Restaurants and other meals on the road	$288	5.6%
Entertainment	$269	5.3%
Other	$169	3.3%
Cash contributions	$157	3.1%
Apparel and services	$156	3.1%
Education	$117	2.3%
Personal care	$64	1.3%
TOTAL SPENDING	**$5,102**	

ASSESSING VALUE

Before making purchases, the Proverbs 31 woman and the 1 Timothy 5:8 man must know something about assessing value. And also, they must first decide whether they really need the product. Wise purchasers are not impulsive buyers. They don't respond to flashy advertisements. That is, they want to be sure that they will get good use out of the product before they buy it. They will assess the value for themselves. And they will consider the quality of the product itself.

A broken bicycle.

Quality is usually your best value, especially if you intend to use the product for more than a year or two. For example, a bicycle should last for at least ten years even under tough conditions. Yet, the average bicycle is a complex assembly of over a thousand parts. Moving parts take a lot of wear and tear, and that includes the brakes, chain, cranks, pedals, sprockets, derailers, wheels, and the gear shifts. A poorly built bicycle might be outfitted with wobbly wheels, poorly adjusted brakes, cheap tires, cheap metal parts, or super heavy or badly fitting parts. All of this would inhibit the bike's movements and durability. The cleats might break off of cheap pedals. Badly adjusted or badly built gears might also jump easily. And cheap shock absorbers could easily bottom out with more intense bumps in the road, making for a very uncomfortable ride. To give you the most speed for the least effort, you want something lightweight, outfitted with dropped handlebars and skinny tires. A good street bike will weigh 17-18 pounds (7.7-8.2 kg). Cheaper street bikes weigh 35-40 pounds (14-18 kg) and run about a third of the price of a good street bike.

If a bike with an aluminum frame lasts for ten years, and a bike with a

Carbon frame bicycle

carbon or titanium frame lasts about forty years, how much would you pay for a bike with the more expensive frame? It might be worthwhile to pay twice the amount for a higher quality bike if it would last longer.

The durability of US cars improved quite a bit between 1980 and 2020. The lifespan of the average car was only 8.4 years in 1995. Twenty-five years later, the average new car would run for 11.9 years.[94] Throughout the 1990s and 2000s, Japanese-manufactured cars generally lasted longer than American-made cars. However, American trucks and SUV's rated high in durability studies. The following table records different models of cars and the percentage of them that made it to 200,000 miles.

Toyota Land Cruiser

Most Durable Passenger Vehicles Manufactured in the 2000s[95]		
Rank	Model	% of Cars Over 200k Miles
1	Toyota Land Cruiser	15.7%
2	Toyota Sequoia	9.2%
3	Ford Expedition	5.2%
4	Chevrolet Suburban	4.9%
5	Toyota Highlander Hybrid	4.2%
6	Chevrolet Tahoe	4.1%
7	GMC Yukon XL	4.1%
8	Toyota 4Runner	3.9%
9	GMC Yukon	3.2%
10	Honda Ridgeline	3.0%
11	Toyota Tundra	2.9%
12	Honda Odyssey	2.7%
13	Toyota Avalon	2.6%
14	Lincoln Navigator	2.6%
15	Toyota Tacoma	2.5%
Average for All Models		1.0%

The most reliable used cars on the market which are most likely to make it to 200,000 miles are listed by order of durability in the following table. If you wanted to buy a used car, the Honda Odyssey, the Toyota Avalon, and the Honda Civic are your best value (by durability).

MAKING WISE PURCHASING CHOICES 352

Honda Odyssey

Best Value for Used Passenger Cars[96]		
Rank	Model	% of Cars Over 200k Miles
1	Honda Odyssey	2.7%
2	Toyota Avalon	2.6%
3	Honda Civic	2.3%
4	Toyota Sienna	2.0%
5	Toyota Prius	2.0%
6	Honda Accord	1.8%
7	Mercedes-Benz E-Class	1.7%
8	Chevrolet Impala	1.6%
9	Toyota Camry	1.5%
10	Toyota Camry Hybrid	1.5%
Average for All Passenger Cars		**0.7%**

The least reliable cars according to consumer studies were the models Ford Focus, Ford Fiesta, Chrysler 200, Dodge Charger, Ford Mustang, Dodge Grand Caravan, the Cadillac Escalade, and the Jeep Cherokee SUV.[97]

If you are a young man or woman purchasing your first car, you should look for durability and reliability. You don't need a lot of bells and whistles, and you shouldn't waste your money on a new car. Most new cars will depreciate by about 15% in the first year, and 5% per year after that. Depreciation is the loss of value that occurs year by year. Unlike houses, cars lose their value year by year. This depreciation is illustrated for three different types of vehicles in the attached chart.

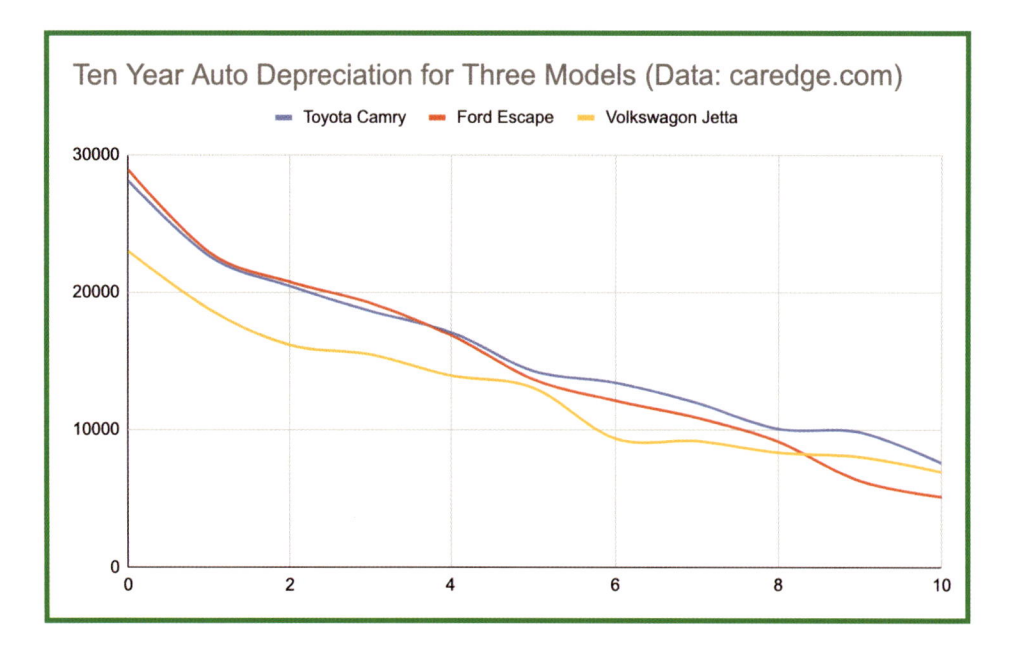

Ten Year Auto Depreciation for Three Models (Data: caredge.com)
— Toyota Camry — Ford Escape — Volkswagon Jetta

When purchasing a car, keep in mind that some cars lose their value quicker than others. For example, if you bought a brand new Nissan LEAF for $20,000, you would only get $7,000 out of it if you sold it five years later (according to Iseecars.com).[98] But then, if you bought a brand new Jeep Wrangler for $29,000, you could sell it for $26,500 five years later. The Jeep Wrangler retains its value far better than the Nissan LEAF. The following table lists several of the best cars and worst cars for retaining value.

Best and Worst New Cars for Depreciation[99]

Type of Vehicle	Car Model	Average 5 Year Depreciation
Electric Car	Nissan LEAF	65%
Small SUV	Ford Escape	50%
Small SUV	Jeep Wrangler	9%
Compact	Nissan Sentra	44%
Compact	Honda Civic	30%
Midsize	Nissan Ultima	49%
Midsize	Honda According	39%
Truck	Nissan Titan XD	39%
Truck	Toyota Tundra	19%

Unless you know how to fix cars, your highest value will be reliability. You don't want to pay a ton of money on maintenance. Some models often require more maintenance than others. Let's suppose you are shopping for a six-year-old used car. Assuming you will drive the car about 15,000 miles per year, compare the following options for purchasing your first car.

	2015 Ford Focus	2015 Toyota Camry	2015 Hyundai Accent
Price in 2021	$14,000	$16,000	$13,000
6 Years' Maintenance	$13,000	$6,600	$9,000
Miles Per Gallon	29 mpg (city)	25 mpg (city)	27 mpg (city)
Gas (90,000 miles)	$10,860	$12,600	$11,600
Total Costs for 6 Years	$37,860	$28,600	$33,600
Average Cost Per Year	$6,310	$4,767	$5,600

Based on this comparison, you would save more than $9,000 over six years if you purchased a more expensive Toyota Camry over the Ford Focus. Because the 2015 Ford Focus and Hyundai Accent were more inexpensive, you might have been tempted to purchase these over the Camry. But you need to consider the reliability of each vehicle. Of course, the maintenance costs might be less expensive if you do the work yourself, but you still have to take into account your time and effort. You don't want to spend more time under the car than in it!

Toyota Camry

Average Maintenance Costs by Auto Manufacturer[100]

Based On Maintenance Costs for the First 150,000 Miles for All Popular Makes

Rank	Make	Cost First 150k Miles
1	Scion	$10,400
2	Toyota	$11,100
3	Honda	$14,300
4	Subaru	$14,400
5	Lexus	$14,700
6	Hyundai	$15,000

Average Maintenance Costs by Auto Manufacturer[100]

Based On Maintenance Costs for the First 150,000 Miles for All Popular Makes

Rank	Make	Cost First 150k Miles
7	Nissan	$15,000
8	Mazda	$15,100
9	Kia	$15,100
10	Volkswagen	$15,300
11	Infiniti	$16,900
12	Mini	$17,500
13	GMC	$18,100
14	Chevrolet	$18,900
15	Acura	$19,000
16	Mitsubishi	$19,000
17	Jeep	$19,400
18	Audi	$21,200
19	Ford	$21,700
20	Buick	$22,300
21	Volvo	$22,600
22	Dodge	$22,900
23	Chrysler	$23,000
24	Mercedes-Benz	$23,600
25	Saturn	$26,100
26	Pontiac	$24,200
27	Cadillac	$25,700
28	Lincoln	$28,100
29	BMW	$28,600

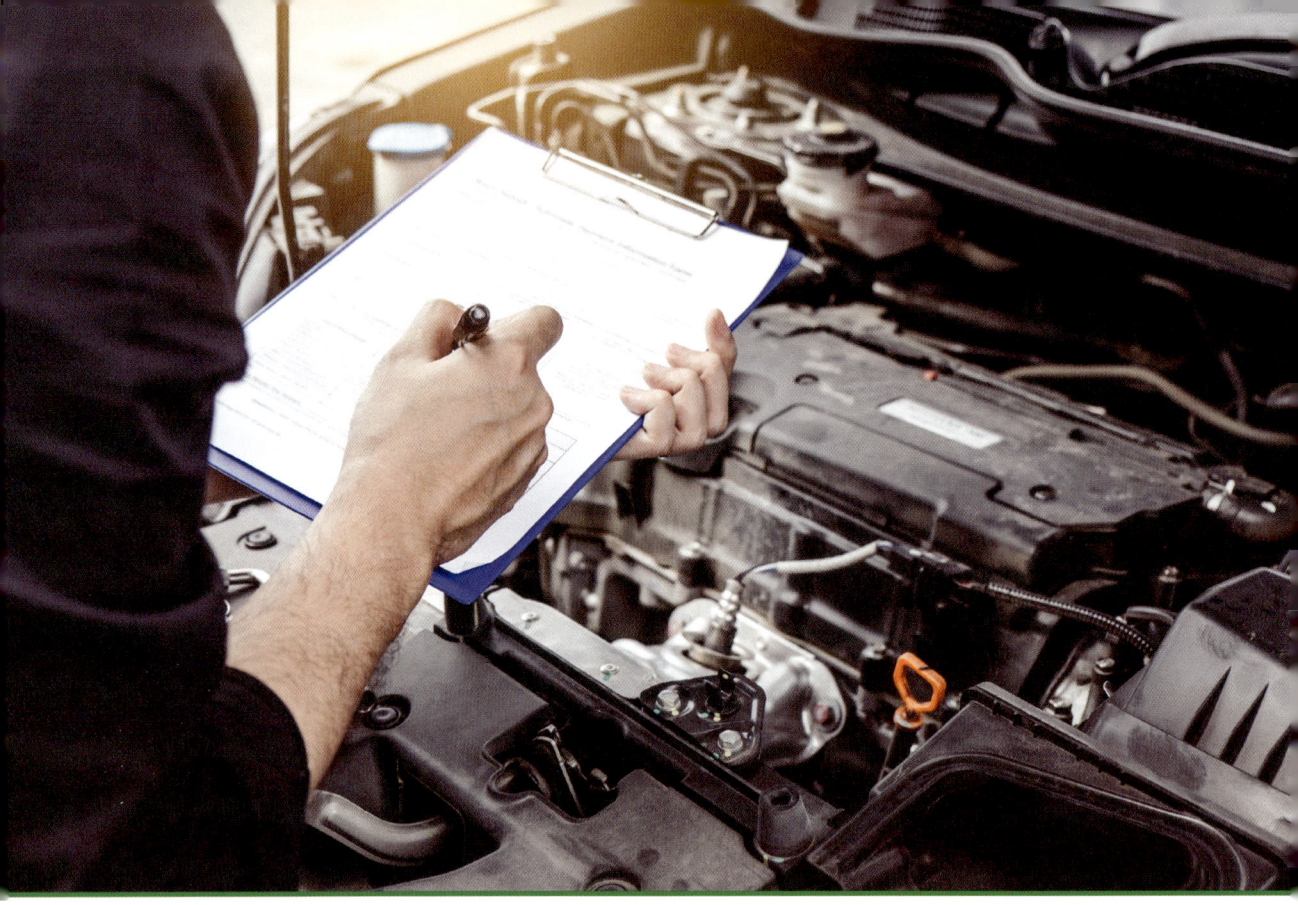

Car inspection

WHAT TO LOOK FOR WHEN PURCHASING A CAR

For most young people just starting out, your automobile purchase and maintenance will be your largest expense. A good discipline for such purchases is to work off a checklist. This prevents an impulsive purchase which you would regret later. Included on the list should be:

1. Inspection of the outside and inside of the car. Small dings and scratches are not all that bad. But be concerned about rusted areas and dents.
2. Open and close the hood, trunk, and doors. Listen for any scraping noises.
3. Check for paint overspray on the inside of the hood or trunk. This gives you some clue as to whether the car has been repainted or repaired (after being involved in an accident).

4. Smell for musty odors, cigarette odors, or excessive air fresheners. Smell the seats for any strange odors. When the air freshener wears out, you might discover the car was owned by a smoker. Check the floor mats for possible leaks.
5. Inspect the seats, upholstery, and floor mats for wear and tear.
6. Take the car for a test drive.

   a. Turn the key to the "accessory" position, and make sure all the dashboard warning lights light up. If they don't, there may be a problem with the electrical system.

   b. The two most important elements of the mechanics of the car are the engine and transmission. Drive the car at different speeds. Accelerate rapidly and make sure the transmission shifts smoothly.

   c. Check out as many of the electronics as possible, including lights, radio, horn, automatic windows, automatic mirrors, and AC fans. Listen for any strange engine noises.
7. Check for leaks after the car has run for a while. Black or brown fluid is usually oil. Green or yellow fluid indicates a radiator leak. A leak in the transmission system is usually indicated by reddish fluid.
8. Check the VIN number (usually located on the driver's door) and

Checking oil levels

run a vehicle history report on that number. This will cost you thirty to forty dollars, but it is well worth the investment. The NHTSA's Safety Issues and Recalls website will also tell you if there are any recall issues with the vehicle.

9. Run price comparisons on the Kelly Blue Book website, or do a web search for other similar vehicles for sale in your area. Be aware that vehicle prices vary throughout the country simply because demand may be higher in some areas than in others.

HOW TO AVOID GETTING CHEATED

> Also the schemes of the schemer are evil;
> He devises wicked plans
> To destroy the poor with lying words,
> Even when the needy speaks justice.
> But a generous man devises generous things,
> And by generosity he shall stand. (Is. 32:7-8)

Nobody wants to be cheated when making important and expensive purchases, but we do live in a sinful world. Young people making their first purchase are often naive, and they can be ripped off by used car salesmen. As followers of Jesus Christ, we have a duty before God to insist on honesty in the marketplace. As much as we commit to integrity and honesty when we are selling to others, we should equally insist upon it when others are selling to us. Stand your ground in every business transaction, regardless of the pressure to cut corners. Here are some of the common tricks used by slippery salesmen:

1. They advertise a price for a car, and then they show you another vehicle (of lesser value).
2. They might roll back the odometer to make it look like

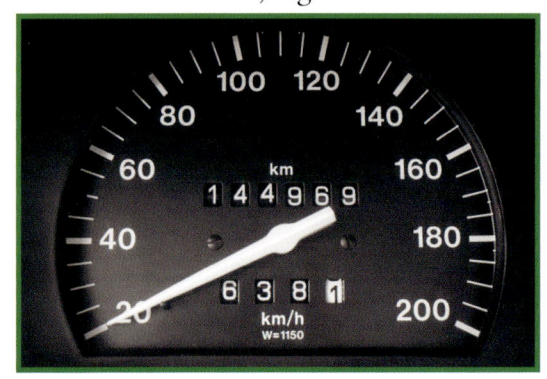

Car odometer

the car has less miles on it.
3. They might provide you with a fake maintenance history on the car. If the car has been in an accident and they cover this up, you could have bought yourself a lemon.
4. They might try to sell the car without allowing you to test drive it or have your mechanic inspect it first.
5. They might sell you a stolen car and then fail to give you a properly-signed title to the car. When buying a car, you need to connect with the current owner of the car as indicated on the title.

MAINTAINING YOUR CAR

When you are starting out in life, you should be saving your money. And you should do all that you can to reduce your expenses. As already mentioned, your highest expenses will be your transportation costs. How much could you save if you performed your own basic auto maintenance and repairs?

Car Maintenance Costs: Professional Service vs. Doing It Yourself			
Maintenance	*Frequency*	*Cost*	*DIY Cost*
Oil Change	2X per year	$80	$30
Brake Pad Replacement	1X every other year	$400	$75
Rotor Replacement	1X every four years	$500	$100
Spark Plug Replacement	1X every other year	$200	$20
Air Filter Replacement	1X per year	$100	$20
Lightbulb Replacement	1X per year	$120	$10
Repairs			
Alternator Replacement	1X per five years	$700	$100
Battery Replacement	1X per five years	$310	$90

Doing these fixes yourself would save you about $760 per year. You would spend about $140 per year on parts, while somebody who had a professional do the work would be spending about $900 per year on parts and labor. However, you do need to budget a little extra time in your schedule to do this work. Most of these tasks wouldn't take more than an hour of time to do. Do-it-yourself videos are plentiful on the internet these days. So, if you have the initiative to figure out how to do these simple tasks, you could save a lot of money.

Replacing spark plugs on a car.

INSURANCE

Just starting out in life, your most expensive costs are going to be automobiles and insurance. Auto insurance rates can vary widely. For a twenty-five-year-old driver, rates vary from $1,200 to $2,400 per year. The best way to save on insurance is to avoid traffic tickets and accidents. Be a safe driver. Some of the best ways to save on auto insurance is to:
- Stay on your parents' auto insurance policy

- Take a safe driving course as recommended by your insurance company
- Maintain high grades in school

Medical insurance for a family of four runs $28,166 per year. A single person pays about $6,000 per year. Using a Christian Medical Sharing ministry, that single person would pay only about $2,000 per year, and the family would pay $6,000 per year.[101] This means a family could realize a substantial annual savings by choosing a Christian Medical Sharing ministry instead of conventional medical insurance.

Just basing our calculations on wise spending for health insurance, automobiles, and automobile maintenance, the average single person could save $7,460 per year or $45,000 over six years. A married couple with a few kids (and two cars) would save $175,000 in just six years! That would pay for about 50% of the cost of the average house in America in today's values. And, so far, we have not even covered the biggest ticket item in a family budget.

HOW TO BUY A HOUSE

Housing is the biggest investment or expenditure the average family will make in a lifetime. Some people will rent a home, while others will buy their home. Wise financial decisions here could significantly reduce costs for a family.

When purchasing real estate, the most important thing to remember is the importance of location. Within the same town, a three-bedroom home could sell for twice as much in one location as it would in another. In some cases, the location is desirable because of nicer views, better foliage, more mature trees, and clean streets. Usually, however, certain locations are better because they are crime free and they have immediate access to public transportation and amenities, or better schools. Also, recent improvements to the neighborhood, the streets, and nearby shops might increase the value of the homes in the area. If others are investing in the neighborhood, no doubt the value of all the homes should rise. The more desirable areas are better taken care of, neighborliness and good character prevail among the people, and there is a consideration for property values on the part of the residents.

The cost of a particular home will be determined by its location.

Here are some tips for getting your maximum value out of a home purchase.
1. Buy a fixer upper in a desirable area. If you make the improvements to the house yourself, you could save a ton of money and make a substantial profit on the investment.
2. Be aware of deal killers—homes with very serious problems. While you are looking to get into a good deal, you might rediscover, to your own chagrin, the old adage: "You get what you pay for."

    Some homes have been used to manufacture drugs, and it might be impossible to remove the toxic conditions residing in the walls and the floors.

    Mold is a major problem in some areas of the country. Radon levels may be high. Spending a few hundred dollars to have professionals inspect for these things might be well worth it. Be sure to attend the inspection so you can ask relevant questions of the professional inspector.

Look out for pest residue in the attic space, the crawl space underneath, or the basement. Knock on the wood on the decks or external door frames to test for damage by termites or carpenter ants. If the wood floors or wood decks feel squishy when you step on them, the wood has likely suffered water damage.

Check for structural problems such as leaning walls, serious cracks in the basement walls and floors, and ceiling cracks.

3. Take a good look at the parts of the house most likely to wear out. Are the roof shingles worn out? Are there any signs of hail damage to the roof or decks? Does the roof leak? Do the faucets drip? Are there any stains on the floor coverings? Does the house need repainting, either inside or outside? Do the floors creak? Are there any cracked tiles in the bathroom? Is there any water damage in the bathroom or kitchen? Be sure to check under every sink for water damage.
4. Turn on every light switch and fan switch. Check all the kitchen appliances. Don't forget to check the ice maker in the refrigerator.
5. Check the heating and air conditioning. Examine the water heaters to make sure the pilot is on and the hot water is accessible in the house.
6. Flush toilets. Turn on the water in every sink and watch for leaks.
7. Determine whether it is a buyer's market or a seller's market. In a buyer's market, there are more sellers than buyers, and in a seller's market, things are the other way around. If you are buying in a buyer's market, you can ask the seller to make more repairs on his own dime—and he will likely agree to fulfill your requests.
8. Purchase a property in a cheaper area further outside of town. You could telecommute instead of driving to work everyday. Or you may have to increase your drive time to the workplace.

HOW TO BUY A HOME IF YOU ARE POOR

> If there is among you a poor man of your brethren, within any of the gates in your land which the Lord your God is giving you, you shall not

> harden your heart nor shut your hand from your poor brother, but you shall open your hand wide to him and willingly lend him sufficient for his need, whatever he needs. (Deut. 15:7-8)

When you are first starting out, you may not have much money saved up to buy a home without debt. Most young couples are poor at the beginning of their financial journey. The following advice should help.

1. Save your money for six to ten years. If you begin saving your money as soon as you get your first job (at fourteen to seventeen years of age), you could be well on your way to buying a house in your twenties. Set a goal to save about 50% of the median house price. Don't spend a lot of money on college, and do not go into any debt for college, for an automobile, or for any other expense. The chart below shows the median house prices in various countries in 2021:

	Median House Price	Median Household Income	Percent of House Price
United States	$385,000	$68,000	18%
Canada	$720,000	$87,930	12%
Mexico	$64,000	$16,000	25%
England	$360,000	$41,500	12%
North Ireland	$205,000	$39,000	19%

2. If you are still young and unmarried, consider living in your parents' home for a few extra years while you save your money.
3. Consider using part or all of your retirement savings for your first home purchase. Check on the legality of this in your particular state or country.
4. As Christians, we would prefer "brother loans." These are forgivable loans. A fellow Christian (or a relative) loans the sum needed, and the borrower sets the interest rate (according to his ability to pay). If he is unable to pay it off for some reason, within seven years, the

loan is forgiven. There must be no breach in relationship if the loan cannot be paid. These sorts of arrangements, of course, involve an extraordinary amount of trust and love for one another, and they are rare these days.

5. Start out with a smaller home with only one or two bedrooms. This will cut your costs significantly. Check out the differences between homes of various sizes in the chart below:

	Hawaii	Wichita, Kansas
Studio	$200,000	
1 Bedroom Condo	$320,000	$75,000
2 Bedroom Condo	$400,000	$100,000
2 Bedroom House	$600,000	$90,000
3 Bedroom House	$640,000	$144,000

6. Build your own house on a piece of property. You can save about 40% of the material cost if you build the home yourself. At current prices, you could build an 800 square foot basic home for $120,000. That doesn't count land or water, septic, and electrical hookups. Building it yourself would save you about $50,000 in labor costs, which means you could build the house for $70,000 in material costs. If you could find a small plot for $50,000 and add in the hookups for $30,000, you could be into the house for $150,000. That would be about 39% of the current median

Start out with a smaller home.

house price in the US.

7. Add on to an existing home belonging to a family member. This is a much cheaper alternative versus building a new home on another piece of property. For 1,000 square feet of living space (as considered above), this would save about $80,000 of the $150,000 price tag. Assuming you did most of the work yourself, you could attach 1,000 square feet, complete with kitchen, living area, two bedrooms, and one bathroom for only $70,000. That's only 18% of the current median house price in the US.

Regrettably, these options are not all available to young families as much as before. Over-restrictive building codes have made it difficult for families to get started without debt. Government tyranny which would prevent a young family from adding on to an existing structure is especially hard on the poor.

FIX STUFF YOURSELF

If you do the easy repairs jobs yourself, you would save an average of $50 per repair on your home. If you can make your own plumbing and appliance repairs, you will save $200-$400 per incident. Electrical malfunctions are the most dangerous to fix, so you should avoid trying to fix your electrical problems unless you are specially trained to do so. If you are trying to replace cracked electrical face plates (which only cost about fifty cents) or any other simple electrically-related repair, the safest thing to do is to turn off the circuit breaker first. Test the circuit by plugging something into the outlet. Or, flip on the switch to make sure the lights are not turning on before doing anything with the light switch or electrical outlet. Unplug all electrical appliances before performing any minor repairs, filter changes, or other routine maintenance work.

Ideally, most new houses aren't going to break down very quickly. Faucet gaskets shouldn't leak for 12-15 years. Exhaust

Fixing door hardware.

fans in the bathrooms should last for about 20 years. The average home will require 20-30 minor repairs or routine maintenances per year and 2-3 major fixes per year. By doing these things yourself, you would save about $1,800 per year.

Let's take a look at the most common simple fixes for the average house. Most of the things that break down are those areas of the house that involve moving parts or water. Every young person should learn to perform most of these basic fixes before graduating from high school. The internet has plenty of how-to videos for anything that can go wrong with a house.

1. Replace door hardware. This is usually a quick job requiring one Phillips screwdriver. Remove two wood screws and two machine screws, and replace the door handles and hardware. If a lock is sticking a little, it may need lubricating. Using a pencil, rub the lead against the teeth of the key, transferring the graphite to the key. This material works like a grease. Insert the key into the lock and turn it a few times. Repeat the process until the lock turns freely.

2. Clean out clogged drains. These are usually easily fixed by one of three methods. None of these solutions will take more than a few minutes.

Faucet repair

a. Run a plastic hair catcher (or "Zip-it") into the drain to pull out as much hair as possible.

b. Disconnect the trap under the sink and clean it out.

c. Snake out the drain using a 20-60-foot plumbing snake (available in most hardware stores).

3. Replace faucet gaskets. The sooner leaks are fixed, the better. Water damage can get very expensive if leaks aren't fixed immediately. The gasket is a little rubber seal in a valve that gets squeezed. It's supposed to prevent water from leaking. When the gaskets get chewed away by chemicals in the water or friction forces, they will need to be replaced. Replacement is surprisingly easy, but be sure to turn off the water under the sink before doing any maintenance.

4. Fix roof leaks as soon as possible. Some roof leaks are tough to locate. Sometimes the water shows up at a ceiling spot distant from the leak. If your ceiling has a plastic vapor barrier between the drywall and the attic insulation, push the insulation aside and look for flow stains on the plastic. Often water runs to openings in the vapor barrier, such as at ceiling light fixtures.

   If you can't see any water marks, and if the leak is fairly small, inspect the underside of the roof for *shiners*. That's a nail that missed the rafters when the carpenter installed the roofing. Moisture that escapes into the cold attic from the rooms below often condenses on cold nails. You might be able to spot the leak on a cold night. The nails will look white from frost. You should be able to fix the leak by clipping the nails with wire clippers.

Oven/Stove

Caution: Always unplug electrical units before trying to fix them.

If an oven doesn't heat properly, most likely the problem is with the heating element (either the one located above the broiler or the one at the bottom used in baking). If the oven heating element doesn't glow red when you turn it on, it may need replacement. The element is plugged in and held in place with a few screws – not a big deal. Get an experienced repairman, adult friend, or family member to mentor you in these basic fixes.

Vacuum Cleaners

The most common problems with vacuum cleaners are either a defective drive belt or blockage in the hoses. Clean out the hoses, replace the dirt bag, or replace the drive belt as needed.

Clothes Washing Machines

If your washing machine isn't draining, check for blockage in filters and hoses. If the washer won't spin or agitate, the problem is probably with the belt. The washer motor turns the belt, which turns the agitator or the tub. Replacing the drive belt takes only a minute or two of work. Remove the washer rear panel and replace the belt.

A defective lid switch assembly might also prevent the washer from spinning or working properly. The lid switch is a safety device to keep the machine from working if the lid is open. Replacement of the lid switch is pretty easy as well.

The other major problems with washing machines are motor problems and electrical problems. More careful research on the internet might help you to correctly diagnose these problems and fix them.

Clothes Dryer

Most importantly, the dryer vent must be cleaned regularly to keep your dryer working. Make a habit of cleaning the lint out of the dryer vent with every cycle. If the blower housing gets clogged, the thermal fuse might blow. This shuts down all heat for an electric dryer. Replace the fuse and clean out the venting and blower wheel.

Lint in a dryer vent.

If the dryer drum isn't turning, the problem is most likely a broken drive belt. Remove the back of the dryer and replace the drive belt. While you are doing that, check for worn rollers, glides, and bearings. These can make for a noisy drying cycle. You might want to replace these as well. Most replacement parts are inexpensive.

The Garbage Disposal

If your garbage disposal won't turn on when you flip the switch, try pushing the reset button at the bottom of the unit. If the machine is making a humming noise when you turn on the disposal, something is probably stuck in the impeller. Using an offset wrench (or an Allen wrench), insert the wrench into the flywheel turn hole and turn it clockwise. You can replace a garbage disposal in twenty minutes. A new disposal will cost about $150. It would cost about three times that amount for a professional to replace it.

UTILITIES

How Much Energy Does the Average Home Use?

Household Energy Use	Percent of Total Use	Average Monthly Cost
Heating and Air Conditioning	46%	$138
Water Heating	14%	$60
Refrigerator, Washer, Dryer	13%	$39
Lights	9%	$27
TV, Computers, and Media	4%	$12
Total:		$276

SAVING ENERGY IN HEATING AND COOLING YOUR HOUSE

Heating and cooling is always the biggest energy cost in the home. An air conditioner can use 1,000 to 2,000 kilowatt-hours per month. At twenty cents a kilowatt hour of energy, this would cost $200-$400 per month. A study conducted in Michigan found that you will pay an extra

$10 per month on your heating bill for every degree heated above 64°F.[102] So, if you set your thermostat at 70°F all day during the wintertime, you would pay an extra $60 per month. And if you set your thermostat at 75°F, you would pay an extra $110 per month for heating. Here are some good ways that every family member can help conserve energy and save money in heating and cooling the home.

1. Be sure your home has good insulation in the ceiling and walls, especially the outside walls.
2. Open and close the front door quickly when you go in and out. A lot of heat escapes the house if you leave the door open when the house is heated. During the summertime, heat from the outside will quickly invade the cool air inside through an open door.
3. Remember, heat rises. If you have ceiling fans, be sure they are pushing cool air downward during the summertime by running them counterclockwise (as you look up at them.) In the wintertime, run the ceiling fan clockwise to pull the cool air upwards and keep the warm air circulating downward.
4. Keep the thermostat at about 78°F in the summer, and keep it under 65°F in the winter. Wear warmer clothes in the wintertime.
5. Keep the window coverings in the sun-facing windows closed in the summer and open in the winter.

Adjusting the thermostat

6. Regularly replace air filters in your heating and air conditioning systems.
7. Don't block vents that are drawing air into your heating or air conditioning systems.
8. Inspect all windows, doors, and attic entries. Identify all locations

where hot or cold air is slipping into the house, and seal these with weatherproofing.

9. About 30% of your house heat or A/C disappears through single-paned windows. Consider replacing these windows with double-paned windows, which provide an insulating air gap between the two panes. This could provide a savings as high as $100 per window per year.

10. An efficient wood stove or fireplace can reduce money spent on gas or electric by as much as $200 per month. This would apply mostly to those who have access to a free source of wood to burn.

Careful conservation of energy would save about 50% on your utility bills.

SAVING ENERGY WITH YOUR WATER HEATER

The water heater is another big energy user in your home—second only to the heating and A/C. Rated at an average of 405 kilowatt-hours a month, water heaters will cost about $80 per month to operate. Here are some tips for keeping the water heater running efficiently.

Wood stove

1. Take shorter showers. Although you may enjoy the luxury of a long, warm shower, remember that showers cost money. A five-minute shower consumes about 10 gallons of hot water, whereas a twenty-minute shower uses about 40 gallons.
2. Make sure that the water heater is covered with an insulation jacket. Also insulate the hot water pipes that are visible in the utility room.
3. Turn down the water heater when you go on vacation. Also, you

can put the water heater on a timer, only keeping it on when people are likely to take showers.
4. Set the water heater's temperature to 120°F or lower.
5. Install shower heads and faucet aerators that conserve water.

SAVING ENERGY WITH APPLIANCES, LIGHTING, AND ELECTRONICS

Although appliances, lights, and electronics do not take as much energy, there may be easy ways to cut costs here as well. Families must be careful, though. Modern appliances and energy sources are meant to make life more convenient. Some people do spend too much time trying to save money, and they end up making their lives more inconvenient and inefficient. Nonetheless, here are some money-saving tips that are not so troublesome and can still save money.

1. Keep your freezer pretty well stuffed and your refrigerator not quite filled up all the way. Frozen foods help keep the freezer cold, but over stuffing the fridge actually increases energy usage.

Keeping a freezer stuffed tight helps keep the food colder.

2. Don't leave the fridge door open very long. Keep things organized in the fridge. This way, you will spend less time with the door open looking for food.
3. Consider using cold water for doing the laundry.
4. Turn off lights when they are not being used. Consider getting a universal switch that turns off all lights and non-essential energy-consuming devices when you leave the home.

SAVE ON PHONE

The average American spends $114 per month on mobile phones and data accounts. Often, the consumer is paying extra for unlimited data. Accounts limiting yourself to 4-12 GB per month will range from $10 to $20 per month. Also, watch out for hidden charges on your mobile phone bill.

HOW MUCH DID YOU SAVE?

Now, let's compare the total amount a small family (two adults and two children) can save on big expenses if they are careful.

Annual Budget Comparing the Careless and Careful Spenders		
	Careless Spender	*Careful Spender*
Auto Purchase/Maintenance	$6,310	$4,000
Auto Insurance	$2,400	$1,200
Medical Insurance	$28,166	$6,000
House Maintenance	$2,000	$200
House Payments (including taxes)*	$20,000	$10,000
Utilities	$2,400	$1,200
Mobile Phone/Data	$1,368	$240
Total:	$62,644	$22,840
Total (without Medical Insurance)	$34,478	$16,840

*Note: House payments are calculated on a 30-year loan (2021).

These numbers do not include food and clothing. But, according to this comparison the careful spender saves $39,804, (the difference between $62,644 and $22,840) if the family chooses the smaller house. If they should prefer living in a median-priced (and median-sized) house, which adds another $10,000 into the budget, the careful spender would still save

$29,804. Adding tithe, taxes, food, clothing, and personal care, the low-budget careful spender would be spending around $30,000-$40,000 per year. In other words, the average family could get by on a rather modest single income if they were more careful with their spending. If the median household income is $68,000, the careless spender is just barely getting by. Actually, most employers will pay for health insurance, so that frees up some extra money for both the careless spender and the careful spender. Removing health insurance still leaves the careful spender spending half of what the careless spender spends on everything else. If the careful spender saves that $17,638 extra (the difference between $34,478 and $16,840) each year over what the careless spender spends, he would save an additional $176,380 in ten years. Using that savings, he could double or triple the living space in his home without going into debt.

SAVING ON GAS

The average American drives 14,263 miles per year. With this many miles, the average family is spending about $167 per month on gas. While you can occasionally buy gas at a cheaper rate here and there, this actually doesn't save much money per year. The better way to save on gas is to carpool with others or use public transportation. Vehicles with better mileage are also a good idea. Unless you have paid off your home, you should stay away from luxury cars. Smaller cars are the best approach to saving on your gas budget. The best small cars for gas consumption are:

Gas Mileage (EPA Combined Highway and Town Driving)		
Car Model	Gas Mileage	
Mitsubishi Mirage	39 mpg	16.6 km/l
Hyundai Elantra	37 mpg	15.7 km/l
Honda Civic	36 mpg	15.3 km/l
Kia Rio	36 mpg	15.3 km/l
Toyota Corolla	35 mpg	14.9 km/l

Gas Mileage (EPA Combined Highway and Town Driving)		
Car Model	Gas Mileage	
Nissan Versa	35 mpg	14.9 km/l
Kia Forte	35 mpg	14.9 km/l
VS Jetta	34 mpg	14.5 km/l
VW Golf	33 mpg	14.0 km/l
Honda Accord	33 mpg	14.0 km/l
Chevrolet Spark	33 mpg	14.0 km/l

Purchasing a fuel-efficient car is the best way to save on your monthly fuel expense. Saving a few cents a gallon by filling up at cheap gas stations will only get you 5-8% savings on monthly expenses. But driving a Mitsubishi Mirage instead of a Toyota Highlander SUV would save you 50% on gas. Driving a motorcycle instead of a Toyota Camry would save you 75% on gas. Less wealthy folks and economies often prefer the use of motorcycles or motor scooters for cost reasons. However, the drawback of motorcycles is the high risk of serious accidents. The National Highway Traffic Safety Association reports a 35-fold increased risk of fatal accidents for motorcyclists compared to other motorists.

SAVE ON FOOD

The best way to save on food is not to frequent restaurants but to limit eating out to special occasions. The average American spends $288 per month eating out. Limit this to an anniversary celebration, two fast-food experiences per month, and two or three other special occasions, and you could cut this down to $70 per month.

The best ways to save on groceries is to:
1. Buy bulk foods, and buy staples. Load up on rice, cornmeal, and oatmeal. The average cereal box will cost $4.00 per pound, while you can purchase oatmeal for less than $1.00 a pound. That's a

75% savings.
2. Don't live "high off the hog." Buy chicken instead of beef. That cuts your per-pound costs by 70%. Choose ground beef over steaks, and you'll save about 50%. Keep in mind Proverbs 23:1-3:

> When you sit down to eat with a ruler,
> Consider carefully what is before you;
> And put a knife to your throat
> If you are a man given to appetite.
> Do not desire his delicacies,
> For they are deceptive food.

3. Keep an eye on the per-pound or per-ounce price of the products you buy. Most grocery stores will advertise the price per pound or ounce on the shelf. Compare brands, and you'll find some brands are 20-50% cheaper than others.
4. Buy a little extra when things go on sale. Sale prices usually run 30-60% off.
5. Buy produce in season.
6. Buy clearance items. These are still perfectly safe for consumption. They will have reduced shelf life, but that's okay if you're shopping for food to consume that week.
7. Cut coupons and keep an eye on the special electronic deals available each week.
8. Plan your meals a month ahead of time. This gives you a chance to shop for good deals ahead of time and to buy in bulk.
9. Shop online for good deals.
10. Avoid expensive drinks. You can save a lot by drinking water, and you might consider purchasing your own water filter (instead of buying bottled water). Keep these prices in mind when you consume drinks.

Mother and daughter reviewing their grocery list

Drink	Price
Tap Water	Free
Bottled Water	20 cents per 16 ounces
Ground Coffee (Regular)	7 cents per cup
Tea (Black)	3 cents per teabag
Iced Tea	3 cents per cup
Tea (Herbal)	16 cents per teabag
Espresso (Home Pressed)	55 cents per shot
Soft Drinks	50 cents per 16 ounces
Milk	50 cents per 16 ounces
Orange Juice	70 cents per 16 ounces
Diet Fruit Drinks	$1.20 per 16 ounces

11. Check out creative new apps like Paribus. Scan your purchases, and Paribus will check the best prices against your purchases and

negotiate refunds for you. Get cash rewards for your purchases on credit cards. Some families have saved up to 80-90% of their grocery expenses by using these methods.

Annual Budget Comparing the Careless and Careful Spenders

	Careless Spender	Careful Spender
Auto Purchase/Maintenance	$6,310	$4,000
Auto Insurance	$2,400	$1,200
Medical Insurance	$28,166	$6,000
House Maintenance	$2,000	$200
House Payment (including taxes)*	$20,000	$10,000
Utilities	$2,400	$1,200
Mobile Phone/Data	$1,368	$240
Gas	$2,000	$1,000
Food	$4,464	$2,200
Restaurants	$3,456	$840
Total:	$72,564	$26,880
Total (without Medical Insurance)	$44,398	$20,880

*Note: House payments are calculated on a 30-year loan (2021).

Based on these numbers, the careful spender saves $45,684 (the difference between $72,564 and $26,880) on transportation, insurance, housing, utilities, gas, and food, if he is willing to start out in a small house. Within ten years, the careful spender would save $457,000, which he could put into a fairly large house (or help some other cause for the kingdom of God). If the careful spender starts out in a larger (median-sized) house, he could save $35,684 per year. And with that, within ten years the careful spender would save $356,840. If medical insurance is taken care of by the employer, the careful spender is still saving $23,518 per year, which would add up to $235,180 in ten years.

This is how the careful spender can pay off his house and live mortgage free.

HOW TO SAVE MONEY ON TAXES

It is almost impossible to save money on social security tax, property tax, and sales tax. These are fixed taxes, and few exemptions are available for the average person.

Income tax is another story. There are hundreds, if not thousands, of exemptions, loopholes, and rules issued for the income tax. Sadly, these advantages usually favor the wealthy and well-informed. Because the tax system is so complicated, most ordinary citizens simply don't have the time or the wherewithal to comprehend it. To make matters worse, the tax code changes every year.

Nonetheless, the general rule is this: The more money you make, the more you need to know about the tax code. Right off the bat, you should know about a few basic tax-saving tips. (Be sure to check out current tax laws with an accountant or by using reputable sources on the internet.)

1. Usually, you can deduct your tithes and charity donations for either national or state/local taxes.
2. In many cases, you can also deduct interest paid on your home mortgage, property taxes, and home insurance. You may also be able to deduct interest paid on a student loan.
3. Business expenses can be deducted, and that usually includes mileage on your car. If you drove your car to your lemonade stands, you can deduct anywhere from 50 cents to $1.00 per mile on your taxes. If you drove five miles per day for eighty days to your lemonade stands, that would account for 400 miles. Where this deduction is allowed, this could give you a $200-$400 tax deduction. Also, you might be able to deduct office space in your house if you use that space exclusively for business.
4. Modern governments are providing tax credits for children ranging from $500 to $2,000 per child. These credits are taken off your tax

bill. So, if you owed $4,000 in taxes and you have three children who qualify for a $1,000 tax credit, you would only owe $1,000 in taxes.
5. You may also be able to deduct education expenses for yourself or family members.
6. Also, income tax deductions are usually offered for retirement savings (called IRA's or 401k's).

LIVING WITHIN A BUDGET

> Not that I speak in regard to need, for I have learned in whatever state I am, to be content: I know how to be abased, and I know how to abound. Everywhere and in all things I have learned both to be full and to be hungry, both to abound and to suffer need. I can do all things through Christ who strengthens me.
> (Phil. 4:11-13)

Careful spenders are disciplined spenders. They are deliberate. They plan ahead. They know where their money goes. They can tell the difference between a need and a want, and they take this into consideration before they make a purchase. "Do I really need this? Or is it just a desire?" They do not worship money or materials. They are not addicted to shopping. And they stay within the guidelines of a budget. Like the Apostle Paul, they are as content with a little as they are with much, always thankful for what God chooses to give them.

Just as a daily planner is one way to discipline your use of time, a budget helps to maintain discipline over your use of God's monetary resources. The budget is one way to maintain intentional and regular self-control over your spending habits so that you don't waste money.

A starter budget for a teenaged child might look like this:

Starter Budget		
Income		
Lemonade Stand	$300	
Lawn Care	$300	
Total	**$600**	
Expenses	Budgeted Amount	Importance
Tithe/Giving (10%)	$60	1
Savings (50%)	$275	2
Cell Phone Bill	$40	3
Car Fuel	$40	4
Car Insurance	$100	4
Clothing/Grooming	$45	5
Entertainment	$40	5
Total	**$600**	

Sometimes you will spend more than the amount you have allotted in a given category. Within the month, you could move money from the less important categories like entertainment into the car fuel category. You can also save up money in a particular category to spend during future months. For example, your insurance bill usually comes due every six months. So you will not spend in that category for six months. All the while, you will save $100 per month and will pay the $600 insurance bill at the end of six months. As you spend money in a certain category throughout the month, you reduce the balance in that particular category. What follows is a running budget over three months. Each time a bill is paid or something is purchased, the expense is noted with a negative sign.

Starter Budget - Three Month

January

Income	Tithe/Giving	Saving	Cell Phone	Car Fuel	Car Insurance	Clothing/Grooming	Entertainment
	60	275	40	40	100	45	40
300	-60		-40	-22.05		-12.00	-18.00
300				-10.86		-5.00	-12.00
						-10.00	-15.00
Balance	0	275	0	7.09	100	18	-5

February

Income	Tithe/Giving	Saving	Cell Phone	Car Fuel	Car Insurance	Clothing/Grooming	Entertainment
	60	275	40	40	100	45	40
Balance	60	550	40	47.09	200	63	35
300	-60		-40	-14.00		-12.00	-13.00
300				-24.00		-35.00	-20.00
Balance	0	825	0	9.09	300	16	2

March

Income	Tithe/Giving	Saving	Cell Phone	Car Fuel	Car Insurance	Clothing/Grooming	Entertainment
	60	275	40	40	100	45	40
Balance	60	825	40	49.09	300	61	42
				-5.00			

12

HOW BUSINESSES RUN

And the Lord said, "Who then is that faithful and wise steward, whom his master will make ruler over his household, to give them their portion of food in due season? Blessed is that servant whom his master will find so doing when he comes." (Luke 12:42-43)

The receipt constitutes a contract between the buyer and seller.

Before engaging in the market economy, it would be helpful to know how businesses actually run. This knowledge will help you figure out how you will fit into it. Businesses are not exactly the same thing as families or churches. All relationships in the business world rely on contracts. When apples are purchased at the grocery store, the seller issues a receipt. This is a contract between the buyer and seller. The receipt records the transaction; for example, stating that the buyer paid $1.50 and received three pounds of apples in return.

Families and churches are covenantal organizations. That means they organize by contract or covenant, but they are maintained by nurturing a relationship. Family and church relationships are connective, and separation is much more painful in these realms than in the business world. The husband-wife relationship is described in Ephesians 5 as a body. Likewise, the church is described as the body of Christ (who is its Head). Ripping the head off the body or tearing a finger off a hand would be painful. The business world does not involve relationships formed on this kind of unity.

Whether you are a steward or manager, an ordinary employee, or the business owner, the Lord calls each of us to be "faithful and wise." We are always stewarding resources with businesses, whether or not we own the business.

There are 7.7 million businesses employing at least one person in America. That's one business for every forty-one people (men, women, and children) in the nation. The following chart gives you an idea of how much income various businesses take in. Keep in mind that this does not equate to profit. Most of this money goes into expenses to run the business.

Annual Income for US Businesses			
	Small	Mid-Size	Large
Restaurant	$300,000	$3,000,000	$7,000,000+
Lawn Care	$30,000	$200,000	$1,000,000+
Coffee Shop	$150,000	$300,000	$2,000,000+
Dog Walking	$20,000	$45,000	
Catering	$250,000	$1,000,000	$3,000,000+
Online Sales	$30,000	$250,000	$1,000,000+
Bed and Breakfast	$20,000	$135,000	$500,000+

HOW TO START A BUSINESS, AND WHAT EVERYBODY SHOULD KNOW ABOUT BUSINESS

Before starting a business, you should first consider whether you are willing to take the risk. This question ties into your calling, to be further discussed in the next chapter. Ask yourself whether God has called you to this. Are you an entrepreneur? More specifically, it would be good to know whether you can handle the pressure of owning and running your own business.

Individual proprietorships are easy to start. You can control all the assets and determine how the business is going to run. These small businesses can be flexible and versatile. Yet, on the other hand, new businesses take time to develop. You will not be successful overnight. It takes years to build trust in your customer base for your business. At the beginning, you need to be able to handle all aspects of the business – a jack-of-all-trades.

Know this, that it is easier to get a job than to start a business. Entrepreneurs need initial capital for the business startup, and normally that money will have to come from their own pocket. Some businesses don't require a large amount of money. One survey found that 64% of small business owners begin with only $10,000 in capital. Some businesses like restaurants are pretty expensive to start up. But all you need for a lawn care business is a lawn mower, a broom, and a pair of hedge trimmers.

Starting a lawn care business does not require much capital.

Yet, not many businesses survive the first few years. Succeeding in business startups takes a great deal of commitment, a humility that learns from mistakes, a willingness to work hard, a resistance to discouragement, a sense of calling, and a persevering mindset that follows through on initiated projects. Only 50% of startups will still be in business in the fifth year.[103] The top reasons why businesses fail include:

1. The business owners failed to understand the market needs. They didn't perform a careful business plan before jumping into the market. Or they didn't stick to the original plan.
2. The business owners failed to count the cost at the outset. They didn't have enough funding for the business, and they didn't realize the amount of time and money it would take to get this business off the ground. Or they just refused to commit the resources. (Jesus refers to this principle when speaking of the Christian life in Luke 14.)

When setting out to do a project, it is important to lay out good plans and count the cost.

> For which of you, intending to build a tower, does not sit down first and count the cost, whether he has enough to finish it—lest, after he has laid the foundation, and is not able to finish, all who see it begin to mock him, saying, "This man began to build and was not able to finish"? (Luke 14:28-30)

3. In some cases, the failed businesses were set up in a bad location. Or they failed to obtain adequate internet presence and effective marketing.
4. In other cases, the business did not meet the market needs or expectations. To succeed in the restaurant business, for example, the start-up enterprise must excel at every point. The business must produce excellent food, offer the best service from a friendly, upbeat waiting staff, and maintain a top-notch ambiance (decor, lighting, background music, etc.). Competition is stiff in this sector. The new business cannot afford to disappoint a single customer in the early years.

    New businesses cannot survive if attended by laziness and complacency. They must be adaptable to customer needs. If customers are asking for lemonade but all you have is iced tea to offer, you're on the road to failure. Both new businesses and older businesses must be adaptable to the ever-changing needs of their clientele.
5. Going into debt and expanding too quickly is another failure point for new businesses. Be faithful in small things first. Before adding new products or new business departments, make sure you have the experience and the know-how to make it work.

STARTING A BUSINESS

Before starting a business, do an honest assessment of what you have to offer. What are your gifts? Are you an entrepreneur type? Have you ever run a business in the past? This is the point at which humility is crucial. How does your idea for a product or service differ from your competitors? Are you going to provide additional features? Will you improve the quality of the product or service over that provided by your competitors? Have you tested your new product on your friends and acquaintances? Have you received honest feedback from others?

The three most important questions to answer before starting up a new venture would be:

1. Do you have enough money to start the business and keep it going for a year? To answer this question, you will need to work out a budget for the first year of the business.
2. Is there a market for your product or service? What is the size of that market? How many people can you reach in advertising? Of these, how many would respond?
3. Who can help you build the business, and how can they help you with their talents?

Before launching a new enterprise, successful entrepreneurs will create a **business plan**. Here are the essential parts:

1. The Players. This includes a description of yourself and key members of the development team. This includes an honest assessment of gifts and calling. Make a list of the other potential team members with their gifts and potential contributions.
2. Previous Experience and Lessons Learned. If you already have business experience or have already established a business, lay out what you have done and what you have learned thus far from that experience.
3. Product or Service Description. Describe in detail the products or services you will provide.
4. Market Analysis. Identify your target market. Describe your customer base.
5. Competition Analysis. Identify your current competitors, their markets, and their products.
6. Marketing and Sales Plan. Write a plan for your business that includes advertising methods, audience reach, and expected responses.
7. Design, Development, and Production Plan. Detail the cost of development and the timeline for production, purchase of tooling, and release of marketable product.
8. Financial Plan. Budget the first year of your business.

Before starting any new endeavor, be sure to pray about it first. Pray for wisdom to assess every part of the business plan rightly. Pray for right motivations, and confess and turn away from all sins of greed, covetousness, and pride.

Market Analysis

The **market analysis** is a key part of the business plan. This is the demand side of the market exchange – the people who will use your product or service.

Demographics

Where will your customers come from? Are the homes in your area maintaining well-cared-for lawns, or do they just let weeds grow in their yards? Is the business seasonal, where grass doesn't grow during the wintertime? What is the average disposable income in your area? Lower income families can't afford to hire these services, so they take care of their own yards.

Consider also, as an example, an internet-based business, where items are sold off the world wide web. If those interested in your product or service will come from internet "neighborhoods," you will have to assess the size of the niche market from your already established network. If you are selling to a niche market, what is the size of this market? If you are selling fingernail clippers, everybody in the world needs fingernail clippers, so that's a pretty big market. But if you are selling mittens for cats, that will be

It is important to consider your market before setting out to establish a business.

a much smaller market. Not many people are in the market for cat mittens.

First describe the type of people who will purchase your product. Are you marketing to men or women? Young or old? Rich or poor? Would your product be largely favored by Christians? Consider all the factors that may limit your market reach.

There are two factors you need to look at when assessing the size of a market: the number of potential customers, and the value the market would place on your product.

Competition

Also, carefully consider your competition before you get into the business. If there are only 200 homes in your neighborhood and ten lawn care businesses, that doesn't provide much opportunity for another operation. But if there are 2,000 homes in your neighborhood and only one lawncare company, then you have real potential for growth. However, if 90% of the people in your neighborhood are too poor to hire a lawncare company (or don't care about their yards), then your market is more limited.

You need to analyze your competition for their strengths and weaknesses and the relative size of their businesses. How many employees does each of these businesses hire? Are they missing some part of the market due to their lack of quality or their limited abilities or offerings? Perhaps you could provide a service the other companies do not offer. This would help you to break into the market.

HOW MUCH MONEY COULD YOU MAKE?

How much money could you make in your business? That's not an easy question to answer. You can hire companies to assess this for you, or make estimates yourself.

For an example, you can estimate the total number of potential clients by counting the lawns in your neighborhood or city. If there were 2,000 lawns available, how much would each customer be willing to pay for lawn maintenance every month? Depending on how wealthy they are, the amount may run between $60 and $200. Your potential income would then be somewhere between $120,000 and $400,000, assuming there were no competitors.

If there are competitors, take the maximum potential income, and divide it by the number of producers (or competitors) in the area. If the maximum potential income for lawncare businesses in your town was $400,000, and there are four competitors (including yourself), that would give each business an average of $100,000 of income per year.

Growth Potential

Prudent entrepreneurs are also looking at growth potential for their businesses. While nobody knows the future but God, there are certain indications of market growth in sectors and geographical locations. For a lawncare business for instance, you should be concerned with all new housing construction in your area. If you learn in your research that there are three new housing developments with 50 homes each planned for your area, that expands your market by 150 homes. That would make room for another lawncare business and more future growth.

New housing developments would provide additional customers for a potential business.

Market Need

There may be a difference between what you perceive the market should need and what the market is really needing. The best way to assess market needs is to talk to people. Ask them about their specific concerns with their current situation. Is there something lacking in terms of quality or offerings with the current businesses from which they receive products and services? Are there certain kinds of weeds growing in people's yards that they want to get rid of? Perhaps you have a product that could make their lawns look better than everybody else's in the neighborhood.

Barriers to Entry

What will be your biggest challenges as you consider going into this business? Examples include limited capital, government regulations, a bad location for your business, safety concerns for your employees, limited access to resources, and so on.

Business Expenses

Before taking on any kind of ministry or work endeavor, let us be sure to "count the cost" as Jesus reminded us. The same principle applies to business. Do you have enough money to pay for the capital expenses, to purchase equipment and tools, for example? If you plan to build houses, you will need to purchase nail guns, screw guns, a compressor, measuring tapes, squares, levels, and five different kinds of saws. If you are opening a lemonade stand, you will need to buy a lemon squeezer/lemonade machine. These tools would cost $1,000-$3,000. These are your capital costs.

But you also need to consider your initial monthly expenses. For any new business, you will have to be patient and work hard without receiving much income at first. Reasonably, it may take two or three years before the income from your business exceeds its expenses. In most of life's endeavors, you have to "pay your dues." You will need to take the time to develop your skills, learn from your mistakes, improve on your standards of quality, and earn a good reputation in the market. And, of course you will need to invest time and money into advertising to get your first customers. The following is a list of basic monthly expenses for most businesses (in this case, a lawncare company).

Business Budget for a Lawncare Start-Up Company	
Item	Monthly Expense
Advertising and marketing	$100
Bonding and insurance	$64
Telephone and internet	$20
Location costs	0
Utilities/Gas	$20
Employee pay	$1,000
Total	**$1,204**

Keep advertising as a regular cost on your monthly budget. Without regular advertising, customers will never learn about your business. They need to hear about your services over and over again—preferably every month for at least seven months. You will have to pay for online advertising and printing flyers to distribute around the neighborhoods.

Insurance and Bonding

Insurance is an important item on every household budget, but also, businesses require this expense. Insurance protects your own property (or assets), while bonding protects somebody else's property. For example, bonding will pay for damage done to the customer's property while you are servicing their lawns. If you back a riding lawnmower or tractor into the customer's plate glass window, bonding will pay to fix it. Insurance protects your own vehicles or equipment in case they are stolen or damaged. In some cases, bonding and insurance are required by law. For example, the state of Colorado doesn't require house builders to be bonded. However, the city of Denver does require this. Government entities often require bonding. Should your lawn maintenance business get a contract with the city for taking care of their landscaping at the city hall, you would probably need to be bonded. Running a lawnmower into an expensive window might result in a $3,000 loss, and that's why bonding is so important for small companies. They usually don't have the capital to fix something expensive if it gets ruined. These systems have their roots in a Christian world and life view. Clearly, Exodus 21 requires restitution when a person's goods are ruined by a neighbor's negligence.

> And if a man opens a pit, or if a man digs a pit and does not cover it, and an ox or a donkey falls in it, the owner of the pit shall make it good; he shall give money to their owner, but the dead animal shall be his. (Ex. 21:33-34)

Insurance on your business investments protects your assets.

PAYING YOUR BILLS

> You shall not oppress a hired servant who is poor and needy, whether one of your brethren or one of the aliens who is in your land within your gates. Each day you shall give him his wages, and not let the sun go down on it, for he is poor and has set his heart on it; lest he cry out against you to the LORD, and it be sin to you. (Deut. 24:14-15)

As emphasized repeatedly in Scripture, Christians are called to faithfulness in paying their bills. It is a matter of honesty and integrity. If you agree to build a deck for $4,000 and the materials will cost $1,000, you must be sure that you have sufficient money to pay the bills before you sign the contract. You should already have access to the $1,000 needed for the materials. Sloppy businessmen and dishonest builders will buy the materials on debt, collect the $4,000 for building the deck, and then fail to pay for the materials they used. In cases like this, the material supplier might put a **lien** on the construction itself (the deck). A lien is a legal claim on the property. If the property is ever sold, some of the money will have to be used to pay off the debt on the material used. By the way, before you purchase a house (or a car), it is a good idea to check for any liens.

Above all, Christian employers must commit to paying their workers on time. God's Word speaks strongly to this in Deuteronomy 24. If your business isn't steady, it would be better to hire temporary employees or part-time employees. A lemonade stand wouldn't be as popular in the wintertime as in the summertime. In colder climates, lawn maintenance is hardly needed in the wintertime.

Christian business owners should pay their employees before they pay themselves. In the situation that the business runs out of money for the payroll, the owner should draw from his or her own savings to pay the employees.

> Come now, you rich, weep and howl for your miseries that are coming upon you! Your riches are corrupted, and your garments are moth-

Christian business owners should pay their employees on time to be faithful to their agreements.

> eaten. Your gold and silver are corroded, and their corrosion will be a witness against you and will eat your flesh like fire. You have heaped up treasure in the last days. Indeed the wages of the laborers who mowed your fields, which you kept back by fraud, cry out; and the cries of the reapers have reached the ears of the Lord of Sabaoth. (Jas. 5:1-4)

JOB DESCRIPTIONS

Before hiring anybody for your company, you should have a firm idea of what your employees will do. The job description is part of the contract between the employer and the employee. Remember that an economy is built on contracts—in this case, an honest exchange of labor for pay. The employee must not be slothful. He must follow through on his commitment to get the job done. And the employer must pay him for his work.

The job description usually includes the following features:
1. A summary of qualifications and skills needed for the job. If you are advertising to hire somebody, you might also list the experience or education needed for the position.
2. A brief summary of the company's mission. Provide some guidance as to how the employee's position will fit into the overall goals of the company.
3. The job title for the employee.
4. The responsibilities and activities involved in the job. As best as possible, list the day-to-day activities required of the position.
5. The job location. This might be an office, a lemonade stand, or their own home office.
6. The company resources available to them. Will they have access to the company equipment, lawnmowers, computers, or construction tools?
7. Salary range and benefits. What will you provide for the employee in exchange for their work?

JOB PERFORMANCE REVIEWS

> We give thanks to God always for you all, making mention of you in our prayers, remembering without ceasing your work of faith, labor of love, and patience of hope in our Lord Jesus Christ in the sight of our God and Father. (1 Thess. 1:2-3)

Keep in mind that feedback is very important for employees. Thoughtful managers and employers will be careful to offer this. Good managers are in constant communication with their workers, and most of it is going to be positive and encouraging. This is the secret to success for most businesses. On the one hand, the employer must avoid flattery or exaggerated commendations. Don't tell people they are doing a good job when they have not done good work. Truth is of essence in business communication and all communication in general. However, honest and grateful affirmation for those who are doing a good job is always in order.

Occasional performance reviews are valuable to employees.

Most companies will provide a job review for their workers every year or so. When people are working for you, consider how important it is to "love your neighbor as you love yourself." They are dedicating a large portion of their lives to your business. To a great extent, their life career is dependent upon you.

And if you are the employee, you want to know if your employer is satisfied with your work. Are you meeting his expectations? Are you honoring the contract or the job description? That is the main purpose of the job review.

Of course, don't be afraid of the job review. This will be one of your best opportunities for personal growth—and even spiritual growth. Come at it with a humble and teachable spirit, and you'll find a great deal of profit in it.

> Faithful are the wounds of a friend,
> But the kisses of an enemy are deceitful. (Prov. 27:6)

> He who rebukes a man will find more favor afterward
> Than he who flatters with the tongue. (Prov. 28:23)

During the review, your employer may tell you things that you are doing wrong or things that you need to work on. He will assess what you have done and how well you have done it. Count the honest assessment of your work as the "wounds of a friend." Be humble as you approach the review, and don't try to defend yourself as if you were the perfect worker. Prayerfully consider the things that are brought up, and seek ways in which you may grow in the upcoming year.

You don't want to be a scoffer. That's the person who doesn't listen to correction and rebuke. And the Book of Proverbs is clear on this: *such a person will never succeed in life. Never.*

> A scoffer seeks wisdom and does not find it,
> But knowledge is easy to him who understands. (Prov. 14:6)
>
> The curse of the LORD is on the house of the wicked,
> But He blesses the home of the just.
> Surely He scorns the scornful,
> But gives grace to the humble. (Prov. 3:33-34)

There are three basic elements to a job performance review.

1. The Employee's Self-Review. Here the employee evaluates his or her own work performance.
2. Progress on Work Goals (from the last review or based on the job description). This asseses the progress made towards accomplishing goals. This part also includes adjustment of goals and the setting of new goals for the following year.
3. Evaluation of the Employee's Character and Work Patterns. An example of a performance review is included at the end of the chapter. The basic metrics that every employer is concerned with include:

1. The Quality of the Employee's Work. How well does he do his job? Does he make a lot of mistakes?
2. The Efficiency of the Employee's Work. How quickly does he do his job? How much does he get done in a day's work?
3. The Character of the Employee. How does he show honor towards management? How does he get along with others on the team?
4. The Employee's Personal Development in Knowledge and Expertise.

Here is the kind of wording you will find on performance reviews.

"Joe has improved his production by 25% this year."

"Joe has produced a new program that achieved these goals or produced these results."

"Joe has exceeded goals set last year by 10%."

"Joe has increased the customer base by 26%."

"Joe has improved working relationships with these customers."

"Joe has provided these innovative ideas that have increased the efficiency of processes by 18%."

"Joe is a problem solver, offering solutions to these problems this year."

"Joe has gone above and beyond expectations for the job by doing this and that."

The best managers play the part of the coach, with the intent of building a positive team-like organization. Coaches are never afraid of providing constructive criticism because they have the best interest of each team member and the whole team in mind. When the review is over, the employee should be encouraged, challenged, more focused, and more in tune with his gifts and his own potential for success in the job.

> Let the righteous strike me; it shall be a kindness. And let him rebuke me; it shall be as excellent oil; let my head not refuse it. For still my prayer is against the deeds of the wicked. (Ps. 141:5)

THE BUSINESS CULTURE

Every business develops its own culture. Some businesses are oppressive and depressing. Most likely the management and owners have provided little encouragement to their workers. Consequently, the employees hate their jobs, and customers can usually detect this. Other businesses are generally bright, hopeful, and happy. Everybody is upbeat and self-motivated, and the customers are well aware of it. The tenor of every business culture is set by those in charge. The president or the owners will be the most influential in setting this culture.

Visit a restaurant or shop at a store, and within ten minutes you will get a feel for the quality of management and the business culture. If the employees are demotivated, grumpy, unloving, confrontational, and unconcerned about the service, they are usually reflecting the company's culture. They are responding to the tone set by the management and the ownership of the shop. If the shop or restaurant is well-kept, and the employees are happy, upbeat, cooperative, and kind, no doubt they reflect a better heart of their management.

The focus of a healthy business culture is never set on money and paychecks. That's a necessary component of happy employees. But, good management will provide more than that – things like daily affirmation, encouragement, a positive outlook, thoughtful coaching, and team building. A healthy and happy business culture makes for the best job satisfaction and job retention. One of the worst problems for businesses is turnover of employees. When people leave their jobs, employers have to invest a lot into rehiring and retraining. Ultimately, for Christians, the right business culture is hopefulness in the goodness of God. Love for God, reverence for God, love for others, gratitude for others, and honesty must form the pillars of a Christ-scented business culture.

Most employees want to be:
1. A vital part of the team. Everybody wants to feel like they are part of a team that is accomplishing important goals.
2. Successful and appreciated. Whenever the team achieves goals and levels of success, that should be recognized by special events and awards.

3. Trusted. If employees are trusted, they don't need to be micro-managed. Most people don't want their bosses looking over their shoulder all the time.
4. Challenged. This means that people want to be given room to grow and to come up with new solutions to problems.
5. Treated fairly. All favoritism and political jockeying should be avoided in the workplace. As with all other human relationships, gossip, evil-speaking, strife, and one-upmanship and proud competition within the organization cannot be tolerated. These are the things which make for an unhealthy business culture.

COMMUNICATION IN THE BUSINESS WORLD

> The tongue is a little member and boasts great things. See how great a forest a little fire kindles! And the tongue is a fire, a world of iniquity. The tongue is so set among our members that it defiles the whole body, and sets on fire the course of nature; and it is set on fire by hell. For every kind of beast and bird, of reptile and creature of the sea, is tamed and has been tamed by mankind. But no man can tame the tongue. It is an unruly evil, full of deadly poison. With it we bless our God and Father, and with it we curse men, who have been made in the similitude of God. Out of the same mouth proceed blessing and cursing. My brethren, these things ought not to be so. (James 3:5-10)
>
> Love suffers long and is kind; love does not envy; love does not parade itself, is not puffed up; does not behave rudely, does not seek its own, is not provoked, thinks no evil. (1 Cor. 13:4-5)

Beyond any other factor, wise and careful speech is the most important secret to success in the business world (and in all human relationships). The power of the tongue to do good or to do evil is huge—greater than you would expect. One of the key elements of love taken from 1 Corinthians 13 is that "love does not behave rudely." The Greek word that is translated *rudely* speaks to behaving strangely and turning people off.

As Christians, we are called not to offend people unnecessarily. This necessitates studying good manners. Bad breath, bad facial expressions, bad body odor, interrupting people when they speak, using coarse words—all these things can turn people off. Your body language can come across as rude. When your manager is speaking, lean forward to listen. Communicate an interest in what others are saying. Check your tone of voice. Are you conveying impatience or anger?

Before speaking, check your attitude and your spirit. And ask yourself the all-important questions: Is it true? Is it respectful? Is it necessary?

Fitting in is important. While we cannot compromise on God's law as Christians, the Apostle Paul adapted his approach to the Jews and to the Greeks.

> For though I am free from all men, I have made myself a servant to all, that I might win the more; and to the Jews I became as a Jew, that I might win Jews; to those who are under the law, as under the law, that

Your body language and speech are important in demonstrating love and respect.

> I might win those who are under the law; to those who are without law, as without law (not being without law toward God, but under law toward Christ), that I might win those who are without law; to the weak I became as weak, that I might win the weak. (1 Cor. 9:19-22)

All our interactions with others in the marketplace should be cloaked in respect and gratitude. When talking with those more experienced or more senior in position, we should show them the honor that is due to them.

> Bondservants, be obedient to those who are your masters according to the flesh, with fear and trembling, in sincerity of heart, as to Christ; not with eyeservice, as men-pleasers, but as bondservants of Christ, doing the will of God from the heart. (Eph. 6:5-6)

Show gratitude to other team members for their work. Everybody has a job to do, and nobody will be successful in this business without the contributions from every other member. Acknowledge a job well done, and thank people for their contributions.

THE MONDAY MORNING TEST

> Do all things without complaining and disputing, that you may become blameless and harmless, children of God without fault in the midst of a crooked and perverse generation, among whom you shine as lights in the world...(Phil. 2:14-15)

The world works for the weekend. Worldly workers will call Wednesday "hump day" because they are anticipating the weekend. They live for recreation and entertainment. Monday is the most dreaded day of the week because this day represents the beginning of the work week. But the Christian lives his life for the glory of God and to serve Jesus Christ, his Lord and Savior. This applies as much to Monday morning as it does to Friday afternoon.

But we will enter into the work week with an infectious enthusiasm, a joyful anticipation, and hopeful aspirations for what the week will bear out.

We take it as a wonderful privilege to serve Christ. Are you the most upbeat in the business on a Monday morning?

Be sure you know why you are working. We are not here for the primary purpose of making money or entertaining ourselves to death. We are here to glorify God and to bless others. In any given moment, know who you are and whom you are blessing. How are those receiving this blessing going to be improved for what you have done for them today? We live in a sinful world. We are taking a hard journey, and our destination is heaven. Let us be the most hopeful, the most loving towards others, and the most willing to serve, even on Monday mornings.

PROFESSIONALISM

Many people live to get to Fridays, and the recreation that happens on the weekend.

To be professional is to meet and exceed the expectations of those you communicate with in the business world. It is to communicate well, as others would like you to communicate with them. But more than this, it is to get things done through proper communication.

Professionals are competent and appear competent. Their gifts are appropriate to their role. They are not over their head in the position in which they find themselves.

Professionals are knowledgeable. They know their field of work. The auto mechanic knows cars. The lawn guy knows all about lawns, weeds, and what makes grass grow. He does his research, and he knows more about it than most of his customers.

Professionals are conscientious. They are organized. They return phone calls. They make sure their work is done right the first time.

Professionals are trusted for their honesty and integrity. They are consistent to their values.

Professionals are especially known for their good manners, respect, and politeness. They are careful never to compromise these values in their communication in the workplace.

Professionals are able to maintain their cool under pressure. They are sensitive to the emotional status of others. They keep their own emotions in check.

Professionals are professional in dress and approach.

Professionals, and especially Christians, are careful not to give way to sexual sin in the workplace.

Professionals have a high degree of confidence. As Christians, our confidence is in God, His Word, His standards, His power, and His forgiveness.

Professionals get things done. They take action items away from every meeting, and they follow up on these things immediately.

HOW TO GROW YOURSELF TO BE A BETTER EMPLOYEE AND PROFESSIONAL

> For this reason we also, since the day we heard it, do not cease to pray for you, and to ask that you may be filled with the knowledge of His will in all wisdom and spiritual understanding; that you may walk

> worthy of the Lord, fully pleasing Him, being fruitful in every good work and increasing in the knowledge of God... (Col. 1:9-10)

When you start out in the work world, you don't feel much like a professional. You might feel a little awkward at first. You might find yourself making mistakes and displaying a lack of ability or character at points. Nobody is perfect, but as Christians we want to be constantly growing. Here are some things you can do to foster growth in yourself.

1. Pray for wisdom. Pray for God's grace. Realize the forgiveness of Christ for your sins, and be eager to forgive the faults of others.
2. Consider yourself. Be aware of your strengths and weaknesses. Be realistic about the opportunities and obstacles that lie before you in the workplace. Commit to grow. Commit to embracing the opportunities and overcoming obstacles, by God's grace.
3. Put to death your sinful tendencies. Believing that Christ has died for you, consider yourself dead to sin and alive to God. With that mindset, you can put to death your sinful deeds and desires. Sins of the tongue, pride, and grumpiness (or ungratefulness) are killers in the workplace (and the Christian life). You must put these to death.
4. Redeem the time while you are at work (Eph. 5:16). Be diligent. Increase your knowledge of the field. Seek out on-the-job training.
5. Watch other professionals. Seek out the best role models whom you can emulate. Lean into mentorships. Turn every job into a mentorship by asking questions of more experienced workers and managers. Take advantage of networking in the field. Learn from your competitors and customers as much as you can.
6. Double check your own work. Never assume you have achieved perfection. Always look for ways you can improve.

DIFFICULT PEOPLE IN THE WORKPLACE

> Then this Daniel distinguished himself above the governors and satraps, because an excellent spirit was in him; and the king gave

> thought to setting him over the whole realm. So the governors and satraps sought to find some charge against Daniel concerning the kingdom; but they could find no charge or fault, because he was faithful; nor was there any error or fault found in him. Then these men said, "We shall not find any charge against this Daniel unless we find it against him concerning the law of his God." (Dan. 6:3-5)

No matter what profession you choose, you will almost always find yourself working with difficult people in this world. When you were a child, you might have run into a bully on the playground. Or you might have met up with the teaser, the tattletale, or the quick-tempered child. Sometimes, these children meet Jesus and are changed by God's Spirit. But most of the time, they don't change very much. They grow up with the same bad temperaments and habits as they had when they were children. Even in their adult lives, they still "don't get along with others well in the sandbox." Here are some tips for getting along with difficult people in the workplace.

1. Be humble, and check yourself first. Why do you overreact to the person in question? Are there problems with your spirit? Perhaps this person is tempting you to sin in anger or unforgiveness, and you are giving way to it.
2. Err on the side of mercy towards others. Some people did not receive the kind of child training or discipleship that you have received.
3. Be aware of personality differences. We can be bothered by others because they have different personalities, different gifts, and different approaches. These things are not sinful. Learn to appreciate the differences. Work with the differences. Don't work against them.
4. Stay calm when the other person is not. Take three deep breaths. Count to ten before responding. Keep your voice very low and speak very slowly when they respond in anger, impatience, or unkindness. The person who remains calm throughout the argument almost always wins.
5. Don't gossip about people behind their backs. Instead, seek counsel from more experienced workers or managers concerning how to

best interact with certain folks in the workplace.
6. Focus upon action items. Remember, we are in the workplace to get a job done. Set personality differences and biases aside, and find ways to work together to get it done.
7. Pray for those who despitefully use you.
8. Do good to them. Bless them. Go out of your way to help them if they need your help.
9. Ask forgiveness when you offend them. As a Christian, this should come naturally. The world is often surprised by humility, and you would be surprised how often this wins over an enemy.
10. Don't assume the worst. While you may think these people are "out to get you," perhaps they are driven by a different motive. Try to get to a place where you can communicate with this "enemy." Perhaps you might find yourself working with them to achieve a common goal.
11. Build a professional rapport with your coworkers. Sometimes, you need to spend more time with them to get to know a little more about them—their family, their lives, their struggles.
12. Try to ignore minor insults. Jesus told us to turn the other cheek when receiving a minor insult. Remember Proverbs 19:

> The discretion of a man makes him slow to anger,
> And his glory is to overlook a transgression. (Prov. 19:11)

13. Speak directly to the person about the problem. While this may not always work (as in the case of the prophet Daniel), sometimes an honest conversation can clear the air a bit.
14. Avoid the difficult person if at all possible. The Proverbs does speak of avoiding the angry person or the "contentious woman." The most uncomfortable workplace is where habitual anger puts everybody on pins and needles all the time. Sometimes taking a wide berth around folks can save you a lot of trouble.

> Make no friendship with an angry man,
> And with a furious man do not go,

> Lest you learn his ways
> And set a snare for your soul. (Prov. 22:24-25)

15. Don't get involved in other people's conflicts. The Proverbs likens this to taking a dog by its ears.

> He who passes by and meddles in a quarrel not his own
> Is like one who takes a dog by the ears. (Prov. 26:17)

16. Avoid complaining about an employee to the manager unless the person is a serious threat to the company's wellbeing.

> Do not malign a servant to his master,
> Lest he curse you, and you be found guilty. (Prov. 30:10)

17. If all else fails, you can always find a new job. The quality of life in a company has a great deal to do with the character of the managers and your fellow employees. A company with bad management and bad employees is bound to fail. Sometimes it may be better to find employment elsewhere. This especially applies when a workplace is controlled by a spirit of anger.

WHAT ARE THE DEPARTMENTS IN A BUSINESS?

What part will you play in the economy? Our last chapter will explore this question of calling in more detail. But for now, we will break down the job opportunities in the business world. Only a minority of the workforce are business owners and entrepreneurs. The rest of us are called to a position within a business. Although there are different kinds of organizations depending on the kind of business, the following gives a rough breakdown of departments and jobs within companies.

Management

> So he shepherded them according to the integrity of his heart,
> And guided them by the skillfulness of his hands. (Ps. 78:72)

The manager of a company is like the captain of a ship. There is a lot going on in a ship that makes its voyage across the ocean. You need a navigator, sailors, engineers in the engine room, cooks, and medical personnel for everybody to make it from here to there alive and well. But somebody needs to be in charge of the whole process. The manager keeps everybody focused on their tasks and holds them responsible for these assignments. Like the ship's captain, the manager charts the course. What path will the ship take to cross the ocean? He makes the tough decisions when the ship is about to sail through a hurricane. Do they sail through it or go around it? The ship's team must work together as a team to make the goals laid out by the captain. They cannot be working on competing or opposing goals.

A good manager leads like a good shepherd. He doesn't drive the sheep. He walks in front of them, and they follow him. There are two qualities involved here. The first is that the manager knows where he is going, and the second is that the sheep want to follow him. What makes this work with the manager is hard to describe. Leadership is a gift from God, whether the leader is leading the family, the church, or a business department. This leadership involves motivating, encouraging, and coaching. The leader must also be accessible to his people.

A good manager leads like a good shepherd.

Some managers are creative and visionary, but not all. Big vision is usually a gift held for the heads of larger organizations.

Good managers must love their people and be concerned about their emotional state. They should be good listeners.

Good managers are peacemakers. They must be able to work through conflicts. They control their emotions, and people are not on pins and needles in their presence. They don't take offense easily themselves, and they always work to bring the team back to a positive, hopeful attitude.

> He who is slow to anger is better than the mighty,
> And he who rules his spirit than he who takes a city. (Prov. 16:32)
>
> Also do not take to heart everything people say,
> Lest you hear your servant cursing you. (Eccl. 7:21)

Good managers understand the vision or the mission of the organization, and do their best to steward the resources they are given to achieve the goals. Often, managers are hired by owners, or executive officers, or board members of the organization. They are men or women who understand how to operate under authority.

Good managers delegate tasks well, and they are aware of what everybody is doing in the organization. They find ways to maximize performance without overly stressing their workers.

Good managers are usually the most knowledgeable about the big picture and the little puzzle pieces in the project at hand. They are able to retain a lot of information without acting like a know-it-all.

Good managers are always looking for strengths in the team members. They will try to fit everybody's strengths to where those strengths can best be used.

Good managers are constantly looking for ways to mentor, especially for those who want it.

Good managers will communicate clearly with their employees. They will go out of their way to make sure they are understood. Does everybody in the organization understand the goals?

Good managers aren't interested in blaming other people for failures.

They will take advantage of mistakes and will use them to help team members learn and grow as contributors.

Good Christian managers will lead as Jesus led. They will see themselves as serving their employees—bearing their burdens, helping with the tough projects, and exercising patient encouragement, coaching, and admonishing. They are willing to suffer more than the rest of the team, if necessary. Those who are gifted to lead and follow the example of Jesus will be good managers in businesses.

This is the picture of good management. Sadly, the world is full of bad managers. Bad managers will rely on anger and control, threats, and manipulation to get people to do what they want them to do. In the long run, though, this kind of management will fail. Ephesians 6 warns against managing people by threats:

> With goodwill [do your] service, as to the Lord, and not to men, knowing that whatever good anyone does, he will receive the same from the Lord, whether he is a slave or free. And you, masters, do the same things to them, giving up threatening, knowing that your own Master also is in heaven, and there is no partiality with Him. (Eph. 6:7-9)

THE GENERAL DIVISION OF LABOR IN A COMPANY

With the exception of self-employed people (who don't have any other employees), every company works like a team. Just like with soccer or football, the team must work together to move the ball down the field and make a goal or touchdown.

A soccer team is made up of the forward striker, center forward, left midfielders, right midfielder, center back, fullback, wingback, and goalkeeper. A business team is made up of the accountant, the sales man, the customer service representative, the production operator and technician, the quality inspector, and the creator or engineer. Several organization charts are provided at the end of this chapter. Organization charts are a good way to see the hierarchy of accountability in the business and how the team members interrelate.

The *accountant's* job is to keep track of money coming in (income) and money going out (expenses). She is usually responsible for filing wage withholding taxes, sales taxes, and income taxes. She prepares reports for management so everybody knows how well or how badly the business is doing.

The *salesman* is responsible for selling the product or service.

The *customer service representative* handles customer questions and complaints. He will answer questions about the product and take care of service

Customer service representative

or repair needs. These team members are usually people persons—they like to work with people.

The *production operators* and *technicians* are the team members who serve as the backbone of the company. They do the core work for the company, so to speak. They make the products or provide the service of the business for the customer base. They mow lawns. They cook the food in restaurants. They make the widgets. They pound nails and build the homes. Technicians are also responsible for fixing the tooling or equipment used to make the products.

The *quality inspector* is responsible for making sure the company is not

A quality inspector makes sure the work was done right.

shipping any defective product. The quality department is committed to zero defects and maintaining high levels of customer satisfaction.

Big companies will also hire a *safety inspector* to make sure all the safety requirements are being followed.

The *creator* or *engineer* is responsible for designing new products and coming up with new ideas for the future. The engineer also adds new features and improves existing products. Every company needs to adapt to changing market demand.

Big companies usually need *lawyers* to help them through government regulations and lawsuits.

Big companies also use a *human resources department* to oversee the hiring of new employees.

Various companies offer different products and services. For example, hospitals and medical centers provide the service of healing. Doctors and nurses are the production operators. And medical researchers are the engineers responsible for identifying new medicines and cures. For restaurants, the cooks are the operators, and the waiters are the customer service representatives or salesmen.

COMPANY ORGANIZATION CHART
infographics for business

- Chief Executive Officer
- General Directors

- Marketing
- Sales
- Advertising

- Operations
- Production
- Customer service

- Administration
- Finance
- Human resource

Systems and sub-systems are found within the above business activities

- Lead Generation
- Lead Conversion
- Sales Presentation
- Product Testing
- Pricing

- Manufacturing
- Inventory Mgmt
- Quality Control
- Purchasing
- Maintenance

- Accounting
- Payroll
- Collections
- Hiring
- Training

Big Company "Org" Chart

Where do you fit into all of this? What are your gifts? What team position will you play in this economy? That's the subject of the next chapter.

General Performance Evaluation Form

Employee: _____ Driver Number: _____
Job Title: _____ Date of Last Evaluation: _____
Evaluation:

	EVALUATION FACTORS	S	A	NI
Dedication	Reports to work on time.			
	Uses time constructively.			
Performance	Good working knowledge of job assignment.			
	Organizes and performs work in a timely, professional manner.			
Cooperation	Willingly accepts work assignments.			
	Willingly accepts changes in assignments not directly related to job.			
Initiative	Performs assigned duties with little or no supervision.			
	Performs assigned duties with little or no supervision, even under pressure.			
	Strives to meet deadlines.			
Communication	Communicates clearly and intelligently in person and during telephone contacts.			
Teamwork	Works well with fellow employees without friction.			
Character	Accepts constructive criticism without unfavorable responses.			
Responsiveness	Handles stressful situations with tact.			
Personality	Demonstrates a pleasant, calm personality when dealing with customers and fellow employees.			
Appearance	Well groomed. Clean. Neat.			
	Dresses appropriately for work.			
Work Habits	Maintains neat and orderly workstation.			
	Maintains neat and orderly paperwork.			

LEGEND: S = Satisfactory   A = Adequate   NI = Needs Improvement

Comments and Recommendations: _____
_____
_____
_____

This performance evaluation has been reviewed with me, and I understand that I may attach my comments, if desired.

Employee Signature: _____ Date: _____
Evaluation Performed by: _____ Date: _____

A sample performance evaluation form.

13

YOUR CALLING IN LIFE

Let each one remain in the same calling in which he was called. Were you called while a slave? Do not be concerned about it; but if you can be made free, rather use it. For he who is called in the Lord while a slave is the Lord's freedman. Likewise he who is called while free is Christ's slave. You were bought at a price; do not become slaves of men. Brethren, let each one remain with God in that state in which he was called.

(1 Cor. 7:20-24)

In this passage from 1 Corinthians, we discover that God calls each of us to a certain place in life. Why does one person become a president of a large company while another digs ditches for a living? Certainly, God puts each of us into various positions in this world. Yet, the same passage describes the preferred state as being free from excessive enslavement at the hands of men. This is why Christians have worked hard to eliminate perpetual slavery during the early centuries (in the Roman Empire) until the 1860s (in the Americas). With all that said, still some are called to be rich and some are called to be not so rich. These words do encourage us to be content with wherever God has placed us in this life. In the words of Paul:

> Not that I speak in regard to need, for I have learned in whatever state I am, to be content: I know how to be abased, and I know how to abound. Everywhere and in all things I have learned both to be full and to be hungry, both to abound and to suffer need. I can do all things through Christ who strengthens me. (Phil. 4:11-13)

God's calling on your life is like a military draft.

A calling is much like a military draft. When a national government drafts a young man into military service, he cannot run away from his position. There are some exemptions allowed, but if a young man is drafted, he has been called by a higher authority to that position. He must serve out his time. If he was to inform his superior, "I don't feel called to this," what would his superior say? Of course, the young man *is* called to it. He has been drafted into the armed forces by the national government. A calling is a responsibility placed upon us from an outside source – a higher authority.

As believers who serve the Lord Jesus Christ and submit to God's will for our lives, we hear God's call and respond to it in obedience.

A calling is something you have to do because you receive the call from God. The calling binds you to pursue it. There are general callings, such as being a husband or a wife or a father or mother. Then there are more specific callings, such as the calling to invent something, or to build something, or to form a business.

The difference between a job and a calling is that there is a higher sense of obligation to follow through on the calling. A higher authority (God, in this case) has called you to this. You cannot quit and walk away from a calling without suffering severe repercussions. Suppose someone signed up for a job as a ferryboat captain across a river. He takes the ferry across the river ten times every day, six days a week. On any given day, he may quit the job. But when the same captain signs up to navigate a ship across a 350,000-mile ocean, he cannot quit halfway across. He is committed to carry the mission through to the end. That is calling.

HOW TO KNOW YOUR CALLING

> Every good gift and every perfect gift is from above, and comes down from the Father of lights, with whom there is no variation or shadow of turning. (Jas. 1:17)

But what is God's calling on your life? The most obvious and foremost way to realize your calling is to consider those things going on in your life right now. Whatever you have received has come from God. He has brought opportunities to your door. Perhaps, He has provided finances for an education. Certainly, He has endowed you with certain gifts and abilities. You have been prevented from achieving certain goals because His providence has placed limitations upon you. Then, on the other hand, you have accomplished certain things, but only because He has allowed you to do them. Contrary to the silly suggestions that come from the positive thinking cheerleaders, you can't achieve whatever you set out to do. Don't listen to people who say, "If you can dream it, you can do it," or "You can achieve anything. The power lies within you." This simply isn't true, and to make such claims is pure arrogance and denies the truth of James 4.

> Come now, you who say, "Today or tomorrow we will go to such and such a city, spend a year there, buy and sell, and make a profit"; whereas you do not know what will happen tomorrow. For what is your life? It is even a vapor that appears for a little time and then vanishes away. Instead you ought to say, "If the Lord wills, we shall live and do this or that." But now you boast in your arrogance. All such boasting is evil. (Jas. 4:13-16)

Mothers are called by God to care for their children.

You can only achieve those goals which align with the will of God for your life. But how do you know what God's specific, revealed will is for your life? Let's define it this way. *God's calling for you is the specific responsibil-*

ities and work opportunities before you which best fit your talents, abilities, interests, and preparation.

Your calling is more than your job.

Your calling includes your marriage if you are married. In this case, you are called to be a husband or a wife.

Your calling includes the gifts you share in your local church body.

Your calling includes raising children, fixing meals, changing diapers, providing hospitality, and discipling your own children.

If you are young and unmarried, here is the best advice: Don't sit around trying to figure out what you are supposed to do when you grow up. Take advantage of the opportunities in front of you. God has placed these opportunities there for you. Perhaps you have run into a manager of a fast food restaurant at your church, and he has offered you a job. Take it. If you are faced with three opportunities, choose the one that best fits your interests and abilities. Early on in your productive years, always prefer the opportunity that offers the most potential for learning. If the manager of one of three restaurants would be most likely to mentor you in the business, that should weigh heavily on your decision.

Between the ages of twelve and twenty-two, you need to be carefully assessing your major gifts and talents. Consider a career and life path assessment, such as that provided by Crown Financial Ministries.[104] A good career test will look at your strengths, interests, values, skills, personality, and motivations.

You should have a general understanding of your aptitude or ease of picking up certain skills or concepts. (For example, some people have more of an aptitude for singing than others.) The following aptitudes are some of those most commonly used in the workplace:

1. Inductive Reasoning Aptitude

This is the ability to collect information and draw conclusions from that information. Research scientists are best at this.

2. Auditory Aptitude

This is the ability to make out sounds and musical pitch. Musicians, singers, and audio engineers need a good ear.

3. Physical Aptitude

This involves physical strength and coordination as well as hand-eye coordination. Those with a physical aptitude are good at sports or as firefighters, personal trainers, soldiers, and construction workers.

4. Linguistic Aptitude

This is possessed by those who pick up new languages quickly. Memorization of Scripture, speeches, and poems come easily for these folks. Missionaries, translators, pastors, and teachers should demonstrate this gift (at least to some extent).

5. Numerical Aptitude

This is the gift of mathematics. Those bearing this gift can memorize numbers, analyze data, and find relationships between data sets. This aptitude is important for those working in finance, higher level accounting, statistics, and economic studies.

6. Clerical Aptitude

This is a gift belonging to highly organized people. They are usually active in accounting, banking, and clerical work. They may or may not be good in math.

7. Analytical Aptitude

This is the ability to organize material logically and identify solutions to problems. These are engineers and practical scientists who can take abstract ideas like math and apply it to the real world.

8. Mechanical Aptitude

This is the ability to figure out how mechanical things work by sight, touch, and visualized cause and effect relationships. Often this mechanical aptitude comes by relating how things work in the present situation to how things have worked in other situations. Auto and airplane mechanics, appliance repairmen, and machine operators usually have a strong mechanical aptitude.

9. Artistic Aptitude

Artists can visualize what might look pleasing to themselves and to others. Anybody with this gift would do well in graphic design, hair styling, and interior design.

Personality assessments like the Myers-Briggs test (and others) are not very accurate. Categorizing personalities is extremely hard to do because in the infinite wisdom of the Creator, He made every person on earth a little bit different.

Therefore, the best way to know what you will do in life is to jump into the business world and do something. With your first job, study yourself as you work.

What part of the job do you enjoy?
What part of the job do you find most tedious?
What part of the job have you figured out?

Artistic aptitude

What part of the job have you not figured out?

Where do you see the most growth in terms of your competence in the job?

KNOW GOD'S WILL FOR YOUR LIFE

When you ask to know God's will for your life, you are speaking of a *revealed* will. You want to know what God wants you to do today and the next day. On the other hand, God also has a *decretive* or a secret will, in which He has worked out the details of your life (much as in the case of Joseph). Being sold into Egypt as a slave and then imprisoned by Potiphar was God's predestined plan for Joseph's life. These details were not known to Joseph until they played out in his life. Likewise, we cannot know God's secret will for our lives until we experience the events He has planned for us.

While we cannot know God's secret will ahead of time, we can seek to know His revealed will for us. This comes first by reading the Word. For example, we know that He would have us make good use of our gifts and

If an opportunity for good work presents itself, take it.

talents. But we must get to know our natural aptitudes before we know what our gifts and talents are. Then we can make use of these talents in the marketplace and the home. That is God's revealed will for us.

Opportunities may present God's revealed will for our lives as well. Suppose, for example, that a roofer in the church has a huge increase in his workload, and he asks for your help. You could stay home and play video games, or you could go out and help him. To turn down that work opportunity might be the most slothful thing and the most unloving thing you could do. The revealed will of God for your life in that situation might very well be to help the brother in Christ with his business.

You have heard the common question, "What do you want to be when you grow up?" Typically, the questioners are asking whether you want to be a civil engineer, an architect, or something else. The college advisor or the teacher is asking about your primary source of income. The emphasis is on money. Their questions are limited to quid-pro-quo money-making career matters. They are really asking, "About how much money will you earn?" "What will the size of your cubicle be?" "Where will you work on the corporate ladder?" This emphasis does not reflect the mind of Christ.

> Therefore do not worry, saying, "What shall we eat?" or "What shall we drink?" or "What shall we wear?" For after all these things the Gentiles seek. For your heavenly Father knows that you need all these things. But seek first the kingdom of God and His righteousness, and all these things shall be added to you. (Matt. 6:31-33)

Economic concerns are not primary when it comes to God's purpose for your life. Don't worry about what you will eat or what you will wear. Rather, seek the kingdom of God, which is righteousness, peace, and joy in the Holy Spirit (Rom. 14:17). That is, we are to seek the things that yield righteousness, peace, and joy in the Holy Spirit. Actually, in some situations, you may have to give up money in order to obtain these things. Peace speaks to your relationship with God and with others. Joy comes in the presence of God, where the church meets together. Joy comes in the realization of God's salvation and the gospel of Christ (Hab. 3:17-18). Joy comes by answered prayer (John 16:24) and by reading God's Word (Ps. 119:111).

Righteousness (in sanctification) comes by obeying God's Word. In the same context as this passage on the kingdom of God, Jesus speaks of this righteousness.

> Do not think that I came to destroy the Law or the Prophets. I did not come to destroy but to fulfill. For assuredly, I say to you, till heaven and earth pass away, one jot or one tittle will by no means pass from the law till all is fulfilled. Whoever therefore breaks one of the least of these commandments, and teaches men so, shall be called least in the kingdom of heaven; but whoever does and teaches them, he shall be called great in the kingdom of heaven. For I say to you, that unless your righteousness exceeds the righteousness of the scribes and Pharisees, you will by no means enter the kingdom of heaven. (Matt. 5:17-20)

Importantly, keep in mind that the law cannot force anybody to keep the law. Rather, it is by grace that we are enabled to keep God's law. This is the point Paul makes in Romans 8:

> For what the law could not do in that it was weak through the flesh, God did by sending His own Son in the likeness of sinful flesh, on account of sin: He condemned sin in the flesh, that the righteous requirement of the law might be fulfilled in us who do not walk according to the flesh but according to the Spirit. (Rom. 8:3-4)

This is the revealed will of God for our lives. As Christians, we are absolutely certain that this is our calling. Seek the kingdom of God and His righteousness first and foremost.

THE GENDER-SPECIFIC CALLING

Increasingly, the modern world has denied gender differences. The world has put men and women in what we call "the gender blender." For instance, Harvard University's president was forced to resign in 2005 because he had suggested that women were different from men. To point out that women are physically or constitutionally different from men would get you laughed to scorn. In this present age, we are forced to deny reality and embrace the ultimate absurdities. But still, those who still think rationally about these things must insist that women can birth children, and men can't. That's an obvious constitutional difference. Men have 26 pounds (12 kg) more muscle mass than women. And women have 40 percent less upper-body strength on average. God designed men and women this way, and this will affect their respective callings. Women have not been gifted with physical strength. They have other strengths, and God will call them to different functions in life than He calls men to.

If we are interested in God's revealed will for our lives, we should look for this in His Word. What does God want of us? It turns out that God's Word contains gender-specific instructions concerning our respective callings.

Are you a young man or a young woman? The Lord has specific instructions for both. Before identifying a specific career path, what is the more fundamental calling? Here is God's vision for your life:

GOD'S CALLING ON MEN

First, God assigned men to take dominion over the ground as well as the thorns and thistles. This is the nature of the curse for the male. When this is shifted to the woman, to be a double curse, society begins to unravel.

> Cursed is the ground for your sake;
> In toil you shall eat of it
> All the days of your life.
> Both thorns and thistles it shall bring forth for you,
> And you shall eat the herb of the field.
> In the sweat of your face you shall eat bread. (Gen. 3:17-19)

Secondly, the Lord holds men responsible for taking care of the material needs of their families (and that includes their widowed mothers and grandmothers).

> Now she who is really a widow, and left alone, trusts in God and continues in supplications and prayers night and day. But she who lives in pleasure is dead while she lives. And these things command, that they may be blameless. But if anyone does not provide for his own, and especially for those of his household, he has denied the faith and is worse than an unbeliever. (1 Tim. 5:5-8)

Thirdly, the young man is assigned to be a protector and defender of his family (Deut. 20:1-5; Neh. 4:14).

> And I looked, and arose and said to the nobles, to the leaders, and to the rest of the people, "Do not be afraid of them. Remember the Lord, great and awesome, and fight for your brethren, your sons, your daughters, your wives, and your houses." (Neh. 4:14)

Fourthly, for men who will be married, the Lord would have them to sacrificially love their wives as Christ loved the church and gave Himself for it (Eph. 5:25, 28).

Fifthly, the Lord would have men to be shepherds and teachers of their

God calls men to take dominion of the ground.

children. This instruction He specifically directs towards fathers in Ephesians 6. Also, He expects husbands and fathers to understand the Word and answer questions about the Word in the home.

> And you, fathers, do not provoke your children to wrath, but bring them up in the training and admonition of the Lord. (Eph. 6:4)

Fathers are responsible for teaching their children God's Word.

The question to ask now is: how can a young man prepare himself for this calling? By learning the discipline of hard work, by studying the Word of God, by sharing the Word with others, by giving of himself for others in sacrificial love, he prepares for this calling. This preparatory work is far more important than taking college courses or military experience. Seek what God wants for your life first, and everything else will come.

GOD'S CALLING ON WOMEN

Even though the vast majority of women in our society are not seeking after God's vision for womanhood, the godly woman should be very interested in what God says about her life. The world is primarily interested in the woman's independence from the family. But what the world will not tell you is that they believe women (as well as men and children) are supposed to be even more dependent on the government for jobs, for welfare, for social security, and for medical help.

Now more than ever, young people need to turn to the Bible for direction. What does God want for you?

For those who will be married, a woman is created to be a helper for her husband in his tasks.

> And the LORD God said, "It is not good that man should be alone; I will make him a helper comparable to him." Out of the ground the LORD God formed every beast of the field and every bird of the air, and brought them to Adam to see what he would call them. . . . But for Adam there was not found a helper comparable to him. And the LORD God caused a deep sleep to fall on Adam, and he slept; and He took one of his ribs, and closed up the flesh in its place. Then the rib which the LORD God had taken from man He made into a woman, and He brought her to the man. (Gen. 2:18-22)

As an ax head upon an ax handle, the woman and the man form an efficient economic team. The woman completes the man as an ax handle attached to the ax head completes an economic tool. Not much more needs to be added to this except to say that every young woman (who will be married) should prepare for this role. What can she do in her developmental years to prepare to be a helper? She will help her husband in the economic element of the home. How can she prepare for this now?

The Proverbs 31 woman doesn't report to a corporate boss. Her economic contribution is more for her husband than for fourteen layers of management in some large business.

WHO CAN FIND A VIRTUOUS WIFE?

> For her worth is far above rubies.
> The heart of her husband safely trusts her;
> So he will have no lack of gain. (Prov. 31:10-11)

Secondly, God calls a woman (who is to be married) to be a home manager.

> Therefore I desire that the younger widows marry, bear children, manage the house, give no opportunity to the adversary to speak reproachfully. (1 Tim. 5:14)

> The older women likewise, that they be reverent in behavior, not slanderers, not given to much wine, teachers of good things—that they admonish the young women to love their husbands, to love their children, to be discreet, chaste, homemakers [home managers], good, obedient to their own husbands, that the word of God may not be blasphemed. (Tit. 2:3-5)

While the wife is a vital element in the household economy, there is a difference between the man and the woman in this economy. They do not fulfill the same role. Nowhere is the man referred to as the "home manager." The man has more of a role outside of the home than the wife, whose focus is to manage the resources of the home. She invests. She keeps accounts. She considers a field and buys it. She produces. Her attention is more toward conserving, investing, and providing needful things for her children and her husband.

God's normal role for most women is that they will get married at some point in their life. But keep in mind that there are exceptions to the norm. About 95% of men and women get married at some point, though many young people are delaying marriage now. Between 1960 and 2018, the average marriage age for women moved from twenty to twenty-eight years old. The blessings of marriage and the social obligation to be married have been greatly downplayed in modern society. Life is lived for self. Children are not considered a blessing. Many babies are killed by abortion or by the use of a device called the IUD. Security is found in the state instead of in the family. The situation for women and families is dreadful because the world has the wrong values.

The character and focal point of the godly woman is presented in 1 Timothy 2:9-15. She is modest in heart and dress, and she is generous in charitable works.

Wives and mothers are to be home managers.

> In like manner also, that the women adorn themselves in modest apparel, with propriety and moderation, not with braided hair or gold or pearls or costly clothing, but, which is proper for women professing godliness, with good works. Let a woman learn in silence with all submission. And I do not permit a woman to teach or to have authority over a man, but to be in silence. For Adam was formed first, then Eve. And Adam was not deceived, but the woman being deceived, fell into transgression. Nevertheless she will be saved in childbearing if they continue in faith, love, and holiness, with self-control. (1 Tim. 2:9-15)

None of this comports with the world's vision for womanhood in the 21st century. But shall we trust a world that has destroyed the family, economies, and human society? Or shall we trust God? If this should be a woman's vision, what can a young woman do to prepare for life? Do you associate with friends who seek after this biblical ideal?

Much of Proverbs 31 and these New Testament passages assume an active home economy. The development of home-based economies will provide income streams, while still providing opportunity for nurturing children and revitalizing motherhood, fatherhood, and a vibrant family life.

The feminist lie told in the 1970s and 1980s promised "you can have it all." Consequently, many women put career first but never got around to having a family. With a home-based economy, women can realize the calling to motherhood, while providing an economic benefit at the same time.

HOW TO PREPARE FOR YOUR CALLING

> Get wisdom! Get understanding!
> Do not forget, nor turn away from the words of my mouth.
> Do not forsake her, and she will preserve you;
> Love her, and she will keep you.
> Wisdom is the principal thing;
> Therefore get wisdom.
> And in all your getting, get understanding. (Prov. 4:5-7)

God's Word underscores wisdom and true knowledge as a value worth pursuing. But this, of course, is that wisdom which begins with the fear of God. This is not necessarily a wisdom that is traded immediately for big money. That is, true wisdom is needed for a successful life, but true success is not measured by monetary wealth. Your first obligation is to seek out wisdom, which comes from God; and sometimes this wisdom may be obtained from wise men or women in your life. One of the most important maxims in life is found in Proverbs 13:20:

> He who walks with wise men will be wise, but the companion of fools will be destroyed.

If you want to be mature in faith, walk with people who are mature in faith. If you want to be successful, walk with successful people.

Whether the parable of talents applies to a spiritual heritage or to the particular economic gifts and talents God has given you, the principle remains the same. You have a responsibility to use these gifts and grow them. Make an inventory of each of your gifts, talents, and interests. How can these be used to benefit others and provide economic increase? Consider how you might hone each of these abilities. Some of these gifts might require college classes for more honing.

College Quadrangle

If you choose the college track, be aware that most college degree programs use a one-size-fits-all approach to preparing young people for life. Should a young man gifted in math take on an undergraduate program in mathematics, he shouldn't forget about his other gifts and interests which will need to be honed. All of our gifts should be brought to bear in life, and the early years are opportunities for honing and learning.

Before leaving the home, all young persons should develop basic business skills or any other skill that corresponds to the gifts God has given them. For example, most young people should learn to type (ideally, at least 80 words per minute). Other important skills that come in handy today include speech and debate, graphic design, negotiating and selling, or basic household and auto repair.

THINK OUT OF THE BOX

The college option is already fading. Over the last ten years, college enrollment has dropped by 4,000,000 students. At this rate, within ten years, college enrollment will have dropped by half. More than ever before, every

Learning to type is a valuable skill in the modern world.

family must be thinking "out of the box" when it comes to this preparation for life. Bootcamps, online tutorials, online college, and mentorships can be far more efficient and effective in the current business environment. Increasingly, large companies are expanding their own training and certification programs. Computer and engineering firms will provide their own education, as will medical facilities for future doctors and nursing staff. Smaller tech companies are more inclined to bring young, bright recruits onboatd for on-the-job training. Now more than ever, young people need to consider their options and use their time and money carefully as they prepare for their economic contributions in the market.

COLLEGE EDUCATION

In some cases, college will offer some economic benefit for those pursuing certain careers. In most modern nations, a college degree is still required for certain professions. America's first college was put in place to train pastors for ministry. The college was a seminary for pastors. Later, liberal arts programs were put in place to present a humanist worldview, and to raise up more teachers to take that worldview into public schools.

Entire university departments are dedicated to opposing God's truth concerning

On-the-job training

economics, man's psyche (psychology), man's problem, the origins of the world (anthropology and archeology), and other areas of study. Education becomes counterproductive when the entire coursework opposes God's truth and replaces it with falsehoods.

College education has become less helpful to the economy as well. The aggregate college student loan programs in the US have now topped $1.73 trillion (as of 2021). That's 8% of the GDP, up from 2.8% of the GDP in 2003. A total of 43 million Americans were saddled by college debt in 2021—over 60% of the twenty-five to forty-four-year-old working population in America.

The average college debt in 1975 was only $1,000 (in today's dollars). That debt could have been paid off in just nine months if 10% of a person's income was put toward paying off the debt. In 2021, the average college debt was up to $32,600; and this would take the average college graduate six years to pay off, assuming about 10% of the person's income was put into paying off the debt. That's eight times the burden of debt carried by the average college graduate in 1975. With 60% of workers taking an average of six years to pay off college debts, this will have a profound effect on human society. This further delays marriage or investment in family life, and extend the implosion of the national birth rate for another generation.

People spend anywhere from $80,000 to $400,000 on a four-year college degree. More and more, young people are asking, "Is it worth it?" Some college degrees will provide a better return on investment than others. This means the college graduate will start earning a good salary right away. This enables the graduate to more quickly pay off the money required to get the degree.

Bachelor's Degree Best Return on Investment[105]	
Bachelor's Degree	Cost Paid off in 5 Years
Electrical Engineering	100%
Communication Engineering	100%
Industrial Engineering	100%
Aerospace Engineering	100%
Registered Nursing	100%
Nursing Administration	100%
Nursing Research	100%
Dental Support	100%
Engineering Technology	100%
Construction Management	100%
Drama	0%
Dance	0%
Zoology	0%
Visual Arts	0%
Film	0%
Ecology	0%
Anthropology	0%
Fine Arts	0%
Music	0%

Based on lifetime earnings, the following table rates each degree from 100%

(the highest income) to 50% (the lowest income).

College Major	Lifetime Earnings (100% = $3.8 million) [106]
Chemical Engineering	100%
Aerospace Engineering	94%
Computer Engineering	92%
Finance	92%
Mechanical Engineering	90%
Electrical Engineering	89%
Economics	87%
Civil Engineering	85%
Nursing	84%
Mathematics and Statistics	82%
Accounting	82%
Construction	81%
Marketing	78%
International Business	78%
Physics	77%
Political Science	76%
General Business	75%
Chemistry	74%
Human Resources	72%
Journalism	71%
Public Administration	70%
Architecture	70%
Computer Programming	70%
Biological Sciences	67%
English Language/Literature	62%

College Major	Lifetime Earnings (100% = $3.8 million) [106]
History	62%
Art History	62%
Psychology	61%
Criminal Justice	60%
Mass Media	60%
Agriculture	59%
Liberal Arts	56%
Film/Video/Photography	55%
Plant Science	55%
Recreation	53%
Fine Arts	52%
Social Work	52%
Cosmetology	51%
Education	50%

THREE BASIC ELEMENTS TO LIFE PREPARATION

> Come, you children, listen to me;
> I will teach you the fear of the Lord.
> Who is the man who desires life,
> And loves many days, that he may see good?
> Keep your tongue from evil,
> And your lips from speaking deceit.
> Depart from evil and do good;
> Seek peace and pursue it. (Ps. 34:11-14)

As the young person gears up for marriage, work, and spiritual maturity, there are three key elements that must be integrated as best as possible on a daily basis: knowledge, spiritual accountability, and life integration. Like three legs on a stool, these three elements should all develop together (at the same time). Modern education tends to separate these things and thereby give an inadequate preparation for life. To separate knowledge from the fear of God, worship, and life usually produces pride and an empty, useless sort of knowledge. Separating spiritual accountability and discipleship from economic preparation usually results in a spiritual downgrade over that period of time in which a young person attends college.

Everybody needs to gain a little knowledge, whatever their economic pursuit, whether it be engineering, home health care, plumbing, pastoring, or some kind of home business. This knowledge is usually obtained through books, lectures, etc. However, the beginning of knowledge is the fear of God (according to the most fundamental lesson found in Proverbs 1:7). So, right knowledge must be centered on the fear of God, reverence for God, and worship of God. Modern education generally neglects this

Whether you are a plumber, an engineer, a chemist, a mother, etc., we must all do our work to the glory of God.

critical component of education. In every case where this is neglected, it will prove to be a fatal oversight. The Christian student, however, must learn his chemistry and his plumbing in the fear of God. In order to be a good plumber or a good engineer, he must fear God. Thus, reverence for God and worship of God should be tightly bound into the education of the student. There should be some daily worship, daily accountability, and daily character formation going on in the life of the young man and young woman. This may come by means of discipleship from parents or pastors in a church. It is a critical component. Good Christian mentorship brings all three of these components together.

The weakness of modern education is especially seen in the failure to integrate knowledge into real life. James speaks of the man who hears the word but does not apply it to his life.

> But be doers of the word, and not hearers only, deceiving yourselves. For if anyone is a hearer of the word and not a doer, he is like a man observing his natural face in a mirror; for he observes himself, goes away, and immediately forgets what kind of man he was. But he who looks into the perfect law of liberty and continues in it, and is not a forgetful hearer but a doer of the work, this one will be blessed in what he does. (James 1:22-25)

Most education is a waste of time because true learning doesn't solidify until knowledge is applied. Education is a two-step process. First, we obtain a fragment of knowledge, and then we learn how to plug that piece of knowledge into life. Learning that the distance travelled by a falling object is $1/2\ gt^2$ is pretty useless for the average person—that is, until he walks by a well and drops a stone and counts the seconds it takes for the stone to hit the bottom of the well. Sitting in a classroom for eighteen years learning the "facts," doesn't produce real knowledge until there is real life application of the facts. In most cases, students finally discover the relevance of that knowledge when they enter the workforce at 24-28 years of age. Most college graduates are of little use to the corporate world until they have worked for several years (in on-the-job training). In fact, a number of companies are no longer requiring four-year college degrees for professional jobs—including Google, Penguin Random House, Costco Administration, Hilton, Apple, IBM, Bank of America, and Tesla.[107] Some are offering apprenticeship programs as a replacement for college.[108] Smaller tech companies are more likely to put young, bright high school graduates into an on-the-job training program.

Percent of Workforce with College Degree[109]	Small Tech Company (1-49 employees)	Larger Tech Company (50-999 employees)
Less than 4 Year College Degree	32%	18%
4 Year College Degree	51%	59%
More than 4 Year College Degree	17%	22%

Every young person (16-26 years of age), preparing for life, should be asking this question: How many hours a day are you studying books, submitting yourself to spiritual accountability and worship, and life applying what you are learning? These three components are essential to create a well-rounded student prepared for life and eternity.

MENTORSHIP

Mentorship can bring these pieces together in a beautiful way. A mentor is first and foremost interested in the character of the student. If the mentor is a Christian, he is also interested in the humility and reverence for God in the life of the student. Finally, the mentor is the one to aid the student in integrating his knowledge into real life work, manufacturing, problem-solving, and economic trade. Whether a young man pursues the entrepreneurial track or the college-corporate track, he needs good mentorship to launch him into his calling in life. Mentorship will give him a true taste for life and give him opportunity to better hone in on his calling. How is he going to know the best application of his gifts, talents, and abilities unless he has actually applied his gifts in real-life situations? How many young people have changed their college major three times, spent themselves into $60,000 of debt, and still don't know what they want to do when they grow up? To avoid the predicament of that lost soul still wandering around California "trying to find himself," or playing games in his parents' basement, mentorship in some field of work at seventeen years of age is a terrific antedote! If a young man is looking at engineering, he can try a mentorship with a mechanical engineer for a time. Here he may discover that he is better suited as a civil engineer. But how would he know this unless he had stepped into the pool at some point and received real life experience under an engineering mentor in the field?

Although this author attended one of the best undergraduate engineering schools in California back in the 1980s, the education itself was still altogether insufficient. Not one college professor was interested in developing character or forming relationships with the students. On my first meeting with the professor assigned as my advisor, he informed me, "Don't come by unless you absolutely need to. If I had things my way, I'd just as soon sit here and contemplate my navel." None of the college instructors took an interest in my character or expressed any interest in my faith. Nobody seemed to care if I was obtaining a sort of knowledge leading to pride or whether I was advancing in love for God and others (1 Cor. 8:1). Moreover, the cooperative education and internship programs popular during these years proved to be hardly useful later in life. Typically, these programs lasted only two to three months with little or no direction and mentorship made available by experienced engineers. Mentorship was hardly the vision.

If a young man decides to pursue a calling in law, he will need to complete six or seven years of higher education. But from the beginning of his college work, it would be ideal if he could apprentice with the best Christian attorney in the state. If he studied his law books in the morning and then worked in the law office each afternoon for seven years, he would be far ahead of the pack at the end of this time. During the first year, he may find himself emptying the waste baskets in the office. With the second year, he will help in research, preparing legal briefs, motions, and stipulations. He will assist in the writing and editing of reports, opinions, legal correspondence, and complex contracts. By the third year, he is sitting next to the attorney in the courtroom and assisting him with critical research. Over the years, that young man will come to see the relevance of what he studies in the classroom, and he will learn how it applies in real life. The attorney mentor takes the time to teach the young man the fear of God, and model Christian integrity in the business of law. A faithful mentor will be interested in the character of the apprentice because he knows that character is the key to success.

As that young man graduates from law school and passes the bar, the aircraft of his life will be off the runway, traveling 500 miles an hour towards achieving his life's calling. But what about the law graduate who has received no mentorship and hardly knows how to apply anything he has learned to real court cases in real courtrooms, or the graduate who thinks he knows something but doesn't really understand the legal profession? On graduation, this fellow's aircraft is still wandering around the tarmac trying to find the runway. This kind of education could very well cripple his implementation of his knowledge for a lifetime, especially if it lacks the life-integrative element.

> Then [Jesus] appointed twelve, that they might be with Him and that He might send them out to preach, and to have power to heal sicknesses and to cast out demons. . . (Mk. 3:14-15)

Here are several basic requirements for an effective mentorship.
1. Mentorship requires a time commitment. If Jesus Christ is our guide, an effective mentorship will take place over *a three-year period,* minimum. Setting the ultimate example of discipleship, the Son of God took twelve disciples with Him for three years. If the mentor is only interested in immediate economic value in the investment of his time, it is doubtful that he will want to take the time to mentor. The mentorship is not immediately productive, so it is the longevity of the mentorship that matters (even more than the

weekly time commitment). It will take at least one full year for the apprentice to recognize the mentor's expectations, approach, goals, worldview, strengths, weaknesses, and the means by which he compensates for his weaknesses. The first year is taken up with "getting to know." By the second year, the apprentice begins to ask more intelligent questions in the long discussions. He begins to understand the rhythms of the work week, and he finds ways to make it more efficient and to contribute to the goals of the project(s).

2. Mentorship involves getting to know the apprentice, and vice versa. After the second or third year, the apprentice begins to understand the "system" of knowledge and expertise used by the mentor.

3. Mentorship gives the big picture and ties in the disparate pieces of knowledge into the whole of life and economy. Any business or ministry has overarching goals and objectives. Multiple aspects of the organization work together to achieve those goals. For example, businesses usually include purchasing, marketing, design, manufacturing, service, and management. An apprentice will discover by real life experience how these multiple aspects interrelate. Young engineers will learn how the 85 different classes and disciplines taken over four years in college interrelate to create a product of value for the marketplace. Young accountants will discover how to implement their learning in business law, accounting practices, administration, and marketing into a real business, and contribute to the success of a real company. Without real experience in the business or ministry itself, the apprentices will never see how the parts contribute to the whole.

4. What is taught in the mentorship is far more than what is conveyed in direct verbal communication. The apprentice will learn the way the master craftsman does his work and how to emulate these precise methods. Whether the master is in the business of framing houses, designing circuit boards for customers, writing letters to supporters in a ministry, or filling cavities, the apprentice will pick up on how the master does his work. He watches the mentor talk

to the customer, troubleshoot problems, answer detractors, inspect his own work, correct his own work, and sell his work. At first, the apprentice is taught to perform the tasks exactly the way the master does it. Only when he has learned that well can he begin to develop his own approach.

5. Mentorship is humbling because the *application* of knowledge is always much more difficult than the *retention* of knowledge. This may be one of the reasons why there is some merit to the old adage, "A students wind up teaching, and B students end up working for C students." It is only in real-life experience that a person will learn how to compensate for his own weaknesses, fix his own mistakes, and apply biblical character to life.

6. Mentorship is particularly helpful in cultivating character. And there is nothing more important than character to bring about success in a calling. As we learned in a previous chapter, Dr. Thomas Stanley interviewed 733 American millionaires and identified the top factors considered important in their economic success. Of the thirty

University lecture hall

factors mentioned, academic degrees and academic success were among the least important. The five most important factors listed as most important by these millionaires were *telling the truth, self-discipline, hard work, getting along with people, and having a supportive spouse.* None of these factors are considered primary in the paideia provided in most college programs. Yet these are the lessons that make up the content of God's book on the education of a young person (the book of Proverbs).

Mentorship is an age-old practice, tried and true. When a workman, a business owner, or a professional of any kind has mastered his craft, by the very fact that he has mastered the craft, he is both qualified and obligated to share his wisdom with the next generation of apprentices. To relegate all education to professional teachers rather than masters in the fields is what has contributed to the sub-standard form of preparation most young people receive today.

Mentorship is valuable for many reasons, but chiefly, a long term mentorship program will bring the young person into the industry or job market. This involvement in the field enables networking, getting to know the business, and merging into new opportunities. Also, mentorship helps the young person to test the waters in a certain field. Before committing to a four-year-college degree, it would be far better for a young person to get some experience in the field. Is this really the best fit for that young person's set of gifts and interests?

Given the breakdown of character and the tough economic straits facing the modern world, mentorship seems to be the most promising solution available now. Our world has sufficient access to information, unlike any time in all of human history. But mere information and knowledge is insufficient for the future of the world economy. The only solution to meet the severe problems of the present day, is spiritual discipleship in faith and character. It is what Jesus came to do. Mentorship is the best and only solution to salvage the present economy. It is the greatest need for future marriages and families. It is the greatest need for the future of the local church.

Mentorship has proved to work in Switzerland. In an age where most other Western countries court a youth unemployment rate of 10-30%, Switzerland's hovers around 2% (the lowest in the world).[110]

Youth Unemployment (2021)[111]	
Spain	31%
Italy	30%
Sweden	25%
Greece	25%
Portugal	24%
India	24%
Romania	21%
Australia	14%
UK	12%
New Zealand	10%
US	10%
Switzerland	2%

High school or secondary education in Switzerland is focused on career and technical education (CTE). Commonly, students will spend only one or two days in school and the rest of time, they apply what they learn at school every week in the workplace. While only 25% of Swiss high school graduates take the college route, 70 percent opt for apprenticeship and early entry into the economy.

CONCLUSION

The world has changed dramatically in the last thirty years. The job market will never be the same as it was in the 1980s and 1990s. Therefore, serious-minded young people who want a life and a family in the years to come must take this paradigm shift in life preparation. There are no other reasonable alternatives. What we are presenting is nothing new. We are merely returning to the age-old, time-tested principles for a good education and preparation for life found in the Bible. As markets tumble and economies stumble, we can be sure that God's wisdom is sufficient to form our lives on firmer foundations. We trust God will use these ideas to equip a new generation of young men and women to rebuild family economies and a new socio-economic system for the next era of human history.

> Therefore whoever hears these sayings of Mine, and does them, I will liken him to a wise man who built his house on the rock: and the rain descended, the floods came, and the winds blew and beat on that house; and it did not fall, for it was founded on the rock. (Matt. 7:24-25)

ENDNOTES

1. M. Shahbandeh, "Total U.S. domestic grain use 2001-2021," Statista, May 14, 2021, https://www.statista.com/statistics/190345/total-us-domestic-grain-use-from-2001/; M. Shahbandeh, "U.S. permanent grain storage capacity 2000 to 2018, by type," Statista, Sep 25, 2020, https://www.statista.com/statistics/802000/top-us-grain-storage-capacity-by-type/.

2. "Corruption Perceptions Index," Transparency International, https://www.transparency.org/en/cpi/2020/index/nzl.

3. Léon Gautier, *Chivalry* (Routledge, 1891), 46.

4. Adam Smith, *The Wealth of Nations: An inquiry into the nature and causes of the Wealth of Nations* (London: 1776), Book I, Chapter II.

5. Smith, *The Wealth of Nations*, Book IV, Chapter II.

6. https://www.theguardian.com/environment/2019/mar/09/american-food-giants-swallow-the-family-farms-iowa

7. Rory Groves, *Durable Trades: Family-Centered Economies That Have Stood the Test of Time* (Front Porch Republic Books, 2020), 26.

8. Harriet Robinson, *Loom and Spindle* (New York: Thomas Y. Cromwell & Company, 1898), 13.

9. John Ikerd, "Is Sustainable Capitalism Possible?" Lecture at The Life Economy Session of The World Life-Culture Forum, Gyengong'gi Province, Republic of Korea, June 20, 2006, p. 5. http://web.missouri.edu/ikerdj/papers/KoreaSustainableCapitalism.pdf.

10. Thomas Jefferson, *Notes on the State of Virginia*, Query XVIII.

11. Thomas Lansford, *Communism* (New York: Cavendish Square Publishing, 2007), 10.

12. Karl Marx, *The Communist Manifesto*, IV.

13. Ibid., II.

14. Karl Marx, Doctoral Thesis: *The Difference Between the Democritean and Epicurean Philosophy of Nature* (1841).

15. Kevin Swanson, *Apostate: Men Who Destroyed the Christian West* (Generations, 2013), 109-110; Casey Chalk, "Karl Marx's Shameful Life Repudiates His Evil Ideology," *The Federalist*, November 30, 2020, https://thefederalist.com/2020/11/30/karl-marxs-shameful-life-repudiates-his-evil-ideology/; Paul Kengor, "Americans Buy Into Marxist

Family Planning" *The Federalist*, June 29, 2015, https://thefederalist.com/2015/06/29/americans-buy-into-marxist-family-planning/; Bill Flax, "Do Marxism And Christianity Have Anything In Common?" *Forbes*, May 12, 2011, https://www.forbes.com/sites/billflax/2011/05/12/do-marxism-and-christianity-have-anything-in-common.

16. Paul Johnson, *Intellectuals* (New York: Harper and Row, 1988), 72.

17. "Cuba - Poverty and wealth," *Encyclopedia of the Nations*, https://www.nationsencyclopedia.com/economies/Americas/Cuba-POVERTY-AND-WEALTH.html

18. Harrison Jacobs, "I traveled to Cuba," *Business Insider*, January 1, 2017, https://www.businessinsider.com/cuba-fidel-castro-death-changes-2016-12.

19. "Pre-Castro Cuba," American Experience, PBS, https://www.pbs.org/wgbh/americanexperience/features/comandante-pre-castro-cuba/; Gladys Martinez, "Cuba Before Castro," *CONTACTO Magazine*,.

20. Allan C. Carlson, "The New Agrarian: An Interview with Allan C. Carlson," *The Grovestead Newsletter*, Volume 3, Issue 4 (2020).

21. Thomas Jefferson, *Letter to John Jay*, August 23, 1785..

22. Carlson, "The New Agrarian."

23. C. R. Wiley, "Against the Recreational Household," recorded at The Grovestead Farm, August 27, 2021.

24. Friedrich Engels, *The New Moral World*, No. 19 (1843).

25. The CDC reports that the birth rate in America "has generally been below replacement level since 1971": Hamilton, Brady, et al., "Births: Provisional Data for 2017," *Vital Statistics Rapid Release*, May 2018, https://www.cdc.gov/nchs/data/vsrr/report004.pdf.

26. Robinson, *Loom and Spindle*, 2; Pitirim Sorokin, *The Crisis of Our Age* (New York: E. P Dutton, 1941), 191.

27. Various studies indicate that between 60% and 90% of youth abandon the faith of their parents after leaving high school (Lifeway Research; Barna Group; Southern Baptist Council on Family Life).

28. Friedrich Engels, *Origins of the Family, Private Property, and the State*, II.4.

29. Karl Marx, Letter to Friedrich Engels on June 21, 1854, published in *Marx-Engels Werke* (Berlin, 1959), XXVIII, 371.

30. Ikerd, "Is Sustainable Capitalism Possible?"

31. Allan Carlson, *The Natural Family Where It Belongs* (Routledge, 2014), 4.

32. Ibid.

33. Wright, Carroll, *Comparative Wages, Prices and Cost of Living* (Mass. Bureau of Statistics of Labor, 1885), 10.

34. Groves, *Durable Trades*, 266.

35. https://wol.iza.org/articles/self-employment-and-poverty-in-developing-countries/long

36. "Employee Productivity: The Data Behind How We Waste Time," Knit, https://www.knitpeople.com/blog/employee-productivity-what-are-your-employees-wasting-their-time-on-everyday.

37. Statista Research Department, "Daily time spent on social networking by internet users worldwide from 2012 to 2020," Statista, September 7, 2021, https://www.statista.com/statistics/433871/daily-social-media-usage-worldwide/.

38. Saima Salim, "More than six hours of our day is spent online—Digital 2019 reports," Digital Information World, February 4, 2019, https://www.digitalinformationworld.com/2019/02/internet-users-spend-more-than-a-quarter-of-their-lives-online.html.

39. Millennials: The Me Me Me Generation," *Time*, May 20, 2013, https://time.com/247/millennials-the-me-me-me-generation/.

40. Kristen Bialik and Richard Fry, "Millennial life: How young adulthood today compares with prior generations," Pew Research, February 14, 2019, https://www.pewresearch.org/social-trends/2019/02/14/millennial-life-how-young-adulthood-today-compares-with-prior-generations-2/.

41. Bialik and Fry, "Millennial life: How young adulthood today compares with prior generations."

42. Data derived from "Facts & Data on Small Business and Entrepreneurship," SBE Council, https://sbecouncil.org/about-us/facts-and-data/.

https://tradingeconomics.com/united-states/households-debt-to-gdp

43. https://medium.com/@ravithinkz/before-you-say-may-warren-anderson-rot-in-hell-f068554c65fb

44. Kim Parker, Juliana Menasche Horowitz and Rachel Minkin, "How the Coronavirus Outbreak Has—and Hasn't—Changed the Way Americans Work," *Pew Research*, December 9, 2020, https://www.pewresearch.org/social-trends/2020/12/09/how-the-coronavirus-outbreak-has-and-hasnt-changed-the-way-americans-work/.

45. https://www.fdic.gov/bank/historical/bank/

46. https://fred.stlouisfed.org/series/FEDFUNDS

47. https://fred.stlouisfed.org/series/WFRBLB50107

https://wolfstreet.com/2021/10/02/my-wealth-effect-monitor-for-our-money-printer-economy-is-out-in-the-pandemic-the-fed-totally-blew-out-the-already-gigantic-wealth-disparity/

https://www.federalreserve.gov/releases/z1/dataviz/dfa/distribute/table

48. https://www.business-standard.com/article/international/elon-musk-is-first-person-ever-to-be-worth-over-300-billion-121103000715_1.html

49. "Nonfinancial Corporate Business; Debt Securities and Loans; Liability, Level," Federal Reserve Economic Data, September 23, 2021, https://fred.stlouisfed.org/series/BCNSDODNS.

50. Wolf Richter, "Top 10 Share-Buyback Queens—Big Tech except Intel, Big Banks except Wells Fargo, Buffett—Incinerate Most Cash Ever in Q2. The Rest Lags," Wolf Street, September 25, 2021, https://wolfstreet.com/2021/09/25/top-10-share-buyback-queens-big-tech-except-intel-big-banks-except-wells-fargo-buffett-buy-back-most-shares-ever-in-q2-the-rest-lags/.

51. https://www.foxbusiness.com/markets/apple-first-3-trillion-company-stocks

52. https://www.atlanticcouncil.org/global-qe-tracker/

53. https://wolfstreet.com/2021/11/17/since-2008-monetary-policy-has-cost-american-savers-about-4-trillion/

54. https://www.heritage.org/welfare/report/largest-welfare-increase-us-history-will-boost-government-support-76400-poor-family

55. Kathy Fettke, "18 Best Places to Buy Rental Property in 2021 for Cash Flow & Appreciation," Real Weath Network, June 3, 2021, https://www.realwealthnetwork.com/learn/best-places-to-buy-rental-property/.

56. "Workers Per Retiree: 2015-2100," EconData US, https://www.econdataus.com/workers.html; "Japan will need reforms to ease economic blow of a shrinking workforce," OECD, November 4, 2016, https://www.oecd.org/regional/japan-will-need-reforms-to-ease-economic-blow-of-a-shrinking-workforce.htm; "Ratio of Covered Workers to Beneficiaries," Social Security, https://www.ssa.gov/history/ratios.html.

57. Nicolas Vega, "Here's how much money each generation has saved for retirement," CNBC, August 20, 2021, https://www.cnbc.com/2021/08/20/how-much-each-generation-saves-for-retirement.html; Brad Tuttle, "Gen-

eration Owe: Here's the Average Debt at Every Age," Money, September 9, 2021, https://money.com/average-debt-by-generation-2021/.

58. Ester Bloom, "68% of young people expect an inheritance, yet only 40% of their parents will leave one," CNBC, June 6, 2017, https://www.cnbc.com/2017/06/06/68-percent-of-millennials-expect-an-inheritance-only-40-percent-of-them-will-get.html.

59. Office of Management and Budget, 2019 Data

60. Trace Bribery Risk Matrix, 2021 Results, https://www.traceinternational.org/trace-matrix.

61. "George W. Bush (R), Top Contributors, 2004 Cycle," Open Secrets, https://www.opensecrets.org/pres04/contrib.php?cid=N00008072.

62. Samuel Stebbins and Michael B. Sauter, "These 30 companies, including Boeing, get the most money from the federal government," *USA Today*, March 29, 2019, https://www.usatoday.com/story/money/business/2019/03/27/lockheed-martin-boeing-get-most-money-federal-government/39232293/.

63. "Defense: Top Contributors to Federal Candidates, Parties, and Outside Groups 2020," Open Secrets, https://www.opensecrets.org/industries/contrib.php?cycle=2020&ind=D.

64. Matej Mikulic, "Domestic and international revenue of the U.S. pharmaceutical industry between 1975 and 2020," Statista, September 15, 2021, https://www.statista.com/statistics/275560/domestic-and-international-revenue-of-the-us-pharmaceutical-industry/.

65. Lev Facher, "More than two-thirds of Congress cashed a pharma campaign check in 2020, new STAT analysis shows," STAT, June 9, 2021, https://www.statnews.com/feature/prescription-politics/federal-full-data-set/.

66. Riley Griffin, "Pfizer Boosts Forecast for Vaccine Sales to $33.5 Billion," Bloomberg, July 28, 2021, https://www.bloomberg.com/news/articles/2021-07-28/pfizer-expects-covid-vaccine-sales-to-top-33-billion-this-year.

67. Peter Loftus and Matt Grossman, "Moderna Turns First Profit, Boosted by Its Covid-19 Vaccine," *The Wall Street Journal*, May 6, 2021, https://www.wsj.com/articles/moderna-turns-first-ever-profit-boosted-by-its-covid-19-vaccine-11620302289.

68. "Subsidy Tracker Parent Company Summary: Microsoft," Good Jobs First, 2021, https://subsidytracker.goodjobsfirst.org/parent/microsoft.

69. "Amazon Tracker," Good Jobs First, November 2021, https://www.goodjobsfirst.org/amazon-tracker.

70. Sissi Cao and Jordan Zakarin, "Big Tech and CEOs Poured Millions Into The Election.

Here's Who They Supported," *Observer*, November 2, 2020, https://observer.com/2020/11/big-tech-2020-presidential-election-donation-breakdown-ranking/.

71. Paul C. Light, "The true size of government is nearing a record high," Brookings, October 7, 2020, https://www.brookings.edu/blog/fixgov/2020/10/07/the-true-size-of-government-is-nearing-a-record-high/; "Executive Branch Civilian Employment Since 1940," OPM.gov, https://www.opm.gov/policy-data-oversight/data-analysis-documentation/federal-employment-reports/historical-tables/executive-branch-civilian-employment-since-1940/.

72. Peter Kastor, "The Early Federal Workforce," https://www.brookings.edu/wp-content/uploads/2018/05/the-early-federal-workforce-by-p-kastor.pdf?utm_campaign=Brookings%20Executive%20Education&utm_source=hs_email&utm_medium=email.https://www.brookings.edu/wp-content/uploads/2018/05/the-early-federal-workforce-by-p-kastor.pdf?utm_campaign=Brookings%20Executive%20Education&utm_source=hs_email&utm_medium=email

73. https://www.washingtonpost.com/news/wonk/wp/2012/09/18/who-receives-benefits-from-the-federal-government-in-six-charts/

74. "Real GDP Growth," International Monetary Fund, 2021, https://www.imf.org/external/datamapper/NGDP_RPCH@WEO/OEMDC/ADVEC/WEOWORLD.

75. "Commonly Used Statistics," United States Department of Labor, https://www.osha.gov/data/commonstats#:~:text=5%2C333%20workers%20died%20on%20the,about%2015%20deaths%20every%20day.

76. David Barstow, "U.S. Rarely Seeks Charges For Deaths in Workplace," *New York Times*, December 22, 2003, https://www.nytimes.com/2003/12/22/us/us-rarely-seeks-charges-for-deaths-in-workplace.html.

77. "How much does the federal government collect in fines?" USA Facts, July 24, 2019, https://usafacts.org/articles/how-much-does-federal-government-collect-fines/.

78. Max Galka, "Quantifying the Government Paperwork Burden," Metrocosm, February 26, 2016, http://metrocosm.com/government-paperwork-burden/.

79. https://usafacts.org/state-of-the-union/transportation-infrastructure
https://www.moneygeek.com/living/states-worst-road-infrastructure/

80. "GDP in England," Our World in Data, https://ourworldindata.org/grapher/total-gdp-in-the-uk-since-1270; Max Galka, "The History of U.S. Government Spending, Revenue, and Debt (1790-2015)," Metrocosm, February 16, 2016, http://metrocosm.com/history-of-us-taxes/; Bruce Bartlett, "How Excessive Government Killed Ancient Rome," https://www.cato.org/sites/cato.org/files/

serials/files/cato-journal/1994/11/cj14n2-7.pdf; "List of countries by government spending as percentage of GDP," Wikipedia, https://en.wikipedia.org/wiki/List_of_countries_by_government_spending_as_percentage_of_GDP; J. J. Scarisbrick, Henry VIII (University of California Press, 1969), 361.

81. "2021 Index of Economic Freedom: Country Rankings," Heritage.org, https://www.heritage.org/index/ranking.

82. "2021 Index of Economic Freedom: Country Rankings," Heritage.org, https://www.heritage.org/index/ranking.

83. https://freedomhouse.org/report/freedom-world/2021/democracy-under-siege

84. "Net official development assistance and official aid received (current US$)," The World Bank, https://data.worldbank.org/indicator/DT.ODA.ALLD.CD?most_recent_value_desc=true.

85. Catherine Bremer, "COVID-19 spending helped to lift foreign aid to an all-time high in 2020 but more effort needed," OECD, April 13, 2021, https://www.oecd.org/newsroom/covid-19-spending-helped-to-lift-foreign-aid-to-an-all-time-high-in-2020-but-more-effort-needed.htm.

86. "The U.S. Government and International Family Planning & Reproductive Health Efforts," KFF, November 11, 2021, https://www.kff.org/global-health-policy/fact-sheet/the-u-s-government-and-international-family-planning-reproductive-health-efforts/.

87. Chad P. Bown, "US-China Trade War Tariffs: An Up-to-Date Chart," Peterson Institute for International Economics, March 16, 2021, https://www.piie.com/research/piie-charts/us-china-trade-war-tariffs-date-chart.

88. Alain Cohn, Michel André Maréchal, David Tannenbaumand, and Christian Lukas Zünd, "Civic honesty around the globe," *Science*, https://www.science.org/doi/10.1126/science.aau8712.

89. Michael Cohn, "Small businesses hurt by unpaid invoices," Accounting Today, March 17, 2017, https://www.accountingtoday.com/news/small-businesses-hurt-by-unpaid-invoices.

90. Amber Raiken, "This Is the Best Fast-Food Chain of 2021, According to Customers," Best Life, October 1, 2021, https://bestlifeonline.com/best-fast-food-chain-2021-news/.

91. Brett Molina, "In-N-Out owner explains why fast-food chain prints Bible verses on food packaging," *USA Today*, October 8, 2019, https://www.usatoday.com/story/money/2019/10/08/in-n-out-owner-lynsi-snyder-interview-bible-verses/3906363002/.

92. Thomas J. DiLorenzo, "The Truth About the 'Robber Barons,'" Mises Institute,

November 1, 2017, https://mises.org/library/truth-about-robber-barons#4.

93. Ibid.

94. "Average Age of Automobiles and Trucks in Operation in the United States," Bureau of Transportation Statistics, https://www.bts.gov/content/average-age-automobiles-and-trucks-operation-united-states.

95. Julie Blackley, "Longest-Lasting Cars to Reach 200,000 Miles and Beyond," iSeeCars, https://www.iseecars.com/longest-lasting-cars-study#v=2020.

96. Ibid.

97. "The Most and Least Reliable Cars by Class," Consumer Reports, October 24, 2016, https://www.consumerreports.org/car-reliability/the-most-and-least-reliable-cars-by-class-a6393284310/.

98. https://www.iseecars.com/cars-that-hold-their-value-study

99. Ibid.

100. "What Are the Total Costs of Vehicle Ownership per Brand?" CRS Automotive, April 30, 2018, https://www.crsautomotive.com/what-are-the-total-costs-of-vehicle-ownership-per-brand/.

101. Based on SamaritanMinistries.org 2021 rates.

102. Kat O'Leary, "How Much is 1° Worth?" EnergyHub, May 15, 2012, https://info.energyhub.com/blog/how-much-is-one-degree-worth.

103. Julija A., "42 Small Business Statistics: Everything You Need to Know," SmallBizGenius, August 26, 2021, https://www.smallbizgenius.net/by-the-numbers/small-business-statistics/#gref.

104. For more information, visit www.crown.org

105. Michael Itzkowitz, "Which College Programs Give Students the Best Bang for Their Buck," Third Way, August 13, 2021, https://www.thirdway.org/report/which-college-programs-give-students-the-best-bang-for-their-buck.

106. "The Economic Value Of College Majors," Georgetown University, Center on Education and the Workforce, https://cew.georgetown.edu/cew-reports/valueofcollegemajors/.

107. Glassdoor Team, "15 More Companies That No Longer Require a Degree—Apply Now," Glassdoor, November 8, 2021, https://www.glassdoor.com/blog/no-degree-required/.

108. Jeanne Sahadi, "No college degree? More employers than ever just don't care," CNN Business, October 12, 2021, https://www.cnn.com/2021/10/11/success/jobs-apprenticeships-college-degrees-feseries/index.html.

109. www.hackerrank.com

110. https://asiasociety.org/global-cities-education-network/apprenticeship-model-switzerland

111. https://tradingeconomics.com/country-list/youth-unemployment-rate

INDEX

0-6

6-Sigma	328

A

Abortifacient	282
Abortion	235, 282, 436
Accountant/Accounting	147, 242, 243, 248, 381, 416, 417, 426, 442, 444–446, 449
Accuracy	321, 323, 324, 326, 328, 329
Advertising	16, 17, 285, 319, 391, 395, 396, 400
Aesop	233
Amazon (Company)	257, 258, 297
Appliances	284, 367, 374, 427
Application	36, 446, 450
Architecture	429, 442
Artist	427
Assets	46, 104, 135, 193, 197, 247, 297, 387, 396, 397
Attorney	447, 448
Augustus Caeser	166
Australia	49, 99, 135, 234, 262, 278, 281, 452
Automobiles	41, 58, 83, 232, 339, 342, 357, 362, 365
Average Deviation	327

B

Bahamas	231, 268
Bankruptcy	134, 135, 175, 196–197, 209, 230
Barter Economy	22, 157
Bitcoin	170–172
Boeing	211, 256, 342
Bolivia	279
Bonding	396, 397
Bonds	11, 110, 115, 180, 181, 191, 193, 208–210, 227

Brands	353, 378
Bribery	39, 42, 68, 79, 168, 253, 255
Broker	210
Budget	225, 228, 256, 287, 346–348, 361, 362, 375, 376, 380, 382–384, 391, 396
Bureaucracy	79, 80, 259, 275, 284
Bush, George W.	255, 256, 287

C

California	59, 226, 447
Campaign Donations	251, 254–257
Capital Costs	333, 339, 395
Capital Investment	48, 203, 204
Capitalism	83, 89, 93, 94, 98–101, 106, 108, 110, 111, 132, 335
Ceylon	60, 61
Charity	109, 125, 197, 222, 223, 227, 230, 236, 267, 334, 381
Checking Accounts	167, 195, 206
Chemistry	442, 445
Chesterton, G.K.	58, 104, 106
China/Chinese	18, 67, 73, 100, 160, 210, 232, 264, 274, 277, 284, 285, 290
Civil Government	21, 39, 40, 42, 45, 46, 67, 99, 106, 115, 164, 168, 183, 209, 235, 265, 275, 285, 343
Clerical	426
Clovis II	72
Coaching	404, 414, 416
Collectivism	110
College/University	39, 126, 186, 192, 343, 365, 429, 430, 433, 438–447, 449, 451, 452
Common Grace	69, 81, 82, 297
Communication	40, 59, 123, 400, 405, 409, 441, 449
Communism	89, 99, 100, 102, 106, 108, 280
Communist Manifesto	99, 100, 108
Competition	7, 27, 106, 251, 331, 338, 339, 341, 343, 390, 391, 393
Condo	366
Congo	83, 282
Consumables	203
Consumers	17, 23, 28, 284, 339
Consumption	376, 378
Contract	32, 76, 128, 131, 132, 256, 285, 315, 316, 386, 396, 399, 401, 448

Contract Labor	127
Copper	32, 60, 62, 166
Costco	446
Counterfeiters	168, 186
Covetousness	17, 19, 46, 88, 198, 290, 391
Coworker	412
Cryptocurrencies	170–172
Cuba	73, 99, 100, 103, 104, 279
Customer	17, 21, 24–26, 30, 121, 130, 143, 144, 167, 269, 285, 300–302, 315–323, 326, 328–331, 335, 388, 390–396, 403, 404, 409, 410, 416–419, 449, 450

D

Debt	56, 70, 74–78, 126, 131–136, 173, 177, 180–183, 186, 189, 192–197, 208, 215, 217, 225, 228–230, 232, 233, 236, 247, 286, 287, 299, 336, 337, 365, 367, 376, 390, 398, 440, 447
Deficit	184, 284, 287
Demand	6–8, 16–21, 27–31, 52, 53, 62, 76, 78, 95, 96, 110, 129, 177, 188, 196, 197, 231, 276, 359, 392, 418
Democracy	80, 94, 268, 274
Demographics	392
Depreciation	247, 353, 354
Depression	76, 77, 83–85, 114, 176, 196, 241, 261
Design	39, 108, 171, 292, 315, 322, 331, 391, 418, 427, 431, 438, 449, 450
Dictatorship	69, 79, 158
Distributism	89, 104–106, 110
Dodge (Company)	353
Dominion	46, 107, 108, 120, 431
Dow Jones Industrial Average (DJIA)	210, 211
Dross	166
Drought	68, 188

E

Efficiency	95, 98, 110, 111, 121, 122, 277, 403
Egypt	68, 70, 72, 88, 248, 315, 336–337, 428

Employment	97, 196, 212, 413
Engineering	148, 292, 439, 441, 442, 444, 447
England	73, 82, 163, 189, 210, 273, 365
Entrepreneurship	32, 126–129, 134, 136, 137, 334, 341, 387, 391, 394, 413, 446
Entropy	66
EPA	376, 377
Estonia	278
Ethiopia	67, 282
Exchange Value	16
Excise Tax	267, 270
Expenses/Expenditures	33, 115, 124, 134, 166, 191, 192, 204, 225, 227, 228, 241, 243–246, 248, 250, 251, 273, 274, 299, 316, 347, 357, 360, 362, 365, 375, 377, 380–383, 387, 395, 396, 417

F

Facebook	122
Family Economy	89, 104, 106–112, 114, 115, 144, 145, 453
Famine	67–70, 336
Farmer/Agriculture	22, 30, 32, 33, 41, 55, 66, 68, 77, 97, 103, 105, 106, 114, 144, 149, 157, 188, 202, 243, 261–263, 313, 341, 443
Federal Reserve	176–184, 186, 190, 191, 194, 209
Feudalism	89–94
Finance	23, 108, 184, 423, 426, 442
Finland	253, 269
Ford (Company)	128, 287, 351, 353–356
Fractional Reserve Banking	184
France	18, 168, 169, 271, 273, 282
Franchises	126, 129, 130
Free Trade	94, 283, 284

G

Gambling	54, 213–215
Gold	48, 84, 156, 159, 161–170, 172, 174, 175, 177, 178, 184, 198, 224, 227, 255, 256, 299
Good Samaritan	223
Gross Domestic Product	76, 182, 195, 267, 273, 274, 278–280, 287, 440

Guatemala	274

H

Hilton	446
Hiring/Hire	32, 48, 80, 85, 126–128, 130, 134, 137, 138, 141, 147, 161, 197, 219, 311, 316, 329, 334, 392, 393, 399, 400, 404, 415, 418, 419
Honda (Company)	351, 352, 354, 355, 376, 377
Honest Money	52, 165, 170, 177, 186, 197
Hong Kong	135, 210
Humanism/Humanist	73, 440

I

Indenture	137
India	68, 130, 269, 281, 282, 452
Individualism	110, 111
Individualized Retirement Accounts (IRA)	240
Indonesia	274, 281, 290
Inflation	76, 106, 184, 188, 189, 191–196, 205–210, 213, 225, 227, 228, 271, 286
Insurance	27, 175, 192, 225, 228, 232, 234, 333, 347, 348, 361, 362, 375, 376, 380, 381, 383, 384, 396, 397
Interest	6, 131, 132, 173, 174, 181, 182, 184–186, 193–196, 205–210, 216, 225, 228, 229, 233, 240, 259, 282, 365, 381
Interview	137–141, 297, 314, 450
Inventory	244, 246, 263, 437
Investment	32, 33, 48, 53, 132, 161, 171, 174, 181, 203–209, 212, 213, 217–220, 222, 225–231, 233, 267, 277, 299, 333–335, 359, 362, 363, 397, 440, 441, 448
Israel	271, 274

J

Jackson, Andrew	175
Japan	160, 191, 210, 232–235, 269, 271, 273, 287, 350
Joseph	212, 311–315, 336, 337, 428
Jubilee	71

L

Labor	23, 32, 39, 41, 42, 44, 67, 68, 83, 93, 97, 98, 102, 109, 113, 118, 120, 125–127, 147, 149, 231, 232, 238, 260, 277, 334, 361, 366, 399, 417
Lamborghini	161
Landlord	90, 226, 261
Lawn Maintenance	329, 393, 396, 398
Lemonade	29, 30, 127, 128, 134, 203, 204, 243–247, 292, 296, 322, 324, 326, 331, 333, 339, 343, 381, 383, 390, 395, 398, 400
Liabilities	247
Lien	398

M

M1 Money Supply	195
Macroeconomy	36
Magna Carta	92
Malthus, Thomas	30
Mammon	20
Management	48, 83, 107, 142, 143, 299, 403, 404, 413, 414, 416, 434, 441, 449
Manufacturing	28, 32, 41, 95, 99, 118, 149, 166, 189, 211, 217, 257, 262, 322, 324, 327, 328, 330, 331, 342, 350, 351, 355, 356, 364, 446
Manumission	72
Market Analysis	391, 392
Marketing	17, 32, 129, 147, 245, 390, 391, 393, 396, 442, 449
Marxism	100, 102, 271
Materialism	110
McCormick, Cyrus	40, 41

Medical	19, 148, 192, 232, 235, 251, 257, 362, 375, 380, 414, 418, 434, 439
Mentorship/Apprenticeship	109, 112, 113, 126, 127, 137, 139, 410, 439, 445–452
Mercantilism	132
Mexico	60, 83, 226, 281, 284, 290, 365
Microeconomy	36
Microsoft (Company)	211, 257
Military	92, 103, 272, 285, 422, 433
Mining	59, 84
Mitsubishi (Company)	356, 377
Monopoly	62, 132, 133, 175, 336, 339–341, 343
Morocco	68, 290
Mortgage	175, 228, 229, 337, 381
Motivation	4, 12, 23, 36, 62, 137, 153, 391, 425
Musk, Elon	183, 215, 217

N

Nails/Nail Gun	31, 32, 39, 41, 369, 395, 417
Namibia	68
Nasdaq Index	210
National Bank	175
Net Revenue	245
Netherlands	82, 253, 290
New Zealand	253, 278, 452
NHTSA	359
Nicaragua	262
Norway	18, 73, 253, 269, 273, 290
Nuclear Power	131
Nursing	440–442

O

Oligopoly	338, 341, 342
Operating Expenses	204
Operators	94, 131, 416–419, 427
Options Market	214
Ownership	45, 46, 94, 96, 98, 104–106, 127, 128, 130, 132, 177, 210, 258, 271, 302, 404

P

Partnership	131
Pencil	58, 59, 61–63, 368
Perceived Useful Value	16, 52
Pharmaceutics	257
Plumbing	32, 129, 367, 369, 444, 445
Portugal	73, 287, 452
Precision	323, 324, 326, 328
Productivity	77, 93, 98, 122, 128, 202, 216, 264
Profit	6, 7, 23, 28, 32, 44, 53, 54, 87, 93, 96, 97, 99, 131, 134, 161, 182, 184, 186, 211, 213–215, 217, 225, 228, 229, 244–246, 266, 270, 299, 307, 319, 320, 333–336, 341, 346, 363, 387, 401
Profit-and-Loss Report	244, 245
Property Tax	225, 228, 268, 271–273, 276, 381
Proprietorship	287
Public Pension	234
Purchasing	183, 353, 354, 357, 362, 377, 378, 449
Pynoos, Morris	39

Q

Quality	7–8, 18, 23–25, 53, 103, 121, 143, 165, 166, 214, 301, 319–323, 325, 326, 328–331, 339, 341, 348–350, 390, 393, 395, 403, 404, 413, 416–418
Quid-Pro-Quo	429

R

Railroads	59, 164, 340, 341
Raw Materials	31, 32, 188, 203, 204, 244–246
Reagan, Ronald	260, 287
Real Estate	224–228, 230, 264, 270, 271, 362
Real Useful Value	16
Reaper	40, 41
Recession	76, 78, 106, 190, 229, 241, 264
Redistribution of Wealth	107
Regulations	39, 42, 80, 94, 260, 262, 265, 267, 280, 284,

	291, 292, 339, 341–343, 395, 418
Rent	27, 33, 84, 94, 163, 171–173, 225, 226, 228, 229, 261, 271, 362
Research	38, 183, 217, 246, 289, 309, 342, 370, 394, 409, 418, 425, 441, 448
Resources	5, 11, 30, 31, 39, 43, 52, 120, 141, 151, 161, 202, 204, 242, 261, 265, 296, 307, 325, 334, 341, 382, 387, 389, 395, 400, 415, 418, 435
Restaurants	144, 319, 320, 322, 348, 377, 380, 387, 388, 390, 404, 417, 418, 425
Retirement	232, 234, 236, 238, 240, 241, 365, 382
Rockefeller, John D.	133, 339–341, 344
Rome	89, 90
Roosevelt, Franklin Delano	170, 177, 178, 259, 268

S

Salary	230, 400, 441
Sales	8, 16, 32, 128, 131, 171, 184, 243, 268–270, 272–273, 276, 318, 319, 333, 334, 336, 359, 381, 391, 416, 417
Savings	167, 174, 180, 184, 190, 193, 194, 204–209, 210, 218, 226, 228, 231–235, 238, 240, 241, 333, 362, 365, 373, 376–378, 398
Scarcity	21, 159, 341
Securities	193, 286
Self-employment	118, 128, 129, 144, 146, 147, 416
Silver	52, 53, 84, 159–161, 163–169, 174, 175, 177–180, 184, 186, 198, 224, 227
Singapore	135, 278
Slave	10, 44, 56, 70–75, 88, 91, 92, 126, 127, 132, 230, 273, 336, 337, 422, 428
Slothfulness	50, 151, 152, 196
Socialism	89, 93, 99–104, 107, 110, 112, 197, 259, 268, 281
Soviet Union	67, 100
Standard and Poor Index	211, 216
Standard Deviation	326, 328
Steward/Stewardship	5, 6, 11, 42, 45, 47, 48, 89, 106, 153, 197, 243, 346, 347, 387, 415
Stocks/Stock Market	48, 53, 54, 85, 114, 130–134, 183, 184, 196, 197, 208, 210, 211, 213–217, 227, 286
Subsidy	63, 133, 183, 257, 258, 261, 263, 340, 341

Subsistence Farming	97
Sudan	67, 252, 279
Suicide	4, 102
Supply	6–9, 16, 17, 25, 27–33, 53, 59, 78, 95, 96, 118, 129, 133, 146, 176, 188, 191, 195, 245, 336
Sustainability	54, 84
Sweden	18, 49, 73, 253, 269, 273, 290, 452
Switzerland	17, 82, 278, 290, 451, 452

T

Talents	5, 11, 43, 44, 107, 124, 131, 147, 149, 150, 152, 154, 173, 202, 213, 302, 334, 391, 425, 429, 437, 446
Tariff	268, 283, 284
Taxation/Taxes	26, 42, 80, 89, 91, 94, 99, 147, 175, 177, 193, 196, 208, 209, 225, 228, 239, 240, 248, 250, 251, 261, 262, 267–277, 280, 283, 284, 286–288, 337, 343, 375, 378, 380–382, 417
Technology	67, 149, 210, 441
Telecommuting	149, 365
Tesla (Company)	215, 446
Texas	63, 208, 226, 263, 268, 271
Tithe	207, 220, 276, 376, 381, 383, 384
Tools	32, 39, 43, 60, 161, 173, 179, 183, 197, 245, 331, 334, 335, 395, 400
Tortoise	233, 234
Toyota (Company)	160, 350–352, 354, 355, 376, 377
Trade	22, 60, 72, 73, 85, 94, 113, 127, 129, 132, 157, 160, 165–167, 171, 214, 224, 276, 277, 283–285, 336
Transportation	232, 233, 250, 347, 348, 360, 376, 380
Trump, Donald	191, 284, 287
Tunisia	68

U

Uganda	282
Unemployment	76, 78, 79, 114, 229, 242, 452
Utility	21, 373

V

Vaccines	114, 257
Venezuela	83, 252, 279, 280
Volkswagen (Company)	127, 356

W

Wages	94, 95, 97, 124
Walmart (Company)	128, 211
Wealth	3, 6, 11, 16, 21, 36, 43, 45–47, 49, 51, 53, 54, 88, 89, 93, 95, 98–101, 103, 107, 110, 111, 114, 125, 132, 133, 144, 159, 161, 182–184, 193, 198, 199, 213, 228, 233, 284, 299, 337, 377, 381, 393, 437
Welfare	85, 99, 196, 197, 250, 267, 289, 434
Workforce	144, 317, 414, 445, 446

Y

Yemen	83, 252

Z

Zacchaeus	199
Zimbabwe	279
Zoning	264